DATE DUE

DEC 0 8 2014			

Demco, Inc. 38-293

Sex, Lies, and Cigarettes

SEX

LIES

AND

CIGARETTES

Canadian Women,
Smoking, and Visual
Culture, 1880–2000

SHARON ANNE COOK

McGill-Queen's University Press
Montreal & Kingston | London | Ithaca

Legal deposit second quarter 2012
Bibliothèque nationale du Québec

Printed in Canada on acid-free paper

This book has been published with the help of a grant from the
Canadian Federation for the Humanities and Social Sciences, through
the Aid to Scholarly Publications Program, using funds provided by
the Social Sciences and Humanities Research Council of Canada.
Funding has also been received from the University of Ottawa's
Faculty of Education.

McGill-Queen's University Press acknowledges the support of the
Canada Council for the Arts for our publishing program. We also
acknowledge the financial support of the Government of Canada
through the Canada Book Fund for our publishing activities.

Library and Archives Canada Cataloguing in Publication

Cook, Sharon A. (Sharon Anne)
Sex, lies, and cigarettes : Canadian women, smoking and visual
culture, 1880–2000 / Sharon Anne Cook.

Includes bibliographical references and index.
ISBN 978-0-7735-3977-8

1. Women – Tobacco use – Canada – History.   2. Women – Canada –
Social conditions – 19th century.   3. Women – Canada – Social
conditions – 20th century.   4. Mass media and culture – Canada –
History.   I. Title.

HV5746.C64 2012   364.1'4   C2011-908268-3

Set in 10.5/13 Calluna with Museo Slab 500, Museo Sans 500,
and Berthold Akzidenz Grotesk
Book design and typesetting by Garet Markvoort, zijn digital

For Terry

Contents

Part III | Enticing Women to Smoke

List of Figures

Acknowledgments

This book would probably not have materialized without trains, planes, and automobiles, and mainly trains. Such a statement in an era of tobacco sponsorship begs to be explained. I began research for this project about fifteen years ago, just as my elderly and treasured mother began a decline with Alzheimer's Disease. My loving father cared for her alone as long as he was able, well into his late eighties. Through this difficult period, he drew on the support of his family, myself included. At the same time, I assumed a demanding administrative position at the University of Ottawa. Over the next seven years, my ability to research and write was episodic as I travelled bi-weekly and usually by train from Ottawa to London, Ontario, where my parents lived. One response to the grief of my parents' decline was an inability to read for pleasure; another was a curious ability to focus, read, and write on the train. After those bleak days had ended, I wrote other portions of this book on the train from Ottawa to Toronto, Montreal, Winnipeg, Saskatoon, Halifax, and Vancouver. The absence of email breaking into my thoughts (a calm since destroyed), the soothing rocking of the train cars on slightly worn rail beds, and my interest in the project itself made the writing a pleasure. While I have written portions of this book on long international flights, plane travel mainly reminds me of why I favour trains. The first full draft was written on an RV trip to Florida during a sabbatical. I am probably not the first person to find that travelling facilitates writing.

When I first began this project, I envisaged something quite different from what has emerged. Trained in conventional historical analysis with an emphasis on written documents, I was regularly frustrated by the lack of commentary about smoking, particularly by the young women whom I hoped to track over a long period. Looking elsewhere for evidence to explain women's relationship with tobacco, I became aware of the importance of the visual performance of smoking. This led me into the field of historical visual culture and quite a different set of analytical approaches, dangers, and rewards from those I had experienced in earlier historical writing. It also brought me into contact with a different archival and scholarly world than I had known. I am very grateful to the many archivists and scholars who have led me to the wealth of expressive visual sources on which much of this book is based. Their knowledge and generosity have enriched my work and made it possible for me to see the problematic that is smoking in different ways.

I am very grateful to the staff of several national institutions, including those at Library and Archives Canada, Dr Sheldon Posen at the Canadian Museum of Civilization, and Dr Amber Lloyd-Langston, Susan Ross, and Dr Tim Cook at the Canadian War Museum. Many provincial-level archivists helped with identification and reproduction of images. In Nova Scotia, Kathryn Harvey, then at the Dalhousie University Archives, and Creighton Barrett provided both images and diaries of the Maritime region, including Cape Breton. In Quebec, Theresa Rowat at the McGill University Archives and Stephanie Poisson at the McCord Museum Archives arranged for rare images to be included in the book. In Ontario, I am grateful to the staff at the Province of Ontario Archives; Carolyn Cross at the Oakville Museum; John Shoesmith at the Thomas Fisher Rare Book Library, University of Toronto; Kathleen Imrie at the OISE/University of Toronto Rare Book Collection; Jane Britton at the University of Waterloo Special Collections, Doris Lewis Rare Book Room; Heather Holmes and Jeremy Heil at the Queen's University Archives; Anne Lauzon at the University of Ottawa Archives; Cindy Preece at Wilfrid Laurier University Archives; and Lawrence Lee, John Huzil, Nana Robinette, and Glenda Williams at the City of Toronto Archives. Stephen Francom, archivist at the Alma College Archives for Elgin County, unearthed conduct codes for this study. Arlene Gehmacher, curator of Canadian paintings, prints, and drawings in the Department of World Cultures at the Royal Ontario Museum, was also helpful. In Manitoba, I wish to thank Maureen Dolyniuk and her staff at the Hudson's Bay Company Archives, Shelley Sweeney at the University of Manitoba Archives, and the staff at the Province of Manitoba Archives. The staff at the University of Saskatchewan Archives in Saskatoon were kind and helpful. In Alberta, thanks to Lia Melemenis and her colleagues at the Glenbow Museum Archives in Calgary. In British Columbia, I wish to thank Erwin Wodarczak, archivist at the Rare Book Room and Archives of the University of British Columbia. I am grateful to Jane Witte of the Ontario Family Studies Subject Association for information on textbooks after 2000.

This book has been enriched as well by many others, all talented and generous people. Very importantly, the research was undertaken and extended by Dr Kenneth Montgomery, who did research on my behalf from the time he was a graduate student, through his early employment, and finally as a tenure-track professor at the University of Regina. Ken's insights over this long period, and especially through his reading of the penultimate version of the manuscript, have added enormously to its depth. I also want to thank Dr Constance Backhouse, Peg Carson, Dr Sarah Glassford, Linda Kupecek, Dr Amber Lloyd-Langston, Dr Eileen O'Connor, Adele Matsalla, Dr Judith McKenzie, Dr Lorna McLean, Allan Rock, and Judy Rebick for their many helpful suggestions and help in locating artifacts. I greatly appreciated the willingness of Dr Kristina Llewellyn from the University of Waterloo to provide a number of oral history transcripts from her research.

An important component of the research base for this book has been the gathering of informal statements from long-time or former smokers. Some have been gathered through casual or formal conversation and email exchanges, others through telephone conversations and written testimony. The many women who have reflected on their reasons for beginning to smoke, their perceptions of how their smoking was received by those around them, and their views on current smoking limitations have provided important insights for me over the past decade. Several women were prepared to have their names in print, and they appear in the notes at the end of the book. Others elected to remain anonymous contributors, and their views are referenced through letters and numbers that I ascribed to each woman at the time of the interview. I am very grateful for the suggestions offered by all of these women, as well as their interest in the project itself.

I am deeply grateful to the two book clubs of which I am a proud member: the long-standing SWIVEL Teachers' Book Club and the Marion Dewar National Capital Region Women's History Book Club for their sustained interest in and support for this project over many years and for having allowed me to attend meetings without having finished the reading. Members of both book clubs have added to the research base directly through their own commentaries on smoking, by suggesting additional secondary literature, and by reflecting as a group on the important role played by smoking in earlier periods.

The Faculty of Education at the University of Ottawa has been gracious and unstinting in its support of this research, extending unexpected kindnesses in particular during the tough years of my parents' decline. Dean Marie-Josée Berger and vice-deans Yves Herry, David Smith, and Tim Stanley have all offered help in many aspects of this work. They made me believe that whatever I needed to continue with my research program would be secured somehow, and all made good on that promise. I am particularly grateful to the research assistants who helped me to keep track of the many images in this book and to secure permissions for their use. In particular, I thank Anita Olsen Harper, Eriola Pema, and Yoriko Aizu, whose enthusiasm and questions have added to this manuscript.

Because of its nature as an interdisciplinary collective, any Faculty of Education shelters and supports a wide variety of disciplinary perspectives. Ours at the University of Ottawa is particularly rich in this respect. I have benefited more than I can say from the wise interventions, scholarly insights, and enthusiasm of my highly intelligent colleagues. Among them, I want especially to thank Dr Cheryl Duquette, Dr Awad Ibrahim, Dr Judith Robertson, and Dr Joel Westheimer for asking questions I would never myself have thought to ask and for having ferreted out "a few other things" for me to consider. Over the past decade, I have co-ordinated a project aimed at encouraging teacher candidates in our B.Ed. program to incorporate curricula relating to peace and development education into the mainstream curriculum, *Developing a Global Perspective for Educators/Developpement d'une perspective globale pour enseignements et enseignementes.* This work has sharpened my awareness of international cartels working in the developing world, peddling new and dangerous products, including tobacco. I thank my dedicated friends and colleagues for carrying on this important program and for finding new ways to introduce this knowledge into the classroom: Tracy Crowe, Dr Ruth Kane, Dr Lorna McLean, and Dr Nicholas Ng-a-Fook. Highly prized of my colleagues are also my academic partners in our Educational Research Unit, *Making Histories/Faire histoire: Narrative and Collective Memory in Education/Récits et mémoires collectives en éducation.* My work has been enriched on every level by these creative, hard-working, public-spirited, and well-read historians: Dr Ruby Heap, Dr Stéphane Lévesque, Dr Lorna McLean, Dr Nicholas Ng-A-Fook, and Dr Tim Stanley.

The broader University of Ottawa community has sustained my research program through such awards as the Excellence in Education Prize, the University of Ottawa Excellence in Teaching Prize, and the Distinguished University Professor Award and by their successful nomination of me for the Ontario Confederation of Universities' Associations' Award for Teaching. Good teaching and public service is reinforced by original research, and the University of Ottawa's support for my work on all levels has been instrumental in the completion of this book.

I have benefited enormously from the good humour and intelligence of the staff at McGill-Queen's University Press. Especially important has been my editor, Jonathan Crago. From debates about the details of Canadian and American copyright law to tracking down better scans of important images, I am grateful for Jonathan's commitment to this project and for his support at the many challenging stages of its production.

Without the sustained support of my family, this book would have been far less fun to write, and it would surely have been a poorer product. My sister, Peg, has remained interested in the topic over the long haul, providing me with information and thoughts as it has progressed. My brothers, Wesley and David, and their partners, Joan and Suzanne, have welcomed me into their homes on research trips. My immediate family has been generous in their support as well. For most of my adult life, I have been surrounded by males, with my husband, two sons, our first dog, Parkin, and our current dog-in-residence, Purple Clifford. (I want to thank both dogs for inviting me along on their daily round of walks during which I reflected on issues raised by the book and occasionally startled passersby with my "conversations." Our dogs are skilled listeners.) To our great delight, the balance shifted about eight years ago with the arrival of our talented daughter-in-law, Sarah, and thereafter our three delightful granddaughters: Chloe, Emma, and Paige. This research is ultimately for the betterment of our triumvirate of perfect grand-girls. They are not yet of an age when they are tempted to smoke, and I am hopeful that this book will contribute to a more informed understanding of why young women are drawn to smoking and to better anti-smoking programs for young women like them.

Our sons continue to astonish me with their productivity and engagement with important academic issues, the continual debate of which has enriched this book. Tim, a multiple prize-winning research historian at Carleton University and Great War historian at the Canadian War Museum, has referred me to tobacco-related research for at least fifteen years. As a graduate student, he acted as a research assistant for me, ferreting out obscure and important documents. His own work has been inspiring for the possibilities of popular academic history in enriching public discourse. Graham, a senior lawyer at the World Trade Organization in Geneva, has added to my research and laughter throughout its duration. As a smoker, Graham has helped me to understand the culture of smokers and the general attractions it has for young people. Through his own legal work, he has also offered international case law findings that have allowed me to better understand several issues, including the current struggle for countries to control flavoured cigarettes, a case under his jurisdiction. His intelligent questions have challenged and helped to shape my thinking throughout the research and writing of this book.

The support, both academic and personal, that has been most meaningful for me, however, has been that provided by my life-partner, Terry Cook. Without his incisive questions, his help in locating useful resources and people, his skills with technology, writing, and argumentation, as well as his unwavering interest in this research and his support for me, this book would have been lighter in all respects. There are no major arguments in this book that have not first been debated with him and then often amended in response to his trenchant questions. The quality of Terry's scholarship has recently been recognized through his appointment to membership in the Royal Society of Canada. I have been fortunate to have benefited from it for the past forty-two years. This book is dedicated to him.

Sometimes, however, the greatest generosity and talent of a supportive family and community are not enough to avoid mistakes or oversights. Any deficiencies in this work are entirely my own.

Sharon Anne Cook
Ottawa, Ontario

PART I

Seeing the Big Picture

Introduction

We live in a period when smoking is almost thoroughly discredited. Given what we know about smoking's dangers to health, and particularly to innocent bystanders or children in a family with a smoking parent through second-hand smoke, it is almost inconceivable that not long ago, women's smoking was widely regarded as sexy, sophisticated, and "classy." Today, smokers are characterized as selfish, undisciplined, and dirty. When women smoke, they are regarded as especially irresponsible.

Popular wisdom holds that we have won the battle against smoking. We congratulate ourselves on steadily decreasing smoking rates, especially among teenagers. And yet, those statistics that we are so pleased about mask a committed group of smokers who continue to puff: girls and young women. The highest rates of smoking of any group in the Canadian population is by women aged eighteen to twenty-four. Smoking rates among this group of young women are declining more slowly than those for males of the same age. Moreover, while male smoking rates internationally are slowly declining, female rates are increasing. The World Health Organization estimates that by 2025, 20 per cent of women will be smokers. It reports an 80 to 90 per cent higher mortality rate in the developed world for women who smoke as opposed to those who do not.[1]

How can we explain young women's self-destructive behaviour? Have we not placed shocking warnings on cigarette packages and in public-service advertisements? Is not every schoolchild warned of tobacco's dangers through health textbooks and educational policies? Have Canadian tobacco manufacturers not been hounded and forced to remove their advertisements, as well as their logos, from cultural events, car rallies, and much else? Are these girls and women simply "stupid," as the Health Canada campaign of the past few years phrased it? What more can we possibly do to make them stop?

In fact, the twentieth-century campaign to deter smoking by young women – and young people generally – has been almost laughably inept. Certainly, these anti-smoking messages have been well-meaning, but both the formal educational campaigns developed for schools and those from government agencies and interest groups have often missed their mark. At the same time, tobacco manufacturers have consistently fashioned inventive and often effective campaigns to entice youths, and especially young women, into smoking culture.

In this study, I explore the relationship between Canadian women and smoking over the course of more than a century. The book begins its examination in the nineteenth century, when women took on the leadership of anti-smoking forces in Canada through temperance, defining smoking as an immoral and dangerous behaviour. It continues through the twentieth century when women themselves became smokers, and it ends in the late twentieth century when smoking yet again was widely regarded as an illicit activity. I trace women's complex historical relationship with smoking – as powerful opponents of others' smoking, as sexualized images for the marketing of tobacco, as protectors of children being drawn into smoking, and as knowing consumers of tobacco.

Throughout this long period, the focus in the book remains fixed on the *social context* of smoking rather than the legislative, medical, or socially prescriptive dimensions of smoking, although those features of smoking are addressed as well. That is, I seek to uncover how the social characteristics of smoking shaped women's smoking practices in the past and into the current age. I explore how women as smokers, decorative objects, or public advocates have been represented by others and how they have represented themselves. I argue that at its most fundamental level, smoking empowered women and continues to do so, despite the many dangers it offers physiologically.

I argue that the lure of smoking for women is a far more complex process than is generally acknowledged and that it is rooted most directly in women's changing identity formation and in strategies for empowerment more than in "liberation." The prime evidence that we both underrate and misunderstand smoking's allure and its palliative qualities for women are the continuing high smoking rates, especially among young women actively engaged in identity construction who are seeking to exercise social power.

Throughout the book, I explore the interaction between women's visual representations as smokers or as anti-smoking advocates and the interconnected processes of modernity, sexualization, and commodification of desire. I do not claim that smoking began any of these features of modern life but rather that smoking, or posturing with cigarettes as a theatrical prop, was and remains a powerful way for women to express themselves and to participate in modernist culture. Nor did this process occur divorced from other social developments and upheavals but often in response to them. Women's harnessing of the power of the visual through smoking was closely associated with other "liberating" ideologies in post–First World War Canada. They included the granting of limited civic rights to women through the vote and as "persons" under the Canadian Constitution, the increasing network of modern communications technology and the range of visual images accompanying it for commercial gain, the consumer revolution, and the growing popularity of Freudianism and eroticism as a feature of the modern intellectual and emotional landscape.

This study does not deny the importance of both consumerism and relaxed norms in fuelling women's interest in smoking. At the same time, it has seemed to me inadequate to explain both the depth and range of the cigarette's attraction for women. It is striking that smoking rates continued to climb during the Second World War and afterwards, when "liberation" was not especially strong in this country. This explanation also does not account for the persistence of smoking among marginalized groups of women who have not often benefited from liberation. Clearly, broader social forces are one part but *only one* part of the story of the allure of smoking for women; beyond this lie other social rewards for the woman smoker.

The evidence shows that from the first period when women took up smoking in earnest, they have *benefited* socially from it. Whether by giving reforming women a prime cause for agitation, by offering women a visually compelling way to construct modern identities and reduce the stress of frustration, or by supplying a means of blunting the despair of difficult lives, tobacco – mainly in the form of cigarettes – has played an important role in defining the modern woman in ways *she has chosen*. In Foucault's terms, women have been subjugated by the dominant discourses of smoking, sexuality, and health, among others. At the same time, women have themselves shaped these discourses as empowered subjects. This book argues that women were active agents in finding ways to use tobacco to their own advantage as individuals and in groups.

In no sense does this book encourage women to take up smoking. On the contrary, it takes seriously the many dangers of smoking for women, once defined as "moral" but certainly also physiological, that have been consistently associated with smoking for women since the nineteenth century. Anyone caring to consult the popular or medical evidence since the 1980s cannot escape the litany of devastating physical effects of smoking on women and their children. Smoking is a lethal pastime and remains the number one killer of Canadian women and men.

In the face of these obvious and documented health dangers, one of the book's aims is to find explanations for young women's resistance to giving up smoking. I posit that the attraction of smoking must be understood beyond its simple, taken-for-granted nature. The choice to smoke is not today and never has been a simple one, and the choice to quit is, and has been, equally complex. Smoking has both emotional and intellectual logic to recommend it to young women, as recent studies have suggested. I argue that this has been so for women since at least the 1920s. Unlike much of the literature available about smoking, I do not accept that women adopted smoking simply because of their role as consumers. They *did* participate in the consumer revolution, but smoking had much deeper meanings for women.

Any young woman wanting to better understand the attraction of smoking has not been much helped by what she finds in the formal school curriculum or community resources in the period from 1880 to 2000. I contend that at no time has the formal school curriculum ever represented accurately or fully the reasons why women smoke. There is no recognition in textbooks that the reasons why women smoke include personal and social power as much as their role as consumers. The implications of this gap are obvious and salient to our stalled efforts to reduce rates of smoking for young women through education.

Factors Drawing Women to Smoking

We know that young women are drawn to smoking through its promise to enhance various prized social qualities: status,[2] sexuality,[3] slenderness,[4] sophistication,[5] and sociability,[6] the so-called Five S's identified by Health Canada. This book is loosely organized around the historical development of those Five S's. Smoking is widely acknowledged to help control stress[7] and anxiety in women,[8] along with other self-management functions such as experiencing pleasure.[9] This in turn allows the smoker to hide negative emotions. The latter is a very useful feature when the smoker lacks authority, as, for example, in certain jobs. Smoking is used by some women to manage the double-tasking necessary when they combine paid work and household responsibilities.[10] It is linked with low self-esteem,[11] negative self-assessments of the body,[12] and dietary restraint.[13] There might well be a connection to eating disorders[14] and to perfectionism in lifestyle.[15] There are suggestive links between smoking, eating disorders, and other substance use as well, all of which are connected to (deficits of) self-esteem, depression, anxiety, and body (dis)satisfaction.[16] Hence, in addition to facilitating the experience of pleasure,[17] smoking also allows women to deny themselves pleasures.

Beyond these factors, smoking offers a route to mild rebelliousness.[18] It is often encouraged by another social ritual, drinking alcohol.[19] Smoking is influenced as well by advertising[20] and by peer, familial, and cultural patterns. One causal factor, which is under-examined in the scanty literature, concerns the visual performance made possible through the act of smoking, a set of visual cues taught to young people through popular culture and carrying with them clear utility for the young woman aiming to construct or reconstruct visual identity. Most of these attractions are either ignored or presented unconvincingly in the anti-smoking literature directed to these same young women, limiting the authority of formal education to disrupt this life-threatening habit which for many emerges as an addiction.

Smoking has key social functions, including meeting and sustaining relationships, claiming space and attention in social arenas. This has been confirmed by tobacco manufacturers' own research.[21] Smoking has been named by young women as having an important "survival function" for dealing with adversity, exclusion, or other difficulties. It is often encouraged among pre-adolescent girls and teenagers in same-sex groupings. A large-scale health-behaviour study of school-aged children in the Americas and Europe at the turn of the twenty-first century showed higher rates of smoking among fifteen-year-old girls than among boys in more than half of the thirty-five countries surveyed.[22] Yet, unlike the careful research carried out by tobacco manufacturers, the study of gendered patterns in youth smoking has only just begun on the part of health, sociological, and educational researchers. From the mid-1990s through to the turn of the century, rates for girls' smoking (ages fifteen to nineteen), as well as those for adolescent women, were found to exceed males'. In 2000 in Canada, the Canadian Tobacco Use Monitoring Survey showed that the rate for girls aged fifteen to nineteen was 27 per cent, compared to 23 per cent for males. By 2005, the gender gap had largely disappeared, with reduced rates for both males and females,[23] when the rate dropped to 18 per cent for both sexes. It remained at about 18.5 per cent for women of all

Age of respondent Smoke cigarettes daily	15–19 years Smoke daily	20–24 years Smoke daily	25–34 years Smoke daily	35–44 years Smoke daily	45+ years Smoke daily
Province of respondent					
Newfoundland and Labrador	12.55%	21.60%	17.27%	18.97%	13.04%
Prince Edward Island	6.11%	13.08%	11.56%	7.03%	15.44%
Nova Scotia	9.30%	27.39%	15.82%	14.22%	15.89%
New Brunswick	9.23%	13.02%	17.27%	21.62%	15.94%
Quebec	10.72%	11.41%	15.61%	10.47%	12.62%
Ontario	6.76%	9.26%	11.33%	14.07%	10.40%
Manitoba	7.78%	15.52%	19.81%	11.79%	7.17%
Saskatchewan	10.48%	14.26%	31.84%	22.95%	9.78%
Alberta	6.78%	14.40%	15.48%	20.22%	10.68%
British Columbia	4.88%	6.86%	12.93%	15.22%	9.99%

Filter: Respondent's sex = Female   Weight: Person weight   © Statistics Canada, 2009

ages.[24] Since 2009, smoking rates for young women have remained high, as shown in figure 0.1, with daily rates in the 25 to 34 age group remaining at about 17 per cent.

These figures illustrate the degree to which smoking remains deeply integrated into women's performative scripts as they interact with their peers. In certain regional and ethnocultural communities, such as Aboriginal communities or in socially or economically marginalized sectors of the population,[25] or for women with limited education, smoking rates are much higher than the national average and show little sign of declining.[26] For example, figures for 2003 show that women with less than a secondary-school education smoke at more than twice the rate of women with more education.[27]

Why Worry?

There are compelling reasons for our society to take seriously young women's historical attraction to smoking and the many ways that young women are induced to begin and continue smoking. For one, there is evidence that the gender gap is closing for the onset age of smoking. Current research indicates that the average onset age for young women is now under fifteen,[28] although it has been estimated to be as low as eleven. There are also particular health threats to women smokers. They include the lethal combination created by some oral contraceptives when combined with smoking, the higher incidence among smokers of cancer of the cervix and bladder,[29] of osteoporosis, and of menstrual irregularities,[30] as well as higher rates of miscarriage[31] and of premature births, stillborns,[32] and lower than average birth-weight in babies,[33] early onset of menopause, a vastly increased risk of developing breast cancer if smoking is begun within five years of the onset of the menses,[34] and much else, including direct effects on female smokers' children[35] through second-hand smoke.[36]

Another reason to be concerned at the rates for women's smoking is the resistance by young women to quit. Many young women of the working and middle classes remain wedded to smoking as a relatively easy way to control their weight, stress, and social interactions. A recent book considers the close interplay of obesity, or the fear of being overweight, and smoking, particularly for young women. It shows that one-third of all deaths from all causes are directly attributable to the effects of smoking and obesity.[37]

The growing awareness of smoking's damage to women's bodies can be traced by taking *The Globe and Mail*'s treatment of the subject as an example. From as early as 1966, the newspaper was reporting that women who smoked had higher than average rates of lung cancer[38] and typical chronic bronchitis,[39] as well as a nine-fold greater chance of developing oral cancers than female non-smokers.[40] They were also at greater risk for cancers of the esophagus, bladder, voice-box, and kidneys[41] and heart disease. They had more colds, produced more phlegm, had limited lung capacity,[42] and had concentrations of carcinogenic chemicals in breast fluid.[43] The steadily mounting list of threats could not easily be ignored. And yet they were not fully recognized until the early 1980s in the general population, and the evidence is still disregarded by many young women today.

We know that cigarettes kill twenty times more people than all illegal drugs combined and that smoking remains the leading cause of death for all of those previously treated for drug and other dependencies.[44] For the general population, smoking is also the leading cause of preventable death. That this powerful evidence now amassed and regularly presented through the media has not caused young women to quit in larger numbers (in contrast to other population sectors) suggests that the process of redefining smoking as a useful behaviour for young women as begun in the 1920s has finally triumphed in the face of clear health threats.

A further reason why women have taken up smoking and then have continued with it are the combined effects of modernism, cultural eroticism, and the emphasis on visual culture.

Modernity, Eroticism, and Visual Culture

For women, smoking provided a route into the pleasures and demands of the modernist revolution. As it applies to this study, modernity can be defined as "the continual production of new products."[45] Jonathan Crary puts capitalism at the root of the process, which "uproots and makes mobile that which is grounded, clears away or obliterates that which impedes circulation, and makes exchangeable what is singular."[46] Closely associated with this aspect of modernity, is the notion of commodification, or the production of commodities for consumer consumption, and the creation of demand for more commodities, linking desire and the search for personal satisfaction with "things," the essence of mall culture.

Cigarette smoking became one more avenue through which commodities could be produced and sold to the public. Through smoking, women also "consumed" paraphernalia that supported the act of smoking: cigarette cases, match holders, cigarette holders, lighters, ceramic and china ashtrays and dishes, specialized clothing, handbags, and many other products. All of these were produced to profile the identity of the woman smoker and set off her performance.

One way to continue to sell lots of things to lots of people, even when those things don't wear out, is to imbue the products with an erotic attraction. Paul Rutherford argues that two distinct but overlapping systems characterized the erotic economy of the twentieth century: the fashion industry with products that framed or embellished the body, masking flaws in the process, and the entertainment industry, which offered various means to represent fashion and the reformed body to a mass audience through movies, television, and the Internet. Following Foucault, Rutherford explores the development of a "regime of stimulation" and its determination of subjectivity and behaviour for both the voyeur, usually a male, and for the object of that gaze, usually a woman, who in turn could manipulate through her control of the voyeur's desires.

Modernism resulted in a vast reorganization of knowledge, a new language to express these hierarchies, and new networks of relationships, spaces, and subjectivities.[47] Essential to the pattern of production and consumption is visual display. Visual methods reveal embodied modernist experience in ways that go beyond what is possible by using narrative means alone. In fact, modernism brought with it nothing less than a new model of visual representation and perception and a new form of the observer."[48] The observer, as one who watches, either passively or actively, operates within a prescribed set of conventions and possibilities. Within this history of the visual, the act of observation changes, asserts Foucault.[49] It has been argued that an emphasis on visual identities became a means by which the subject was shaped by this "regime of truth" and who in turn could actively alter conventions. Foucault suggested that this process was most obvious when fault lines appeared through the struggle over social power.

This scholarship has encouraged me to chart the process of visual representation in Canada as it applied to women's smoking, suggesting the effects on the observer, both men and women, and on the object of that gaze, the woman smoker. Feminist scholars argue that the gendering of the "surveyor and the surveyed" mirrors patriarchal society.[50] Carson and Pajaczkowska identify a feminist version of visual culture in which the goal is to "see" visual representation through women's eyes.[51] Generally speaking, feminist analyses seek to include women's voices where they would conventionally be absent.[52] More recent work also points to the power of the observed to captivate the observer through enticement, creating an "unstable relationship of power between the one who looks and the one who displays."[53] This examination takes up the question of how the gaze – especially women's gaze – alters and is in turn altered by the spectacle of woman as smoker. Wherever possible, it adopts a feminist perspective on this process.

Within this context, photographs and other like representations of "reality," such as lithographs and drawings, assumed new significance. They became a chief expression of the process of commodification. "Photography is an element of a new and homogenous terrain of consumption and circulation in which an observer becomes lodged."[54] The observer might also be the creator of the image, or the arranger of the images, as in the case of the family photograph album.[55] Along with other visual records, photography became a study of social practice.[56]

Whereas our senses had been joined in pre-modernist times, with touch often working in tandem with sight to give an object meaning, modernism re-sorted the senses in a new hierarchy of meaning. Sight dominated over all others. The unrelenting emphasis on visual elements – external ones, of a streetscape or the home, as well as personal features relating to clothing and the body – meant that appearance became a quantifiable indicator of social capital. If one were to be a consumer, sight would be the primary means by which this world of endlessly reproduced objects would be surveyed, assessed, and, finally, consumed. In the process, however, consumers and especially female consumers were themselves "consumed" as their bodies were evaluated according to new and demanding visual standards.

The new predominance of vision as a marker of value and the many products to be purchased, displayed, and then rejected for a new fashion took place in Canadian society as it was urbanizing after 1921, when for the first time, more than 50 per cent of the population lived in cities. The urban experience encouraged a particular kind of observer, one who moved through space on foot, taking in products, advertisements, and other consumers in spaces lit by artificial light. Spaces were often visually confused and enlarged by mirrors and high ceilings. Space was also shortened through public transportation where one travelled with strangers through a landscape that changed regularly with advertising placards. The collage of images, colours, sizes, movement, and object depth created a kind of multiple vision in the modern observer, one where some objects were necessarily filtered out but whole sets of others were absorbed in a glance.

Through modernity, women's roles in a secularized, acquisitive, and urbanized culture were profoundly changed. Whereas women had defined themselves as active participants in broad social change and as morally exemplary caregivers of their families and society in general before the First World War, by the 1920s they were called upon to become junior partners in public life through the portal of shopping as the family's consumer specialist. Smoking allowed young women during this transitional period to imagine new expressive techniques that would mark them as modern and sophisticated rather than (arguably) backward-looking and repressed. A parallel process was occurring with young university men, for whom smoking had long been a symbol of maturity.[57] Smoking had already acquired social meaning as a sophisticated, mature, and intellectual act before women took up the habit. Women actively shaped and reshaped the meaning-making processes so that it could serve as an appropriate symbol for their desires and needs.

As a function of modernity, women consumers were (and remain) under enormous pressure to be "perfect," at least in their appearance. The new beauty cult was fuelled by film stars, like Marlene Dietrich in figure 0.2 or Mae West in 5.23, who became templates on which women of the era modelled themselves. Many of these stars smoked both on and off the screen. Their air-brushed images underscored for women the importance of youth,[58] including unlined faces and sparkling white teeth, as well as slimness. The promise of sophistication offered a reinscribed respectability for women and presented a new and alluring possibility for creating "social magic," subverting the older prescriptive code. The image of the independent, sophisticated, but disciplined woman smoker, waged or not, was inserted into a larger canvas of optimistic Canadian development and carefully developed by advertisers of many products, tobacco included.

Types of Evidence Used in This Book

Necessarily, the range of visual, written, and material cultural sources as the basis of this examination are diverse. Generally, they fall into two categories.

First, visual representations generated *by* women, both in opposition to smoking and in support of it, are used. They include individual photographs, both staged and candid; photograph collages with or without labels and other products of undergraduates' yearbooks; as well as posters. Oral testimony has been provided by women who have smoked for many years, some of whom began in the interwar period and others from the 1960s or later. Primary literature, including diaries and letters of non-smokers, provide insights into the women who chose to smoke and those who decided against it. Additional accounts by women smokers have been given to me by other generous researchers; these visually rich descriptions provide context for other written accounts, both personal and official. Other written sources by women include pamphlets, autobiographies, institutional histories, journals, poetry, women's club minute books, organizational official reports and awards manuals, teachers' manuals, songbooks, and elocution guidebooks.

Lest it be thought that all nineteenth-century Canadian women objected to tobacco use and that all twentieth-century Canadian women took up smoking, I have included life narratives that represent a range of decisions in every period. Analyzing life narratives requires that one attend especially closely to the context of the woman's life and agency. For example, did the woman have a real choice about whether or not to smoke, whether or not to condemn tobacco? Ideological patterns of the time must be examined, as well as relationality to others in the woman's family, social orbit, or workplace. The audience being addressed is important, as is the embodiment suggested by the narrative, or ways in which the narrator's body is imagined.[59]

For the most part, in comparing the accounts of smokers and non-smokers, it is striking that the smokers were less reflective in explaining their decision to smoke than the non-smokers were in explaining their decision not to. In part, this demonstrates that the choice to smoke seems often to be an emotional one, frequently not intellectualized or explained very fully. At best, the factors impelling these women are hinted at but not explicated. This apparent reticence reminds us that without the visual evidence for such women, from which we would undoubtedly learn much, we cannot hope to reconstruct the full range of reasons for smoking based on these accounts. Nevertheless, in contrasting women's personal accounts, we are able to fill in some of the gaps.

Second, visual representations, written accounts, and material culture *about* or *for* women in a number of forms are presented and analyzed. These include print advertisements, posters, billboards, movies, individual and group photographs, and educational illustrations. The secondary literature has provided an essential context with which to understand the prescriptions associated with the performance of smoking. Important here are biographies of notable women who took a strong position on smoking. Popular cultural sources have also been important: advice literature, medical commentary, short stories in women's and family magazines, novels, pulp literature, newspaper and periodical articles, formal regulations, poetry, textbooks, teachers' guides, Sabbath-school teaching materials, and students' assignments have all been very useful in understanding the reported relationship women constructed with tobacco.

Interpretive Frameworks

Judith Butler has enriched our understanding of modern social systems as a constituent of identity. Particularly sensitive to detecting counter-discourse, Butler argues that stylized and repetitive images and actions must be studied and mined for meaning.[60] She argues that repetitions of acts, both social and linguistic, eventually take on the power of ritual, creating a kind of "social magic"[61] for the performer. Such repetitive acts have particular meaning for the socially disenfranchised, creating behavioural codes that, she argues, constitute the person and can eventually take on hegemonic authority in cultural terms. Butler's insights are applied most often to sexual roles that are "transgressive" or boundary-breaking, such as transgendered women, or, we might add, women first taking up public smoking after 1918 or women living on the margins in our own period.

In my quest to understand the process by which identity is constructed and reconstructed through smoking, I have drawn on Michel Foucault's work, particularly his notion of "technologies of the self."[62] These, he argues, "permit individuals to effect by their own means or with the help of others a certain number of operations on their own bodies and ... thoughts, conduct, and way of being, so as to transform themselves in order to attain a certain state of happiness, purity, wisdom, perfection, or immorality."[63] Technologies of the self work in tandem with other types of power to allow domination in social contexts. He terms the point of contact between various technologies of domination of others and the self "governmentality." These concepts have been useful to me in understanding the power and identity formation that accompanied the women who lead anti-tobacco campaigns in the past and present and the ways in which young women smokers position themselves in opposition to formal medical and educational discourse.

Decoding Evidence

In seeking to understand the nature of women's relationship with smoking, this study analyzes both conventional historical text and visual records. It begins with the premise that a primary appeal of smoking for women has been the variety of visual statements that cigarettes allow women to make. By decoding how women presented themselves as opponents of smoking and as smokers, as well as how others represented morally exemplary women who decried tobacco's curse and the morally compromised woman smoker, we can uncover other meanings held by smoking for women. It follows, therefore, that visual representations, both constituent of the discourse of a culture and influenced by other broad discursive patterns, are critically important in a study such as this one.

By discourse I mean "statements which structure the way a thing is thought, and the way we act on the basis of that thinking."[64] Discourse is a powerful influence on subjectivity, but while there is no single discourse operating in any period or society, and while discursive patterns can change in response to socio-economic conditions, political upheaval, or ideological constructs,[65] dominant patterns do emerge that ascribe taken-for-granted meanings to particular acts like smoking. At the same time, Penny Tinkler reminds us that "[d]iscourse is also not a straitjacket: women may take up dominant meanings, seek to resist them, or position themselves in a counter-discourse. Women may also seek to invent new discourses."[66] It is clear to me that women have done just this – invented new discourses – around smoking.

"Reading" Visual Texts

To "read" a photograph or other visual image, one must accept that images are "visual text," complete with a range of "signs." This requires close attention to the details and levels of meaning contained in these images and circulated, their reception, and the context that produced them.[67] As important as it is to distinguish the visual source's provenance and subject, it is also necessary to consider the specific cultural contexts within which the visual record was produced. When were these visual artifacts generated, with what intention(s), and how do they compare with other cultural artifacts of the same era and place? How accessible were these visual products to women and, indeed, to the general culture? Who is caught in the gaze of the photograph, and why? Who is controlling the gaze, and why?

Film had been an important cultural outlet for men and women since the turn of the century. The popularity of movies had generally increased by the First World War, and by 1916 more than twenty million tickets were sold weekly at the cinema in England alone.[68] By the 1930s, cigarettes were commonly placed in movie actors' hands and "used to invest characters and scenes with a range of meanings."[69] Alan Brandt argues that films "both reflected and reified cultural norms at the same time that they created styles and fads."[70] Mitchell and Reid-Walsh note that "[f]ilms offer a window into culture and, more generally, into our society's perceptions of gender, family, and social life ... films offer a means by which we understand who we are and how we should behave. Films ... reflect as well as shape our images of ourselves and others."[71] As important as the record of film is as a source of social norms and identity imagery, the public reaction to it is important to track. Did Canadian women make time in their busy lives for the movies? During times of particular financial constraint, did women find the money for movies or choose other forms of leisured "watching"? Oral testimony, letters, and diaries of Canadian women help us to appreciate the general importance of movies in their lives, especially in a pre-television era.

Despite the widespread recognition that visual records are an important historical source, a debate exists as to whether the effective use of visual records for academic investigation requires specific skills of "visual literacy." Paul Messaris argues that "[w]hat distinguishes images (including motion pictures) from language and from other modes of communication is the fact that images reproduce many of the informational cues that people make use of in their perception of physical and social reality."[72] Thus, he posits, we possess innate visual intelligence. Similarly, Ronald Barthes holds that the photograph is "a message without a code."[73] The constructed nature of the visual record, together with its essential ability to either reinforce or break unmediated "visual orders," suggests that attending to certain semiotic functions can be productive in understanding the power of visual records. With this in mind, Janne Seppanen (after Barthes and others) sets out the concepts of "denotation" (the visual

0.2 | Marlene Dietrich, c. 1930. © Bettman/ Corbis. Image BE063084

record's obvious meaning), "connotation" (its "surplus" meanings), and "myth" (in which the 'historical' becomes 'natural').[74]

One way in which the mythic meaning of the visual record can be made to appear as a natural representation of a phenomenon, rather than as one that has been carefully constructed, is by drawing out the photograph's metaphoric content. As in spoken language, metaphors alide two images, a primary one, usually the subject, and a secondary, culturally significant image that is broadly recognized. Metaphoric strategies invite the observer (or the listener, in spoken language) to apply some features of the culturally significant image to a visual record's subject, thereby creating a "parallel implication complex," as Charles Forceville puts it, where either or both the primary and secondary image(s) are strengthened by the power of their association.[75] The image of Marlene Dietrich in figure 0.2, with her cigarette held high and the smoke emphasizing the cigarette's position, is a case in point. I argue that movies were exceedingly important in creating mythic images around the stars and the cigarette. Cassandra Tate reports a study of American films of the late 1920s and early 1930s regarding who smoked and the characterization of the smokers. Sixty-five per cent of the male movie heroes smoked, while only 22.5 per cent of the "bad guys" smoked. Similarly, of female movie heroines, 30 per cent smoked, but only 2.5 per cent of "bad girls" were shown smoking.[76] Hence, the connotations of smokers were very positive in this influential source of popular culture in the interwar period when smoking by a woman was first integrated into popular culture.

In the case of Dietrich as shown here, a culturally powerful and recognizable image of femininity was developed by aliding a beautiful and mysterious woman with cigarette-smoking (the denoted meaning) and smoking in a particular way. Here the connotated meaning of smoking to connote feminine wiles and sexual knowing came to be so recognizable through the many films that Dietrich made that it assumed mythic proportions. It thus strengthened both images – that of any woman smoking in this fashion and of Dietrich herself, who became iconic for her sexual prowess, her smoking, and tough-talking. Dietrich was one of the starlets photographed so often while smoking that the cigarette became an identifiable part of her cinema image. In this photograph, her image is softened with an elegant evening gown, a halo effect on her soft hairstyle, and a decorative stairway on which she is posed.

The most common stance for the woman smoker was to hold her cigarette in a "flag" position in which the cigarette was held at chin level, just as Dietrich has done in this photograph. This pose connoted femininity, even exaggerated femininity, in the smoker. For decades afterwards, even to this day, women have perfected that characteristic stance of crooked arm, cigarette held high, staring evenly ahead. The mythic nature of that stance will be observed repeatedly in this book as woman after woman replicates it closely, likely copying the many movies and female movie stars who had taught her *how* to smoke and still remain a lady.

To illustrate other principles outlined above, we might use as an example a cover of the *Canadian Home Journal*, the so-called "Macdonald Lassie" by cover artist Rex Woods. Beginning with the denoted meaning, anyone familiar with Export "A" cigarette advertising will immediately recognize the image of the Scottish woman with her distinctive highland hat and her Macdonald plaid scarf. Denoting a Macdonald Tobacco product for more than a century, the highland imagery seems naturalized.

We know too little about the artist of this famous piece. Unofficial accounts have Woods born in 1903 in Lincolnshire. Immigrating to Canada during the early 1920s, he attended the Ontario School of Art and became a prolific cover artist for *Maclean's* and, as can be seen in figure 0.3, the *Canadian Home Journal.* He has been called "the Norman Rockwell of Canada," and indeed, his art is strongly reminiscent of Rockwell's.

0.3 | An early version of the Macdonald Lassie – cover of *Canadian Home Journal*, 1936

Given the conservatism of both Rockwell and Woods, one wonders how he could be celebrating the classic image of the Macdonald Tobacco Company and in an era when women's association with smoking was still heavily contested. The answer lies partly in chronology. This winsome gal appeared on the cover of the *Canadian Home Journal* in January of 1936, long before the image was popularized by Export "A." Macdonald Tobacco reportedly hired Woods to execute the original image based on this cover art, and it was updated by the company several times thereafter by artist Will Davies and others.

Having addressed its provenance as far as can be determined and its denotated meaning, let us now turn to the image's connotated meanings. The young woman is presented as the very image of beauty for the 1930s: she faces the camera with a shy smile framed by coloured lips, rouged cheeks, and shaped eyebrows in the style of that era. She is "fair" in all respects, with almost mustard-coloured hair, perhaps to bring out the bright yellow in the tartan scarf. Her headpiece is a traditional part of the highland dancer's costume, and while we are not offered a full-body view, we can assume that she is athletic and skilled. The connotated meaning, therefore, is of a fully respectable, even conservative young woman in the full bloom of youth and beauty. The mythic meaning of this piece of art is shaped by the woman's caucasian beauty, the contested nature of smoking for women at the time, and the power of tobacco advertising. The resulting reading of the Macdonald Lassie would be something like "Export A is such a fine cigarette that even young, conservative, and pure women can safely support it." We do not know whether the Macdonald Lassie was meant to be portrayed as herself a smoker, of course, but regardless, by the alison of a pretty young woman of privileged ethnicity with smoking, the act itself is normalized.

Who is caught in the Macdonald Lassie's gaze? Readers of the *Canadian Home Journal* would largely be female, with the model's age group included. Yet the association with Macdonald Tobacco would not yet be set, so her utility in peddling cigarettes with this image would be in the future. A product of magazine art first and tobacco advertising art thereafter, the young woman pictured here had a long run in influencing women whether to smoke or not. Her model as a beautiful woman was powerful in itself in suggesting visual identities that could be taken up by observers.

The Macdonald Lassie's fair complexion was not by chance. As a model of conventional beauty, comeliness, and modesty, the Macdonald Lassie's visual qualities ran counter to the usual depiction of the woman smoker or tobacco worker. As will be seen in succeeding chapters, the only place where women of colour were represented in tobacco iconography was as déclassé labourers in the cigar or cigarette industries or as unrespectable performers. It was very rare to find a racialized non-white woman represented in Canadian cigarette advertising through to the 1980s. The Macdonald Lassie is fully representative of the bleached models invoked to sell cigarettes to both men and women.

Starting in the interwar period, photographs became much more common in Canada as a result of less expensive cameras, including ones that non-professionals could easily use like the Kodak Brownie. Women took pictures of their pals and were in turn photographed. These visual records, which appear to be "candids" or largely unmediated in source or construction, such as one finds in a student-produced photograph album or unposed shots in a movie magazine, tell us different things about the subjects, their era, and locale than do studio-produced photographs by professional photographers. This research aims to "read" all of these visual documents, comparing them wherever possible.

It must be acknowledged, however, that visual documents can rarely ever be considered unmediated. Generally, the greater the photographer's skill in constructing the image, including the choice of subject, the more the product looks to be "candid." Even in instances where photographs are genuinely extemporaneous, a selection must have been made among other like photographs from which this one was selected. Beyond that, photographs are mounted in a given pattern, "framed" or coupled in a particular spatial relationship with others, and these groupings influence the meanings made by observers. Exclusions as well as inclusions produce their own narratives and narrative shifts. These can only be detected with a "sufficient" number of examples to uncover the pattern at play, allowing the observer to attend to categories such as poses, props, people, and places.[77]

The Historiography of Women's Tobacco Use

This analysis has benefited enormously from the secondary literature bearing on the history of smoking. Until very recently, the literature related to smoking has been preoccupied with the long-standing battle between governments and corporate tobacco giants in which the tobacco interests have been exposed as rapacious and unethical.[78] And such stories have been exceedingly well told: Richard Kruger's *Ashes to Ashes* won a Pulitzer Prize.[79] This study does not dispute that aggressive marketing campaigns by tobacco manufacturers have helped to convince men, women, and children to try smoking. Indeed, anyone familiar with the literature documenting the actions of tobacco manufacturers since the late nineteenth century could not reasonably conclude otherwise. However, unlike many academic works in this area, this study argues that women were willing accomplices in normalizing smoking. Women took an active role in shaping smoking's meanings, thus contributing to the smoking woman's identity. This was not, nor is it today, a passive process whereby women were victimized.

Interest in the social history of smoking is much more recent. Across North America, there have been a few studies of tobacco as representative of other moralized behaviours, such as drinking, drug-taking, and gambling, generally associated with temperance[80] and with the professionalization of doctors.[81] A small international literature in social history has appeared over the past decade, which includes women but which is by no means exclusively concerned with women's decisions to smoke or their representation.[82] Of particular importance, Matthew Hilton has produced an impressive cultural history of smoking in Britain, concentrating on the male smoker. Many of his insights about the significance of visual and artifactual culture have enriched this study of women's smoking.[83] Cassandra Tate has shown how the anti-cigarette movement in the United States took on "Big Tobacco" between 1890 and 1930 and lost. The forces arrayed against the cigarette included Progressive Reformers, evangelical moralists, and tobacco farmers supplying manufacturers of cigars and chewing tobacco. Yet the social influences favouring a product like the cigarette were too powerful. Her investigation of the American WCTU's (Woman's Christian Temperance Union) role in the anti-tobacco movement has been very useful for this study, showing how less invested it was in anti-tobacco agitation than I have demonstrated for Canada.[84]

Allan Brandt's masterful *The Cigarette Century* is the latest addition to tobacco scholarship.[85] Brandt explores the process by which the cigarette played a "prominent and popular role in the rise of a consumer age for America." His incorporation of the cultural history of smoking, the scientific debates that muted health concerns about smoking's effects, and the political and legal attempts to control Big Tobacco give the book an impressive range. He argues that "historical exploration of the cigarette reveals the advantages of problem-centered histories that call for disrupting some of the traditional boundaries of disciplinary inquiry."[86] Like Brandt, I have attempted to bridge disciplinary boundaries in exploring smoking's importance to women. Acknowledging that smoking does support social exchange and adolescent identity formation, his analysis also positions women as mainly acted-upon, not as actors, in the performance of smoking.

In Canada, Jarrett Rudy has explored changing public views of tobacco consumption on the part of women and men in Quebec between the late nineteenth and mid-twentieth centuries. Rudy's main argument is that smoking served to promote liberal ideals related to gender, class, and racial norms. Even the rituals of smoking were structured by liberal concepts, he argues. These changing ideological frameworks, which stressed views of personal rights, supplanted earlier moral explanations.[87] Rudy's scholarship is helpful in explaining some of the arguments about smoking specific to Quebec culture but is less relevant when applied to women's entry into smoking culture elsewhere. After all, the popularity of smoking among women occurred during the Second World War and into the 1970s, long after liberalism's modernist influence had reached its nadir. Nevertheless, Rudy's interpretation of the failure of the Montreal WCTU anti-tobacco campaigns to generate much interest is illuminating in comparison to the stronger response from English Canada. He concludes that the combined weaknesses of English anti-tobacco advocacy and the opposition of the Roman Catholic and Anglican churches to state involvement in moral training meant that "dominant notions about smoking as a sign of respectable and mature masculinity were less successfully challenged by the W.C.T.U. in Quebec and Montreal than elsewhere in Canada."[88]

The foremost source on the "Canadian Tobacco Wars" is Rob Cunningham's study, *Smoke and Mirrors.* Cunningham adopts the same explanation for women's interest in smoking as is characteristic of most of the rest of the literature: that women took up smoking through becoming "liberated" consumers. He presents for us in impressive detail the two major efforts to gain legislation in Canada to control packaging, advertisement, and sponsorships of tobacco products, always resisted by the tobacco interests and often successfully. His account of the battle to gain passage of two critical bills informs the context in which women were wooed by tobacco producers in the 1980s. Cunningham credits much of the success of this belated legislative protection to effective alliances of citizens, medical doctors, and political strategists, welded, he says, for the first time in the late 1980s in the war against tobacco. In positioning the alliance as a late-twentieth-century development, however, he ignores the many effective women-led shifting alliances that operated in Canada throughout the nineteenth century. As well, Cunningham's study is primarily a political one, privileging the drama of legislative change (or failure) and largely ignoring the social world of smokers.

The historical literature focusing directly on the history of women and smoking is even smaller and more recent. In Canada, my own work has explored women as opponents of smoking through temperance leadership,[89] while Cheryl Krasnick Warsh has analyzed advertising campaigns in postwar Canada to encourage women to drink alcohol and smoke cigarettes.[90] She argues that tobacco advertisers represented the woman smoker as glamorous, wealthy, sophisticated, and liberated. "The freedom of women to smoke and drink was an inevitable development of the culture of consumerism."[91] However, as valuable as Warsh's scholarship is in tracing patterns used by advertisers, the women as presented in this analysis are their creations. I have sought to build on this base by also exploring the role taken by women themselves over a long span from the late nineteenth to the early twenty-first centuries. I have pursued the views of smokers through personal accounts, oral histories, diaries, letters, journals, photograph albums, biographies, and other sources.

Penny Tinkler's stimulating work is grounded in the British experience. She argues that between 1880 and 1980, cigarette smoking became progressively feminized. Her contentions do not appear to hold for Canada or the United States.[92] Like this study, hers is based largely on visual culture[93] and offers much insight methodologically.

In all of these works, women's introduction to smoking is seen as closely aligned with their growing role as consumers from the 1920s and with women's expanding social, economic, and legal freedom. Increased access to motorcars and unchaperoned dance halls, civic rights gained through the franchise, less constraining dress, and higher rates of paid employment for women all have been seen in these histories as leading to women demanding the right to smoke.[94] In so arguing, both the popular and academic literature have largely adopted the arguments put by advertisers in that era. While this study does not deny that consumerism and greater social freedom stimulated Canadian smoking rates among women, it digs far deeper than these time-worn explanations, drawing on more recent educational, medical, and sociological literature.

Within the educational and medical literature on smoking, gendered analyses or those stressing the social utility of smoking are rare.[95] Research into the health effects of smoking has tended to adopt a model stressing individual choice, with smoking presented as a poor life-decision. This remains the dominant stance of health textbooks and much community-based literature, which carry the burden of the anti-smoking message to young women. The power of the smoker's social group in these sources is acknowledged, but the implication is that personal decisions can, and must, weigh against these deleterious habits adopted by the "crowd."[96]

Some recent studies on smoking in the international health and sociological literature have explored the influence of social context in smoking onset and persistence.[97] A recent article explores the importance of cigarette and packaging design for women smokers.[98] In Canada, Lorraine Greaves has made an important contribution to charting the relationship between mature women's smoking and social disadvantage,[99] while a study by Frohlich showed the importance of smoking as a shared social practice among Canadian teenagers.[100] The importance of female adolescent social hierarchies in interrupting or encouraging smoking has also been explored by Mitchell and Amos.[101] There is increasing recognition that adolescent society constitutes its own culture within which young women must find a place. Smoking can facilitate inclusion in this social framework,[102] although just how this occurs is still not well understood.[103] Several studies indicate the importance of smoking as an adolescent route to identity formation and re-formation.[104] This book builds on a number of those findings and explores that process historically for women of all ages.

The Boundaries of This Study

This book is limited in a number of ways. First, the discussion is rooted primarily in the historical representation of English-Canadian women, despite the use of some francophone sources for purposes of comparison. The subjects of this study are also primarily racialized white women, since the source material is far stronger for that sector of the population than for any other. It is clear that rates of smoking differ by ethnocultural community in Canada as elsewhere,[105] with Chinese and South Asian Canadians smoking less than European or Latin American Canadians.[106] Still, there is much that we do not know about the nature of the relationship of smoking to women in various cultural contexts.[107]

Second, the time period is long: from 1880 to 2000, and within this span some themes are developed for shorter or longer periods. The book follows both chronological and thematic patterns. By no means do all themes address each period in Canadian history. To take one example, because the height of the close association between women's waged work and smoking was in the period from the 1940s to 1980s, that becomes the emphasis of the period addressed in chapter 8.

Finally, the sources for this study are Canadian whenever available. Some sources from entertainment, such as the interwar movies and the stars they spawned, are transnational in influence. Hence, on occasion non-Canadian sources are used to explicate Canadian themes.

How This Book Is Organized

This book explores Canadian women's general representational patterns in the nineteenth and twentieth centuries and depictions of cigarette use. It does so to inform both patterns: perceptions of women smokers and women opposed to smoking were *shaped by* views of smoking and gender in a given period, and in turn the smokers and non-smokers themselves *influenced* how smoking was perceived and marketed. To make this dual process and the interlinkages evident, a general social history of Canadian women is offered. Women's arguments for or against smoking over time is cast against this backdrop. Smoking itself has a social history with strong visual and artifactual evidence. In addition, it has a business history, a history of tobacco technology, a medical history, and a distinctive history of advertising, all influenced by the gender, class position, and interests of the representational "observer" or consumer. The book attends to these various intersections and resists any easy conclusions as to which domain most influenced the others.

Did advertising "create" the market of women smokers, or did women "demand" this guilty pleasure? I argue that no clear causality exists; advertisers and the market they sought influenced each other over the course of this century. The book does not support the contention that Canadian women were merely seduced by the glamour of smoking and forced into addiction. Rather, it argues that whether women were opposed to smoking or participated in that culture, they had good reason to do so and that their interests helped to shape official prescriptions for smoking in every era. Women were subjected to powerful discourses tying glamour with smoking, but this pressure was not a one-way process. Conversely, the imperative for cigarette manufacturers to make money through their product, the changes in manufacturing processes, and the broader anxieties and goals of Canadian society helped to determine what products were offered to women, how, and with what normative values. Thus, this is not a simple narrative of women either entrapped or liberated, nor of tobacco manufacturers as rapacious or conventionally entrepreneurial. To put a human face on the analysis, I have profiled as many women as possible, including those who opposed smoking, those who ignored it or resisted its lure, and those who took up smoking. Taken as a group, these profiles aim to suggest the complex connections between smoking and women's lived motivations and experiences.

The book's first section contains this introduction and one overarching chapter. The latter offers a brief history of women's relationship with smoking in Canada between about 1880 and 2000. It shows that women's decisions to agitate against smoking, to accept others as smokers, or to themselves take up smoking were strongly influenced by broad social forces such as the dominance of temperance or Canada's involvement in war. As well, women who participated in these national movements and who articulated a position on tobacco use helped to shape social views about addictions generally, women's rights and roles, and appropriate interventions.

At the beginning of the period, most respectable racialized white women of the middle class actively opposed smoking by their fathers, brothers, husbands, and sons. The largest Canadian women's organization of the era, the Woman's Christian Temperance Union, became a leader in the anti-smoking movement in nineteenth-century Canada, maintaining that leadership position until about the First World War. Beyond women who were involved in scandalous occupations like prostitution or the music hall or those who self-consciously defined themselves as bohemians or artists, very few women smoked, and almost none smoked in public. By the end of the twentieth century when the book concludes, smoking had again become unacceptable in polite society, but the movement to stamp it out was no longer led by women. Furthermore, the majority of women smokers were no longer only members of the underworld or disreputable women but young women between the ages of 18 and 24, daughters of the middle and working classes using tobacco for their own purposes.

The book's second section is divided into three chapters and concentrates on the nineteenth century. Chapter 2 offers a detailed survey of how Canadian women's leadership in the anti-smoking movement developed. Grounded in their commitment to the temperance movement, dutiful Christian women accepted this responsibility by portraying themselves as moral exemplars of Canadian society. Many of these women identified as first-wave (maternal) feminists and demanded a public role in society based on their moral superiority. Other women in the anti-smoking movement would more accurately be described as proto-feminists. Their campaigns against tobacco were part of a multi-faceted moral movement that afforded them political prominence. Women used anti-tobacco campaigns to develop and foster identities of unblemished subjectivity in contrast to the impure "other": men and those few women who smoked. Their identity as "pure" women supported a particular racialized and classed image of the Canadian nation and their rightful place within it. As an example, Bertha Wright, an intrepid leader of the Young Woman's Christian Temperance Union in Ottawa, is profiled. By 1930, this style of moral leadership had waned, and the anti-smoking forces were in retreat as Canadian society gradually came to accept smoking as a benign pleasure for both men and women.

Chapter 3 takes up the theme of the many routes through which women acted as "gate-keepers" to shield children from tobacco products. During the nineteenth century, women parlayed their traditional role as children's protectors and educators into a broad program directed mainly at boys. By the twentieth century, women joined forces with male colleagues and health advocates to expose tobacco manufacturers' attempts to lure children (and their parents) into the company of smokers by offering treats like collectors' cards, prizes, and other enticements.

Chapter 4 explores how the formal educational system has dealt with the issue of youth smoking and especially the phenomenon of the "girl smoker." When school textbooks and community resources bemoaned child and adolescent smokers, they almost always assumed them to be male. The chapter surveys the woeful inadequacy of school curricula and some community materials to acknowledge the girl smoker from the time that smoking was first treated in textbooks from the 1880s until after 2000. This banal and unconvincing curriculum is contrasted with the creative and effective informal curriculum mounted by tobacco manufacturers. Failing to find themselves in formal educational resources, girls have been informally taught why, how, and when to smoke in the socially prescribed ways through popular culture, including that fashioned by tobacco manufacturers. Profiled here is the "invisible" girl smoker, standing just out of focus and behind the text of educational materials intended to dissuade male youths from smoking.

The book's third section considers the many enticements by which women have been drawn into smoking culture. Chapter 5 explores the origins of smoking's sexualization. Almost from the cigarette's introduction, it assumed a feminized quality, allowing mythic sexual meanings to be projected onto the object and act of smoking. In turn, it imbued the woman smoker with sexual attraction. Sexualized women's images were used as marketing symbols for tobacco in all forms – loose tobacco in tins, cigar boxes, and cigarello and cigarette packages – and in advertisements in a wide variety of print and graphic media, as well as in the movies and on television. All of these images helped to develop mythic sexualized meanings associated with smoking. I hypothesize that the sexual allure of the woman smoker has helped to attract women to the ranks of smokers because it allows otherwise "respectable" women to develop and exercise a sexually charged persona in ways that would otherwise not be possible, given societal norms governing female behaviour. The long tradition of sexuality and smoking is explored through the fictitious "girls on the cigar boxes."

Benefiting from this sexualization of the respectable woman smoker as well as the long-standing tradition of sexualized bohemian, artistic, and intellectual women smokers, the twentieth-century "sophisticate" often used the cigarette to hone an identity marked by independence and talent. In chapter 6, the "New Woman," the first powerful symbol of the sophisticated woman, is examined. These women were early entrants to the professions, women who supported themselves in the arts, or took up places in academia, often asserting their rights by brandishing a cigarette. Several women diarists and teacher and artist Doris McCarthy offer case studies for this chapter.

One of the many attractions of smoking for young women was the promise that if they smoked, they would have less difficulty remaining thin. From the 1920s, Canadian women were presented with an unforgiving formula if they hoped to meet the new standard of physical beauty: a thin figure, with clear, unlined skin and sparkling teeth, sweet breath, polished nails, a youthful face improved by cosmetics, and a perfumed aura. Fashions began to change more quickly. Chapter 7 argues that cigarettes helped to construct a woman's fashion statement. Smoking gave the additional advantage of focusing attention on the woman smoker's carefully constructed appearance. From the 1930s billboards showing the slender and pretty "Winchester" cigarette girl to the Canadian version of the Virginia Slims advertisements of the 1970s (for example, du Maurier "Slims"),

Canadian women could find examples like themselves pictured in magazines, on placards, in movies, and eventually on television, reminding them of the idealized female physical form and cigarettes' helpful quality of suppressing appetite.

For a woman to take full advantage of this visual attention, she needed to spend a good deal of her time in public. Middle-class women had some opportunity to hone their public performance in "society," but freedom was given as well to the waged or salaried woman who had occasion each day to practise her smoking pose. Chapter 8 discusses the role of waged and salaried women in popularizing smoking. Before the Second World War, many women engaged in particular kinds of work were not permitted to smoke on the job. However, war work bestowed respect on waged women, and the opportunities for them to smoke with their friends and co-workers were vastly expanded. It was not until this time that unremarkable and respectable women in large numbers chose to claim the right to have themselves photographed as smokers. Smoking became a commonplace for many waged women until the end of the twentieth century when public space for smoking in the workplace was again restricted. Chapter 8 illustrates this trend through the work-life of nursing sister Evelyn Pepper and her famous cigarette lighter.

If smoking had been adopted by salaried or waged women alone, it would never have obtained the level of public support in Canada that it enjoyed from the 1940s onwards. To become a performance that conferred status, smoking had to be adopted by middle-class women. Chapter 9 explores smoking among Canadian women faculty members, undergraduates, and other post-secondary students. Although slow at first to accept smoking, once academic women did so in the 1940s and 1950s, the visual records show that smoking became almost ubiquitous on Canadian university campuses and in other post-secondary institutions. Female students were often portrayed as smokers, perhaps as a marker that they belonged in this traditionally male world.

The rates of smoking for Canadian women continued to climb until the mid-1970s, during the same period when second-wave feminism became established in this country and the United States. Chapter 10 traces the symbolic alignment of women smokers and second-wave feminism as self-defined feminists carved out careers and established new social codes. One of Canada's most identifiable icons of that period, Joni Mitchell – songwriter, performer, artist, and lifelong smoker – has made the cigarette an important component of her visual identity.

Chapter 11 addresses the appeal of smoking for women in marginalized sectors of Canadian society, particularly exploring its power to reduce stress. It examines such women through the lens of third-wave feminism. Women caught in poverty, those of racialized non-white identity, women disadvantaged through addictions, women with non-mainstream sexual orientations all have high rates of smoking. Despite now being a woman of privilege, the profiled persona for this chapter is k.d. lang, a woman who has declared her lesbianism, her fondness for cross-dressing, vegetarianism, and political protest movements. Not herself a smoker, lang has mined the ambiguous and rich symbolism associated with smoking, weaving it into striking visual and aural tableaux. Lang has managed to use smoking as a means of announcing and even popularizing representations of lesbianism and cross-dressing rarely exercised in mainstream culture.

A social history of Canadian women reveals that tobacco and women have had a long and rich history. Indeed, the hidden story is that women have often been at the heart of the matter: through anti-tobacco agitation, in tobacco advertising and marketing, and as smokers themselves. The historical roots and development of this close association is worthy of investigation.

1

Women and the Weed

A BRIEF HISTORY OF SMOKING IN CANADA
THROUGH WOMEN'S EYES

Canadian women have been closely associated with tobacco use in this country, either opposed to or supportive of it, since at least the nineteenth century. In that era, Protestant women pushed their way to the front ranks of the temperance movement as implacable opponents of smoking on moral and physical grounds and as protectors of children. Women themselves had long been smokers in rural settings in Canada – for example, in Quebec, where *les fumeuses* escaped censure by smoking *tabac canadien* with other members of their families.[1] By late in the nineteenth century, however, gender prescriptions had hardened, and most women living in urban areas gave up smoking. There were so few women smokers at this time that no accurate figures exist. Enumerating women smokers is also difficult for this period because in addition to rural women, most came from marginalized sectors of society as public performers, as prostitutes, or as other participants of the criminal and poor underclass. At the other end of the social continuum, members of the artistic world and intelligentsia regularly adopted habits that set them apart and gave them public notoriety. Smoking was a prime example. For such women, smoking gave licence to transformative bodily gestures, supporting this distinctive "technology of the self."

In the early days of women's public smoking, race acted as a further demarcating factor. The link between tobacco and racialized non-white status was a long-standing one. Southern European women, in particular those of Turkish and Spanish origin, had since the nineteenth century been workers in cigar and cigarette factories. Stylized versions of the lightly clad young women of colour made their appearance on posters and decorative covers of cigar boxes in the windows of tobacco emporiums. The exploitation of racialized non-white women models by advertisers helped to sexualize the act of smoking, reproducing privileged meanings of smoking as an activity that would make women more sexually attractive to men. These were not the only representations of racialized non-white women in circulation, of course. Among Canada's First Nations, women who favoured clay pipes as a remnant of fur-trade days developed their own iconography of an Aboriginal type of woman smoker, distinctive and proud.

Women smoked alongside men in First Nations' communities. This native form of tobacco-growing and curing was adopted by pre-industrial rural French Canadian society, where women also freely enjoyed their tobacco pipes. A powerful image from the Hudson's Bay Archives of an Aboriginal woman smoker can be seen in figure 1.1, which shows an Inuit woman. Here we see no hint of the sexualized "squaw" image that so disparaged Aboriginal women in the twentieth century:

Aboriginal women typically chose the corncob or clay pipe for smoking, as did women in other traditional communities, such as women in the Orkney Islands or Appalachia. Because she was protected by her location and culture from norms that sexualized and debased the woman smoker, the pleasure this woman takes in her pipe seems for her own purposes alone rather than for the visual effects of the gaze. This image is part of a larger archival collection in which the culture and society of Inuit in the Chesterfield Inlet area were documented for archeological and cultural purposes. Hence, the image of Aboriginal-woman-as-smoker is almost incidental to the larger ethnographic study.

Tobacco seems to have originated in South America, spreading northward in prehistoric times.[2] Various kinds of tobacco, including tabacum and rusticum,[3] were cultivated by the Eastern Woodlands Aboriginal peoples, especially the Iroquois Confederacy and Algonkians. Among the First Nations, tobacco had long been considered to hold spiritual and healing properties, and it was often consumed as part of shamanistic or governance ceremonies or when collaborative approaches were required for the community. Because of its high nicotine content, this early form of tobacco could produce hallucinogenic experiences.

In Canadian tobacco iconography, the Aboriginal "brave" was frequently associated with tobacco in various forms, even though most tobacco-tilling was done by the community's women. Emphasizing the masculinity associated with smoking, tobacco shops in the late nineteenth century often decorated their doorways with an image of an Aboriginal man in

1.1 and 1.2 | Chesterfield Inlet woman with corncob pipe, 1939; "The Indian Pocohontas," Calgary, 1885

full headdress, holding tobacco products of some kind to welcome patrons to the shop. Sometimes this "nod of the head" to the Aboriginal contribution to early tobacco production was in the form of a picture, but on occasion, when the cigar or tobacco store could afford it, a full statue graced the entranceway.

Figure 1.2 is a rare example of an "Indian maiden" or "Pocohontas" figure that dates from 1885. Purchased by the Glenbow Foundation in 1967, its provenance is somewhat obscure. As an artifact of cigar-store art, it is an exemplary if unusual depiction. The maiden is highly decorated, as was the custom with such figures. She has red, green, blue, yellow, brown, and black painted on her cast-metal surface. She is physically imposing, standing more than five feet tall on an eight-inch cast-metal base that would bring her to roughly the same stature as many men (or less likely, women) frequenting the store. She holds a bunch of cigars in one hand and tobacco leaves in the other.

1.3 | An Aboriginal woman at Sandy Lake, Ontario, 1955

Aside from the obvious commercial value of such a carefully wrought object at the storefront door, what does an artifact of this kind tell us about common perceptions of First Nations' women's roles in the tobacco industry of the late nineteenth century? Given the many hyper-sexualized images of non-white racialized women associated in some way with tobacco in that same period, as discussed in chapter 5, it is striking that the maiden is asexual in her presentation. This might have been due to the respect with which merchants *believed* Aboriginal women were held in the general economic exchange of that era. Countering this, however, were the sexualized Aboriginal images that appeared on cigar-box labels, which graced shelves in the same stores. Alternatively, the representation might have simply followed the depiction of male models for the "cigar-store Indian," which were far more common than female and which typically avoided sexualizing the man.

Figure 1.3 of a First Nations woman in 1955 shows that pipe-smoking in that community lasted long into the twentieth century. Clay pipes became common from the earliest days of tobacco trade from the Americas to Britain in the seventeenth century.[4] Such pipes had been used by both men and women during the fur trade when First Nations women interacted with fur-trade post officials and their families. Most clay pipes were originally made in London and distributed by the Hudson's Bay Company. Tobacco was recognized as a domestic product, interwoven with Canadian First Nations' culture and achievements. This image is part of an archival collection taken by a southern photographer of the lands and people surrounding the woman's community of Sandy Lake. Less a study of the woman smoker, the image aims to document the lifestyle and culture of native peoples, especially habits that contrasted with southern society.

The photographer for this image has taken the picture of the woman in an uncharacteristic pose, one favoured by Western cigarette-smoking women and commonly displayed in the cinema or on billboards: neck extended, her hand raised to the tobacco, and with eyes downcast. Contrast this image with that of the conventionally posed Chesterfield Inlet woman in figure 1.1, for example. Now consider the pose struck by Marlene Dietrich in the introduction – figure 0.2. The set of the head of the woman from Sandy Lake and that of Dietrich are very similar, as are the downcast eyes, the grip on the cigarette or pipe, and much else.

How can we understand the photographer's decision to impose a stance on the woman that she would likely not have adopted independently? Or can we be sure that this was not the woman's choice? The woman in this photograph, whether or not striking a conventional pose for her time and place, is obviously enjoying the experience of being photographed. We are reminded by this that the subject of the photograph has been offered the power to represent herself in a way she finds pleasurable, and this woman clearly revels in her opportunity. The image can most productively be understood as a cooperative one between the photographer and the subject.

Along with respectful depictions of Canadian First Nations' women as smokers, *les fumeuses* of Quebec also seem to have escaped the most negative assessments made of women who smoked in this period and later. This might have been partly because of the long-standing tradition of pipe-smoking among rural canadiens in the nineteenth century. Quebec historian J.-Edmond Roy quoted an American observer who reported that canadiens were "perpetual smokers. You could say that every man, woman and child had to have their pipe and tobacco and used them constantly."[5]

Tobacco Consumption Came in Many Forms

Smoking tobacco in pipes was actually a later development in Western society than taking it in the form of snuff, a popular pastime in Britain from the end of the seventeenth century,[6] especially among the British upper classes. Snuff was a finely desiccated tobacco meant to be inhaled in order to produce sneezing. As it became less conventional, snuff-takers were often satirized, especially in North America, as effete, flamboyant, and dirty. Snuff was also favoured by some women, stereotypically by older women. By the nineteenth century, men and women choosing snuff were resented for demonstrating moral lapses through their snuff habits and general dishevelment. There are many accounts of snuff-users, eyes permanently inflamed, nose reddened and even ulcerated, having destroyed their sense of smell. The violent sneezes doubtless made snuff the "untidiest form of using tobacco," leaving users like Frederick the Great "disfigured by being covered with snot and snuff."[7] Never as popular in North America as in Europe, it steadily lost ground in the later nineteenth century to chewing tobacco, which accounted for 58 per cent of the tobacco market in the United States by 1880.[8] In time, chewing tobacco too came to be satirized and associated with ill-mannered frontiersmen and oafs, habitually taking poor aim at the spittoon.

By the early twentieth century, chewing-tobacco spittle on the floor or on pathways offended many women whose long dresses were soiled by the tars. Norms of cleanliness among the middle class were on the rise at the same time that women's dress fabrics were voluminous and difficult to clean. This seemingly wanton disregard for women's use of public spaces gave fuel to first-wave feminism, which demanded, among other things, that women's public lives be respected. Even women and men who were unsympathetic to the feminist cause could find much to support in the anti-tobacco movement of that era, which took aim at smoking, chewing, and spitting as odious male pastimes.

One effect of snuff's frequent representation as a feminized tobacco product was that male snuff-takers' masculinity was often called into question. Reports of the male snuff consumer's effeminate gestures and appearance helped to make snuff itself an object of ridicule in literature and in the cinema. On the other hand, the masculinized images of chewing tobacco in similar popular cultural sources, as well as those in advertisements, re-established tobacco's legitimacy as a male leisure activity. The lesson of snuff's representations, however, was that some types of tobacco use had the potential to destabilize gender norms, as would be demonstrated more strongly by cigarette-smoking.

In its turn, the popularity of chewing tobacco waned before that of pipes and cigars. Along with snuff, it became a product used by a niche rather than a mass market, such as baseball players. A survey in 1987 showed that fully half of major-league players had used chewing tobacco, or "smokeless tobacco" as it came to be called, and that a third were current users.[9]

Smoking tobacco overtook chewing varieties in the United States by the start of the twentieth century, with cigars slowly taking on the connotation of middle-class male respectability and even statesmanship through strenuous advertising. Cigars had become the most common form of smoking by Americans between 1880 and 1890 with the importation of better-quality tobacco from Spain after the Napoleonic Wars.[10] They retained a significant portion of the Canadian market until the First World War.[11] In time, cigars would develop their own transgressive qualities because of their strong odour and size, but until the 1920s they shared the market with pipes in providing a presumably harmless and respectable middle-class male diversion. Women took up cigar-smoking in small numbers in the 1920s and again in the 1970s, and they figure in the current buoyant cigarello market.

Cigarettes were defined almost from the beginning as "foreign" because of their use by European immigrants. In the period before the First World War, they were considered to be a "deviant"[12] form of tobacco, since they were favoured by these same immigrants, bohemians, and disreputable women, many of whom were represented as racialized non-white.[13] Of course, not all "foreigners" were people of colour, but a racialized discourse of both cigarettes and smokers was taken up by many Canadians in the pre–First World War period. This construction of cigarettes as un-Canadian (vs home-grown), lethal (vs health-giving pipes and cigars), and as favoured by youths and women (vs middle-class males) drew on older racist tropes whereby the Other threatened a pure, prosperous, and stable male-controlled Canada.

To add to this threatening construction of cigarettes, smoking was closely associated in the public mind with the consumption of illicit drugs such as opium, which many anti-tobacco advocates claimed was mixed into the tobacco or imbedded in the wrappers. That the term "cigarette" is the feminine diminutive of "cigar" indicates its suspicious origins and (for the period) weaker status. It foreshadows as well the sexualization of both the product and the process of smoking, with tobacco often placed in competition with women's charms. For example, Rudyard Kipling wrote love poems to his tobacco and insisted that if the women in his life demanded that he make a choice, tobacco would be his life-love.[14]

Well into the twentieth century, the argument was made that tobacco-smoking, especially in the form of pipes and cigars, was harmless for mature men but dangerous for youths and women. This popular wisdom, as expressed by Canadian legislators[15] and medical authorities,[16] held that grown men were protected against many of the worst physical effects of smoking through moderate use. In this echo of alcohol-control rhetoric, many of the same opinion-makers invoked the distinction between youthful excess and mature moderation.[17] A sympathetic and even admiring profile was constructed for adult male smokers, principally by advertisers but supported as well through authoritative commentary in family magazines like *Saturday Night* and *Maclean's*. Print advertisements claimed that pipes and cigars were a "harmless pleasure,"[18] a "comfort and solace"[19] to the overburdened man of the world, even a quick corrective and source of improvement in athletic performance because of its calming effects.[20] Articles in these magazines claimed that cigars and pipes acted as reasonable companions for the lonely or bored, a replacement for snacks, and a means to blunt "the edge of hardship and worry."[21] Columnists portrayed male smokers as discriminating,[22] prosperous, artistic, and athletic. By the 1970s, when tobacco manufacturers were courting the woman smoker, smoking was said to reduce their "nervous irritation."[23]

The construction of pipe- and cigar-smoking as manly undertakings added further to the definition of cigarette-smoking as a feminized activity. Like snuff-taking before it, cigarette-smoking had the power to further destabilize gendered behaviours and weaken masculinist claims to certain kinds of leisured acts. This was, for instance, the view of the *Canadian Cigar and Tobacco Journal* in 1932: "When women first commenced to smoke cigarettes the majority of men objected on the ground that it made the men appear effeminate."[24] Some might argue that destabilization of gender norms caused by cigarettes was resolved long ago. Yet as late as 1975, Dr Ray J. Shephard of the University of Toronto Department of Environmental Health asserted that men who smoked heavily were "feminine" while women were made "masculine" by smoking.[25]

Making Cigarettes Accessible and Attractive to Women

In the early 1880s, American James Bonsack patented the cigarette-rolling machine. By the time it was fully operational in 1884 and first introduced in Montreal in 1888,[26] mass-produced machine-manufactured cigarettes were on their way to replacing the hand-rolled variety because of their much lower cost. The manufactured cigarettes were also cleaner to use, since new varieties of tobacco could be more tightly packed into the wrapper, reducing the flaking on clothing and the disintegration of the cigarette if held too long on the lips.[27] Rolling one's own cigarettes remained a prized male rite into the twenty-first century, but it had never been popular among women. The machine-rolled cigarette also eventually allowed for various fancy paper wrappers to be used for women's decorative cigarettes, and very importantly, it accommodated filters. These were much valued by women because they have been widely believed to make smoking safer, inviting as well decorative possibilities, with coloured filters to match lipstick and nail-polish colours.

The tobacco used in these machine-rolled cigarettes was milder than that used in cigar, pipe, or plug tobacco production, making cigarettes even more attractive to women and particularly young women, who had been found to favour mild over strong taste in cigarettes.[28] The tobacco was "flue-cured," adding further to its mild taste[29] and its consequent popularity among women. This encouraged as well the inhalation of the cigarette smoke, which in turn promoted nicotine addiction and with it a wide variety of illnesses.

A further incentive to smoke cigarettes resulted from American James (Buck) Duke's aggressive marketing strategies, starting in the 1890s. Duke consolidated the tobacco industry in the United States, creating the first tobacco trust, and introduced new technologies of production and commercialization, including modern advertising. "James Duke almost single-handedly invented the modern cigarette," claims Allan Brandt.[30]

The "short smoke" offered by the cigarette necessitated a quick light. The development of the self-striking match and the advertisement-heavy matchbook in the 1890s meant that lighting the cigarette was much easier than it had been in the past. Soon after, mechanical lighters joined the array of lighting devices. All of these advances succeeded in making cigarette-smoking an inexpensive, portable, and independent act. The performative possibilities for women also developed: the cigarette became a favourite theatrical prop as the woman smoker selected her pre-rolled cigarette, lit it with one of the many decorative lighters, and then held it prominently at chin level.

Home-grown tobacco encouraged smoking among both men and women in Canada. Tobacco had been grown commercially in Canada since before Confederation, but production did not reach significant levels until the 1930s when cigarette manufacturers sought sources of tobacco that would not be vulnerable to fluctuating import tariffs. Smokers also demanded varieties that were milder than the native-cultivated tobacco used in *tabac canadien*.[31] From the 1930s, tobacco-growers have constituted a significant element of the agricultural sector in Ontario and a somewhat lesser percentage in Quebec and the Maritimes. For example, in the 1960s when tobacco production peaked, there were about 4,500 Canadian farmers for whom this was the principal crop. By 2005, there remained only about 680 growers, the vast majority of whom are in southwestern Ontario.[32]

During the heyday of women's smoking, locally grown tobacco was cheaply available. Lobby groups such as the *Canadian Cigar and Tobacco Journal*[33] maintained pressure on the government and ridiculed efforts to reduce smoking rates. Throughout much of the twentieth century, smoking was encouraged among women through the government's reticence to point to the health threats that were becoming increasingly clear. The government was accused repeatedly of remaining silent because it was addicted to tobacco taxes.[34]

Canadian Women Take Up Smoking

In the period before the First World War, women were active participants in smoking culture in Canada as both opponents and participants. By the 1920s, public smoking by women was becoming more common and by a broader range of women. At the same time, anti-tobacco women – that is, those who deplored smoking as a personal pastime and who mobilized others against smoking – were still well represented in Canadian society. This would remain the case until after the Second World War. And yet that orientation was already perceived as old-fashioned by the late 1920s as public support slipped away.

The woman smoker of interwar Canada was likely to be a waged or salaried worker. Based on oral testimony of women who lived in that era, it appears that smoking was common, though not always in public. Nevertheless, one working woman who learned to smoke in that period reports, "we all smoked everywhere all the time."[35] At the same time, there continued to be many who objected to women's smoking, including some Quebec tobacco manufacturers who argued that women who smoked strong tobacco could become addicted more easily than men because of women's tendency to hysteria and lack of will to control their impulses.[36] Not everyone accepted their severe assessment of smoking for women, and the walls of resistance to the woman smoker were beginning to crumble.

Statistics were first systematically collected in Canada on the number of women smokers in the mid-1960s when the link between smoking and cancer was definitively traced. Numbers for the earlier period are therefore necessarily impressionistic and reliant on international comparisons. Despite the lack of statistics for American women smokers before 1935, contemporaries asserted that the quadrupling of cigarette sales there between 1918 and 1928 was due in part to the advent of the woman smoker. One estimate puts the percentage of American women smokers at 5 per cent in 1923 and 12 per cent in 1929.[37] A Canadian estimate puts the Canadian rate of women smokers also at 12 per cent in 1929.[38] Estimates from the period put the rate of smoking by women between the ages of twenty and fifty at 40 per cent in the interwar period for at least occasional smoking.[39] Another source puts the figure at 18 per cent of American women smoking by 1935 and 36 per cent by 1944.[40] We can assume that Canadian figures were close to this, if not greater, since Canadian rates have consistently topped American ones through the decades. In summary, then, before the Second World War a minority of Canadian women adopted smoking.

The real break-through for the woman smoker occurred during and after the Second World War. In the relatively short period of the 1940s when women's labour was both desperately needed and valued and when social mores reflected that respect, the "girl smoker" was accorded far more liberty to light up than had ever before been the case or would be for several more years. It was during this period that Canadian women first typically claimed the right to be photographed as smokers in such settings as workplaces or university spaces. While this demand might at first seem unremarkable, it signalled women's acknowledgement of the powerful, indeed iconic, importance of being seen as smokers as a constituent part of a modern female identity. In this period too, women attending post-secondary educational institutions were often identified by cigarette marketers either as smokers or as sympathetic to smoking. The closing down of much of women's paid work in the 1950s, when Canadian women were persuaded to return to their kitchens and classrooms, produce more children, and remove themselves from the paid labour force, remained a period of tolerance for public smoking by both women and men.

To establish women's smoking rates in Canada for the 1940s and 1950s, we are limited to a few surveys, and they give wildly contradictory figures. In the first survey of women smokers in Montreal in 1947, almost half of the approximately 1,300 women *who responded* declared themselves to be smokers.[41] Of this group, 58 per cent were anglophone women and 40 per cent were francophone.[42] A Canadian Daily Newspaper Association consumer survey in 1953 credited 69 per cent of Canadian men and 55 per cent of Canadian women as smokers.[43] If accurate, this appears to have been the apex of smoking rates for women in Canada, also placing women in Canada ahead of their American sisters. It was estimated that between 1922 and 1954, cigarette-smoking had increased by almost 1,000 per cent in Canada while the population had increased by roughly 72 per cent.[44] A private survey conducted by the Canadian Daily Newspaper Association in 1956 indicated that about 68 per cent of francophone women in Montreal and 28 per cent of anglophone women admitted to smoking,[45] showing historical and socio-cultural influences on smoking patterns.

The damning report of the American surgeon general in 1964 followed a major Canadian conference in 1963 that had investigated the link between cigarette-smoking and cancer. The Canadian Medical Association (CMA) reached conclusions similar to those of the American Advisory Committee on Smoking and Health, chaired by Surgeon General Luther Terry. In the words of the American report, "cigarette smoking is causally related to lung cancer in men ... The data for women, though far less extensive, points in the same direction."[46] Health Minister Judy LaMarsh, herself a reformed smoker, noted the report's significance and broadcast the government's goal to prevent youths from taking up smoking.[47] The American report had an almost immediate chilling effect on smoking rates in both Canada and the United States. The *Financial Post* quoted estimates that the general rate of smoking had fallen from 63.3 per cent in 1962 to 52.2 per cent in 1963. In 1963, the Canadian Medical Association had taken a strong stand against cigarette advertising through its journal.[48] "The campaign to seduce the young and to recruit them into the ranks of regular smokers (with the consequent curtailment of life expectancy for at least 10% to 15% of those who succumb) is virtually unopposed in this country."[49] By 1964, newspaper accounts reported that rates were again climbing in Canada based on sales reports from tobacco producers and stock prices, which recovered quickly.[50] Worried authorities noted that more teenagers had taken up smoking by 1965 than ever before,[51] although this had been a fear long before 1965.[52] By the time official statistics for Canadian smokers were available in 1965, it was estimated that about 39 per cent of women[53] and about 62 per cent of men smoked. As male rates for smoking slowly declined after 1965, women's rates climbed into the mid-1970s, culminating at just under 40 per cent.[54]

In the same period, smoking rates for those between twelve and eighteen also climbed, with girls' smoking rates in both Canada and the United States matching boys by the mid-1970s.[55] These are the first official, age-specific figures available, and since there are no comparators, we can only assume that they represented higher rates of smoking than had earlier existed. One explanation for the increase in girls' smoking in this period is connected to the introduction of new shapes and types of cigarettes, as discussed later in this chapter. Filter cigarettes, the longer king-size lengths, and menthol-flavoured cigarettes all were favoured by women from the time of their introduction.

Cigars also recovered market value, possibly to mimic the same longer aesthetic of the 100 and 120 mm cigarettes. Cigar-smoking was another response to the fears created by the 1964 American surgeon general's report, which especially targeted the dangers of cigarette smoking and the deep inhaling common with cigarettes.[56] Some women took up cigar- and cigarello-smoking in this period, further swelling the cigar's market share.[57]

While women's rates of smoking declined slightly in the mid-1960s with the dawn of the women's movement, another developing population demographic was being progressively courted by tobacco manufacturers. As second-wave feminism gathered momentum in the 1970s, grounded in and influenced by other reform campaigns such as civil rights and resistance to the war in Vietnam, smoking again became fashionable, especially among well-educated activist women who self-defined as feminists. The well-worn trope of the woman smoker in the vanguard of some social or educational movement found a comfortable place in Canada during the 1970s and 1980s. This phenomenon is discussed in more detail in chapter 10.

Smoking rates in Canada differ according to region. As can be seen from figure 1.4, current numbers of women smoking are fewer than men in all territories and provinces, with women almost matching men in such areas as Nunavut. This is especially striking, since men still outnumber women there. Considering women's rates, some provinces have consistently higher rates than others. For example, consider the data in figure 0.1. Newfoundland and Labrador and the Maritime provinces currently have higher smoking rates for women of all ages than does British Columbia. Thus, smoking patterns are determined in part by cultural experiences, some of which are regional and others ethno-cultural. Familial and community-based influences also pertain. In addition, there is a split between rural and urban women, with more rural women smoking than urban women, as was the case historically. These latter factors have an influence on regional smoking patterns, making it difficult to assert with assurance that more northern women smoke because of their location alone.

By the turn of the twenty-first century, almost one-third of young women aged twenty to twenty-four smoked,[58] and this group remains the most resistant of any to smoking cessation programs, which are often less relevant to young women.[59] For instance, nicotine replacement therapies are considerably less successful with women than with men.[60] Figures 0.1 and 1.4 demonstrate that the rate for that age group is declining slowly at the end of the first decade of the twenty-first century. This slice of the Canadian population comprises all classes and many vocations. Further-

1.4 | Table II. Smokers, by sex, provinces, and territories (number of persons)

	2004	2006	2008	2009
		number of persons		
CANADA	5,874,689	6,112,442	6,009,311	5,730,321
Males	3,155,944	3,337,112	3,370,225	3,169,054
Females	2,718,745	2,735,330	2,639,086	2,561,267
Newfoundland and Labrador	103,663	111,851	108,884	103,409
Males	51,390	63,001	58,339	59,944
Females	52,273	48,851	50,545	43,465
Prince Edward Island	26,031	25,555	25,235	24,694
Males	14,447	15,060	13,745	12,793
Females	11,584	10,494	11,490	11,901
Nova Scotia	180,176	194,307	188,488	186,514
Males	91,422	98,832	102,057	99,178
Females	88,754	95,476	86,431	87,336
New Brunswick	143,543	149,124	149,932	142,147
Males	77,332	85,382	72,005	73,654
Females	66,211	63,743	77,927	68,493
Quebec	1,577,008	1,650,863	1,542,295	1,499,501
Males	807,396	889,644	832,206	780,823
Females	769,611	761,219	710,090	718,678
Ontario	2,186,991	2,242,443	2,172,468	2,055,964
Males	1,210,839	1,260,170	1,259,886	1,183,121
Females	976,151	982,274	912,582	872,843
Manitoba	190,762	211,692	230,436	197,714
Males	100,018	116,116	128,043	106,909
Females	90,743	95,575	102,393	90,805
Saskatchewan	187,522	204,209	201,824	175,651
Males	96,579	103,414	112, 615	94,834
Females	90,943	100,795	89,209	80,817

/continued

	2004	2006	2008	2009
		number of persons		
Alberta	610,996	628,853	660,351	695,369
Males	344,530	360,072	375,203	405,608
Females	266,466	268,780	285,148	289,760
British Columbia	639,351	662,026	700,691	617,778
Males	347,419	368,833	400,559	335,648
Females	291,932	293,193	300,132	282,131
Yukon Territory	8,257	9,655	8,594	9,870
Males	4,457	5,028	4,515	5,371
Females	3,800	4,627	4,079	4,499
Northwest Territories	12,495	12,858	11,728	12,271
Males	6,089	7,091	6,876	6,402
Females	6,405	5,767	4,853	5,869
Nunavut	7,896	9,006	8,384	9,437
Males	4,026	4,470	4,177	4,768
Females	3,870	4,535	4,207	4,669

Note: Population aged 12 and over who reported being a current smoker.
Source: Statistics Canada, CANSIM table 105-0501 and Catalogue no. 82-221-X.
Last modified: 2010-07-13.

more, young women are becoming devoted smokers at an earlier age. The average onset age for young women is now about fourteen. We have yet to successfully address this particular group of smokers through smoking cessation programs or in formal school curricula, largely because of a failure to accurately and fully represent the reasons why women smoke. I argue that these reasons are as much about personal and social power as they are about consumer roles or access to public health knowledge.

The Battle to Limit Tobacco Consumption in Canada

A long-standing movement to eradicate or reduce tobacco consumption existed in Canada since the early nineteenth century. Led principally by evangelical Protestant sects like the Methodists and the many temperance lodges, women's temperance associations, and their youth groups, they discouraged tobacco users from smoking through moral suasion and terrorizing, as can be seen in chapters 2, 3, and 4. These groups argued that tobacco was the "evil twin" of alcohol and that by smoking, chewing, or taking snuff, a person became predisposed to crave even more dangerous products like alcohol or drugs. By the late nineteenth century, smoking came to be associated with opium. The belief that drug use began through a gateway product like tobacco continues to be invoked by those worried about smoking among the young.[61]

"Prohibition" was never imposed on cigarettes in Canada, although there were several attempts. The first piece of federal legislation of this type was a 1903 free vote in the House of Commons to ban cigarettes entirely; however, the vote was lost. A private member's bill to the same effect later that year also failed. Part of the problem with both bills was that adult males would have been denied the pleasure of smoking along with (male) youths, always the main focus of concern. There was an attempt to forbid the sale of tobacco to anyone under eighteen through an amendment to the Criminal Code, also in 1903. This too failed, although a bill setting the age of purchase at sixteen was passed in 1908 as the Tobacco Restraint Act.[62] Maximum fines were set at $10 for a first offence, $25 for a second, and $100 for a third. This act remained on the books until it was replaced in 1994.[63] Despite these attempts at legislation, one should not conclude that Canadians were particularly worried about tobacco. In the same year that the Tobacco Restraint Act was passed, Parliament also enacted the Opium Act, setting a fine of $1,000 for anyone convicted of the "import, manufacture, sell[ing] or possess[ion] for the purposes of selling opium."[64]

In 1914, just as war was brewing, another bill was proposed to prohibit cigarettes. However, at the last minute, the government named a Commons Commission on the Cigarette, which was to suggest amendments to the 1908 Act.[65] When the parliamentary session ended, the commission was adjourned and eventually disbanded. With the start of the First World War, "smoking seemed positively safe compared to the profound violence" of the trenches.[66] Smoking rates for both men and women accelerated during the war, further developing a climate in which smoking was accepted.

Similar attempts to limit youth access to tobacco were taken at the provincial level. Legislation to outlaw the selling of tobacco to minors was enacted in most provinces between 1890 and 1901. For example, New Brunswick passed a law prohibiting the sale of tobacco to "minors," in this case anyone under sixteen, in 1890 and then strengthened it in 1893 by providing for incarceration for those found in contravention of the statute.[67] In 1891, British Columbia passed legislation prohibiting the sale or giving of tobacco (or opium) to those under the age of fifteen.[68] Ontario's law of 1892 applied to youths under eighteen,[69] and the Northwest Territories enacted the same age limit in 1896.[70] The Nova Scotia law was passed in 1900 to prevent the "use of Tobacco and Opium by Minors,"[71] and PEI passed a much tougher law in 1901 to control the sale and possession of tobacco, providing for imprisonment of minors found with "cigarettes, cigars, or tobacco in any form" on their person.[72] Thus, while the legal age to smoke varied across provincial jurisdictions, there was a common legislative will to keep tobacco away from young people. By 1922, sixteen American states had either prohibited or limited the sale or promotion of cigarettes.[73]

If the anti-smoking forces were active during this period, they were also heavily criticized in the popular press throughout the interwar period. Anti-smoking education in the schools and community remained connected to anti-alcohol and drug education through to the end of the twentieth century. But whereas anti-tobacco women had managed to directly influence the school curriculum in the nineteenth century, their leadership was largely lost after the Great War.

Medical opinion on smoking's dangers was divided from the nineteenth century until after the Second World War. By the early 1950s, however, increasing evidence of smoking's carcinogenic effects was appearing in the scientific literature. The first large-scale study, conducted by Canadian Dr Norman DeLarue, compared fifty patients with lung cancer with fifty who were hospitalized for some other reason. He found that more than 90 per cent of the cancer patients had smoked, while fewer than 50 per cent of those free of cancer had done so. Although the causality was not yet clear, the association between smoking and cancer was strong.[74] Another major study in 1950 explored the relationship between smoking and lung cancer, when 51.2 per cent of 605 men hospitalized for lung cancer were found to have smoked twenty or more cigarettes daily over the previous twenty years. Only 19.1 per cent of a control group of patients without cancer smoked at that rate, while 14.6 per cent were non-smokers. Published in the *Journal of the American Medical Association* that year, the study was widely discussed.[75]

Partly in response to the study, a private member's bill was debated in Parliament in 1950. It called for a special committee of the House of Commons to consider the "cigarette problem," especially smoking's effect on "mental, moral and physical health" and most particularly on "teenagers and unborn children."[76] In 1951, the Canadian Cancer Society also drew public attention to a possible link between cancer and cigarette-smoking, and in 1954 it issued its first warning about the dangers of cigarette-smoking.[77] Later that same year, the Department of Health and Welfare carried out its own study of smoking among Canadian veterans. By 1960, it had published results indicating that the group of cigarette-smokers experienced 60 per cent more deaths than the group of non-smokers.[78]

The weight of medical evidence continued to mount. In 1960, the Canadian Medical Association reported its concern about the relationship between smoking and bronchitis, bronchiectasis, emphysema, and coronary heart disease. By 1961, the CMA had accepted that smoking was strongly implicated in the incidence of lung cancer.[79] With the 1962 report of the Royal College of Physicians in the UK, which asserted that "cigarette smoking is a cause of lung cancer and bronchitis,"[80] a Canadian conference drawing the same conclusion in 1963, and the subsequent publication of the American surgeon general's bombshell report in 1964, the evidence was so strong that only renegades questioned the causality between smoking and cancer, especially lung cancer. The evidence considered by the ten members of the surgeon general's advisory committee included animal experiments, clinical or autopsy studies, and population studies. Their conclusions that "[c]igarette smoking is a health hazard of sufficient importance in the United States to warrant appropriate remedial action" emerged from the causal relationships between cigarette-smoking and lung cancer as well as cancer of the larynx, esophagus, and urinary bladder as found in studies of men. It also established a relationship between cigarette-smoking, pulmonary emphysema, chronic bronchitis, and coronary heart disease, all in trials of males.[81] The report acknowledged that smoking was a "probable cause" of lung cancer in women.[82] The link between smoking and disease etiology was now incontestable. The old battles within the scientific and medical communities were a thing of the past.

Legislative efforts to extend controls on cigarettes in the later twentieth century were frustrated by several factors. From 1963, with the second wave of anti-tobacco efforts, legislation to limit smoking faced strong resistance from a combination of tobacco manufacturers, consumers who opposed limitations on presumably "private" and benign habits, and groups hungry for the sponsorship money that had made certain sports and arts events possible. With the crucial Canadian Medical Association's meeting in 1963, which had declared a link between cancer and cigarette-smoking, and the American surgeon general's report the next year, the Canadian government was forced to define a stronger position on cigarette-smoking, particularly by youths. Health Minister Judy LaMarsh announced increased funding for research and anti-smoking education in 1965 but refused to consider a tobacco prohibition. Critics, for example on the path-breaking CBC current affairs television program *This Hour Has Seven Days*, insisted that the Canadian government needed to further limit cigarette advertising. In 1965, tobacco manufacturers spent two million dollars on television advertising alone.[83]

Bill C-75, introduced in 1963, would have placed cigarettes under the jurisdiction of the Canadian Food and Drug Act, restricted advertising, demanded warning labels on packaging, and reduced tar and nicotine levels. Predictably, it failed. Members of Parliament from Ontario's tobacco-growing area hysterically opposed the bill, calling it "the first step toward doing away with everything for which democracy stands."[84] The following year, Canadian tobacco companies issued a voluntary advertising code. Yet another parliamentary committee worked through 1969 on warning labels and restrictions to advertising. The tobacco manufacturers continued to object to the "extreme and unsubstantiated propaganda that is spread about the so-called evils of smoking."[85] For its part, the Canadian federal government spent $120,000 on smoking prevention and research in 1964–65; in the same period, it devoted $575,414 to research and to further support tobacco-growers.[86]

At the end of 1969, the parliamentary committee tabled its report, calling for a phased-in ban on advertising, health warnings on packages and vending machines, and maximum allowable tar and nicotine levels, all of which had to be declared on the packages. It also called for more public education and surveys. In 1971, Canadian tobacco manufacturers announced they would no longer advertise on television or radio.

The debates on how to control the cigarette industry in Canada had no discernible effect on the rates of women's smoking, which continued to rise throughout this period.[87] It is possible, of course, that the effect was simply delayed. And yet the apex of Canadian women's smoking rates occurred in the mid-1970s. The probable explanation for the continuing high rates of women's smoking is to be found in the influence of second-wave feminism, as discussed in chapter 10. By the late 1970s, however, the tide began receding as many public spaces denied both men and women the right to smoke and as the damaging reports of cigarette-smoking took hold.

Community groups also became more vocal. In 1974, registered nurse Rosalee Berlin founded the Non-Smokers Rights Association in Toronto. Early efforts to convince cities to enact bylaws restricting smoking in public spaces prompted Toronto Mayor David Crombie to call the group "the most impressive and intelligent lobby I have ever known."[88] The result of these and associated campaigns was to limit smoking areas in cities and towns. In 1976, Ottawa passed a bylaw prohibiting smoking in many public spaces, including supermarkets, hospitals, elevators, and school buses.

The Toronto Board of Health led the way by banning smoking advertising in Toronto Transit Commission subways, streetcars, and buses in 1979,[89] followed by other transit authorities the next year.[90] Subsequently, certain public areas such as lunchrooms and restaurants, retail establishments, and finally private workspaces in public buildings were declared off-limits by the late 1980s.[91] A similar pattern was observed in other Canadian centres so that by November 2005 Halifax had extended its smoking ban to restaurant patios, and even Quebec, with among the highest smoking rates in Canada, banned smoking in bars and restaurants as of January 2006.[92]

But Canadian tobacco manufacturers did not remain inactive during the gathering storm of opposition to cigarettes. Manufacturers regularly introduced "improved" versions, some of which found a ready market with women. The first of these was the filter. Filtered cigarettes had been introduced with the "Parliament Premium" brand in 1931. The composition of the filter occupied much research and advertising space. This first version was made of cotton. In 1952, as a result of research during the Second World War, Kent Cigarettes introduced a filter derived from asbestos, which was marketed as "the greatest health protection in cigarette history." Smokers, however, complained that it was like smoking through a mattress.[93] In the 1970s and 1980s, research continued, including piercing the filter with small holes. The notion was that air flowing through the holes would dilute the smoke entering the mouth, thereby reducing the amount of tar consumed. However, if the holes were covered by fingers or the mouth, they had no effect.[94] Clearly, this "innovation" was as overblown as claims about healthy smoking.

In the early 1960s, several Canadian producers, including Rothmans and Imperial, introduced the longer king-size cigarette with a filter specifically for the male market.[95] Women took to the longer format almost immediately. In the late 1960s, shorter "mini" cigarettes were introduced by the Imperial Tobacco Company.

In figure 1.5, a publicity photograph provided by the Imperial Tobacco Company in 1968, a woman stares happily at the range of cigarettes available to her, as published in the *Winnipeg Tribune*. By the early 1970s, the "100s" had been reworked to appeal to women, claiming "more" flavour and less tar. Presumably, the longer cigarettes also offered an attractive aesthetic to match the ideal of thinness for women's figures. The "Virginia Slims" were the iconic version of this marketing campaign in the United States, but many brands adopted the longer cigarette in Canada too, including Matinée. By 1975, the length of several types of cigarettes had been further extended to 120 mm in what the media termed "a clas-

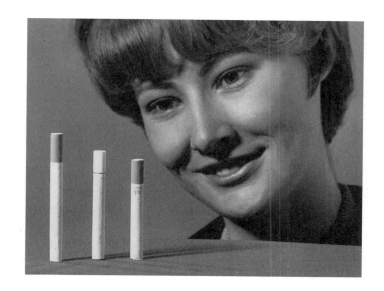

1.5 | More choices for cigarette lengths, *Winnipeg Tribune*, 1968

sic exercise in gamesmanship," with the market leaders becoming Benson and Hedges's "Plus" and Macdonald Tobacco's "More."[96]

Finally, the development of "light" or "mild" cigarettes further extended the cigarette market to women. Introduced in 1976 in Canada, "light" cigarettes had tar levels reportedly reduced to 14 mg or less. These brands were heavily advertised in women's magazines and by the late 1970s were the most popular among women: Player's Light, du Maurier Special Mild, Cameo Extra Mild, Matinée Special Filter, Matinée Extra Mild, and Peter Jackson Extra Lights[97] all captured a significant portion of the growing female market in Canada because of the claims that they were safer than regular brands. In 1976, it was estimated that the twenty-six light brands on the market accounted for approximately 15 per cent of all sales; by 1979, there were forty-nine light brands accounting for 40.1 per cent of market share.[98] Later that year, the "ultra lights" were introduced with a tar rating advertised at 7 per cent or less.[99] However, because there was no single standard for the "light" or "mild" designation, tar levels varied widely across the industry. To capitalize on the success of the "ultra light" cigarettes, marketers introduced a new disposable lighter, the "Ultra Lite," intended to compete with the Bic and Cricket disposable lighters currently holding most of the market share.[100] In 2001, Health Minister Allan Rock introduced legislation to ban the "light" or "mild" terms on cigarette packages. The legislation never passed. In 2003, the government asked tobacco companies to voluntarily remove these terms from the market; this request was refused. Nevertheless, tobacco companies have replaced the "light" designation with a range of other euphemisms such as "Special," "Smooth Taste," and "Elite" to approximate the older terms of "regular," "light," and "extra light."

By the mid-1980s, a new front had been opened in the battle against the tobacco companies: reports of the dangers of second-hand smoke. The phenomenon was first reported by the American surgeon general in 1972, and studies of the specific effects of second-hand smoke began in the early 1980s when non-smoking wives of male smokers were found to have elevated rates of lung cancer. An American study in 1984 found that between 500 and 5,000 non-smokers died yearly from exposure to second-hand smoke. In 1986, the American surgeon general produced a report devoted entirely to second-hand smoke or what was then called "environmental tobacco smoke," or ETS. The report indicated that "involuntary smoking is a cause of disease, including lung cancer, in healthy non-smokers."[101] This source of disease remains a major concern to Health Canada. (See figure 4.18.)

In 1988, two important Canadian bills passed into law. Bill C-204, the Non-smokers' Health Act, restricted smoking in federally regulated workplaces, planes, trains, and boats. It placed tobacco under the Hazardous Products Act, thereby prohibiting all advertising and sales except what was permitted by specific regulation.[102] Bill C-51, the Tobacco Products Control Act, banned tobacco advertising and sponsorships and required rotated health warnings on packages.[103] "Tobacco use is no longer socially acceptable as an activity among Canadians," noted Health Minister Jake Epp when introducing the bill in 1987.[104] The furious battle to push both bills through Parliament is a story in itself, told with insider knowledge by Rob Cunningham in his book *Smoke & Mirrors*.[105] After enormous pressure from both the anti-smoking pressure groups and the tobacco interests, both bills passed the House of Commons in May 1988. Bill C-51 was eventually successful in surviving legal challenges in the Quebec Court of Appeal as well as in the Supreme Court of Canada. One important result of the legislative battle was to further roll back spaces where smoking could legally be enjoyed as well as to reduce public display space for cigarettes. This indicated in a graphic way that smoking had moved from a majoritarian act into one practised by a devoted minority, usually furtively, in doorways, alleys, and other hidden spaces.

Nevertheless, the battle continues. Beginning in 1991, the smuggling of tobacco across the American border provoked a major public debate, particularly since it involved First Nations peoples whose lands straddle the border. In 1993, *Maclean's* estimated that smuggling was a $1-billion-a-year operation.[106] A forensic accounting firm estimated in 1991 that in excess of one of every nine cigarettes smoked in Canada had been smuggled.[107] To control the smuggling, the federal and several provincial governments reduced taxes on cigarettes in 1994. One almost immediate effect, in addition to curtailing the smuggling, was an increase in teenagers' rates of smoking. Twenty-three per cent of young men smoked in 1993; 28 per cent smoked in 1995. Similarly, young women's rates jumped from 25 per cent in 1993 to 28 per cent in 1995.[108] And while it seems clear that tobacco manufacturers have forever lost important segments of the North American market, a study from the late 1990s indicated that the war in the media continued to give the advantage to tobacco producers. An analysis of front-page American newspaper coverage of tobacco issues between 1985 and 1996 – a total of 179 articles – showed that tobacco producers consistently framed their message more effectively than did tobacco-control interests.[109]

The issue of cigarette packaging provoked new struggles in the 1990s and again in 2010–11. As the body of evidence grew that cigarette smoking was very damaging to health, cigarette packages assumed new importance as a site for warnings to potential smokers. Prior to 1990, warnings on cigarette packages appeared on the sides of the package. However, with new legislation that year, warnings were required to cover 25 per cent of the front and back of the package and 25 per cent of all six sides of the carton. The warnings were to be bilingual and only in black or white on a plain background. Despite the fury of the resistance from both tobacco producers and smokers, the warnings finally appeared only in 1994, eliciting yet more resistance. Health Canada investigated the effect of plain packages, concluding after a full year of study that youths would likely be influenced by undecorated packaging. However, no action was taken. Since 2001, warning messages have become even more graphic. Stark messages ("Cigarettes hurt babies") and luridly coloured photographs were required, profiling the effects of smoking on the lungs, teeth, and mouth. These graphic warnings, required to cover 50 per cent of the package, appeared first in Canada. This was a source of some pride to many anti-tobacco and health advocates. The new regulations, introduced in January 2011, require warning labels to cover 75 per cent of each package of cigarettes and mandate shocking images, including one of a dying anti-smoking advocate, Barb Tarbox, under the heading: "This is what dying of lung cancer looks like. Barb Tarbox died at 42 of lung cancer caused by smoking."[110]

Cigarette-packaging policy is one thing, but establishing that images on packages have a real effect on smoking rates has been a slow process. In fact, it was not until 2008 that a team of researchers at the University of Waterloo showed conclusively that a clear link existed between packages with warning labels and rates of smoking. Geoffrey Fong, David Hammond, and Mary Thomson are now applying their research skills to help control smoking in middle- and low-income countries where rates are climbing steeply.[111]

From the heyday of temperance agitation in the 1870s to the present, women's social experiences have been influenced by, and in turn have influenced, the place of tobacco in Canadian society. From nineteenth-century notions of female purity and women's moral superiority to the modernist period when women were charged with the task of being the family's consumer specialist, smoking has offered a platform from which women could exert leadership against smoking or take up the habit themselves. Women's modern identities, often supported by smoking, were based fundamentally on visual cues and embedded in popular culture. By the 1960s, the link between cigarette-smoking and various cancers had been confirmed. Through a supreme effort, anti-smoking legislation was enacted in the late 1980s. Women contributed to this final and seemingly successful battle, but they did not lead the charge.

PART II

Fighting the "Little White Slaver"

2

Women as Moral Exemplars

So she buckled right in with a lift of her chin,
If she had any doubting she hid it,
She started to sing as she tackled the thing
Which couldn't be done – and she did it.[1]

The women of the late nineteenth and early twentieth centuries who became most closely associated with anti-smoking campaigns were those
who supported temperance. The largest and most powerful women's
temperance organization was the Woman's Christian Temperance Union
(WCTU), founded in the United States and Canada in 1874. By 1891, the
Canadian Dominion WCTU reported a membership of almost 10,000 women. By 1914, 16,838 members were on the rolls, and by 1927, 30,043 members were recorded, making it the largest non-denominational women's
organization in Canada. Thereafter, membership fell off, eventually slid-
ing to its present figure of around 2,000.[2]

The WCTU is remembered mainly for its opposition to alcohol, and indeed this was one of its prime targets.[3] But its activism extended far beyond this single goal. The WCTU tried to improve social conditions that
gave rise to intemperance and violence, especially against women and
children. It insisted on reasonable working conditions for waged women,
it demanded prosecution of men who had been violent against women,
and it was one of the first Canadian women's groups to support women's
right to vote.[4] It championed various forms of childhood and adult education and homes for abandoned and "fallen" women, as well as poor, aban-

doned, or orphaned children; it lobbied for and provided humane care of the indigent aged; it set up residences and "Travellers' Aid" for single working women; it helped establish women's hospitals, coffee houses, and reading rooms and supported travelling lecturers and missionaries. In short, its interests ranged far beyond public control of alcohol to a wide array of other public and private social problems. All of their causes served to support the nuclear family and particularly mothers as moral leaders of the family in a period of rapid industrial change.[5] Temperance women are frequently identified as "proto-feminist," and many were supporters of first-wave feminism.[6]

One of many reasons for the WCTU's success as a women's organization was its structure, rooted as it was in the local network of women's groups. Women were not asked to choose between this group and others; most women belonged to a network of groups with interlocking memberships. It would not have been uncommon, for example, for a woman to belong to her church missionary society, to the Ladies' Aid, to the Local Council of Women or YWCA, to the local Orphans' Home Committee or the Women's Institute in addition to the WCTU. The resulting network of women gave them a powerful base on which to lead large-scale movements such as temperance. Tobacco use was one of the prime "gateway" products on the temperance hit-list, a suspected route through which youths took up drinking and other dissolute pastimes.

A second reason for the success of the WCTU was its organizational model. The WCTU was remarkably democratic in its functioning. The executive officers at all levels were usually chosen by election. As a general rule, the executive did not set policy, although it did establish the agenda to be debated at each convention.[7] Through a system of local (urban, town, or rural) "unions," provincial assemblies, and national meetings, the WCTU sought to involve women in every community across Canada in monitoring their local living spaces, demanding a voice for women in civic activities. While WCTU unions lower in the hierarchy were expected to report to those above them, there is no indication that the higher levels controlled the local unions by monitoring their adherence to official policy or by disciplining infractions. The local groups operated in a loose confederation to form the next level of the hierarchy, deciding the degree to which they would support the provincial or national structures financially and ideologically. Sometimes this autonomy resulted in provincial unions breaking with policies set by the national organization, as in the case of the Quebec WCTU not supporting the federal bill to prohibit cigarettes.[8] This relative autonomy may account for the longevity and vitality of the local and provincial unions in otherwise difficult circumstances long after the federal organization had become moribund.

The organizational model pioneered by the WCTU – locally, provincially, nationally, and internationally – has been credited with creating a sophisticated design to promote temperance,[9] dubbed by one historian "moral bureaucratization."[10] One can see much evidence of this new form of bureaucracy in the many artifacts left behind by the WCTU as it struggled to rid society of ills, including tobacco. As an instance of this, the national level of the organization condemned smoking by everyone but focused its energies on youth smoking. To support its youth programs, it offered teaching materials for public and Sunday Schools, medals and other prizes for youth competitions to members at the local level, as well as suggestions on how to influence local politicians and policies to ensure that youths could not buy tobacco products in local shops. Local unions were free to make their own choices about what issues they championed in their own communities and with what materials as well as how they proposed to wage these campaigns.

Yet another source of these women's power and authority rested on their world view, which was profoundly religious. The mainstream religious culture of late nineteenth-century Ontario and the Maritimes was evangelicalism.[11] The pattern for the WCTU's religiosity had been set by the founder of the WCTU in Canada, Letitia Youmans. Youmans's evangelicalism[12] was characterized by a view of salvation as personal and experiential. That is, salvation was dependent on a spiritual awakening of the soul. The moral health of a Christian society was thought by evangelicals of all Protestant denominations to be undermined by such frivolous activities as dancing, gambling, smoking, and alcohol consumption. Education held an important function in serving evangelical goals by promoting more edifying activities, with the development of new skills and the encouragement of service to the saviour and community.

The touchstone of this ideology was the moral superiority of women in a world that had become degraded. Frances Willard, founder of the National (American) WCTU had put the case in her autobiography, *Glimpses of Fifty Years*: "But now the savage world is under foot, and man lifts his strong hand up toward woman, who stands above him on the hard-won heights of purity that she may lead him upward into freedom from the drink dominion and the tobacco habit and that he may learn that highest of all human dignities – a chastity as steadfast as her own."[13] Women's moral superiority gave them enormous strength, argued Willard, if only they would take up the challenge.

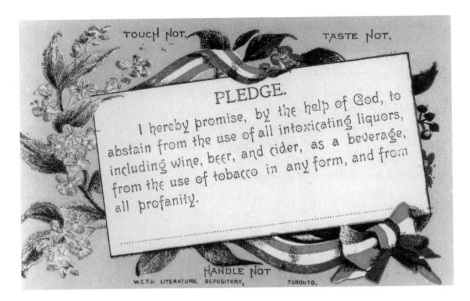

2.1 | WCTU Triple Pledge Card, nineteenth century

Temperance groups, the WCTU included, developed new strategies to keep the temperance message in the forefront of their members' everyday lives. For example, the original "Pledge" produced by the WCTU for all members is shown in figure 2.1. "Touch Not, Taste Not, Handle Not," it warned, as if by some kind of evil osmosis an innocent could forever be lost to the evil of profanity or intoxicating liquors or tobacco just by touching them. The notion held by most temperance groups in nineteenth-century Canada was that by using one relatively benign substance, like strong foods or cider, an appetite would be created for ever stronger indulgences. The unaware user would be drawn into the vortex of hard drugs, alcohol, and unspeakable sexual desires. Smoking was one habit that enslaved the user to its own pleasures and to other more base desires as well. As naive as this message might appear to us today, the approach is actually very modern and supported by many anti-addiction groups. If one is to stop the offending behaviour, whether drinking, smoking, or anything else, one must resolve to do so with the support of others and then avoid situations where these products might be encountered.

This pledge card's presentation features deserve more than a passing glance. Produced by the Dominion WCTU, it takes a conventional pledge card, as was commonly distributed by male-organized temperance societies, and rests it on a feminine backdrop of a sprig of blossoms intertwined with a tricolour ribbon. The latter feature dates the card as having been produced early in the WCTU's history, because the white ribbon, indicating purity, came to dominate the WCTU iconography by the late nineteenth century. The resulting card signals its feminine qualities, the moral message of the triple threat to purity, and the necessity of the temperance supporter to declare her support by writing her name on the dotted line. In an age when few women were asked to sign their name to any kind of official document, her signature would have signalled unusual seriousness of purpose.

The Members of the Young Woman's Christian Temperance Union

One of the many ways that the WCTU sought to invigorate public debate and private commitment to "clean living" was by mobilizing other members of Christian families to take on their own projects. Mothers were encouraged to enrol their babies in "The Little White Ribboners," and children were invited to join a network of youth groups where they could be educated in the hard work of temperance. But it was the single young women in every community who were regarded as the real strength of local projects. Pious, single women aged between about fifteen and thirty joined the Young Woman's Christian Temperance Union, the YWCTU. Founded in 1880 by Frances J. Barnes,[14] it was active in Canada by the mid-1880s. Like its mother organization, the YWCTU was committed to an evangelical interpretation of personal salvation, to the eradication of harmful substances like alcohol and tobacco, and to reducing social ills suffered by all Canadians but especially women and children. It is the members of the YWCTU who are the subject of the poem at the beginning of the chapter in which the young woman is lauded for tackling seemingly impossible projects. As a demonstration of this ethic, the YWCTU took on the challenge of discouraging friends and family from indulging in products particularly favoured by the young, like alcohol and tobacco.[15]

As a subsidiary group of the WCTU, the YWCTU also had specially designed pledge cards. Figure 2.2, for example, is a "Pledge Book" distributed by the Alberta YWCTU, with a pledge card included. Produced by the National (American) WCTU, this pledge card dates from the nineteenth century when the evangelical ethic was prominent and the campaign for young women was focused primarily on alcohol. Young women were encouraged to sign and date a solemn promise to forswear alcohol and to "employ all proper means to discourage the use of and traffic in the same." The pledge against alcohol typically included as well a pledge to eradicate tobacco and swearing.[16]

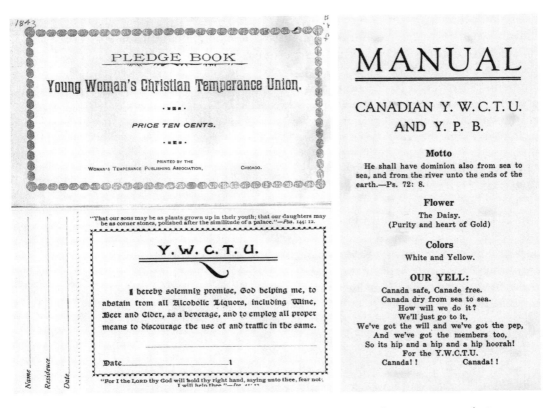

PLEDGE BOOK

Young Woman's Christian Temperance Union.

· ▪ ▪ ·

PRICE TEN CENTS.

· ▪ ▪ ·

PRINTED BY THE
WOMAN'S TEMPERANCE PUBLISHING ASSOCIATION,   CHICAGO.

"That our sons may be as plants grown up in their youth; that our daughters may be as corner stones, polished after the similitude of a palace."—Psa. 144: 12.

Y. W. C. T. U.

I hereby solemnly promise, God helping me, to abstain from all Alcoholic Liquors, including Wine, Beer and Cider, as a beverage, and to employ all proper means to discourage the use of and traffic in the same.

Date_____ 1

"For I the LORD thy God will hold thy right hand, saying unto thee, fear not; I will help thee."—Isa. 41: 13.

Name
Residence
Date

MANUAL

CANADIAN Y. W. C. T. U.
AND Y. P. B.

Motto

He shall have dominion also from sea to sea, and from the river unto the ends of the earth.—Ps. 72: 8.

Flower

The Daisy.
(Purity and heart of Gold)

Colors

White and Yellow.

OUR YELL:

Canada safe, Canada free.
Canada dry from sea to sea.
How will we do it?
We'll just go to it,
We've got the will and we've got the pep,
And we've got the members too,
So its hip and a hip and a hip hoorah!
For the Y.W.C.T.U.
Canada! !   Canada! !

2.2 and 2.3 | YWCTU "Pledge Book," Calgary, nineteenth century; YWCTU/YPB "Manual," cover, nineteenth century

And what gave young women the power to purge alcohol and tobacco from their midst? In the words of the WCTU, "That our sons may be as plants grown up in their youth; that our daughters may be as corner stones, polished after the simultitude of a palace." It is not difficult to detect which was the more precious, the plant-like male or the polished cornerstone of the young woman.[17] Beyond this claim, young women's authority derived from their privileged relationship with Christ through their evangelical world view, from that empowering purity of spirit they strove for relentlessly, and from their communal efforts to reform a debased society. The evangelicalism that drove this group of young women is also identified through religious text at the bottom of the pledge card. Young women are reminded that God both sanctions and protects them against any fears associated with their spiritually motivated anti-drink and anti-smoking campaigns.

The power felt by these young women to change the circumstances of their society speaks of Foucault's "technology of the self." Young women who might have been drawn to the YWCTU were not only intensely religious and dutiful but also self-improving. Members constituted themselves as ethically aware and pure, particularly in contrast to those who acted as if they were ethically obtuse and impure, such as smokers. Thus, their identity formation was nourished by this contrast and kept continually in view through their projects where they regularly encountered the "impure." Their performance of these qualities in private worship and public reformism conferred on them a sense of their own superiority, encouraging them to present themselves as virtuous and to undertake daunting projects to prove that superiority. Their power arose from the interplay of a range of interlocking structures including religion, class, the moral bureaucracy of which they were a part, and state sanction. In Canada, the YWCTU drew its membership from the same societal ranks as did the WCTU: the upper working and middle classes. Often without the advantage of formal education, the YWCTU girl hungered to be recognized as exceptional. The manual pictured in figure 2.3 justified the YWCTU's existence by identifying itself as a "training school for leadership in religious and moral movements" and as providing "a University of Reform" to its membership through "its sweep of vision."[18] The cover of the manual for the YWCTU and Young People's Branch announces that their symbol is the daisy to signal the young member's purity and generosity ("heart of Gold"). Following on this, the young women celebrated the daisy's colours of white and yellow, working them into many events they sponsored and donning appropriately coloured costumes. But like the poem that opens this chapter, it is the YWCTU "Yell" – a choral recitation at top volume – that defines the ideal YWCTU member as one brimming with energy, moral conviction, and fervent patriotism.

Canada safe, Canada free.
Canada dry from sea to sea.
How will we do it?
We'll just go to it,
We've got the will and we've got the pep,
And we've got the members too,
So its hip and a hip and a hip hoorah!
For the Y.W.C.T.U.
Canada!! Canada!!

The girls and women of the YWCTU not only constructed themselves as pure of heart and action but, very importantly, as the ethical and Christian inheritors of the true Canadian nation. This claim to their position in a "Canada dry from sea to sea" is striking and ironic, since it was made in a time when women were denied full citizenship through their vote or as "persons" under the BNA Act. Regardless, the YWCTU "Yell" defines the Y member as a loyal subject of the state, intent on keeping it "safe" and "free."

The young women of the YWCTU were to be devoted to the entire temperance agenda, with control of alcohol at the root and other associated evils, like smoking, to be eliminated. Because their male friends and brothers were thought to start on the road to alcohol through tobacco use, however, the YWCTU soon took up the anti-tobacco cause with greater enthusiasm than it devoted to alcohol elimination. The YWCTU would eradicate this bane from the breadth and length of Canada through their energy, their numbers, and their unshakeable will to do the right thing. Although from a twenty-first-century perspective this might appear to have been a naively optimistic blueprint of what would be possible for any youth group, there is no doubt that the membership was meant to feel that they could achieve anything, including a self-identity that defined them as "pure" and others as "impure" through their dedication and spiritual force.

Despite the expectation that these young women would one day join the WCTU, many stayed on in the YWCTU "farm team" well into adulthood, carrying on the many projects the local groups had initiated. Their unwillingness to leave this enabling culture, to be folded into the mother organization with its own norms and projects, is not surprising. Along with the Bands of Hope (the WCTU's popular youth group for boys and girls), the YWCTU was the most active group created by the WCTU. In fact, it often rivalled the mother organization in the range of activities it undertook and the successes it enjoyed, especially in childhood education and evangelical proselytizing.

Training the Young Woman in Anti-tobacco Advocacy

If the YWCTU girl were to be an effective advocate for a tobacco-free society, she herself needed to be educated in the special role she could play, the dangers presented by tobacco use, and how to successfully put her case to others. In many instances, the members of the YWCTU had previously been members of other temperance children's groups. Here they were trained in elocution and argumentation through a catechistic process of rehearsing arguments against temperance, along with the appropriate retorts. (See accounts of Medal Contests in chapter 3.) A special YWCTU leaflet series in methods of persuading the public was published by the National (American) Woman's Christian Temperance Union and distributed across Canada by the Dominion (Canadian) WCTU. The pamphlets educated the young women in how to make effective use of the media, how to structure petitions, and to whom they should be presented for maximum effect. Others took up thorny organizational problems, such as convincing the mother organization to establish Y groups in the first place.[19]

Cassandra Tate suggests that in American temperance organizations, including the WCTU, "cigarettes were never more than a secondary issue for most of those who supported the campaign against them."[20] For the Canadian YWCTU and WCTU, however, this was not the case. Tobacco served as a unifying feature of their program, allowing the young women members to take on leadership fortified with moral justice. Through their anti-tobacco agitation, the YWCTU could exercise a powerful "technology of the self," aggrandizing their self- and social authority through urging the adoption of moral behaviours, including rejection of tobacco use.

Since young women might be unaware of their power to attract sinners to the movement, these upright and impassioned women needed to be warned about the less than honourable intentions of some of the male sinners they hoped to save and against whom much of their identity was constituted. One can only be convinced of one's virtue if a competing model of evil is available for comparison. Unreformed smokers were an apt example of evil-doing in their own families and social groups.

Take as an example figure 2.4, a pamphlet distributed by the Ontario WCTU to its members and to the YWCTU groups under its authority. The pamphlet warns its readers of the many dangers to youths who took up smoking cigarettes, physically, mentally, socially, and above all morally. A pamphlet like this one did not stand alone, however. Young women in the YWCTU were flooded with incendiary literature about the urgency of the smoking menace to their brothers, male friends, and fathers. Stella Irvine's pamphlet "Sound the Alarm!" (figure 2.5) left no doubt of the ravages caused by cigarettes.

As hyperbolic as such statements that cigarettes "steal the brains" or that smokers "are committing suicide on the instalment plan" seem to us today, Stella Irvine's sentiments mirrored much temperance and some popular Canadian commentary on the cigarette's dangers in this period, particularly for young men. There was widespread support for such notions in the popular press,[21] in pedagogical literature, and in textbooks used in physiology and health classes until the Second World War.[22] In 1881, Letitia Youmans spoke to the provincial convention about the many

TO CURE THE CIGARETTE HABIT

Ontario
Woman's Christian
Temperance Union

SOUND THE ALARM!
Mrs. Stella B. Irvine

SAVE OUR YOUTH!
THE CIGARETTE habit destroys the moral stamina necessary for any line of success.
CIGARETTES UNDERMINE EVERY PRINCIPLE OF MORALITY.
CIGARETTES lead to MORAL DEPRAVITY; LYING, CHEATING, IMPURITY, loss of MORAL COURAGE and MANHOOD and a COMPLETE DROPPING OF LIFE'S STANDARDS.
CIGARETTES introduce the boy to IDLERS and STREET CORNER LOAFERS
CIGARETTES KILL THE FINER INSTINCTS. The CIGARET-SMOKING GIRLS lose the peculiar characteristics of young womanhood which are its charm.
CIGARETTES STRIKE A BLOW AT EVERY VITAL ORGAN. Scientists affirm that "tobacco is the greatest single menace to the health, efficiency and longevity of the race
CIGARETTES UNBALANCE THE MIND. "Many of the most pitiable cases of insanity in our asylums are cigarette fiends."
CIGARETTES STEAL THE BRAINS. High school testimony is, "Memory impaired; clearness of thought hindered; application made more difficult; ambition deadened; the power of will broken."
CIGARETTES GRADUALLY KILL THE POWER OF DECISION. The ability to say "No" is lost
THE VERDICT IS: "CIGARETTE-SMOKERS ARE COMMITTING SUICIDE ON THE INSTALLMENT PLAN."

SOUND THE ALARM!

W.C.T.U. LITERATURE DEPOSITORY,
97 Askin Street   London, Ont.

2.4 and 2.5 | "To Cure the Cigarette Habit," pamphlet, nineteenth century; "Sound the Alarm," brochure, London, Ontario, about 1900

dangers of tobacco. As filtered through the views of the WCTU's recording secretary, Mrs Youmans is reported to have presented the testimony of the presidents of two colleges and of a Dr Hayes of Pennsylvania, who said that "no pupil who begins to use Tobacco when a boy ever attains to excellence in his studies. Every brand of cigars, every species of Tobacco has the Tobacco soaked in Alcohol. She would rather a child of hers would be in his grave than use Tobacco,"[23] reported the secretary. These terrorist statements about tobacco's evil effects served to remind the YWCTU member of what she was *not*. It secured her place in a cosmology of virtue, in support of a moral state and school system and as implacably opposed to both tobacco and tobacco-users.

Once the young YWCTU woman had been schooled in the many dangers associated with smoking, she needed purpose-designed pedagogical materials for younger children if she were to convincingly teach them. Very often, the YWCTU served as leaders of these groups. Boys were especially encouraged to attend on the principle that they were the most likely smokers of the next generation, but predictably, the group had more success with girls.

In one manual devoted to convincing children to avoid tobacco,[24] the leader is directed to begin her lesson by explaining the definition of slavery as illustrated by images from *Uncle Tom's Cabin*. Teachers were instructed to refer directly to Abraham Lincoln and his (moral) determination to free the African-American slaves. Discussion was then to lead to habits and how we become enslaved to them. Good and bad habits were to be distinguished, culminating in the habit of using "the little white slaver," or cigarettes. "Why is it so called?" the teacher is to ask. "It is a slave driver. It does away with personal liberty. It leads to other bad habits, e.g. drink, profanity and juvenile delinquency." This information is to be followed by expert testimony, one of which is provided by Judge Margaret Patterson of Toronto who asserts, "There is no future for girls who smoke." Finally, the lesson is capped with a short review, "We all want to be free will agents. Then do not begin a habit or practice which will end by enslaving you."

How are we to understand this use of metaphoric American slavery as a touchstone for discreditable and evil habits like smoking? Is the American source of the teaching materials and the ready example of the parallel evil of slavery enough to explain its use? Are we meant to associate the evil of smoking with the evil displayed by "slave-drivers"? Or are we to overlay the weakness of the African-American slave with the moral weakness of the smoker? Perhaps all of these were intended to a degree, allowing the child-listener to take from this clumsy parable what he or she chose. There is no doubt, however, that the African-American slave was to be *pitied* while the racialized white child was to be *admired* in these stories. The identity construction of a temperance-led child, particularly a moral little girl, would be furthered if she accepted the merit of these teachings. But we cannot ignore the implicit racism contained in such texts.

Another resource used in boys' childhood education was Ella Wheeler Wilcox's poem, "Two Boys and a Cigarette."

> Two bright little boys named Harry and Will
> Were just the same size and same age, until
> One day in their travels it chanced that they met
> A queer little creature, surnamed Cigarette.
> This queer little creature made friends with the boys
> And told them a story of masculine joys
> He held for their sharing, "I tell you" quoth he
> "The way to be manly and big is through me."
> Will listened and yielded, but Harry held out,

"I think your assertions are open to doubt,"
He said. "And besides, I'm afraid I'd be sick."
"Afraid," echoed Will. "Oh, you cowardly stick –
Well, I'm not afraid, look ahere." As he spoke
He blew out a ball of cigarette smoke.

Five years from that meeting I saw them again,
The time had arrived when they both should be men.
But strangely enough, although Harry boy stood
As tall and as strong as a tree in the wood,
Poor Will seemed a dwarf; sunken eye, hollow cheek,
Stoop shoulders proclaimed him unmanly and weak,
A cigarette, smoothing each wrinkle and fold,
And the smoke that he puffed from his lips, I declare,
Took the form of a demon and grinned from the air,
And it said, "See that wreck of a man that I made
Of a boastful young fellow who wasn't afraid."[25]

In this resource, male students are encouraged to construct a particular form of masculinity that stands in direct contrast to the pure and spiritually enlivened young woman's femininity profiled in the Loyal Temperance Legion (LTL) manual. What constitutes moral manliness in the temperance landscape? A good man shuns tobacco. He is tall and strong. That's the sum of it. This seems a much simpler prescription than the one women are called upon to assume and one that would result in a less agential and confident youth. The temperance woman's identity was complex but powerful.

Poems like this one were used in a variety of ways. This poem or other readings to support the lesson could be committed to memory by the children and used as recitations by heart in the medal contests (see chapter 3). Recitations might also comprise part of the "demonstration" section in the youth group meetings in which children would be asked to present a poem and analyze its message. For children with weak literacy skills, reading skills would be developed by using resources like this one in which rhyming helped the child to decode and then pronounce words correctly. This "practice" of prepared scripts allowed the child to incorporate the ideas of such readings into a steadily developing and self-improving identity.

Beyond childhood education, the YWCTU girl was offered a challenge: to convince young men her own age to reform and reject both alcohol and tobacco. This was to be accomplished mainly through informal socializing when young men would be told repeatedly that no decent girl would have anything to do with a man who drinks or smokes. But how were they to do so and not risk losing the romantic attachments that ultimately added to their authority by making them wives and mothers? The YWCTU girl was to prepare herself through another of the leaflets intended especially for her. In "A New Regime,"[26] a typical conversation is staged among young women who are considering their choices. Some of the girls insist that they must tolerate their male friends' stinky cigars. Others argue that they will lose both the men and the entertainment and companionship that come with them. The heroine of the piece, ambiguously named Dune, sharply chastises them all for their faintness of heart:

> I blame the men, but candidly, girls, I blame you more, for it lies with you to check this evil in large measure, if not entirely. How can you have so little spirit, so little womanliness, as to lay aside your own self-respect to win the favor of these men, to lower your own standards of what is true and sweet in character, for a few paltry attentions from men whom you ought to despise. [She ends by quoting Ruskin] Ah, wasteful woman! She who may on her sweet self set her own price, how has she cheapened paradise!

In addition to uplifting and didactic fiction pieces like this one, the young women of the YWCTU were tutored in ways to convince boys to reject tobacco and alcohol through pedagogical discussions at meetings, in the WCTU's *Woman's Journal*, and through personal mentoring.

By no means, however, were the hardy young women of the YWCTU alone in attempting to reform their male friends. This moral work was a well-understood rule of young women's socialization before the Second World War and, in many places across Canada, well beyond that date. The Belleville School for the Deaf regularly ran columns and descriptions of in-school events and conflicts in its bi-weekly paper, *The Canadian Mute*. A number of references emerge of the young women disagreeing with the boys' chewing tobacco. For example, in April of 1892, correspondent Mary Lynch reports on the young women's efforts to stamp out chewing tobacco: "On a late Saturday evening the pupils gathered in the chapel. Mabel Ball stood up first, and pointed out to the boys the results of chewing tobacco. The boys replied by sending Francis Hunt up to point out to them the wickedness of chewing gum. The boys got their 'mad up' when a few more lectures were given them. The girls meant well."[27] In postwar

Canada, most girls' groups, including the Canadian Girls in Training and the Girl Guides, all opposed girls' smoking and expected their members to discourage boys and young men as well.

The self-identity encouraged for "decent," self-improving, Christian, and white racialized young women until at least the 1920s in Canada was to eschew smoking themselves and to take on the education of vulnerable male friends and relatives as well as romantic partners. A large proportion of young women held loyally to this set of expectations, with some even exceeding them.

An Exemplary Female Tobacco Critic: Bertha Wright

For many young women of late nineteenth-century Canada, the message of the YWCTU fell on keen ears and hearts. Women like Bertha Wright developed a wide range of literacy and numeracy programs around temperance and evangelical-laced education, which she and her YWCTU sisters offered to working boys and girls in after-hours coffee houses, gyms, and reading groups.

As a temperance advocate, educational reformer, and Christian activist, Bertha Wright is the model of the YWCTU woman. In many respects, she represents young women in other Christian youth groups as well. Seen in figure 2.6, a photograph taken in the famous William James Topley Studio on Sparks Street in Ottawa, Bertha presents herself with a direct gaze and partial smile. She has chosen for her photograph a smart vested suit and an overcoat trimmed with fur, a fashionable style for the middle-class woman of the 1880s. A tall hat and simple hairstyle draws the eye to her arresting eyes. To be a serious woman social activist did not require that one be plain or careless of appearance. Bertha Wright is a striking figure on the nineteenth-century model of the temperance woman.

Wright came by her visible confidence and considerable ability through family privilege and personal determination. Descended from the founding family of Hull (now Gatineau), Quebec, through her great-grand-father, Philemon Wright, Bertha found a place in Ottawa's economic and political elite circles. She lived for a time with her aunt and uncle, Hannah and Joseph Currier, at 24 Sussex Drive. Uncle Joseph was a wealthy timber baron and member of Parliament in the 1870s and 1880s. Bertha had attended the Ottawa Ladies' College and by the time this photograph was taken had cultivated a wide range of good works and controversial public missions for which she had become known in the Ottawa region. Still, none of this activism was accomplished as a flaming radical. One observer noted admiringly of Bertha that "[a]fter hearing Miss Wright, one does

2.6 | Bertha Wright, Ottawa, 1889

not wonder at her success. One element of that success, we should imagine, is her 'womanliness,' there is nothing of the 'new woman' about this charming speaker."[28] Indeed, Bertha Wright had refined an identity that was the epitome of the serious, capable, and deeply religious woman activist of the nineteenth century.

From the beginning, Wright used her class privilege and personal authority to improve the lives of women around her through her evangelical mission. While still a young woman, she published her autobiography, detailing her motives and staggering number of projects, most of which operated under the banner of the YWCTU. This was one of six books authored by Wright. In describing her primary task as "the work of winning souls,"[29] Wright and the YWCTU organized marches and urban missions, mainly across the river in Catholic Hull, to entice women and men departing from the bars and looking for a "short open air service" to come to Christ for salvation.[30] Two serious riots resulted from her intrepid marches with the women of her Bible study group, stirring comment from as far away as the House of Commons.[31]

2.7 and 2.8 | Home for Friendless Women, Ottawa, exterior, 1891, and interior, 1895

Women who had "strayed" and/or who had suffered abuse at the hands of men were sought out through visits to the jail or by standing on street corners and distributing leaflets. "Fallen" or abandoned women with children were invited into the Home for Friendless Women (HFW) where the women would be clothed and sheltered along with their children as long as they agreed to stay for a full year. In the early years, by far the largest group of women were admitted for intemperance, including smoking in various forms.[32]

Were the women exhorted to give up drink and smoking? Very likely. Certainly they could not engage in either under the watchful eye of the paid matron and YWCTU sisterhood. Beyond moral reprogramming, the women were given vocational training. The HFW ran a public laundry, as can be seen in figure 2.8 of the folding room. The hot, steamy, grinding work was intended not only to teach useful skills but also to remind the women of how they had come to a place like the HFW. Judith Walkowitz notes that in the many women's reformatories that housed laundries, "women could do penance for their past sins and purge themselves of their moral contagion. Clear starching, it would seem, cleanses all sin, and an expert ironer can cheerfully put her record behind her."[33] Joni Mitchell recorded a memorable version of this life in "The Magdalene Laundries."

"Flower Missions" were designed to bring the infirm or aged to temperance and Christ. The YWCTU held evening events and classes to reach "students, society girls, young women in the civil service, girls in business, and working girls."[34] One very important component of Wright's mission was to reach working-class children through the Loyal Temperance

Legion, the Bands of Hope, the Youth Temperance League, Bible study groups, Sabbath school groups, literacy groups, after-school home-craft clubs for girls, callisthenics groups for boys, and more. Bertha Wright was more than a dutiful daughter and niece: she was an impassioned proponent of temperance and personal salvation and tireless in her mission.

All of these projects undertaken by the members of the YWCTU were important acts of self-improvement and identity formation in which the sisterhood pitted itself against errant forces – a culture encouraging intemperance and vice, women caught in immoral lifestyles or addictions, various "forces of evil" holding back men who smoked – and triumphed, by their own and others' assessments. These discourses of triumph over evil and narcissism are what Foucault refers to as "technologies of the self," and through them the young women actively shaped their own subjectivities or identities.

The Image of the Young Temperance Woman

If the young temperance woman like Bertha Wright presented herself as a stylish, if serious and pious, middle-class woman of her age, other temperance advocates also adopted this "reading".

In 1897, the Canadian WCTU hosted a convention of the international (World) WCTU in Toronto. To acknowledge and celebrate Canadian women's temperance leadership, *The Templar Quarterly* published the graphic shown in figure 2.9. Not affiliated with the Canadian WCTU, the journal was nevertheless an affiliate in the temperance cause. It presented the Canadian president, Mrs Rutherford, welcoming her temperance sisters to Canada in awkward Shakespearean mimicry, "Welcome to our fair Dominion! Welcome to our hearth and heart; / Welcome here, from every nation; our best welcome we impart!" The graphic presents the United States representative as first in line for this warm greeting, robed in stars and stripes. Next comes Mother Britain with her trident and imperial hat, setting off her Union Jack–inspired skirt and cape. These two nations comprised the strongest members of the World's WCTU, making them logical candidates to be in the foreground. Behind these two luminaries stand various other women's representatives, including one in burqua despite there being no WCTU in societies where the burqua would be commonly worn or seen. Perhaps they were being hopeful. Perhaps it was an attempt to illustrate their own multicultural recognition or celebration in a way that preceded the Canadian state's eventual move in this direction. However, the claim that women in far-off lands also attempted to control drinking and smoking was accurate. Here, the Canadian delegation

2.9 | *The Templar Quarterly*, 1897

is led by a remarkable young woman, resplendent in an off-the-shoulder dress with hints of a Union Jack and many maple leaves. She approaches her international sisters with warmth and evident pride. Behind her are arrayed older, plainer, conservatively dressed women, comprising the remaining Canadian delegation. The scene is completed, and the youth underscored, with a child Knight Templar, another associate in temperance work, guarding the canopied podium. It must have been an irresistible impulse to include a Knight Templar somewhere in the scene, given the publication's commitment and readership.

But this wishful example of cooperative internationalism for the temperance cause could not mask the fact that Canadian WCTU temperance leadership was still controlled by anglo, Protestant, and racialized white women, just as it was in most other places in the world. The WCTU had experienced disappointment and distress in its inability to make headway in Quebec beyond Montreal or into other than Protestant women's groups in the rest of the country. The organization did reach out to women from other ethnic and racial communities in Canada. It had tried to reinvigorate the organization by encouraging racialized non-white women to become leaders in their own communities by setting up "Coloured" Unions at the turn of the twentieth century. This had worked reasonably well, particularly since temperance was promoted by modern Pentecostal and Evangelical sects with strong representation of racialized non-white women and men. But the aim of extending the movement to other religious orientations, particularly Catholic, Jewish, or Islamic, frustrated the temperance forces. Women in burqua were not likely to join the WCTU or any of its international affiliates any time soon.

In comparing Bertha Wright's image and this graphic as representations of temperance women during the heyday of temperance, there is much common ground. Despite Wright's clothing – a necessity in frigid Ottawa – she could stand in for "Lady WCTU" without raising comment. This image of the young temperance woman as beautiful, confident, and prosperous, racialized white, middle-class, and heterosexual was both calculated and a reflection of the sort of woman drawn to temperance generally in this period.

However, the Bertha Wright image was not the only way the temperance woman was portrayed. Arrayed against these complimentary images of temperance womanhood was a persistent societal view that gathered steam as the twentieth century progressed. This representation defined the temperance woman as intrusive on others' personal space and lifestyle, censorious, humourless, and bound to Bible and outworn conventions. It was especially apparent during times of national stress, as during the First (and Second) World War, when temperance women were vilified by Canadian soldiers as misunderstanding the nature of the war and the need for comfort and fortification by the fighting men. This position was not always adopted by their officers, however, many of whom could see the advantage of sober combatants.[35] Almost all men in uniform, and a good proportion of the public besides, supported the men by sending tobacco to the front as an allowable pleasure in the midst of horror.

Young Women Training the Next Generation to Reject Tobacco

One of the primary ways through which the YWCTU influenced younger children and their own peers was youth groups. The YWCTU was the primary force from which the leaders of the Bands of Hope and the Loyal Temperance Legions, both children's temperance groups, were usually drawn.[36] The children thought to be most in need of direction by attractive and skilled young women were poor working boys, such as the shoe-

2.10 and 2.11 | Shoeshine boy, c. 1900–10; Newsboy, Montreal, 1905

shine lads shown in figure 2.10. Working children constituted an important element of the family-based workforce, both within the home and on the street. By selling newspapers, acting as domestic servants, and serving in other forms of employment, these children made an essential contribution to the family economy.[37] They were also hungry for recreation, comradeship, and, of course, sustenance. The YWCTU recognized the needs of these urban working boys and developed extensive and often sophisticated educational anti-smoking programs. The aim was to capture children's loyalty early, particularly that of working-class boys, and maintain it through to a temperate adulthood. There is evidence that in addition to racialized white children, children of colour were also encouraged to attend these youth groups.

Bertha Wright studied the problem of effective education for poor children and became the organization's most visible authority on it, regularly contributing a column to the WCTU *Woman's Journal*. A proponent of careful planning and orderly presentations, Wright recommended strong lesson motivators (including snacks for every class) and opportunities for boys to apply what they had learned to the building of other life skills. This we would now identify as progressive education. Bertha also recommended the use of personal testimonials and salvation narratives, prayers, and recitations of scripture. Like any gifted teacher, she drew from a variety of traditions and pedagogical styles while insisting always on the primacy of the teacher as a moral exemplar. "Occupy the ground so thoroughly," she advised (untrained) youth leaders, "that there will be no

PLEDGE

"I promise, by God's help. to abstain from all intoxicating drinks, and to try to induce others to do the same."

Name ....

Date ....

The man who indulges in Alcohol lays himself open to chances of tubercular infection. His children are born with a diminished power of resisting this disease.—SIR VICTOR HORSLEY.

Mothers! Taking of Alcoholic drink such as beer or wine

Before Birth, it Starves! After Birth, it Stunts!

Orders for Requisites for the working of this Department to be obtained of

CANADIAN NATIONAL W.C.T.U. LITERATURE DEPOSITORY

97 Askin Street - London, Ontario

Price of this Leaflet—2c each, 50c per 100.

"The Little White Ribboners"

●

A Department of Work of the

CANADIAN NATIONAL WOMAN'S
CHRISTIAN TEMPERANCE
UNION

●

NATIONS
are gathered out of
NURSERIES

LITTLE WHITE RIBBONERS

BADGE—A Band of White Ribbon tied in a Bow on Left Wrist.

Dear Friend:

Thousands of little ones (from babies up to 7 years of age) are already enrolled among the

"LITTLE WHITE RIBBONERS"

by mothers who wish to bring up their children with a record of Total Abstinence, and to dedicate them at the very beginning of life to this great cause.

We hope you may wish to add the name of your little one to our Roll by signing the promise given on the next page and handing it in with TEN CENTS* to your Local Superintendent. We will then give you a Card to certify enrollment, and on which to keep a yearly record, which we trust will keep us in touch with you both.

"The Hope of the Race is in the Child," and we invite your hearty co-operation in our effort to train up a race that shall not know the taste of alcohol.

Yours very truly,

THE SUPERINTENDENT

of the Little White Ribboners.

Adopted by the Canadian National Woman's Christian Temperance Union.

THE MOTHER'S PROMISE

"I hereby place my child's name among the Little White Ribboners, promising not to give or allow him (or her) to take any intoxicating Drink."

|No Mother who takes alcohol during the period of nursing can enroll her baby until it is weaned.|‡

Child's Name ....

....

Age .... Date of Enrollment .... 19....

Mother's Name }
and Address }

....

Is Mother herself a Total Abstainer? ....

*The only expense in connection with this Enrollment is TEN CENTS, to be paid before name is entered on the Roll.

Date of Payment: Name of Receiver:

....

‡For Pledge See Over

2.12 and 2.13 | WCTU Pledge, The Little White Ribboners; WCTU Promise, The Little White Ribboners; nineteenth century foot-hold for the enemy [disorder]." But even if adversity were encountered, she advised them to "Keep on teaching; keep on trying new plans; keep on expecting; keep on praying."[38]

Working youths, like the Montreal-area newsboy from about 1905 shown in figure 2.11, were self-reliant, practical, and sometimes aggressive in their rejection of temperance instruction. Teaching them to read and write would have been a challenge, but temperance instruction would have been that much more difficult. The WCTU records speak time and again of how trying this area was for them. In taking on the leadership of groups in which this paper boy would have been welcomed, the YWCTU became widely recognized and admired for their skill in group instruction. Any young woman like Bertha Wright had cause for pride in her success with youngsters.

Another difficulty in trying to run successful working-class children's groups was that the WCTU tended to sentimentalize all children, as was common during the Victorian period, setting up unrealistic hopes that were rarely realized. This sentimentalizing, even eugenist, tone was obvious in much of the group's literature, including its promotional leaflets for "The Little White Ribboners," the smallest children (from birth to seven years of age) to be organized into a corps. "The Hope of the Race is in the Child," "Nations are gathered out of Nurseries," intoned the pamphlets, shown in figures 2.12 and 2.13, as a eugenist blueprint and representative of the era. While the Little White Ribboners was a mother's support group for abstinence, the image is of unblemished children, almost baptized in temperance. It speaks of a child who is pure and helpless, not one who helps to support the family through his labour or one who has a class-based appreciation for the bonding effects of drinking and smoking. Strikingly, too, the purity and "hope" of children is defined through the image of racialized whiteness and expressed throughout as childhood purity. Children who were racialized non-white and working-class would have felt the sting of falling outside the preferred definition.

Confronting the Spectre of the Girl Smoker

By the 1920s, the fears for Canada's young male smokers were accompanied by worrisome observations that even girls were taking up the habit. Some anxiety had earlier appeared as temperance leaders faced the painful possibility that the young women, on whom they so depended to carry out their childhood educational plan and to reform the young men with whom they socialized, might themselves be drawn to smoking. In 1910, the president of the Newmarket WCTU raised this possibility. As reported by that union's recording secretary, "The President read a resolution on the Evil of the Tobacco habit – oh! what can be accomplished when men of high degree in prominent positions indulge in the habit setting a bad example for young boys even women and girls are taking to the habit in some places not far distant."[39] Thus, while the blight of women's smoking had not found Newmarket yet (or so imagined the secretary), it was not far away. In 1922, the "women of the Oxford County WCTU place ourselves on record as being strongly opposed to the use of cigarettes by anyone, but more especially our women and girls; and we pledge ourselves to fight against this evil which is destroying the youth of our nation."[40] The problem was not confined to Ontario. The Manitoba WCTU wondered, "Are Women Really Smoking in Winnipeg?" Hearsay suggested that among young women at supper-dances, "Winnipeg's so-called society young women, dressed in the height of the scantiest evening attire, EVERY ONE OF THEM PUFFING A CIGARETTE."[41]

However, a less invested reading of the records, both text and visual, indicates that young women with these affiliations rarely smoked in the period before the Second World War or afterwards. The diary accounts of young women involved in Christian youth groups, such as those of Lauretta Sluenwhite, Ethel Fry, and Bernice Robb discussed in chapters 8 and 10, all demonstrate that Christian ideals and familial associations helped to discourage these young women from smoking. At the same time, respectable young academic women who were not allied with temperance, as discussed in chapter 9, were also slow to take up smoking in any numbers. For those young women on the margins of society, the very poor, the rebellious, the artistic, and the sexually explicit, smoking offered an ideal prop to perform that rejection of conventional standards of womanhood and to define new modern identities. These were the young women whom the members of the YWCTU and their mother organization had very little power to dissuade from smoking and about whom they fretted at their meetings and in their records.

The Transformation and Decline of the Young Woman's Christian Temperance Union

The YWCTU attracted significant numbers of Canadian women in its heyday. In 1914, for example, when the Dominion WCTU boasted a membership of more than 16,000, there were about 1,596 young women in the YWCTU, as well as 11,535 children enrolled in the Bands of Hope or Loyal Temperance Legions.[42] Not coincidentally, that year saw the third major attempt to bring in federal legislation to control smoking. And yet by that time, the exciting pioneer years and popularity of the YWCTU had passed. The organization did try to change with the times. By 1905, the YWCTU was on record as supporting the abolition of drinking and smoking, a "living wage," the eight-hour day, conciliation and arbitration to settle labour disputes," and social purity, "one standard of purity for both men and women and in the equal right of all to hold opinions and to express the same with equal freedom."[43]

In 1910, despite this forward-looking and modern statement of principle, they were a mere shadow of the whirlwind groups that had worked magic during the 1880s and 1890s. Their numbers were in decline, and their actual programs were a sad parody of what had been a robust agenda to change society. And the decline not only took place in Canada. Internationally, the YWCTU organization was reduced to suggesting that local groups organize costume pageants.[44]

The YWCTU declined as well because of the new century's consumer-based ethic and dramatically different standards for young woman in society. By the 1920s, for example, the Winnipeg District WCTU issued a "Call to Young Women" in its magazine, *The Prohibition Watchword*, to support temperance in Manitoba. There was almost no response, and by 1926 *The Prohibition Watchword* itself had ceased publication[45] when prohibition had become provincial law. By that date, most young women were caught up in Canada's postwar acceptance of women's paid employment, relaxed standards of propriety that allowed for unchaperoned socializing, and a new fascination with rapidly changing "fashion" in personal presentation, as was the modernist norm. As Tim Cook observes in *Shock Troops*, the war had "changed everything." Even veterans remarked that "[t]he place we left off wasn't there anymore."[46]

And yet, although the image of the young temperance woman had become unfashionable by the twentieth century – indeed, a parody of a proud tradition that was sneered at rather than respected – the ideology of morally upright women leading by example did not die. Popular literature reflected these notions well into the twentieth century in light novels, while fiction appearing in women's and family periodicals celebrated it, as did the cinema. Works like Reta Gray's *Queer Questions Quaintly Answered* from the turn of the century, for example, featured a chapter entitled "The Boys Who Smoke." Although unaffiliated with the temperance movement, the account could comfortably sit with any of the temperance literature of the previous half-century. It features a doting mother and her daughter, Gladys, who stare out of a window at boys who are secretly smoking in an abandoned house. The mother determines to do something to rid the world of tobacco, since boys "are being diseased in body, made weak in mind, and vicious in morals; are filling our reformatories with truants and thieves, and giving us useless and bad citizens."[47] This "typical" mother could work miracles in the lives of the boys around her because "God had given her more strength in some things than He had given man; she was stronger to resist temptation."[48] Her reference to the necessary self-improvement of all citizens as well, especially wayward boys who smoked, is consistent with discourses developed by temperance advocates.

The ability of a reinvigorated moral citizenry to support the nation-state is both reminiscent of much temperance discourse and a foreshadow of arguments made throughout the twentieth century. The moralizing of tobacco use continued to be a concern of Canada's Protestant denominations, among others. In 1950, for example, the London, Ontario, conference of the United Church of Canada asked the general council to take a firm stand against tobacco. Non-use of all tobacco products is "unquestionably Christian and of positive moral significance," they argued. "[P]ositive Christian values inhere in the abstention" of smoking.[49] Here too we find self-improvement supporting and legitimizing the nation-state. The notion of powerful, moral women had travelled far beyond the temperance halls, infiltrating multiple spatial dimensions of Canadian society, as it does still. This I will discuss further in forthcoming chapters.

3

Luring Child Smokers with Prizes

A popular self-help book of the nineteenth century, *Search Lights on Health: Light on Dark Corners*, "sold only by subscription," set out the two paths for the young male smoker (see figure 3.1). "What will the boy become?" it asked and answered by showing the downward spiral into moral and physical decay of the boy who allowed himself to indulge in "idleness and impurity, vice and dissipation." To demonstrate the precipitous slide, the young man is shown smoking. Unsurprisingly, boys who avoided these traps, and who instead chose industry and purity, could expect to find success, honour, and, not coincidentally, good health. The nineteenth-century view of human nature was that these choices were largely under the boy's control. Young men embarked on a life of dissipation needed to be shown the error of their ways. This was to be accomplished by presenting lifestyle choices to youths as if they were separate worlds unto themselves: packages of attitudes, abilities, and consequences were available only to those who chose the complete program. The "high" path brought the young man into a world where elders were respected, salvation sought (and granted), and the individual subsumed his desires to his responsibilities. The "low" road offered short-term pleasures of the body and mind at no apparent cost. Yet narcissistic pleasures lead inevitably to indolence and irresponsibility for one's personal improvement and others' needs. To the youth, the difference often seemed to be which path offered more easy enjoyment; to educators and other moral leaders, the issue was one of responsibility, whether accepted or rejected.

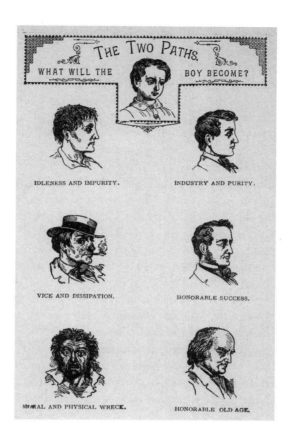

3.1 | "The Two Paths: What Will the Boy Become?" nineteenth century

But even if young men were well disposed to take up the hard work of the righteous path, it was widely acknowledged that he could rarely succeed alone. This was particularly so for youths from poor circumstances or with immoral models to follow from their own families. Vulnerable boys needed to be helped along the positive path of character development through trustworthy moral exemplars. These exemplars included the male authority figures of school, church, community, and possibly family, exercising "technologies of the self" by demonstrating to boy smokers an alternative approach to living. And since these were boys in need of nurturing, many of their guides necessarily were women. Mothers, sisters, daughters, female community activists, Sabbath or state school teachers, all were charged with the task of helping the young man find his way along the right path before he chose badly and ruined his life. This task both flattered and frustrated Canadian women, forcing them into a position where they competed with other (nefarious) forces for the minds and souls of boys.

By the twentieth century, the analysis of character development was increasingly based on environmental notions. Although parentage could either help or hinder the child's progress, broader community influences – particularly those offered through the formal educational system – were thought to have the power to reshape a badly directed boy into a character success. In reinforcing the young man's efforts to do the right thing, women were presented as having a pivotal role. An influential woman could rein in boys' bad behaviour by calling on those finer influences that only a woman could exert. Sometimes the woman led through her role as a teacher, other times as mother, aunt, friend, sister, or youth worker. Even though young women themselves had first taken up public smoking in significant numbers in the 1920s, the concern of the anti-tobacco forces remained firmly fixed on young men well into the century and even to our own period.

In the early twenty-first century, tobacco companies and the broad reach of consumer culture are vilified for ever stronger enticements to both boys and girls to smoke and through an ever-expanding range of clever techniques. These techniques include the unofficial marketing of cigarettes through product placement and showing models of sophisticated smokers in movies and in other corners of the entertainment industry such as music. Smoking continues to be a mainstay of "cool" on the Internet and in other unregulated strands of popular culture. The old arguments by educational authorities that refusing to smoke was a prescription for good character have largely fallen by the wayside. Furthermore, the new "character programs" developed by anxious ministries of education across Canada in the first decade of the twenty-first century are more situated in an "active citizenship" model than in one stressing good health.

As governments seek to close off routes where smoking is valorized, new entry points have been found for this enticing and (now) counter-cultural expression of identity. One notable element of the current anti-smoking programs developed for youths remains their non-gendered approach. Most attempts to control smoking among the young by convincing them to choose the right "path" ignore the young woman smoker. The assumption is that boys and girls are enticed into smoking culture by the same baubles and fantasies. This is inaccurate, as the history of enticements, protective measures, and research shows. Girls are drawn to smoking for reasons different from those that influence boys. The story of trying to protect children from using tobacco is gendered in every possible dimension, from the victims to the advocates.

We have known for some time what it takes to mount an effective anti-smoking program for young people. The ingredients were restated in a 2006 American court decision that heavily criticized tobacco manufacturers' youth smoking prevention programs. Four strategies are known to reduce youth smoking: increasing the cost of cigarettes, eliminating marketing practices that make smoking appealing, implementing empirically validated school-based prevention programs, and conducting media campaigns directed at youth, using locations that have been shown to influence youths' smoking.[1] Tobacco manufacturers have managed to subvert all of these strategies. The pro-smoking forces have managed to maintain marketing practices that make smoking appear "cool" and benign, even subverting media campaigns that were intended to be anti-smoking products into smoking encouragement programs. On the other hand, anti-tobacco forces, including the provincial and federal governments, health agencies, and most particularly schools, have failed to effectively protect children by implementing any of these strategies consistently or believably.

This chapter explores the historical contest between cigarette manufacturers and advertisers and those who have fought to eliminate smoking by the young: community groups, educators, and governments. In the process of trying to draw young people into either the anti-smoking or pro-smoking camp, both sides have used enticements. In many cases, these lures have been material objects, or "prizes." In other instances, the reward has been social. This struggle has characterized the history of youth smoking since the 1880s, with the anti-cigarette forces holding the edge before the First World War and the manufacturers and purveyors of cigarettes gaining strength from the 1920s to the 1990s.

Luring Children to Smoking through Prizes or Promotions

They come in fruit flavours, cost about $1 each, and are widely available at gas stations and convenience stores across Canada. They're cigarillos, mini-cigars that contain nicotine, carry few if any health warnings, and are smoked by a significant number of Canadian teens, according to statistics recently released by Health Canada.

Cigarillos, dubbed the "new cigarettes," are a growing source of worry for anti-smoking groups and politicians who say they're being marketed to youth as a result of a legal loophole that critics say needs immediate attention from the federal government.

Many of the cigarillos on store shelves in Canada feature brightly coloured packages and come in a variety of flavours, including strawberry, peach, coconut, vanilla and rum.

Health Canada has numerous restrictions that limit cigarette advertising and require prominent warnings on packages. But cigar products are considered to be a distinct product category subject to different rules, which means that individual cigarillos can be sold without any warnings. Those sold in packages require smaller, less prominent health warnings than those on cigarette packages. But anti-smoking advocates and politicians in some provinces say the tobacco industry is taking advantage of those rules to create flavoured cigarettes in trendy packages in order to appeal to youth and get them hooked on the habit.[2]

This account from a *Globe and Mail* article in February 2008 speaks to one of the most consistently reported reasons why young people begin smoking: to be "cool" among peers. In this case, the reward is a fruit-flavoured cigarillo laced with nicotine, which can be sold individually instead of in a package. This new front in enticing children into smoking culture is representative of the creative and effective ways that tobacco manufacturers have approached children as a market. How effective is this particular approach? The most recent Youth Smoking Survey identifies fruit or candy-flavoured cigarillos as responsible for slowing the reduction of youth uptake of smoking. As much as 35 per cent of young Canadians admitted to having tried these enhanced cigarillos.[3] Furthermore, Health Canada's tobacco-use monitoring survey shows that more teenagers have tried cigarillos (12 per cent of those aged 15 to 19) than the comparative general population (4 per cent of all Canadians, aged 15 and older, in the previous 30 days).[4]

The effectiveness of this ploy to draw younger and younger children into smoking has been recognized by the federal and several provincial governments. In March 2009, the Canadian government introduced Bill C-348, An Act to amend the Tobacco Act (cigarillos, cigars and pipe tobacco).[5] It seeks to make a broad range of specified "additives" to these products illegal, including spices and sugars but not including menthol, an additive dating back to the 1970s and more popular among youths in the United States[6] than among those in Canada.[7]

How did the competition for and against child smokers through the use of rewards begin? The rapid expansion of media in the late nineteenth century, with power presses, mill-produced paper, colour lithography, and large-scale distribution systems by rail, meant that advertising assumed new significance in the developing consumer culture.[8] Commercial artists' skills were in great demand to feed the growing appetite for personalized advertising, especially in the tobacco industry. This resulted in a wide variety of enticing graphic advertisements for consumers of all ages.

3.2 | York and Front Streets, Toronto, 1925

In a 1925 photograph (figure 3.2), a concentrated display of advertising in the form of tobacco placards is shown on a corner of York and Front streets in Toronto: Players Navy Cut Cigarettes have pride of place and number with at least twelve placards on the two faces of the Quick Lunch & Soda Fountain. In front of the shop is an open kiosk with advertising for Old Chum Tobacco. On the roof are two more tobacco placards. It might be argued that the simple visual exposure of so many tobacco billboards, most in bright colours, represented a pleasure of its own. But with the cigarettes being marketed on these signs are a variety of additional treats for the consumer. The MacDonald's British Consuls billboard, for example, offers collectors' cards. These inclusions in packets of cigarettes featured cars, sports and movie-star personalities, and playing cards in which a full set of the card pictures could be redeemed for a pack of cards, as seen in figure 3.3.

Tobacco manufacturers had first begun placing "girlie" pictures of scantily dressed attractive women in cigarette tins before the First World War. Girlie cards drew on a long pornographic tradition of erotic postcards, which flourished between the early 1890s and the end of the First World War. Most were photographs of women showing a bit of flesh, and many were women of colour, or elite women, shown in degrading positions. It

3.3 | Macdonald Tobacco/British Consols playing cards, 1926

has been estimated that between 1894 and 1919, 140 billion postcards of this type were sent around the world, making it the most widely distributed form of commercial pornography.[9] Only the mildest of pornography could be sent through the mail, of course, with the more raunchy versions available for sale in news shops and by tobacconists.[10] From tobacco shop to tobacco package was a short hop for the girlie pictures.

"Buck" Duke, founder in 1890 of the American Tobacco Company and relentless promoter of cigarettes, installed his own print shop at his Durham factory in order to produce new colour lithographs on his cigarette cards. He also offered premiums and coupons to purchasers of his cigarettes.[11] Duke had first placed trading cards with pictures of lesser actresses and "sporting girls" in his cigarette packages before 1900, ostensibly to prevent the package from crushing the cigarettes. American tobacco manufacturers also offered large posters to be redeemed with tags, some of which were photographs and others lithographs. For example, advertisements from the National Tobacco Works (New York) for Newsboy plug tobacco offered "Beautiful Pictures Free for paper tags of tobacco." "The pictures can be seen in the cigar store windows, and will beautify any home. It will not take long to get the entire set."[12] It can easily be forgotten that tobacco, along with many other products, was fodder for self-improvement, however defined.

3.4 | Card pictures: "Aviary and Cage Birds," 1926, album cover

The women shown on these posters or cards were typically bare-armed, with décolletage and tights. These "lascivious photos" raised general alarm, even on the part of Duke's own father, who freely acknowledged that the cards were directed to young men and boys.[13] Although they appear mild to the modern eye, tobacco art on the girlie cards operated at the very boundaries of North American public standards of decency. Most of the artists working in tobacco lithography and some in photography were European-trained, transporting European skills and combining them with colonial notions to produce their images.[14] Duke's and other Canadian manufacturers' cards mimicked those found on cigar boxes in the ubiquitous cigar store on most street corners. Often posed in "cheesecake" positions, the female models were frankly sexualized. The cigar-box beauties are discussed in chapter 5. The heyday of cigarette or trading cards in Canada came a few years later, but many still circulated until the Second World War.

More than sexualized images were offered to the collector, however. In Canada, cards could be collected on such imperial themes as celebrated ships of England, Dickens's England (with biographies of Dickens's characters and line drawings), Burns's Scotland, animals of England, the 1937 Coronation, Egyptian kings, queens, and deities, fish and bait, flags and coats of arms, and "Aviary and Cage Birds," as in the two collages shown in figures 3.4 and 3.5. In this instance, the cover (figure 3.4) is that of an

3.5 and 3.6 | Card pictures: Aviary, 1926; Card of Henri Groulx, Paris, France, 1920

album into which the collected cards could be glued. An attractive graphic on the inside matches the cover art and provides appropriate spaces for the bird pictures, as shown in figure 3.5. In general, "card pictures" were meant to be collected or traded with friends until a full set had been assembled. Typically, larger cards were included in cigarette packages of ten than in the smaller packages of four: more cigarettes meant bigger prizes. To extend the possible holdings, for example of movie stars, still images were taken from movies and grouped with studio-produced promotional photographs. There was little chance that the producers of movie-star cards would soon run out of materials. One run featured 50 "Famous Film Stars," another "Film, Stage and Radio Stars." In addition to fetching photographs, the cards gave extensive text with a faintly risqué tone on the subject at hand. In this way, they also reflected their origins as "girlie cards" from the turn of the century. Others featured sports and adventure stars, military generals, and flags and stamps of foreign countries.

Some cigarette cards were merely quirky or comic. Figure 3.6, French in origin, might well have been one of these cigarette cards, but just what is being collected in this image is unclear: perhaps comic pairings such as one might encounter in the music hall. The WCTU's response to cigarette cards was indicative of other anti-cigarette forces. Much time was spent strategizing on how to deal with this threat to childhood but with little success. In 1926, for example, the members of the Grey and Dufferin County (Ontario) WCTU seriously considered buying up all available cigarettes for the coloured cards displaying "birds," distributing the cards without the cigarettes. "Would it pay?"[15] they asked themselves, eventually giving up on the idea as too labour-intensive.

While the pre-war period was the heyday for prizes in tobacco, a second phase of prizes from Canadian manufacturers was offered in the mid- to late 1960s. Belvedere Cigarettes advertised in 1965 a full range of prizes available in packs of cigarettes.[16] Other media reported in 1969 that cigarette manufacturers, including Rothmans of Pall Mall Canada Ltd, Benson and Hedges, and Macdonald Tobacco Company, all offered cash games like poker, gifts, and coupons in cigarette packages. They reported that the prizes had increased their market share from 23 per cent to almost 60 per cent in fifteen months.[17] Gift certificates offered prizes from coffee mugs and alarm clocks to fur coats, sports cars, and trips to Hawaii.[18] Having witnessed the Canadian Broadcasting Corporation's voluntary removal of cigarette advertisements in May of 1969,[19] and anticipating the Canadian government's banning of tobacco advertisements in the broader media, the tobacco manufacturers resolved to use good portions of their advertising budgets as incentive programs. In the modern case, the so-called "in-pack promotions" eventually raised fears about the effect of these prizes on their profit margins.[20] By 1970, more than 60 per cent of all cigarettes sold in Canada carried cash and gift promotions.[21]

The disastrous conclusion to promotional advertising for the Canadian tobacco advertising industry occurred in 1970 when Imperial Tobacco advertised "instant winnings of from $5 to $100" in a new brand called Casino. A printing error on the game cards resulted in some purchasers winning prizes repeatedly. There were reports of individuals claiming prizes of between $20,000 and $30,000. Imperial Tobacco eventually paid out vast sums to consumers despite its rapid removal of Casino from the market. What began as a ploy to lure children into the market ended in an undignified debacle.[22] Nevertheless, this does not suggest that the policy of treating potential customers failed.

Most of the prizes were directed at young adults, but Imperial Tobacco also sent out promotional letters to some 200 children in Ontario. Children were urged to buy a pack of Embassy Cigarettes and win a bicycle or even a Cadillac. One child's mother sent the letter to Barry Mather, an MP who strongly supported a total ban on cigarette advertising, adding valuable fuel to the campaign that year.[23] By 1972, all advertising for tobacco on television and radio had ended in Canada, and the promotions were a thing of the past, at least in Canada.

Despite the advertising ban, tobacco manufacturers in the United States continued throughout the 1980s to offer promotions with free cigarettes, many of which were offered to youths. In Canada, there were complaints that tobacco marketing continued to be directed to youths. For example, when Temp Cigarettes were introduced to the market in 1985, many contended that the marketing campaigns targeted young people with the use of few words on advertisements, colour choices, and pictures of hip youths.[24]

At the same time, "Big Tobacco" developed "youth programs" throughout the 1980s and 1990s with the avowed goal of preventing youth smoking through education. The agreement reached between Big Tobacco and the state attorneys general in 1997 required that tobacco manufacturers spend $500 million annually on youth anti-smoking programs.[25] One of these appeared in 1999 as the "Tobacco is Whacko – If you're a teen" campaign. The graphics for this campaign were cool and interesting, lending the campaign credence as a bona fide anti-smoking campaign. The poster campaign was accompanied by an expensive series of television advertisements in which youths discussed the importance of ending domestic violence, protecting against natural disasters, but mysteriously, little on quitting smoking. It eventually emerged that the tobacco sponsors had spent far more on the advertising campaign ($100 million) than on social activism ($60 million).[26]

But the complaints against this campaign were centred on more than budgetary decisions. Critics noted that the "Tobacco is Whacko" campaign amounted to a pseudo anti-smoking message: "Tobacco is for adults only. Wait until you're 18, *then* light up."[27] While at first blush the argument might seem to discourage smoking, in fact the message to media-savvy youths was the direct opposite of what was stated. Rather than presenting smoking as madness, as in "Tobacco is Whacko," the advertisement has been accused of promoting smoking as a form of rebellion, a known factor in the lure of smoking to youthful populations. As well, critics targeted the word, "Whacko" as being so far out of teenage parlance by 2000 as to be laughable.[28] It seems clear that these advertisements were intended to show the merits of curbing smoking but actually accomplish the opposite. There is evidence that this campaign and other pseudo prevention campaigns have increased smoking among teenagers.[29] Further, it has been shown that ineffective campaigns like this one, combined with slick advertisements directed at adults, increase youth smoking rates. Exposure to this combination of advertisements resulted in lower perceived harm of smoking, stronger approval of smoking, stronger intentions to smoke in the future, and a greater likelihood of having smoked in the past 30 days.[30]

These pseudo-smoking-reduction programs have not gone unnoticed by American jurists. A 2006 American court decision heavily criticized these "youth smoking prevention efforts" as "not only minimally funded – given the vast sums they spend on marketing and promotion to youth – and understaffed both qualitatively and quantitatively" but also because no effort had been made to validate the programs' effectiveness.[31]

Further research has shown that to be an effective deterrent, anti-smoking messages must stress the social unacceptability of smoking.[32] In contrast to the proven strategies, tobacco manufacturers have instead adopted school-based and community prevention programs, media campaigns, and programs targeting parents[33] with the message that smoking is an "adult decision."[34] This message too would have the effect of encouraging smoking, not discouraging it. Personnel associated with the youth smoking prevention programs are often too inexperienced to be effective. Further, they are under-resourced.[35] For example, in 2003 Philip Morris budgeted $110 million for youth smoking prevention in comparison with $7.1 billion for sales incentives and product promotions.[36] There is no evidence that tobacco manufacturers on their websites or in their campaigns ever broach the damage done by smoking to teenagers and their families or the fact that quitting is difficult once smoking is taken up.[37] This research has led the US Supreme Court, and indeed most observers, to conclude that the tobacco manufacturers' youth smoking prevention programs are *intentionally* inadequate in discouraging smoking or that they actually encourage smoking. This conclusion is supported by an internal Big Tobacco document quoted in the Court's decision from 1991. It indicated that a "youth program" would be important to the tobacco industry because it would "support the Institute's objective of discouraging unfair and counterproductive federal, state, and local restrictions on cigarette advertising, by: (a) Providing on-going and persuasive *evidence* that the industry is actively discouraging youth smoking and independent *verification* that the industry's efforts are valid; (b) Reinforcing the belief that peer pressure – not advertising – is the cause of youth smoking [and] (c) Seizing the political center and forcing the anti-smokers to an extreme."[38] The strategy of positioning smoking onset as a function of peer support does have some credibility in the literature. However, the conscious attempt to reduce the assumption of advertising's influence on youths demonstrates the depth of the industry's cynicism and manipulation, a position that has been well demonstrated by popular culture in the past two decades.

Beyond the advertising of tobacco manufacturers that was intended to draw youths into smoking, there has been a wide range of other social incentives that young people have found supportive during their early teens when identity formation is in process. Especially for young women, smoking confers the possibility of taking on different personae according to the needs of the stage of development or situation. Smoking allows a manipulation of the visual orders to "become" a rebel brandishing a cigarette one hour and a demure but thoroughly "modern miss" the next. Smoking gives a young woman something to do with her hands and something to talk about. It suggests a meaningful small gift to be given during a break from classes or other responsibilities to a friend without her "smokes." It helps to reduce stress; it supports weight control; it adds glamour to an otherwise lacklustre appearance. All of these incentives for women's smoking have been validated by smokers interviewed for this study, and all appear repeatedly in tobacco advertising campaigns. In short, tobacco manufacturers and others understand that smoking has given, and continues to give, many more rewards to youths intent on developing an identity than trading cards or even a trip to Hawaii. The multi-faceted allure of smoking and its reinforcement of modern cultural norms helps to explain why it has always been a practice difficult to counter and why strategies such as those adopted by tobacco manufacturers in their highly sophisticated advertising campaigns meant that opposing smoking would be a hard sell.

Until the 1920s, the struggle to protect children from the manipulation of commercial and cultural forces encouraging smoking was led mainly by women, both individually in their role as caregivers and collectively through their own associations, the youth groups they sponsored and led, and pressure groups on the formal school curriculum. The story of women's attempts to reduce the lure of cigarettes for children is a proud but ultimately sad one. Until the Second World War, they waged a reasonably effective battle, but with the 1950s and the very powerful societal forces that supported smoking, they steadily lost ground, eventually producing outdated programs that reached children from only the most anti-smoking families, children who very likely would not have been attracted to smoking in the first place.

The Campaign to Oppose Kids' Smoking: Prizes Offered through Anti-Smoking Programs

Nineteenth-century evangelicalism had been one of the primary agents in empowering women to declare their leadership of anti-tobacco agitation in Canada. By calling into question traditional authority figures, by declaring salvation a matter between the sinner and Christ, and by arguing that salvation required "nurturing" of children and vigilance by adults, women claimed an important role in saving themselves and others.[39] This powerful position was further buttressed when women organized themselves into interlocking networks of social activist and religiously based groups in the late nineteenth century. Groups like the WCTU, the YWCTU, women's missionary societies, and Ladies' Aids, as discussed in chapter 2, all gave women the authority and means to lead campaigns, including those to wipe out tobacco.

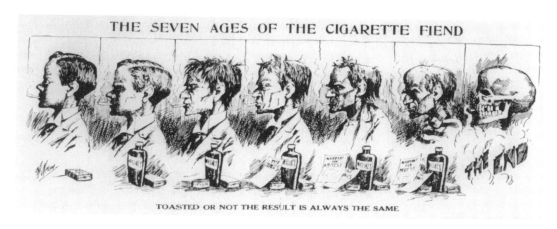

THE SEVEN AGES OF THE CIGARETTE FIEND

TOASTED OR NOT THE RESULT IS ALWAYS THE SAME

3.7 | "The Seven Ages of the Cigarette Fiend," nineteenth century

Children who attended evangelical youth groups in the nineteenth century were presented by their female leaders with graphics such as figure 3.7, the "Seven Ages of the Cigarette Fiend." The physical danger of tobacco, temperance advocates argued, was that tobacco users acquired an "unnatural" appetite for stimulants, which would drive the victim, and particularly young people, into alcohol and drug use[40] and away from God. "The tobacco road, though reeking with smoke and the filthiest kind of filth, is the broadest, and by all means the shortest and most direct route to that river of death, Alcohol."[41] In the first frame of figure 3.7, a well-groomed boy smokes from a package of cigarettes. In the second "age," whiskey has joined the cigarette in the boy's arsenal of pleasures, and the lad is noticeably more gaunt. By the third frame, the boy has aged, become unkempt and thinner, and opium has been added to the pile of playthings. In the fourth age, the man's cigarette remains firmly in place in his clenched and thin mouth; he is gambling at the races and indulging in alcohol and drugs. In the fifth age, the smoker's clothing has become tattered, his tie lost, his hair stringy and thin, and a warrant for his arrest has joined the paraphernalia of his doom. The boy has become a pathetic old man. In the sixth age, his hair is thinner yet, his frame collapsed, and the articles of his impending decline grow. Finally, "the end" arrives, with only the skeleton remaining. "Toasted or not the result is always the same," warns the label, alerting young men to distrust the claims of advertisers for pleasurable products like "toasted" tobacco.

A young man presented with this frightening caricature, a girl whose brother or father smoked, or a mother whose sons or husband indulged in tobacco use would be asked to identify with the end-results of smoking and suggest other ways that the boy's life could be lived, free from this scourge. Children and mothers received the same message from popular literature. Pye Henry Chavasse's *Advice to a Mother on the Management of Her Children and on the Treatment on the Moment of Some of Their More Pressing Illnesses and Accidents* from 1880 directed his recommendations to mothers everywhere:

> I am addressing a mother as to the desirability of her sons, when boys, being allowed to smoke. I consider tobacco smoking one of the most injurious and deadly habits a boy or young man can indulge in. It contracts the chest and weakens the lungs, thus predisposing to consumption. It impairs the stomach, thus producing indigestion. It debilitates the brain and nervous system, thus inducing epileptic fits and nervous depression. It stunts the growth, and is one cause of the present race of pigmies. It makes the young lazy and disinclined for work. It is one of the greatest curses of the present day.[42]

Reta Gray warned boys in 1899 in her *Queer Questions Quaintly Answered, or, Creative Mysteries Made Plain to Children* that chemists "were surprised to find how much opium is put into [cigarettes]," with wrappers "sometimes made of common paper, and sometimes the filthy scraping soft rag-pickers bleached white with arsenic. What a thing for human lungs."[43] And Maud Cooke of London, Ontario, in her helpful book on *Social Etiquette*[44] in 1896, reminded the newly engaged young man that slang, profanity, drinking, and smoking should all be eliminated from his life if he had fallen into these disreputable habits. All of these self-styled authorities were exercising Foucault's "technologies of the self" in offering advice to mothers and boys about the dangers of cigarette use. Rather than developing the personal authority that accompanied maturity, smoking would impoverish the young man on every conceivable level.

Before the First World War, the children and youths whom these authorities so longed to save from lives overshadowed by tobacco and alcohol came mainly from the working class. Anti-tobacco advocates practised their own brand of luring, promising these children – and especially the boys, their greatest worry – a panoply of diversions and socially improving activities, such as literacy training for those who could not attend school regularly because of the need to help support themselves or their families. Here too, technologies of the self were being invoked in campaigns to convince boys to model their lives on a different template than that offered by their own parents. Anti-smoking programs for these children in the evenings and on weekends and for middle-class school-attenders at the end of the school day were provided through such groups as the Bands of Hope, the Loyal Temperance Legions, or paramilitary youth groups like the Boy Scouts.

Pre-war anti-smoking youth groups garnered good numbers of children. Often the children were decked out in a variety of association-specific regalia. In the case of the temperance-led Bands of Hope, for example, this regalia included bright banners to use in marches, as well as sashes, hats, and decorative medals for personal adornment. Children were provided with drums, cymbals, and other noise-makers for the marching exercises, and these exercises were often choreographed to the temperance songs. So that all of the children could participate in the singing, a few songs were practised at each meeting from such sources as "Prohibition Songs" (see figure 3.8). As noted in chapter 2, time was set aside at the weekly meetings for formal lessons on the dangers of tobacco. Temperance curriculum writers recommended that the lessons be interactive and feature choral and individual reading exercises. Especially if the group had weak reading skills, the poem would occasionally be performed by one of the students who was a strong reader or by the leader as an example. In this way, many children without the benefit of consistent formal schooling learned to read and "declaim," or speak persuasively. The often sentimental selections would be accompanied by expansive gestures and exaggerated facial expressions to give full meaning to the elocution, providing children with the public speaking skills needed for self-improvement in business, education, or culture. The goal was to enrol a child who would one day become a persuasive anti-tobacco advocate and who could speak convincingly for the movement.

In all of these public meetings, the programs copied and sometimes improved on the pedagogy of the public school system. The "lesson" (shown in figure 3.9), with its careful graphic organizers and message, would have been used at one of the temperance-led youth groups. Its mimicry of the conventional school curriculum was one reason why temperance "lessons" struggled for legitimacy as more children were educated by the state. Graphics like this were meant to be confused with "unbiased" school materials. Such materials and strategies were designed to attract male children first and girls when possible as helpers with the temperance message. In fact, except for the Boy Scouts, girls came in much larger numbers to most of these groups, and since the teachers were almost all women, temperance education quickly became a feminized zone. To counter the perception that anti-smoking groups were meant only for girls, temperance groups bought supplies that would have a particular appeal to young men – for example, barbells for weight training. The lads were encouraged

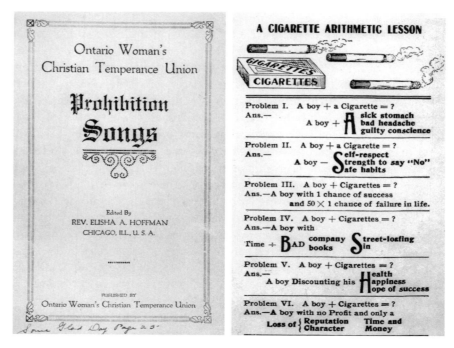

3.8 and 3.9 | Ontario WCTU "Prohibition Songs," 1920s; "A Cigarette Arithmetic Lesson," nineteenth century

to come and use the facilities much like a fitness club but with the provision that they would attend the "meeting" while on the premises. This seems to have worked for short periods in centres where the financial outlay was possible for the weakening temperance forces. The children and youths were almost always fed at the meetings on the simple principle that such treats would bring the children back repeatedly.

To give the children confidence and practice in declaring themselves as anti-tobacco advocates with the ability to convince others to follow their lead, the WCTU began running a series of medal contests, first developed by American prohibitionist W. Jennings Demorest and his wife in the 1880s. By 1895, the (American) National WCTU had made the medal contests a centrepiece of their vast extra-curricular educational program with children, and in 1905 medal contests were also officially adopted by the (Canadian) Dominion WCTU. By this time, however, they had operated for many years in various provinces, particularly Ontario, Manitoba, and Quebec.[45] An active program of medal contests continued in Canada well into the 1980s.[46] The WCTU adaptation of the old Demorest system

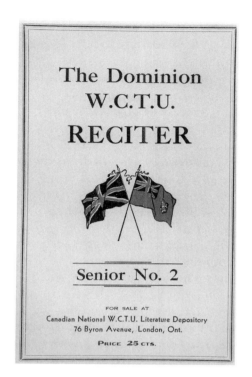

3.10 | "The Dominion W.C.T.U. Reciter" for medal contests, London, Ontario, early twentieth century

was to charge admission to contests, in which "scholars" competed for medals in recitation, music, or, eventually, art and essay contests. In short order, thousands of children were reached, much-needed money dropped into the chronically poor temperance coffers, and children who otherwise might have been drawn into smoking through commercial means were kept engaged at a formative period of their lives while learning how to self-improve.

Youth groups sponsoring medal contests made a selection from one of the sanctioned reciters, such as the one issued by the Dominion WCTU, shown in figure 3.10.

> I'm going to keep my temperance pledge
> And come here when I can
> Because I want to do some good
> When I become a man.
>
> For little boys and girls must learn
> To study and to think;

The L.T.L. is a training school –
Where we train to fight strong drink.

We are the hope of this fair land.
And as we live and grow,
True temperance principles you will
Observe in us, I know.

No wicked word shall pass my lips,
No stale tobacco breath;
The temperance pledge I mean to keep
Till life shall close in death.[47]

The above recitation was produced some time in the 1930s, by which time both tobacco and alcohol were firmly integrated into working-class culture. The "rum jar" had kept many soldiers' morale up during the First World War,[48] and both smoking and drinking carried on long after the war. Yet although conditions did change after the Second World War, anti-tobacco forces maintained the same pattern they had developed in the early part of the twentieth century. The 1979 *Medal Contest Book* for Manitoba featured this recitation with agricultural themes:

MEN OR MULES
Ever see a mule-race?
        It's a perfect scream.
Watch the mule that's in the lead!
        You would never dream
How the rider has to watch, –
        For if the mule looks back
And sees that he's ahead, he'll turn
        And run – to meet the pack.
Some folk, in the race of life,
        Are too much like mules, –
Scared to death to leave "the bunch";
        THEY'RE such silly fools
That, though they're "superior"
        (Have they much more mind?)
When they find themselves ahead
        They'd rather stay behind!
That's why some folks start to smoke, –
        They don't dare to lead.

> They're afraid to stay ahead.
>   Brains are what they need.
> Why on earth don't folks be folks,
>   Following human rules?
> Why run back to meet the pack
>   Like a lot of mules?[49]

This selection betrays the self-perception of the non-smoking youth as "inferior" to the smart "bunch" where smoking has clearly been incorporated into adolescent culture, both male and female. The rather unconvincing attempt to define the non-smoker as "superior," as more intelligent than his peers, and as a proto-leader demonstrates another instance of "technologies of the self" whereby the non-smoker is encouraged to regard himself as the inheritor of leadership in the "race of life." Here, they must be dissuaded from running with the pack where they "don't dare to lead." Regardless of its weak effort to turn the tables on twentieth-century "cool," this approach to anti-smoking education is marked by its outdated pedagogy. By the 1970s, long gone were the days when learning was demonstrated by reciting poetry, particularly the doggerel that had become standard in much temperance education. The weaknesses of the anti-smoking program, modelled on practices that had been common a century earlier, would have been obvious to most youths.

Children in the many temperance youth groups also performed their temperance messages in musical medal contests, and increasingly, the musical versions were favoured over the giving of recitations, possibly as a mirror of public education where recitations became rarer. Recitations were put to music and sung or instruments played as accompaniment. The medals given to the winners are shown in figure 3.11. Available in silver or gold with chains and diamond details, the medals were intended to be a significant motivator for children to become active anti-smokers and to advertise that fact to their friends and school authorities by wearing the fruits of their labour.

Increasingly in the twentieth century, contests that had depended on declaiming or musical demonstrations were discarded in favour of essays or poster competitions. The results of a British Columbia WCTU poster contest from the 1960s are shown in figure 3.12 as models for other anti-cigarette groups to show aspiring artists. Youth group leaders sought out potential smokers in every venue where it was common and where young people were inclined to meet, providing literature and personal testimonials to counter the insidious effects of peer-group smoking. Anti-smoking leaflets and posters were typically placed in railway waiting rooms, in bar-

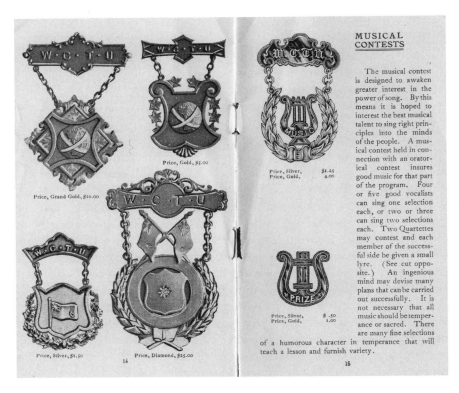

Price, Gold, $5.00

Price, Grand Gold, $10.00

Price, Silver, $1.50   Price, Diamond, $25.00

Price, Silver, $1.25
Price, Gold, 4.00

Price, Silver, $ .50
Price, Gold, 1.00

14

MUSICAL CONTESTS

The musical contest is designed to awaken greater interest in the power of song. By this means it is hoped to interest the best musical talent to sing right principles into the minds of the people. A musical contest held in connection with an oratorical contest insures good music for that part of the program. Four or five good vocalists can sing one selection each, or two or three can sing two selections each. Two Quartettes may contest and each member of the successful side be given a small lyre. (See cut opposite.) An ingenious mind may devise many plans that can be carried out successfully. It is not necessary that all music should be temperance or sacred. There are many fine selections of a humorous character in temperance that will teach a lesson and furnish variety.

15

3.11 | Rules and medals for the Canadian WCTU musical medal contests, 1920s

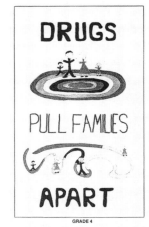

GRADE 4

GRADE 5

GRADE 5

3.12 | British Columbia WCTU poster ideas

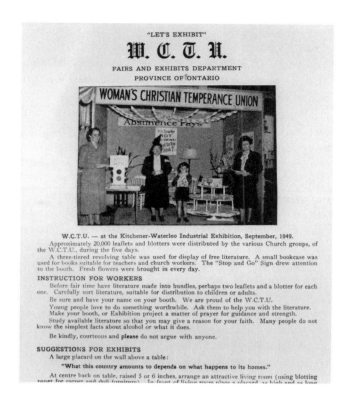

3.13 | WCTU fairs and exhibits plans, Ontario, 1949

ber shops, and in commercial establishments of sympathetic merchants. Local fairs and exhibitions were a particular worry, because these meeting spots for young (and mature) men were often unchaperoned (by women), encouraging youths to drink and smoke over long days spent in single-sex conviviality. To combat these tendencies, groups staged exhibits to advertise the virtues of a temperate life.

In figure 3.13, a photograph and didactic pamphlet, the Kitchener-Waterloo WCTU booth is shown at the annual Industrial Exhibition in 1949. The three women staffing the exhibit booth have brought along a winsome boy who carries his own literature, presumably to appeal directly to children. This was not by chance. The women were assured that "[y]oung people love to do something worthwhile. Ask them to help you with the literature." Since boys were the prime audience of this exhibition, the child's presence would be useful. At such events, signage was evidently very important. Signs announcing "Stop" and "Go" drew the public closer to the booth. The sign behind the four figures shows the pedagogical style favoured by anti-cigarette forces in this period. A large banner states the case directly: "Abstinence Pays." Directly below is a sign inviting discussion and debate on alcohol (and its companion, tobacco): "It's smarter NOT to drink. What do you think?" Having drawn the public to the booth, workers were instructed to "[b]e kindly, courteous and please do not argue with anyone."

The description below the photograph points out the kinds of literature distributed in that era: leaflets and blotters, the latter intended especially to appeal to students. On the tiered table, the women offer free literature, likely in the form of leaflets, while a bookcase holding longer works "suitable for teachers and church workers" ensured that no population important to the anti-cigarette cause would be missed in this opportunity to engage with fair-goers. Workers were instructed to ensure that the literature was properly sorted so that the correct materials would reach the right audience. The fresh flowers visible at each corner of the booth presumably announced that by not drinking or smoking, life could be filled with beauty and hopefulness.

And yet by the postwar era when this sample exhibit was offered to anti-tobacco activists, such strategies had the old-world look of temperance campaigns that predated prohibition. There is a sense of desperation about this and other suggested exhibits that cause the observer to distrust the enthusiastic assessments by the workers of the extent of their influence. If one were to compare the give-away prizes offered by tobacco manufacturers in packages of cigarettes with this fair-exhibit sample, there seems little contest about which approach would win over Canada's youth.

Even so, if the temperance forces had become outdated by the mid-twentieth century, other community-based groups, like the Non-Smokers Rights Association (see chapter 1), had stepped into battle by the 1970s. The new formulation of anti-cigarette forces did not turn their attention with the same energy to youths, however. In most cases, these groups were most concerned about the rights of all Canadians to function in no-smoke environments, youths included.

Male-Sponsored Anti-smoking Programs

The struggle to attract – and hold – the potential male smoker long enough to convince him to give up smoking was shouldered by more than women's temperance forces, although very often men and women collaborated in this daunting challenge. Like their female counterparts, the bulk of anti-smoking groups sponsored by men operated most effectively before the First World War. For example, the Anti-Cigarette Leagues, of which there were both American and British versions, were a major provider of boys' anti-smoking clubs and materials and had both male and female leaders. In the United States, Lucy Page Gaston ran the groups in the nineteenth century with determination and unflagging energy, with the support of the American WCTU.[50] Groups had also been founded in Canada before the First World War. The Anti-Cigarette Leagues put their case against tobacco to boys of all classes.[51] Middle-class boys were approached mainly through the print media where icons, such as famous sportsmen, provided testimonials of clean living. The leagues pursued young men in the working classes through these same channels as well as through other sympathetic organizations, including the Sunday schools, the Bands of Hope, and the Young Men's Christian Association. All of these groups agreed to disseminate league materials and sponsor anti-cigarette speakers.

As was common with the temperance organizations, the Anti-Cigarette Leagues conveyed their message to young men through formal instruction, culminating with the signing of a pledge "for the good of ... [the] country." Like the Bands of Hope and the Young Men's Christian Association, the cigarette abstinence message was mixed with requirements for orderliness and discipline in dress, speech, and bearing. Hobbies were introduced at meetings to replace lounging and smoking, including reading, board games, collecting, body-building, fishing, and other much more competitive sporting events condoned and participated in by the middle class.[52] Performances were often staged, and they also acted as a means to an end: discipline was required to present the theatrics as well as mastery of other discrete skills such as declaiming convincingly, literacy, and numeracy. As well, meeting other supportive fellows embarked on the same self-improvement journey helped to keep the young men from backsliding. The aim of the leagues was to support clean living while also encouraging upward class mobility.

The Anti-Cigarette Leagues were also avowedly patriotic and in the British groups even imperialistic. One of the earliest advocates of the British organization was Lord Baden-Powell, whose address to the Liverpool Anti-Cigarette League in 1906 had attracted 2,500 boys. By 1908, the British Anti-Cigarette League boasted more than 80,000 members,[53] while the American membership stood at about 300,000 in this period.[54] The astonishing rise in membership in the leagues was not sustained, however. While the British and American Anti-Cigarette Leagues did not survive the First World War, their methods, which had been copied from other youth groups, were in turn taken up by newer boys' organizations such as the Boy Scouts.

3.14 | *The Cigarette News*, 1931

In Canada, these clubs survived until after the Second World War, although they never commanded the huge membership of either the British or American organizations. Here they were sustained by an evangelical-like commitment to ridding the world of tobacco and by a belief in the power of positive example. One journal produced by the Anti-Cigarette League was *The Cigarette News*. It was produced in the form of a newspaper with cartoons, uplifting news items, and jokes. Broadsheets of this type could provide the program for a meeting of the club, or selections from several issues might be cobbled together for a program. Otherwise, they were meant to offer the individual boy an uplifting diversion through reading. Other publications from anti-cigarette groups offered moralized fiction for the boys to read or for teachers to present to school children.[55] The anti-cigarette clubs never rivalled organizations like the WCTU in Canada, but they did add much-needed support to the informal anti-smoking lobby.

In addition to the course of activities to convince boys to reject tobacco, childhood anti-cigarette education was also offered by the many nineteenth-century temperance lodges – for example, the Sons of Temperance. Groups like the Young Men's Christian Association, the Boy Scouts, and the Salvation Army all had active anti-smoking educational agendas. Sometimes women ran the clubs for the younger children while men taught the older boys for whom fears were greater. At other times, the men and women cooperated in presenting different aspects of the anti-tobacco message. Of course, none of these clubs imagined that girls were smokers, so the education was tailored almost exclusively to males.

Another male-directed and dominated group with an active anti-smoking program was the Salvation Army. Introduced to Canada in 1882, the Salvation Army grew rapidly in its early years among young and predominantly female workers in major cities and small towns[56] as it took advantage of rifts in other Protestant denominations to quickly build its membership.[57] Commanding attention in the way of revivalists through colourful marching, complete with uniforms and banners, duelling bands, "Hallelujah lasses" with tambourines,[58] and enthusiastic evangelism, the Salvation Army set out to attract converts by stressing its affinity with and its celebration of working-class culture. In this way, it distinguished itself from other evangelical groups, such as the WCTU, which sought middle-class respectability. In its pitch to young male smokers, it presented its version of the "slippery slope" for the young man trying to kick the tobacco habit without the fortifying power of divine intervention. The imagery in much Salvation Army anti-smoking material was heroic and militaristic, contrasting with the WCTU's dominant maternal imagery: "The terrible appetite is now fully aroused, and feeling unable (in his own strength) to battle with the enemy, he again yields to the temptation, and the 'tobacco fiend' with grip like steel, holds him in its loathsome embrace, fastens its poisonous fangs so tenaciously around him that escape seems impossible, and he begins to realize His Peace With God is Broken."[59] The tobacco fiend's "loathsome embrace" is strengthened by its partners in crime, as can be seen in the cover from *The War Cry*, the Salvation Army's national Canadian magazine, in a feature from 1910 (figure 3.15). Here, the ghostly "smoking" is joined in battle by other nefarious habits: gambling, murder, crime, and drinking. Garbed in flawless Roman armour, the virtuous forces of Righteousness with their shields of Faith and their helmets of Salvation wrestle these forces of evil to the ground. One Righteous Soldier calls for help as he prepares to take on a bottle-shaped wraith called "Drink" busy strangling a young man in the foreground. The Knight in the shiniest armour ignores the requests for help, however, as he stares longingly into the "Tent of Retirement" where the observer can imagine there is rest, quiet, shelter, and possibly the company of an illicit relationship. Despite being the best equipped to fight for righteousness, the tired

3.15 | Salvation Army, *The War Cry*, cover, 1910

(and dispirited?) Knight longs for a break from his labours. He stares into the void with his hand resting on his dagger, having forgotten his original purpose of waging the battle for Righteousness.

In an invitation for the reader to ponder the meaning of the graphic, the cover sheet didactically quizzes, "What Does This Picture Mean?" The editors helpfully follow up with an explanation, the denoted meaning, at the bottom of the graphic in case any reader missed the central point: "It illustrates the condition of those who have got tired of fighting against the foes of mankind, and who have made up their minds to sheathe their swords and take it easy. They turn a deaf ear to the entreaties of their comrades, and turn their backs upon those who are in the grip of the demons of hell." To underline the connoted meanings of the graphic, the explanation continues, "What are you doing? Are you active in the strife, or a laggard in the tent? God and man call to you to wage a good warfare." The mythic qualities of this graphic are also clear:

men who actively struggle against adopting a lifestyle of indulgence are not just common men but rather "knights in shining armour." They are promised honour and respect, the greatest prizes of all in life, if only they will continue the struggle to free themselves and others from the "grip of the demons of hell."

Much of the argument put by the Salvation Army in this graphic, and otherwise in the energetic *War Cry*, was consistent with that of other temperance forces. This allowed for joint efforts in the battle against tobacco and drink. For example, the Salvation Army organized its own anti-cigarette leagues in some American centres.[60] Yet there were a number of features of the Salvation Army's anti-tobacco message that set it apart. Despite having appealed early and powerfully to women, women were neither given a role in convincing the young man to resist smoking or chewing, nor did any part of the message address itself to the woman smoker. The youth who sought to give up tobacco and its vicious associates of gambling, carousing, and drink or to avoid taking up these pernicious habits was to be supported through strong male mentoring and supportive male friendships from within the community. As with all evangelicals, friends and guides would ensure the young man's security in his faith and, ultimately, in his salvation.

Most of these male-led organizations, evangelical and otherwise, directed their efforts specifically to working-class boys. There was a general acknowledgement that smoking, along with other pernicious habits like drinking, had become a mainstay of working-class male culture more powerfully than of the middle class. In this drive for self-improvement, the working-class boy needed all the help he could get, and that included breaking the hold of tobacco on his spirit. Writers in Canada's popular press were more prepared, if rather condescendingly, to excuse the transgressions of working-class boys than those of young men from the middle class. "If young fellows and children in the upper and middle class indulge in the habit one can scarcely wonder that the lower classes act in the same way. The poor little beggars have very few joys in life, and they may be more easily excused than their betters."[61]

Boys' youth groups with strong anti-cigarette messages were dealt a lethal blow by the First World War.[62] In short order, young men who had been protected from tobacco's evils were welcomed into the Canadian Corps as Canada's fighting force. Public opinion about cigarettes' value for young men swung 180 degrees, from a dangerous and soul-destroying evil to an essential balm for the fighting man's ragged spirit. In the new style of trench warfare, the young soldier's enemy was as much boredom and fear of silent gas attacks as the embodied enemy and shell-fire.[63]

Cigarettes, it was argued, "enabled [the soldier] to endure suffering and win victories."[64] This view was even propounded by the eminent medical journal, the *Lancet*, which noted in 1915 that smoking "undoubtedly affords relief and diversion in all nerve-straining tasks."[65] Even the WCTU defended itself against charges that they had banned cigarettes from gifts to soldiers. *The Globe* reported a WCTU spokeswoman as insisting that "[n]o cigarettes, of course, were ever included in our boxes, since we disapproved of them, but we made no effort to check their use." Nevertheless, 400 veterans booed the WCTU during a march in Toronto in April 1919.[66]

Tobacco was freely offered to soldiers – by the major tobacco producers, service organizations, and the public – to bolster their morale.[67] Tobacco was considered to be so essential that the Canadian Expeditionary Force and other Canadian overseas military forces through their journal, *The Maple Leaf*, defined cigarettes' importance to potential female benefactors in England and Canada: "Cigarettes are to them what pretty clothes are to you; neither they nor you are content without those things."[68] It was argued as well that tobacco would keep soldiers from drinking too much alcohol. Cassandra Tate quotes an estimate by Benedict Crowell, American assistant secretary of war, that 95 per cent of the American Expeditionary Forces used tobacco in some form.[69]

But the war did not end anxieties about young men's smoking. One youth group that had existed before the war and gained in popularity afterwards was the Boy Scouts. The Scouts consciously prepared their members to be accepted into middle-class society, aspiring to become leaders, first of boys, later of men. Its newsletter, *The Scout*, warned readers in a column entitled "Easily Led" that sometimes young men took to smoking to avoid being called a milksop or a "goody-goody" or to invoke younger boys' admiration in a cheap bid to be seen as a leader. "But, make no mistake about it," the column warned, "he who is easily led, at least in the wrong direction, is lacking in manliness. He is not 'the captain of his soul,' he has no mind of his own, he is a mere follower and imitator."[70] The Scouts' founder, the same Lord Baden-Powell who had championed the Anti-Cigarette Leagues, regularly reminded Scouts that it was their moral and imperial duty to shun tobacco in all forms while still young. And although he could imagine some former Scouts as grown men taking up tobacco, he could not imagine that they would smoke cigarettes: "they're what women and little boys smoke."[71] Needless to say, the women smokers to whom Lord Baden-Powell referred were not appropriate companions for Scouts.

In place of cigarettes, the Scouts offered young men instruction in a wide variety of skills, including outdoor opportunities for city-dwellers.

Like the many organizations that had preceded and coexisted with it, the Scouts offered badges and prizes as evidence of their abilities and membership.

In the official rhetoric of all of these groups, cigarettes presented compatible but distinct dangers to working- and middle-class male youths. Thought to sap physical, moral, and emotional vigour in the developing male, the future leader and responsible citizen of the Canadian state, cigarettes were feared both for a range of articulated threats to young men and for those lurking, unexpressed anxieties fuelled by rapid societal change. At the same time, cigarettes' availability and performative possibilities offered young men a means to contest the civil code into which they were being inducted.

Anti-smoking groups for youths faded from view after the Second World War in most parts of Canada, surviving longer in Alberta than in Ontario. "The fact that the anti-smoking movement centered so forcefully on smoking among women and children ultimately undercut its legitimacy," asserts Allan Brandt.[72] The message would thereafter be taken up by multi-purpose youth groups like the YMCA and, of course, the school curriculum.

The battle over the child and youth smoker through various kinds of rewards, prizes, and lures continues in the twenty-first century, both in Canada and abroad. Recently, Margaret Chan, chief of the World Health Organization, accused Big Tobacco of being "on the march" in enticing new young smokers in developing countries. This "new frontier" contains those most vulnerable to tobacco's ill effects and chronic disease because of the shortage of health care and poverty, she noted.[73] Clearly then, despite the efforts of women's and men's groups, anti-tobacco interests, and pressure groups, the battle to save youth from themselves as smokers has not yet been completely won.

4

Smoking (Mis)Education

THE "INVISIBLE" GIRL SMOKER

Allan Rock sneaked his first cigarette in the basement of his school, now Tabaret Hall at the University of Ottawa, when he was twelve.[1] Ironically, his office is now three floors above that dark corner, where he is currently university president. The health curriculum to which young Allan Rock was exposed did not stand in the way of him adopting a twenty-three year career as a committed smoker, nor did it serve other students very well either.

Formal education has particularly failed to take the young woman smoker seriously. This has meant that curricula intended to dissuade young people from smoking has not recognized the particular reasons why young women choose to take up smoking, what factors support the habit for women, or how women might be convinced to stop. For the most part, women have simply been ignored in school curricula, but in some cases the arguments marshalled in school textbooks to convince young men to stop smoking have inadvertently encouraged girl smokers.

Anti-tobacco topics first entered the school curriculum in Canada in the late nineteenth century. In Ontario and other eastern provinces in English Canada, the study of health began as a course called "scientific temperance instruction" and treated tobacco use as a close companion to drinking. The graphic shown in figure 4.1, from A.P. Knight's 1919 textbook used to teach hygiene in Ontario and other Canadian classrooms, aimed to show boys "the up and down grade; how we climb and how we may fall" after drinking alcohol. The objective was for youths to develop self-control over their bodies, including their senses, emotions, and judg-

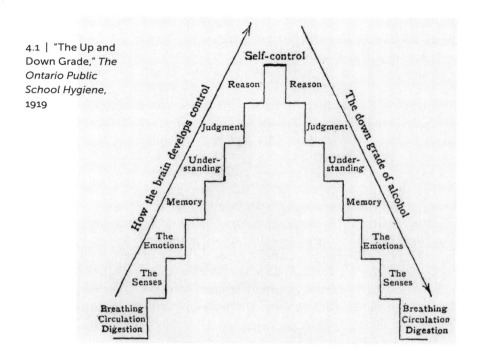

4.1 | "The Up and Down Grade," *The Ontario Public School Hygiene,* 1919

ment. This would occur by nurturing the brain and soul's ability to take on increasing challenges. The downward slide, accelerated by drinking alcohol and, implicitly, by taking tobacco in any form, reduced the brain's and soul's capacity to govern the body. The graphic argued that by giving in to base desires, the body became unable to carry out even basic functions like breathing and circulating blood and air. The message of this graphic, then, was a classic temperance tale of the dangers of deadening the spirit, mind, and body with pollutants like alcohol and tobacco. The young observer of this textbook message, whether male or female, was shown how one important "technology of the self" operated to attain governmentality over errant bodily desires. Self-control could also bring with it social power. The subject, as shown here and elsewhere, was consistently assumed to be male.

Introduced in the 1880s in most eastern Canadian provinces, courses in scientific temperance instruction (STI) mixed temperance messages with newer notions of physiology to redefine "health" as based on scientific principles. STI courses peaked in popularity during the 1890s and in the first decade of the twentieth century. In Ontario, for example, the curriculum area was renamed "hygiene" in about 1910, then "health" from the mid-1920s, and expanded to encompass physical education and personal development as well from the mid-1940s. By this date, the temperance message had largely fallen away in favour of modern conceptions of health, bringing with it new technologies of the self and imagined rewards.

Tobacco use was addressed in other than health textbooks as well. For example, *The Dominion Educator* for 1920, the so-called "peace edition" of this educational encyclopedia, helpfully included the following reference to the cigarette: "a small cylindrical roll of tobacco, encased in a paper wrapper, used for smoking ... Tests of boys who smoke cigarettes and of those who are not addicted to them show on the part of non-smokers more alertness, greater endurance and better health."[2] In addition to drawing attention to smoking as an addiction, the reference uses the language of science to assert that non-smoking boys would have an edge intellectually and physically. Mirroring much of the school textbook messages of the era, it would have appealed to young men who imagined a future for themselves as leaders in academia or sports, both widely considered as almost exclusively male domains. It completely ignored young women smokers.

Another subject in the late nineteenth-century curriculum that acted as a vehicle for health education and was directed specifically to girls was domestic science. It first became an optional course at the fourth- and fifth-form levels in the 1890s and was extended to secondary schools in the mid–twentieth century as home economics. It began its slow decline in the 1970s and was then renamed family studies. The health and family studies curricula were distinctive within the school program for their gender-specific programming. While health classes were usually single-sex because of the sex education component,[3] domestic science was originally developed as a course exclusively for young women. Although it has been a coeducational course since the 1980s in most places, it remains the only curriculum area rooted in women's knowledge and employing a largely female teaching force.[4] Hence, one would expect to find information of special significance to girls and young women about smoking, drinking, and much else in both the domestic science/family studies and STI/health courses. Yet here, as in the remaining formal curriculum, the young female smoker was (and is) all but invisible.[5]

By no means were all youths reached through the school system. Children in school were a captive audience, but this group often did not include the most committed smokers among both boys and girls – working-class youths. If smoking were to be wiped out as a tantalizing but lethal pastime by young people in and out of school, other agencies would need to take up the challenge of educating youth through informal means. Some of the nineteenth-century groups to engage anti-tobacco education were discussed in chapters 2 and 3. Other community influences and government health agencies are discussed at the end of this chapter.

As important as the textbook was in defining official prescriptions for correct living, it competed with other pedagogical forms of representation in presenting pleasurable activities and forbidden substances, including and perhaps especially smoking. This continues to be the case. Put differently, the "social rules" to guide budding smokers as they learned this new form of social exchange were developed and taught through a parallel informal educational system that often undercuts that of the formal school system. Often, it is termed the "hidden curriculum."[6] It shapes students' opinions, teaches skills both in and outside the classroom, and is directly influenced by popular and peer culture. Much of it was, and still is, based on didactic visual representations found in popular culture. These representations are considered throughout this book, since they have informed everyone's views about how and when to smoke. This chapter will consider formal anti-smoking education for young women and men in the school curriculum over the long span of 1880 to 2008 as well as some examples taken from non-school sources, all of which aimed to shape youth behaviours. Every source consulted focuses particularly on how young women are addressed in the formal or informal curriculum, if at all.

Textbooks, Girls, and "Correct Living"

Many of the official messages delivered to children in the formal educational system come through the textbook. Textbooks represent an important conduit through which society's leaders aim to pass on intellectual and moral capital to children through carefully selected facts, value-laden assertions, and even threats.[7] As had temperance advocates of the nineteenth century,[8] twentieth-century health educators reasoned that if values for "correct living" could be inculcated early in children's school experiences and then supported throughout their youth to the point when healthy habits became second nature, even children from dissolute families, where "bad habits" were thought to be endemic, could be reformed.[9] For both boys and girls, the message was delivered primarily through the hygiene and health curriculum[10]; for girls, it also found its way into domestic science/home economics/family studies.

An examination of textbooks and resource materials supporting the two school subjects of domestic science and health opens a window into how the formal school curriculum responded to the perceived dangers of smoking and to other challenges. The majority of the textbooks examined here were produced for Ontario schools, though many of them were adopted for use in other provinces as well. Textbooks allow us to examine through a curriculum lens issues of race, class, and gender by charting the various behaviours that were considered to be injurious for Canadian youths and which ones were deemed to be normal, and why.

A study of textbooks and the supporting educational resources that facilitate teaching from them does not tell us how they were used by teachers in the classroom. We have access to pedagogical recommendations to teachers, which were contained in teachers' guides for textbooks and other pedagogical directives from the mid-twentieth century onwards. However, we do not know what use teachers actually made of these recommendations once they faced their own students. Assuming that knowledge is constructed by both the learner and the teacher within a particular community and by utilizing class, race, gender, and familial norms, we also cannot know what actual meanings readers made of the textbook message. What we can assess with some accuracy, however, is how closely given textbooks mirror other resources and societal referents over time. Based on the continuities and discontinuities of rhetorical patterns in the text and society, we can draw some conclusions about the contribution made by the formal curriculum to a topic like smoking. We can also trace dominant discourses about smoking intertextually as a way of gauging the privileged meanings of smoking in cultural circulation.

The textbooks and other visual artifacts relating to the school curriculum include authorized and recommended textbooks for the teaching of scientific temperance instruction, hygiene, or health to students in public school (Grades 1 to 8) and the early years of high school.[11] For domestic science, the central sources include Adelaide Hoodless's first textbook for public and high school instruction, the *Ontario Teachers' Manuals for Household Management and Household Science* from 1916 to 1918, and the official "Programme of Studies" for domestic science, which framed the Ontario course throughout the twentieth century. In addition, a number of family studies textbooks in use across Canada show how the subject of smoking was presented from the 1960s to 2008. In an age when teachers likely depended even more on the textbook than is true today because of their own limited formal education and fewer alternative sources and because of widespread respect for any published source, we can assume that the textbook's message on smoking was held in respect by most students and teachers.

4.2 | Girls cleaning their teeth at Forest School in High Park, Toronto, 1917

Health and Hygiene Textbooks

The earliest hygiene textbooks[12] were compendiums of folk and quasi-scientific approaches to personal and family health in the home and barn. The temperance base of early textbooks' structure and argument is obvious. They were written in a conversational tone, organizing the subject into lectures that contrasted "pure" and "polluted" bodies and households and offering advice on animal husbandry and easy cooking alongside the chemical properties of whiskey and its effect on the blood. Insofar as women make any appearance at all in such health textbooks, it was to warn against the physical damage incurred by tight lacing, not the effects of smoking or drinking.

In the 1890s, textbooks for scientific temperance instruction typically expanded their physiological discussions beyond moral lessons. The public health or hygiene movement of this era aimed to improve Canadian society through the health and vigour of its children.[13] The scientific basis for much of the discussion around healthy living encouraged better diets, lots of exercise,[14] and the avoidance of harmful substances like alcohol and tobacco. Other healthy habits encouraged in these textbooks were good ventilation in living and working spaces, access to natural light, keeping scrupulously clean and tidy – including brushing teeth – and discouraging self-abuse.[15] The 1917 photograph shown in figure 4.2 includes many of the

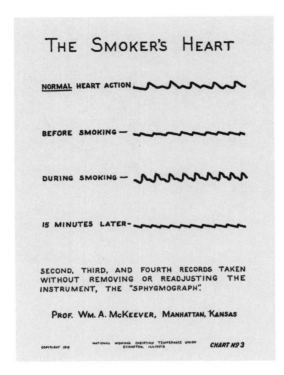

4.3 | "The Smoker's Heart,"
*Graded Scientific Temperance
Lessons: For the Use of
Teachers*, 1913

healthy habits promoted for schoolchildren in this era. The girls are being instructed in the fresh air and in a natural setting about the importance of cleanliness and being taught the best way to brush their teeth. Garbed in a variety of "middies" – dropped-waist dresses with nautical collars – and many with enormous bows in their hair, the girls watch a teacher closely while another teacher supervises from the line. The class of about sixteen reminds us that for health, the boys and girls were separated.

Most health textbooks concentrated on physiological arguments to discourage smoking, such as this account from the much-used Benjamin Richardson *Temperance Lesson Book* of 1883. He noted that the effects of smoking included "faintness, nausea, vomiting, giddiness, delirium, loss of power of the limbs, general relaxation of the muscular system, trembling, complete prostration of strength, coldness of the surface, with cold, clamming perspiration, convulsive movements, paralysis, and death." In addition, the smoker could expect to experience, "dilation of the pupils, dimness of sight, a barely perceptible pulse and difficulty breathing."[16] A diagram such as the one shown in figure 4.3 from one of the STI teachers' manuals from 1913 was consistent with what might aptly be termed a terrorist approach to anti-smoking education. A graphic like this one would have been used both in the public schools and by children's and youth groups. The argument is based on popular "scientific experiments" of the era. In this case, a set of readings from a "Sphygmograph" machine shows a "normal" heart rate contrasted with a resting heart, before and after smoking. The lesson was that the effect of smoking on the heart is to overexcite it, creating dangerous spikes in the heart's rate. The scientific gloss for this lesson can be seen both in the simple experiment and in the unpronounceable and imposing name for the machine that underpins the demonstration.

Even when hygiene textbooks from this period ostensibly addressed both boys and girls by using the collective noun "children," the reasons offered to discourage smoking suggest that the perceived subjects were exclusively male. For example, the teacher's manual for *The Golden Rule Books*, dating from 1916 and widely used in Ontario, suggested that

> there is a general consensus of opinion on the part of students of hygiene in regard to the effects of cigarette smoking on children. It appears to have been established that the poison of the nicotine in cigarettes weakens the action of the heart, irritates the nerves, and retards physical development. Many school principals attribute to it the mental inefficiency which in many cases leads to truancy, and from truancy to crime. Even if there were a doubt on this subject, there is no gain from the practice, and abstinence from cigarette smoking on the part of boys should, accordingly, be taught as a virtue.[17]

Thus, the argument that teachers were to present to (male) students was clearly defined: tobacco induces physical and mental chaos that can, and likely will, lead to truancy and crime. It can injure a physical system and stunt intellectual growth by sabotaging concentration. In a throwback to Victorian worries, many post–First World War textbook authors pointed to smokers' lack of ambition as a major threat, with this erosion of the soul over-casting all other fears. All of these negative effects, many of which are admittedly unconvincing today, were demonstrated through case studies of young men's promise being unrealized, of illness overtaking a previously healthy lad, of young men turning to crime through associating with "bad boys" who smoked. If the concern had also been extended to girls, there would undoubtedly have been some mention of girls' moral sensibilities being compromised or their reproductive abilities reduced in school materials of the era.

The multiple threats of smoking for young men were felt beyond each boy's soul, physical health, and intellectual development, however. The dangers extended right to the nation-state. One of schooling's prime functions from the nineteenth century was to develop a moral and competent workforce for the rapidly industrializing nation. If young men dropped out of school before these skills had been inculcated, were lost too early to on-the-job training by virtue of their skill deficits and attitudinal lapses, they would not be able to contribute to Canada's development. Young men shut out of Canada's stable workforce because of their addiction to smoking were a visible insult to the nation's ability to control its workforce or to train the next generation of leaders.

The 1920s was the first decade in which significant numbers of women began smoking in public. Many schoolgirls would have had occasion to see a woman smoking, and diary accounts from the interwar period show that many others experimented with smoking in the privacy of their bedrooms. Nevertheless, girls' attraction to cigarettes went unmentioned in textbooks of the era, along with any legitimate reasons girls might have had for taking up smoking – for example, reasons relating to identity formation, peer socializing, enhanced status and sexuality, developing sophistication, and remaining slender.[18] Textbooks from the 1920s until after the Second World War offered a message that cigarettes paved the route to self-abasement rather than improvement.[19] Pedagogically, these hygiene textbooks were made more attractive to girls by extending the range of issues addressed to nutrition and health, exercise, healthful rest, nature study, ventilation, and even first aid.[20] But the temptation for girls to smoke was not discussed.

The link drawn between tobacco and pathogenesis presented even more possibilities for anti-smoking education to be applied to both girls and boys.[21] Tobacco's carcinogenic properties remained contested within both the scientific and medical communities, however, and would remain so until the 1950s.[22] However, anti-tobacco advocates had no trouble finding doctors who would testify to the damage it wreaked on individuals.[23] The result of the disagreements over linking smoking with any particular disease, and the particular problem of proving causality, was that anti-smoking educators fell back almost exclusively on hygienic and moral arguments and particularly on the negative effects of tobacco on athletic and academic performance. Both of these were regarded at the time as primarily male concerns. Hence, until the 1960s the messages circulating most widely and publicly were not about smoking's dangerous association with disease but rather smoking's erosion of physical strength and its blunting of ambition, alertness, and positive character formation in

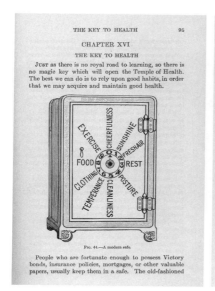 

4.4 and 4.5 | "A Modern Safe," *Ontario Public School Health Book*, 1925; "Food and Finest Development," *Highways to Health*, 1933

males. Given this trend, it is easy to understand why almost all textbooks of the interwar period grouped tobacco with other feared drugs – hashish, cocaine, opium, and, of course, alcohol – and why girl smokers did not see this as applying to them.

Health textbooks produced and used during the 1920s and 1930s based their health message on physical, mental, and social "efficiency." One popular textbook of the period represented health as a "modern safe" (figure 4.4), one in which the growing child invested dividends like rest, fresh air, sunshine, exercise, (good) posture, food, and of course, temperance. The mental hygiene movement of the same period, which aimed to control the damage "mental defectives" and feeble-minded youths could have on the general population, can also be seen in figure 4.4. Children and youths were exhorted to dispel depression through purposeful "cheerfulness," one of the keys to the "modern safe."

Textbooks could be subtle in their presentation of health's essentials or overtly racist. In a graphic illustrating the importance of food to physical and mental development (figure 4.5), the child learned that "food of the temperate zones is most suitable for man's growth."[24] To explain the difficulties faced by other than racialized white peoples, the textbook breezily offered the explanation that their regions "furnish diets which lack the

4.6 | Entrance to Sunnyside Bathing Pavilion, Toronto, 1923.

essentials for man's finest development." Apparently that was reserved for strapping males from Canada, Norway, Scotland, and England.

The late nineteenth and early twentieth centuries also supported the "playground movement," which sought wholesome outlets for children during their leisure hours. Good health resulted from the body's careful nurturing through organized play, as is suggested by a photograph of the entrance to one of Toronto's swimming pools, developed to support healthy play in a supervised setting (figure 4.6). In the case of the Sunnyside Bathing Pavilion, the pool was very likely built for disadvantaged children and as part of a thrust to situate recreation for all children in more natural settings. This was also the period when city parents first sent their children to residential summer camps. City living was increasingly seen as damaging to all people, especially children, with the natural environment of camps and playgrounds serving as a balm to the body and spirit.[25]

The argument in support of healthy exercise and against tobacco use could best be appreciated in the 1920s through physiological and chemical explanations rather than moral precept. The argument was buttressed by damning clinical studies. In figure 4.7, the clinical demonstration was designed to measure the effect of tobacco on the time required for a subject to recognize and pronounce a word. The apparatus had a revolving drum on which bands with words were placed. The instant a word was shown, "the chronoscope was automatically set in motion by electricity … the subject pronounced the word as quickly as he recognized it."[26] The time taken to identify the words was carefully logged. Then the subject was given tobacco and repeated the experiment. A table of figures claimed

4.7 | Apparatus to determine smoking and mental efficiency, *Tobacco and Mental Efficiency*, 1923

to demonstrate the results of this clinical trial. "Some of the subjects lost in efficiency under the influence of tobacco, while others gained, though taken as a whole the losses were greater than the gains."[27] Such demonstrations hearken back to impressive-looking machines like the "Sphygmograph" mentioned in figure 4.3, which had been ahead of its time in invoking scientific reasons for rejecting tobacco.

In the interwar period, such "tests" appeared regularly in textbooks. A student could observe the smoker blowing into a calibrated machine, demonstrating weak "wind," or the smoker's uneven pulse rates and episodes of nausea,[28] showing a relative inability of the smoker to withstand physical stress. Or a student could see a boy blowing cigarette smoke through a dampened handkerchief to produce a nicotine stain (which was actually a tar stain). All of the experiments, it need hardly be pointed out, related to typical life experiences of male students, leaving females out of the discussion entirely. The same demonstration with the male experimenter and females either enabling or standing around supportively was still being used in public displays by community-based groups well into the 1980s.

To appeal directly to male readers, the authors of interwar health textbooks invoked the horrifying image of a schoolboy losing interest in sports: "Now one of the most important things for success in games is staying power, and one cannot have that if his 'wind,' as it is called, is not good."[29] Next, he loses his appetite. "A boy smoker, with his stained fingers, his pale face, and general listless manner, is far from being at his best."[30] The fashion aesthetic of the 1920s was one of boyish thinness. When female readers of health textbooks were informed that smoking was problematic because it reduced appetite, we can safely assume that this would have been read by many girls as a good reason to smoke rather than as a recommendation to avoid or stop smoking. Despite educational authorities' identification of girls as endangered by cigarettes and as requiring special physiology and hygiene courses,[31] texts continued to ignore them as imagined readers.[32]

The Second World War left a deep mark on health textbooks throughout the 1950s. The message presented to the adolescent male about the value of smoking, as well as the cost to the smoker, was different from the message that had been common before the war. The war experience clearly influenced notions about acceptable behaviours generally and specifically about the importance of positive social interaction. As well, educational psychology made itself felt in teachers' manuals, stressing the need for the male student to be aware of and analyze his own behaviours. The 1942 Programme of Studies for Ontario, for example, noted in its first paragraph that educators must attend to the development of social skills because they "enable the individual 'to work with other people,' 'to get along with others,' 'to act in a socially acceptable manner,' 'to develop a socially satisfactory personality,' and 'to be a good citizen.'"[33] This heightened attention to positive social interaction was also predicated on new definitions for health itself. A 1951 health textbook adopted the definition of the World Health Organization: "social health [is] the ability to live in harmony with other people of other kinds."[34] Far from being an absolutely unhealthy habit, smoking was now considered by textbook authors to be one activity that could help a person develop this "socially satisfactory personality."

The imagined task in these health textbooks for postwar adolescent males was to learn to smoke (and drink) responsibly in public. In other words, smoking and drinking were recognized as having *visual* power. The young male citizen would perform his social health through smoking. The imagery and ethos in textbooks in the 1940s and 1950s is that of the male combatant: intensely competitive ("life is dominantly a competition for prizes"[35]) but socially supportive ("stay cheerful and friendly and generous, yet fight for your own rights and for the rights of others"[36]). Social smoking was considered as cementing these important male friendships and to do so visually. As one textbook approved for use at the high school level put it: "smoking is a social custom that makes for friendliness and comradeship." This same text stressed that smoking was "fairly universal." In supporting smoking as a normative and sanctioned masculine activity, it noted, "[n]o one likes to be different from his friends."[37] High school yearbooks of the era freely advertised tobacco and tobacco shops.[38]

By the late 1950s, the case against smoking as reflected in textbooks had become stronger once again. A health textbook from 1958 credits nicotine as considerably more harmful to the system than the same authors had admitted in the 1951 edition.[39] While recommending that smokers not inhale and enjoy cigarettes and pipes by smoking slowly, the text also credited tobacco use as the cause of high blood pressure, heart disease, lung cancer, reduced life expectancy, and restricted blood flow to the extremities. Thus, death as a direct result of tobacco use made a weak and for adolescents unconvincing comeback. Then, as now, it would be difficult for any "invincible" adolescent to imagine himself succumbing to high blood pressure, heart disease, lung cancer, or numbness of fingers or toes. And, it might be noted, none of these maladies had a visual expression, making them even less "real" to the adolescent lad of the mid-twentieth century.

How can we explain the changed message about the physical damage caused by cigarettes over the course of a single decade? The demands of the Second World War on combatants, their need for some kind of allowable pleasure, however momentary, and the perceived social needs of these young men to defend each other as members of a solid social unit all suggested to contemporaries a legitimate use for cigarette-smoking. The situation was reminiscent of the First World War when a popular way to show support for the troops was to send tobacco overseas. New textbooks often need almost a decade to be developed, so the 1951 edition would have retained its wartime flavour. By 1958, this lag had been bridged.

As discussed in chapter 1, studies began to appear from the 1950s in Canada tracing the causal link between cigarette-smoking and cancer.[40] Based on these studies, a private member's bill in Parliament called for a special committee of the House of Commons to consider the "cigarette problem."[41] Undoubtedly, textbook writers as well as the general public would have been aware of this debate and the widespread concern about youth smoking. None of the studies involved women, and so the invisibility of the female smoker was reinforced.

By 1961, the Canadian Medical Association acknowledged that smoking was strongly implicated in cases of lung cancer.[42] The 1962 report of the UK Royal College of Physicians asserted that "cigarette smoking is a cause of lung cancer and bronchitis,"[43] and a Canadian conference drew the same conclusion in 1963. Finally, the publication of the American surgeon general's report in 1964 marshalled such strong evidence that no

4.8 and 4.9 | "Relax, Girls!" *Canadian High News*, 1965; "Matters of Good Taste,"
Canadian High News, 1966

one could seriously deny the causality between smoking and cancer. And
yet the new recognition of public endangerment from cigarette-smoking
took a long time to make its way into educational materials.

Spurred on by the now clear evidence of smoking's causal role in cancer,
the Department of National Health and Welfare in the mid-1960s began
producing a periodical for Canadian high school students, *High News*.
Demonstrating far more recognition of young women's investment in
smoking than any textbook of the era or for long afterwards, the department targeted young women in a series of articles. These articles reviewed
particular reasons why girls had taken up smoking in this period. "You
don't have to smoke to be smart," asserts one, depicting a pretty young
woman with a modern hairstyle and stance. "Matters of good taste," leads
the second graphic, which then itemizes what constitutes true status: "a
clean fresh breath ... sparkling white teeth ... lovely unstained hands ..."
none of which was easily available to the girl who smoked. This graphic
caps its argument in a way similar to the first, "It's smart not to smoke,"
and offers an appropriately coiffed and made-up young woman as a visual representation of good taste. Both graphics were also centrally placed,
adding weight to the message in contrast to the limited print, and the
complete message was tailored to women's concerns. If Canada's national
agency for health could acknowledge the young woman and her reasons
for smoking, why did health textbooks ignore her?

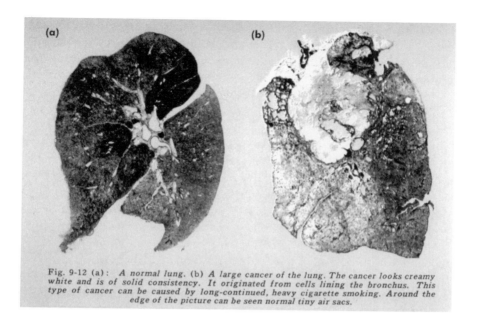

Fig. 9-12 (a): *A normal lung.* (b) *A large cancer of the lung. The cancer looks creamy white and is of solid consistency. It originated from cells lining the bronchus. This type of cancer can be caused by long-continued, heavy cigarette smoking. Around the edge of the picture can be seen normal tiny air sacs.*

4.10 | Two lungs, *Health, Science and You: Book 1,* 1967

By the late 1960s, most health textbooks had finally caught up with the new research. They devoted much more space to the dangers of smoking than had their predecessors and presented them in a terrorist campaign to shock young men into recognizing the many types of damage. Figure 4.10 shows a health textbook from 1967, where students are presented with two lungs, a normal one and one riddled with cancer. "The cancer looks creamy white and is of solid consistency. It originated from cells lining the bronchus. This type of cancer can be caused by long-continued, heavy cigarette smoking." The 1971 textbook, *Tomorrow Is Now: Today's Psychology and Your Health*, published by Holt, Rhinehart and Winston,[44] devoted a complete chapter of thirty pages to a careful examination of smoking, its causes and multiple deleterious effects on the body's physical and emotional well-being. Even in this extensive and impressive example of health education taking smoking seriously as a topic for adolescents (again grouping tobacco in all forms with other drugs), girls were addressed only marginally.

Health textbooks from the 1960s onwards treated smoking in the by now popular "spiral" format so that students at younger and older age levels received similar messages but with increasingly more complexity as they matured. Hence, in Ontario for example, the dangers of cigarettes were now first presented to children in Grade 4 health classes, but each year afterwards the message was reinforced, using illustrations and examples in keeping with the young person's stage of development. Since the 1970s, curricula such as these have also been designed to take into account a variety of different learning styles and ability levels. Considering this increasingly sophisticated messaging, the absence of a gender variable is all the more striking and troubling.

At the same time, history textbooks of the 1960s and 1970s undercut the message of health dangers by presenting the history of smoking by women as an act of "determination," a "defiant sign of their quest for freedom,"[45] as a bid for a public life when women "discovered that [their] place need no longer be only in the home,"[46] and as a means to compete directly with men in careers when they "began to smoke cigarettes quite openly ... cut their hair short ... [and] dresses became severe in line or shapeless."[47] In celebrating smoking as a liberated and modernist behaviour, such historical renderings of smoking's appeal to women earlier in the century would likely have served to fuel young women's interest in smoking in the 1960s too rather than warn them away.

During the 1980s and 1990s, health textbooks presented students with a formulaic anti-smoking discussion that emphasized the danger of smoking to the cardio-respiratory system. More positively, students have been encouraged to increase their levels of exercise, eat healthily, and control stress in ways other than smoking. Less positively, the treatment of smoking is notable in this period for its gender-blindness and until 1994 for arguments that persistently point to the concerns of the middle-aged authors rather than to those of their adolescent readership. For example, smoking is cited as contributing to hypertension or high blood pressure, to emphysema, and to heart attacks. Women's issues do make an appearance beginning in the 1970s, though in a form not likely to resonate with adolescent girls, as girls-as-mothers became the common focus. To take one instance, danger to the fetus is consistently noted as a reason to avoid smoking.[48] Yet what adolescent girl then or now believes that she is likely to become pregnant? To the charge that no adolescent with a history of reasonable health believes that he or she is a candidate for degenerative heart disease, the texts make an unconvincing case that autopsies of young people "killed in accidents or war have found that many 20-year-olds have blood vessels already up to 50% closed by atherosclerosis."[49]

Clearly, part of the explanation for so little in the way of adolescent-centred arguments is the same as for the paucity of female interests reflected in these texts: the research base was itself androcentric and carried out with mature males and therefore blind to the kinds of issues that might have persuaded female adolescents of smoking's many dangers. It was only in 1994, after the passage of the Tobacco Sales to Young Persons Act the previous year and the consequent prohibition of smoking in all Ontario high schools, that adolescent-directed anti-smoking resources from the community became more common.

While girls were first addressed as imagined readers of these textbooks in the 1970s, modern health textbooks continue to ignore the particular concerns of girls in deciding whether or not to smoke. Not a single textbook from the 1970s to the 2000s offers a gendered approach in its attempts to discourage smoking. It is notable as well that teacher-prepared resources for classroom instruction often disregard girls' particular reasons for smoking. The major resource guide for Ontario health teachers produced by the Ontario Health and Physical Education Association for the new guidelines in 2000 presented no strategies or resources of particular interest to girls and included a single case study of reasons to begin smoking featuring two boys.[50] Further, the mandated Ontario government curriculum guideline makes no suggestion of gendered reasons for smoking. For example, there is no discussion of female-related goals of status enhancement, of smoking's promise to keep girls thin, of the claim of increased sophistication, of the bid to demonstrate sexuality, or of female-centred social exchanges through smoking and borrowing cigarettes. At least some of these reasons had been acknowledged by the Department of National Health and Welfare's anti-smoking materials in the 1960s. Because of health textbooks' failure to address fundamental and distinctive reasons why young women are drawn to smoking, they have played only a minor role in disrupting a behaviour that ends in addiction for many women.

Domestic Science/Home Economics Textbooks

If health textbooks largely disregarded the female smoker, we might ask whether a female-centred curriculum with a predominantly female teaching force like domestic science/home economics/family studies did any better. The short response is – no. Certainly, girls have been ascribed a special role in maintaining a healthy diet and home life from the beginning of this curriculum area in the 1890s. Adelaide Hoodless, the founder of domestic science in Canada, asserted in her first textbook,[51] from which the engraved plate reproduced in figure 4.11 is taken, that "[p]hysiology and temperance principles permeate the whole course of study." Here, a domestic science student stands in her scientifically designed and orderly kitchen, waiting to support the health of her future family through proper

4.11 and 4.12 | Domestic science student in her ideal kitchen, frontispiece, *Public School Domestic Science*, 1898; Domestic science class, Ontario Normal School of Domestic Science and Arts, Ottawa, 1886

living and nutrition. As in the early STI courses, temperance was to be supported through the development of habits of "neatness, promptness and cleanliness, all of which Domestic Science inculcated through study and practise." The Hoodless textbook, on which all others were modelled well into the twentieth century, mainly addressed the safe preparation and disposal of food through nutritious recipes. Increasingly, the course focused on general principles of household management and was divided between food preparation and sewing.

The domestic science course taught such topics as the parts and function of the body, just as physiology courses of the era did, but added to the agenda the preparation and classification of appropriate food for different individuals and situations, as can be seen in this photograph of a domestic science normal school class in Ottawa. The young women shown in figure 4.12, dressed in their purpose-designed aprons, protective hair-covers and neckties, take instruction from a master teacher educator who has set out the scientific principles on the blackboard. The young women are surrounded by equipment to simulate a modern kitchen, replete with scientific paraphernalia. Proper cooking instruction on this scale was much more than a typical mother could offer her daughter. Here, the technology of the self, as Foucault describes it, is intended to produce a young woman with authoritative knowledge sufficient to wield power over other young women who would be her students. Ultimately, the girls under her

4.13 | First Nations residential school sewing class, Resolution, NWT

direction would exercise authority in their own households. By virtue of the knowledge bestowed on young women through domestic science, the properly schooled girl would have the means to develop a "technology of domination" over both men and women without this advantage.[52]

Instruction in homemaking went beyond training Ottawa's best-heeled girls. In the photograph shown as figure 4.13, domestic science is being taught to young First Nations girls for all of the reasons noted by Hoodless: to bestow on these Aboriginal girls the same technology of domination in their own households and communities that their racialized white sisters obtained through domestic science. The setting for the First Nations girls is probably a residential school, established in part to compensate for these girls' presumably weak mothering and knowledge base.[53] The role of domestic science or home economics instruction for First Nations girls was to create happy, well-organized homes of their own on even a minimal income, using a colonialist model.

By the turn of the twentieth century, household science was recognized as an optional course in Ontario and in several other provinces as well, generally taught in the upper grades of elementary schooling.[54] At the secondary level, it was more rarely taught. Because of its optional status, there were generally no compulsory or even recommended textbooks for its teaching. This remained the case through much of the twentieth century. Nevertheless, sampling some of the many textbooks that were produced for this area of the curriculum helps us to decode the assumptions behind the course and its teaching.

The *Ontario Teachers' Manuals for Household Management and Household Science* from the First World War do not mention smoking by anyone as an issue of concern.[55] This is not surprising, given the low rates of women's smoking for that period. However, the same absence is found in the 1930s when smoking rates for women were higher. The Ontario Programme of Studies in the 1930s shows from the suggested outlines for home economics courses in Grades 7 and 8 that smoking was still officially ignored as an issue for young women.[56] Lack of official recognition in textbooks, teachers' manuals, and classroom resources does not mean that this topic was never addressed in classrooms, however. Smoking could and likely would have been broached through a theme identified for Grade 8 students, "use of leisure time," in which teachers were encouraged to discuss safe and healthy pastimes such as reading books and magazines, practising hobbies, and sharing in family games. It would have required only a short leap to place smoking on the list of unacceptable leisure-time activities, and it is likely that some teachers would have spent time discussing this with their classes.

The Ontario Programme of Studies also offers a rationale for studying home economics at all:

> Chief among these educational values is the development of a girl's natural interest in her home, together with the cultivation of desirable attitudes towards the privileges, duties, and responsibilities of life in the home. Scarcely less important, educationally, is the opportunity afforded by the work in Home Economics to train the girls in proper habits relative to their personal appearance, the care of their belongings, and the conservation of their health. Far reaching, too, is the influence of the Home Economics room and its activities in cultivating in the girls standards of good taste in clothing and home-furnishings and an appreciation of scrupulous cleanliness in person, dress, and surroundings.[57]

Hence, home economics would continue to provide the young woman with the skills and knowledge, the technologies for self-improvement, for herself and her future family. Her developed "good taste in clothing and home-furnishings" in 1939 apparently did not include smoking, a message contradicted by popular cultural texts of the period.

Home economics textbooks from all periods, from the 1890s to 2008,[58] are silent on the particular reasons for young women making the decision to smoke. The subject is approached obliquely in some texts but always as if the choice were gender-blind, as with health textbooks, and primarily one to be made by males. Women as smokers are ignored as much through an absence of text as by the way the lifestyle of a proper and responsible young woman was framed. For instance, the ideal figure shape of the 1960s, as presented in home economics textbooks, was fuller than today's, removing one important reason for the young woman to take up smoking in the first place. A 1965 textbook counsels the thin girl to cover her body as much as possible to hide this unsightly condition: "Your throat is scrawny? Your collarbones stick out? Cover them with scarves, roll collars, Peter Pan collars, shirt collars, turtle-necks, or cowls."[59] Manicured hands are emphasized in a 1968 textbook, with hand-care occupying a full page of detailed instructions.[60] Smoking is notoriously hard on the hands, discolouring fingers and nails. These textbooks argued that the knowledge and skills contained in them would fit a young woman for "the rest of your life. The family unit is a basic part of every community, and you, as a young woman, will be responsible for a particular family in the future. Knowing how to budget wisely, how to serve dinner on time, and how to sew your own clothes, will help you to have a well-organized and happy home."[61]

Textbooks worried about the company kept by vulnerable young girls moving into the city. A textbook concerned primarily with making a home cautioned that "[t]he single girl coming to a new urban centre and separated from her family for the first time faces many problems. Before she selects living accommodation, she may stay at the local Y.W.C.A. or some similar hostel providing supervised living quarters for girls. This is a recommended procedure because it brings her in contact with girls in similar situations, and provides her with mature guidance from older and more experienced people associated with or supervising the hostel."[62] Hence, smoking was emblematic of a lifestyle far removed from the blueprint being recommended for young women in these textbooks. It might have seemed superfluous to engage the topic at all, considering the model of young womanhood presented here.

By the 1970s, the field had been renamed family studies and became co-educational in many provinces in an attempt to revivify the subject through male support.[63] A popular pedagogy of the period was the decision-making model introduced by Laurence Kohlberg. Textbooks of this period provide many case studies and ample opportunity for both male and female students to consider their options in making life-forming decisions. These textbooks bear a striking similarity to health textbooks of the same era, denoting the field's general erosion as an area where women's knowledge had been privileged. More important was finding a place for itself in the curriculum. Family studies textbooks lost their female-centric focus, attempting to appeal to all students. One result of this reorientation was the introduction of smoking as a topic, though almost always as a male activity. One textbook devotes a section to diverse problems faced by adolescents. One of them is the damage caused to the body by smoking. It is instructive to quote the full question and answer to see how the problem is conceptualized and focused:

> *Question*: I've started smoking, and I've been told that smoking is not only harmful to my lungs, but also to my eyes. How can smoking affect my eyes? *Answer*: Because of certain gases present in the smoke, vision can be reduced greatly. The carbon monoxide present in smoke reduces the ability of the blood to combine with and carry oxygen. A lack of oxygen interferes with night vision, and with the size of the total visual field which is so important, especially for drivers who need to have "side" vision. When smoke gets into the eyes, it causes eye irritation. So with each cigarette you smoke, a potential danger exists that your eyes will not function normally.[64]

In this selection, the "problem" behaviour is located exclusively in physical well-being as befits a modern conception of health. Care has been taken to remove any gendered connotations in both the statement of the problem and its solution. And yet eye or lung problems are likely not reason enough for any "invulnerable" adolescent to be inclined to give up smoking. Without directly taking aim at the reasons why young people take up smoking in the first place, and especially why young women do so, the best-intentioned anti-smoking advocates would make only limited progress by using these resources. Textbook messages like these demonstrate as well that very little pedagogical progress had been made in arguing the anti-smoking case in textbooks in over close to a century. The pedagogical pattern is still modelled on the question-and-answer format of the catechism, as was common in the nineteenth century. In the same period, as discussed in chapter 3, tobacco manufacturers had developed sophisticated pedagogy and messaging, further challenging the formal school curriculum to find its mark with adolescent smokers.

In other family studies textbooks, smoking is represented but only as a topic peripheral to larger concerns of dependency and well-being. For example, a full chapter in *A Family Is ...* (1979) is devoted to drugs and alcohol, further reflecting the principles of the health curriculum. Smoking makes a single appearance in this book, with the time-tested anecdote of the athlete who defies his coach by smoking when he is clearly warned that the basketball team will have no smokers. In this instance, Jeff's girl-friend listens patiently to his quandary and helps him make a reasonable decision, but there is no sense that the unnamed girlfriend is, or even possibly could be, a public or closet smoker.[65] Most other textbooks throughout the 1970s and 1980s simply ignore smoking altogether.[66]

By the 1990s, one popular family studies textbook addressed smoking by using the health rubric so common in health textbooks and that applied to both sexes but mainly to the middle-aged. Under the category of "Lifestyle Habits and Involved Risks," students are told that "tobacco smoke contains nicotine and carbon monoxide. While the nicotine stimulates the heart to beat faster, the carbon monoxide deprives the heart of the oxygen it needs to function. Smoking tobacco is the major risk factor for cardiovascular diseases in Canada and attributes [sic] to about one-third of all cardiovascular-related deaths."[67]

How can we explain the failure of both health and domestic science/home economics/family studies textbooks to address the particular interests and needs of young women smokers? Textbook markets in Canada are small enough that a given textbook would reasonably be expected to serve both sexes in several provinces and for some years. As well, avoidance of smoking was but one area of "correct living" that textbook writers needed to promote, and as the twentieth century wore on, new sections needed to be added on venereal diseases, HIV/AIDS, and other seemingly more pressing health concerns. Nevertheless, research completed in the 1980s by Health Canada on the special and separate reasons for young women taking up smoking and the particular dangers presented to the young woman and her unborn children was widely available to textbook writers, as to others.

Omitting the female smoker is a reminder that official textbooks still carry strong moral messages, whether overtly or not. The young female smoker remains a representation that textbook writers and educational policy officials refuse to acknowledge. Young women's invisibility as smokers in official texts signals the continuing male-stream nature of most school curricula, including an area once based in women's knowledge systems. Finally, it is possible that educational officials are operating on the old but misguided principle that in erasing the young female smoker from school curricula they are removing negative models. Instead, they are forcing young women to look elsewhere for direction. The silence of the formal educational system in these two curriculum areas meant – and means today – that young women receive almost no usable information through the formal curriculum to guide their decisions about smoking.

Anti-Smoking Education through the Hidden Curriculum

It must be acknowledged that despite the lack of any mention of girls' smoking in the official curriculum, there might well have been efforts to teach about smoking's dangers through informal means in the so-called "hidden curriculum." Some teachers were responsible for formally teaching about tobacco because of the subjects they taught, but since the 1950s, all teachers have been encouraged to monitor the school plant and grounds, routing out smokers. Evidence of how teachers approached this part of the curriculum has been provided by oral histories from former teachers. One Toronto secondary school teacher describes her refusal to allow entrance to her class by any students who stood on the nearby street corner smoking.[68] Phoebe[69] recalled this occurring in the 1950s: "It [smoking] was a big problem. Now it wasn't school property and the people on that corner didn't like it but they were awfully generous about it. There was a kind of wall built around the place. Well, my husband and I used to drive around the corner and I told my home form, the pupils I taught, if you're going to be standing out there and smoking, you are not coming into my class. You can go to the principal and tell him you are going to take your English or History somewhere else. And I got away with it." Looking back, Phoebe registers her surprise at her own temerity in making this claim to her students, particularly in light of how such an assertion would be received today. Yet throughout her testimony about her teaching days, she offers many examples of her resolve to save both the children and her community from the blight of smoking by providing a clear and unambiguous code to both boys and girls who she believed did not recognize the implications of their behaviours

Efforts by teachers were supported in this era too by the Canadian Teachers' Federation and school board officials, who ran reports in their professional publications of how other jurisdictions were discouraging youth smoking.[70] And yet a proactive position by the schools was still several decades off. These halting efforts and actions by individual teachers show how far behind well-meaning anti-smoking advocates fell in the struggle to win over youths in postwar Canada.

Interestingly, in light of this concern with young people, the federal government had an explicit policy not to be involved in any "smoking-related education"[71] in this period. The educational initiative was expected to remain with the formal school system and an informal system of interest

Aswers to the True and False Test

(Editor's note: For the facts on which these answers are based, we are indebted to an article in the January 1950 number of Reader's Digest, written by R. W. Riis).

1. False. They are only less irritating than other brands.
2. True.
3. False, or at least not recommended from the health standpoint.
4. True, but this does not mean it is harmless.
5. True.
6. False. In any form of athletics smoking is a handicap.
7. True.
8. True.
9. False.
10. True.
11. False. It soon returns to normal
12. True.
13. False. The nicotine reaction seems more powerful than that of alcohol.
14. True.
15. True.
16. True.
17. False, only 4/9 as much.
18. True.
19. False, though some claim the former is more irritating.
20. True.

(Reprint from July 1950 Temperance Review)

Before You Offer Yourself as a Slave

Ask About the Wages!

4.14 | "Before You Offer Yourself as a Slave," Calgary, 1950

groups. This policy was revised only in the 1970s. When the government chose to act at all, its intervention in the period before 1963 was limited entirely to legislative enactments against *youth* smoking, taking care to exempt the adult male smoker.[72]

Other Community-Based Responses to Anti-smoking Education

With the decline of clubs specifically or primarily devoted to stopping youth smoking, as documented in chapter 3, other community agencies and eventually government-sponsored ones stepped into the breach. Until late in the twentieth century, the materials produced by most

TRUE OR FALSE?

If some young person in your household is itching to demonstrate his or her sophistication by getting inured to the scented weed, let him try his wits on the following test questions.

1. Certain brands of cigarettes are soothing to the throat.
2. Rapid smoking may inject gases into the lungs at a temperature as high as 135° Fah.
3. For those who are overweight tobacco is an effective reducing agent.
4. Smoking does not cause any more harm or any different harm to pregnant mothers than to any one else.
5. Heavy smoking causes excessive acid secretion in the stomach, which may favor the growth of stomach ulcers, if not actually causing ulcers.
6. An athlete gets an immediate "lift" after smoking due to the constriction of his blood vessels and consequent speeding up of the blood flow.
7. Smoking may increase the pulse rate by as much as 28 beats per minute.
8. The pulse of an unborn baby is raised when its mother smokes.
9. Seasoned smokers find their blood pressure does not increase to the degree their first smoking caused.
10. The higher your blood pressure is the more sharply tobacco lifts it.
11. When a smoker stops smoking the resultant tension causes his blood pressure to climb more dangerously.
12. Surface temperature of the extremities e.g. finger tips drop as much as 15 degrees after smoking and remain so for an hour afterward.
13. The disturbance of the circulation due to smoking may be overcome by drinking beer at the same time, for beer relaxes the blood vessels.
14. Nicotine is used as an effective insecticide by horticulturists.
15. A pipeful of tobacco gives the smoker more nicotine than a cigar and four times as much as a cigarette.
16. Buerger's Disease has been found only among smokers. In this malady the circulation may be so faulty as to call for amputation to check gangrene. Cessation of smoking arrests the disease.
17. More is spent for tobacco on this continent than for liquor.
18. 99½% of lung cancer occurs with smokers.
19. Benzo-pyrene the ingredient which turns your teeth brown is more harmful than nicotine.
20. Out of 100 non-smokers 66 can be expected to live to 60.
   Out of 100 light smokers 61 can be expected to live to 60.
   Out of 100 heavy smokers 46 can be expected to live to 60. Habitual smokers have 62% more gas on stomach, 65% more colds, 76% more nerve disorder, 100% more heartburn 140% more shortness of breath, 167% more throat irritation, 300% more coughs.

4.15 | Quiz from "Before You Offer Yourself as a Slave," Calgary, 1950

community-based groups had a curious old-world look to them, framing arguments that seemed out of place for the time. With some exceptions, these materials ignored the female smoker in any other than misguided and limited asides. Take as an example the brochure produced in 1950 reproduced as figures 4.14 and 4.15. As a bridging document from older temperance scripts, this pamphlet by the Temperance Review and adopted at some later date by the Alberta WCTU for distribution to youth groups and schools, is entitled, "Before You Offer Yourself as a Slave, Ask About the Wages!" It sports a graphic that could easily have been produced in the 1880s. Aside from the fact that the opening title/question makes very little sense without context, the catechism-like set of questions and answers

4.16 | *Smoking and Cancer,* 1963

direct the youth's attention to picayune issues of little interest to young people. For instance, one question asks for equivalent nicotine levels in cigars, pipes, and cigarettes when youths far and away favoured smoking cigarettes. Would high levels of nicotine disincline young men from smoking a particular product? Any typical young person is unlikely to care or need to know this arcane snippet of information. Or one might reflect on the value of this question/statement: "Did you know that less than half the amount spent on alcohol is expended on tobacco?" Do the writers hope that current smokers will celebrate this fact? These questions reflect older adult and middle-aged concerns of family finances and would likely be considered useless information to a young person considering taking up smoking. They also seem poorly considered in their logic. Moreover, some items are so poorly phrased that they confuse even sympathetic readers. Others are misleading and dangerous. In 1950, the evidence was already in that smoking mothers did their unborn children no favours, and yet question 4 is directed exclusively to the health of the mother.

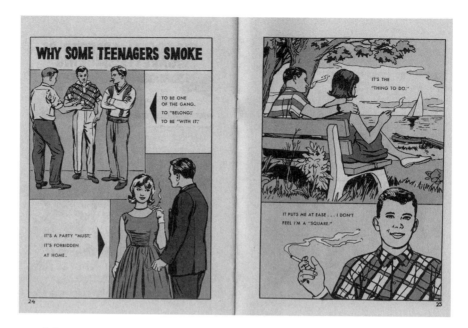

4.17 | "Why Some Teenagers Smoke," *Smoking and Cancer,* 1963

A second example of community-generated anti-smoking resources comes from the 1960s. *Smoking and Cancer* is representative of this period. Produced as a general information booklet but with a clear focus on youth smoking, the booklet was privately produced with support from the Canadian Cancer Society (figure 4.16). Burdened with another graphic that defies understanding on its cover,[73] the booklet tells the story of tobacco by using caricatures, graphs, and other visual elements. It mimics 1960s comic books, giving an early example of a graphic narrative, presumably to interest young men who would be familiar with this format. The pamphlet demonstrates that rates of lung cancer had been steeply climbing in Canada since 1945 in both men and women and that there was a positive correlation between the number of cigarettes consumed each day by men and cancer rates in both the United States and Britain. It also notes that there was a dramatic decrease in smoking among physicians. Girls are included with boys in the general category of "teenager," as shown in figure 4.17. To explain why some youths feel the need to smoke, the pamphlet acknowledges social pressure, stress release, adolescent rebellion, and modern codes of behaviour that seem to mandate smoking. And yet the discussion, while broaching some of the reasons why adolescents are indeed drawn to smoking, neither develops them nor genders the discussion. The reasons offered are so vague as to be unsatisfying for any reader, youths or adults.

The Canadian Department of Health and Welfare introduced its first educational materials in the 1960s in response to the (by now) clear link between cigarette-smoking and various forms of cancer. Its first campaigns were tentative and as unconvincing as school-based and other community groups' materials by framing the argument in terms that did not relate to adolescent culture. By the 1970s, however, more convincing materials were provided to schools.

Educational posters from the 1970s presented giant diseased lungs to be hung in classrooms or other public spaces. They supported the arguments in textbooks by visually presenting the horrors of cancer. Part of a broader campaign to shock youths into a recognition of the effects of smoking on the body, it drew on a long tradition of ghastly images that had appeared in school textbooks from the 1880s. Nevertheless, this is another example of a campaign missing its mark. Few young persons could imagine themselves ending up with cancerous organs.

This poster from 2007 (figure 4.18) carries on that tradition, with the added feature of the dangers of second-hand smoke. Nevertheless, it shocks the observer by providing visual evidence of this invisible danger. By this date, Heather Crowe had contracted cancer from second-hand smoke in the restaurant where she worked. Her motherly example, on television ads, on posters, and in news accounts, helped to give a female face to the victims of cancer who did not smoke. This visualization of a woman's unmerited sadness because of the cancer struck a deep chord with many Canadians. But did it impress young women who saw their grandmothers in Heather Crowe rather than themselves?

By the turn of the twenty-first century, after youth rates of smoking had risen again, new youth-generated campaigns were mounted, which targeted youths specifically. Poster campaigns were developed for bus shelters, buses, and other public spaces where adolescents tended to congregate. In 2004, the *stupid.ca* campaign was developed by the Ontario Ministry of Health and Long Term Care in an attempt to construct smokers as uncool. An advisory panel of youths aged fourteen to twenty-one was named.[74] This campaign seems finally to have struck a chord among youths, although it too has been criticized as stereotyping all young smokers as "stupid."[75]

The essential difficulties with all of these brave attempts to reduce youth smoking has been a misunderstanding of the fundamental motivations for youth smoking and especially female adolescents' attraction to it. The assumptions that underpin virtually all educational campaigns

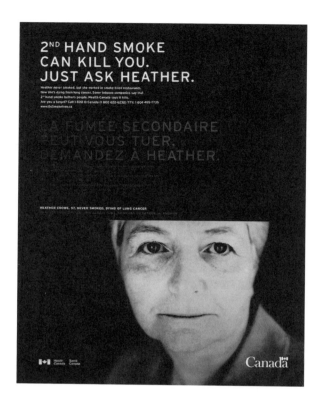

2ND HAND SMOKE
CAN KILL YOU.
JUST ASK HEATHER.

Heather never smoked, but she worked in smoke-filled restaurants.
Now she's dying from lung cancer. Some tobacco companies say that
2ⁿᵈ hand smoke bothers people. Health Canada says it kills.
Are you a target? Call 1 800 O-Canada (1 800 622-6232) TTY: 1 800 465-7735
www.GoSmokefree.ca

LA FUMÉE SECONDAIRE
PEUT VOUS TUER.
DEMANDEZ À HEATHER.

HEATHER CROWE, 57, NEVER SMOKED, DYING OF LUNG CANCER

Health   Santé
Canada   Canada

Canada

4.18 | Heather Crowe

directed to youth over the course of the last century and into the new
millennium is that youths take up smoking because of pressure from
peers, admiration of older models, and ignorance of the long-term effects of smoking. Recent research into reasons why girls begin smoking
reduces the significance of peer pressure and questions the power of the
other stated causes. It has been shown rather that women are more likely
to smoke to reduce stress, while men take up smoking to reduce boredom and fatigue.[76] Young women's decisions are often rooted primarily
in the social repertoire of girls and women to facilitate social exchange.[77]
Smoking appears to promote social cohesion, most particularly where the
practice is not condoned. To understand the process as based simply on
peer pressure, ignorance, or fantasy, therefore, misses the complexity of
the choices being made and the significance of the social exchange. In
addition, to present strongly moralistic messages in anti-smoking campaigns often results in rejection by youths, who see such strategies as
shaming.

Learning How to "Do" Smoking outside the Academy

If young women have been offered little or no useful instruction in their school textbooks, where did/do they learn how to "do" smoking? What skills exactly had and have to be mastered to be a competent smoker? Surveying the knowledge and skills involved in amassing this type of social capital is reminiscent of both Foucault's technologies of the self and Butler's notions of performance theory. In a closely studied process, young women transform their bodies, conduct, indeed their very selves to attain a state that telegraphs governmentality, with evidence that they can be considered experienced smokers.

Learning to smoke has always required that the novice first obtain her cigarettes. In the case of underage smokers, of which there continue to be many, this alone can be daunting. Young women have likely always "borrowed" cigarettes from older family members or friends if they could not buy them themselves. The current practice is often called "bumming" whereby single cigarettes are exchanged on school grounds or in shopping malls, whatever public space can be found for smoking these days. Testimony from adolescent women smokers indicates that there is a widely acknowledged economy of bumming that must be learned in order not to break the implicit rules.[78] "Adolescents describe 'building up' their smoking identities and amassing social capital which results from others recognizing them as skilled or 'real' smokers."[79]

Lighting the cigarette represents another challenge to the girl smoker. In the era of screen starlets who smoked, women were taught that a gallant man might light their cigarette for them, but in the current climate of self-reliance, young women would usually need to do this for themselves. Lighting the cigarette smoothly requires practice, and some report developing visual tricks, such as "sparking" with a lighter.

The most demanding skill to be accomplished is performing inhaling safely and demonstrably. Novice smokers often avoid inhaling deeply for fear of coughing or worse. Screen stars who provided the most direct instruction on this made a full performance of inhaling the smoke, often in mid-sentence, to focus attention. In the 1920s, a young woman's deep inhaling of smoke, with the movement of the diaphragm, the lengthening of the torso, and the throwing back of the head, was regarded by many as disturbingly and sexually explicit.[80] In today's adolescent world, young women report watching others closely to find out whether the smoker is "real," even calibrating the thickness of the exhaled smoke to ascertain whether it has been appropriately inhaled.[81] They report studying television and movie actresses who accomplish this performance successfully, such as Carrie Bradshaw in *Sex and the City* or the women in the television series *Mad Men*.

Holding the cigarette between inhalings constitutes another skill to be mastered: the height of the cigarette's position, its proximity to the face, and the manner in which the ash is expelled are all definable features through which the smoker displays competence in the skill and in bodily control generally. The fingers between which the cigarette is poised constitutes a ritualized component of smoking. Women generally hold the cigarette between the middle and index fingers, although in cases where strong rejection of norms is being telegraphed, it might be poised on the lips with no hand contact or cupped in the hands, as discussed in chapter 11. There are distinctive gendered rituals for the holding of the cigarette, with gay men and butch women transgressing the rituals through their non-compliant ritualized "holding" performance.

Finally, the stubbing of the cigarette can elicit a whole other performance, often signalling or marking strong emotional responses. Stubbing the cigarette is often aligned with stubbing a conversation or suggestion.[82] It seems to be accepted that these skills can only be acquired through both modelling and practice. This education was – and is – accomplished through the educative function of popular culture – peer models, movies, and television – rather than through formal educative means. The knowledge is extended by peers and older family members, including mothers, as well as by popular culture Obviously, this information must be acknowledged in anti-smoking campaigns directed to young women if they are to be effective.

Smoking allows the young person to hone her identity with many practical and imagined advantages and to develop a range of skills and identity qualities as she moves toward maturity in a modernist era. Formal and much community-based education has been unhelpful to young women as they make choices about how they will shape their own identities. Until formal and informal education acknowledges the deeper uses for smoking by women, the chance of anti-smoking campaigns having the desired effect are limited. This is particularly so with young women who are disadvantaged.

We now turn to the successful marketing of cigarettes to girls and women, with their promise of producing a facsimile of the modern aesthetic. In turn, women's eagerness to meet this standard helped to shape advertising through popular cultural texts.

PART III

Enticing Women
to Smoke

5

Eroticism

In *A World Made Sexy*, Paul Rutherford surveys the rise of what he terms the "Eros project," a process through which our society has become saturated in eroticism.[1] He argues that as a result of continual stimulation and an intellectual climate born of Freudian psychology, sexual satisfaction through visual means has become a primary cultural goal. Visual representations of the erotic – in photographs, billboards, film, television, and the Internet – have assumed iconic importance.

In this chapter, I closely examine images for evidence of the origins of erotic associations of women with tobacco. Women have often been employed in highly sexualized ways to sell cigarettes, cigars, loose tobacco for pipes, and other products associated with smoking and chewing tobacco. I explore the relationship between tobacco in its many forms and women's sexuality. To a degree, the sexual allure of cigarettes and of women who smoke is a reflection of the growing climate of eroticism generally in our culture. At the same time, there has been an undeniable sexual connotation in the representations of women with tobacco products for more than two centuries. Women smokers have had a deep investment in this erotic culture and have pushed the front forward in eroticizing elements of everyday smoking.

Women have used smoking for their own purposes, and other agents, including tobacco advertisers, have also welded allowable displays of sexuality with twentieth-century norms of femininity. This has resulted in one of the most prolific representations of women smokers: the woman as sexual creature, young, sexy, frankly alluring, and intent on having her own pleasures. This image has survived throughout the nineteenth and into the twentieth century, culminating in the feminist smoker of the 1970s to the 1990s.

Early Representations of Sexualized Women and Tobacco

It has been observed that in the nineteenth century, women had only two options available to them. They could accept the demanding mantle of the morally superior and asexual woman on the model of the women discussed in chapter 2, which required women to be respectably self-sacrificing and self-effacing as well as pious. Or women could forge an identity characterized as pleasure-seeking, sexually active, and self-pro-moting.[2] That this second choice was a distinctly more modern pose and increasingly common in the twentieth century did not soften the criticism most such women received. Angel or vamp/slut: those were the choices, and sometimes the second was not a choice at all but a default position into which women tumbled because of economic circumstance and/or the taint caused by their active sexuality.

In the nineteenth century, the portrayal of the woman who worked in cigar or cigarette manufacturing was often as a racialized non-white and sexualized creature. Prosper Merimée's 1845 novel, *Carmen*, picked up harem images from popular literature and transposed them to an Anda-lusian site to develop the sexually provocative image of Carmen. Carmen works in a cigarette factory where the women work in their undergar-ments because of the heat. The lack of clothing allowed the racialized non-white complexion of the "other" to be even more obvious, reinforcing old notions of women (and men) of colour *as possessed by* their sexual na-tures rather than as able or willing to discipline their own bodies.

To add to her boundary-breaking portrayal, Carmen is presented as a gypsy, a sorceress and a smoker who "enslaves her lovers as much as to-bacco does."[3] Carmen exercises a powerful "technology of the self" in her interactions with men. Carmen is said to love the smell of tobacco smoke, to relish the act of smoking itself, choosing her own lovers at will. She is not portrayed as a prisoner of her base instincts but as glorying in her sensual pleasures. Bizet's opera, based on the novel, opened in 1875, and Carmen's licence and that of the other cigarette girls smoking on stage sent shockwaves through the audiences. The onlooking male chorus in the opera sings: "Look at them! Bold looks, flirting ways!"[4] The Spanish or Turkish woman as cigar- and cigarette-maker remained a popular racial-ized image in popular culture, creeping even into Canadian school text-books.

The "Turkish Cigarette Girl" is shown in figure 5.1 under the subtitle "Selfish Slaves of Injurious Drugs" in a textbook used in Ontario schools, likely dating from the last quarter of the nineteenth century. In naming the cigarette girl as a "selfish slave," the image emphasizes the woman's insistence on her own pleasure but also her seemingly helpless slavery to the product. As in the case of *Carmen*, cigarette girls were often depicted as sexually ravenous, selling their wares in revealing clothing. To help explain to the reader of this textbook why a discussion addressing drug addiction would have an image of a young dancing woman who presumably makes or sells cigarettes for her living, the first paragraph asks:

> What is the most devilish, subtle, alluring, unconquerable, hopeless and deadly form of intoxication, with which science struggles and to which it often succumbs; which eludes the restrictive grasp of legislation; lurks behind lace curtains, hides in luxurious boudoirs, haunts the solitude of the study, and with waxen face, furtive eyes and palsied step totters to the secret recesses of its self-indulgence? It is the drunkenness of drugs, and woe be unto him that crosseth the threshold of its dream-curtained portal, for though gifted with the strength of Samson, the courage of Richard and the genius of Archimedes, he shall never return, and of him it is written that forever he leaves hope behind.[5]

What schoolchild could forget the images conjured up by this purple prose? As a cigarette-maker or seller, the young woman might not herself indulge in the drugs she prepares (although given Carmen's example as a smoker, this too is possible), but other "tobacco fiends" were considered to be lost, in the same straits as drug addicts. Nevertheless, how this young woman as a worker in any way typifies drug addicts remains a mystery, unless the link is her connotative identity as a racialized non-white, dangerous, and sexual "other" – the portal into all manner of uncontrolled, undisciplined, and dangerous "technologies of the self." In this construction, the cigarette/dancing girl is powerful, but the user of tobacco, an addicted man, is powerless. The male addict "lurks," "hides," and "haunts," with a "waxen face," "furtive eyes," and "palsied step." Meanwhile, the cigarette girl dances on, apparently in perfect health.

In such textbooks, nicotine was classified as a drug, one with a particularly insidious nature. As a "gateway drug," it was thought to be a substance that facilitated the consumption of stronger and more dangerous substances such as alcohol and hard drugs. The outwardly attractive and alluring woman is used to explain the process whereby victims were en-

Figure contents (as printed within the image):

440   *Selfish Slaves of Injurious Drugs.*

A TURKISH CIGARETTE GIRL.

The Selfish Slaves of Doses of Disease and Death.

1. **Most Devilish Intoxication.**—What is the most devilish, subtle alluring, unconquerable, hopeless and deadly form of intoxication, with which science struggles and to which it often succumbs; which eludes the restrictive grasp of legislation; lurks behind lace curtains, hides in luxurious boudoirs, haunts the solitude of the study, and with waxen

FEATURES FOR WOMEN   **The Toronto Sunday World**   AMUSEMENTS MUSIC. CLUBS
Sunday, May 14. 1916

"HABIT" A CARTOON SERMON BY RODNEY THOMSON

PLEASURE

5.1 and 5.2 | "A Turkish Cigarette Girl," *Search Lights on Health,* nineteenth century; "Habit," cartoon sermon, 1916

ticed into an underworld of addiction, sickness, and, ultimately, death. The explanation of crossing the threshold of the "dream-curtained portal" foreshadows the next image and reinforces the message that was offered to readers a few decades later.

The woman in the next graphic is also sexualized, beautiful, and apparently free of addiction to any dangerous substances. Her powerful nature is thus underscored along with that of the dancing girl. At the same time, she is suspect because of her association with these substances, including tobacco. The "cartoon sermon" above comes from *The Toronto Sunday World*, later known as *The Star Weekly*. It was not a product generated by the temperance forces but by the mainstream press, demonstrating how deeply imagery initiated by temperance advocates had infiltrated general society. This included the sexualized nature of women associated with tobacco. Several of the young men streaming through the "Pleasure" gate are smokers. The denotative meaning has them welcomed by alluring women chiselled into each side-post of the door and by a warm, beautiful, and scantily dressed woman in the flesh. The real power of the graphic shown in figure 5.2, however, emerges from the connotative meanings. The young men's decline into habits that bring no pleasure at all but rather enslavement is fully predictable and abetted by the apparently winsome young woman as she works in league as the "front person" with her evil associate-monster, "habit." Sexuality, smoking, and other such narcissistic pleasures will eventually enslave and demean all who take that route, the connotative meaning warns, for there is no exit in this hellish landscape, only a sheer wall with "A" ("Addiction"?) carved into it, a wall that cannot be scaled, certainly not by the prematurely old, wizened, and dopey wrecks found here. Hence, women who themselves seek pleasure through sexuality, often marked by the presence of tobacco, self-adornment, and enticement of others, are a danger to themselves and to all who respond to their entreaties to take up a life that is inevitably one of debauchery, although it might appear harmless at the start.

Throughout the late nineteenth century and the early twentieth, prostitution was considered the major social evil in Canada, presumed to be imposed on women against their will. Hence, the so-called "white slave trade" terrified many. The assumption was that young, unblemished women were being lured or snatched into prostitution, not that women were willingly engaging in the sex trade.[6] That the cigarette in this period was also called "the little white slaver" traces the close association between illicit sexuality and cigarette-smoking.

Even sympathetic assessments of smoking invoked imagery that was often sexualized. When J.M. Barrie decided to publish a collection with smoking as its theme, he chose the title *My Lady Nicotine*.[7] (The same title was used for a popular one-reel film during the First World War starring screen star Billie Rhodes. It emphasized soldiers' need for tobacco.[8]) Connecting feminine wiles with smoking was so common by 1913 when Barrie published his work that it elicited no comment. Barrie's book constructs his pipe as a virtual woman, one who does his bidding, whatever that might be. In so doing, the creator of *Peter Pan* conferred sexual feminized power on his daily companion, his pipe. Barrie's popular and sentimentalized love letter to his pipe foreshadows the twentieth-century sexualized image of women associated with tobacco.

Sexualizing Women and Tobacco in Advertising: The Girls on the Cigar Box

By far the clearest examples of sexually explicit messages associated with smoking were introduced to Canadians through advertising in the form of "girlie cards" (see chapter 3), posters, and the coloured lithographed labels on the inside covers and exterior tops of cigar boxes. Other examples appear on packages of loose and plug tobacco and on cigarette tins. Many of the images used on tobacco packages in Canada were faintly risqué, illustrating women with thick flowing hair, rosebud lips, and heavily rouged cheeks. A common representation too was of the racialized female Other, with exotic robing adding to the sexualized and bountiful woman's appearance. Favourite images were of Turkish, Spanish, Roma, and First Nations peoples. In a study of American tobacco art at the turn of the twentieth century, Dolores Mitchell found that the most common representations on cigar box labels and in posters were Turkish, Spanish, Amerindians, and African-American women.[9] Although the boundaries of her study are unclear, the examples she cites indicate convincingly that the American market supported more frankly pornographic lithographs than did the Canadian market. Penny Tinkler contends that one effect of having these artistically decorated tobacco and cigarette boxes on sale to the British masses was to make tobacco products more visible and accessible.[10] In addition, however, such tobacco art further aligned women's sexuality with tobacco products.

The late nineteenth century, when tobacco art on cigar boxes was at its zenith, was also a period when media was disseminated at a rate never before possible. Such mass communication technology as power presses, the ready supply of paper of various grades, the means to produce colour lithography relatively inexpensively and transport the products across the North American continent all contributed to the development of advertising. With the rise of mass production of tobacco products, manufacturers were eager to have their product purchased in as many outlets as possible, the cigar store included. Thus, by the 1880s in Canada a symbiotic relationship between cigar-store owners and tobacco manufacturers had developed. Individual merchants could order their own specialized labels for cigar brands, displaying them proudly in the storefronts and on racks in the shop. A limited number of firms printed the labels, but the range produced between 1885 and the First World War was impressive. In the United States, only ten printers supplied most of the lithographed labels, requiring up to a month to produce each one, with twelve press runs apiece.[11]

Hundreds of these made-to-order cigar-box labels appear in the recent virtual exhibition by the Canadian Museum of Civilization (CMC), "Canada in a Box: Cigar Containers That Store Our Past, 1883–1935,"[12] and many other examples can be found in museums across Canada and in private attics and cellars. From the 1880s, federal regulations for the use

5.3 | Cigar box with broken seal

(but never the re-use) of cigar boxes were strict: packages of cigars were inspected, and a stamp was then affixed to the exterior. Once the stamped seal was broken, the contents could be consumed as a package or sold individually, usually in tobacco shops. Figure 5.3 shows one such tobacco box with a broken seal. The box would be set out on the counter with the decorative label facing outwards. Shop proprietors could design a personal label, and the holdings of both the CMC and the McCord Museum indicate that many did so as corporate advertising. Thus, the decorative posters are useful not only as examples of popular art of the period but also as personal promotional statements by Canada's mercantile class. Popular imagery was employed to promote the self-image of sponsoring shop owners.

Cigar-box labels took as their subject local and national events and institutions; they celebrated heroes, both mythic and real, and also lampooned those figures through inversions of the social hierarchy. Huge numbers of surviving cigar-box labels feature pretty women, many with sexualized images. Images of women can generally be sorted into three categories: the exotic, the sexually explicit, and the refined, with the categories blurring and mixing. Figures 5.4, 5.5, and 5.6 show women dressed in exotic but decorous attire, with ample bosoms and low-cut dresses. Still, none is intended to be taken for a Carmen-like cigar-maker. "Flor" sports a fur collar and an elaborate hat; "Irma" too has been given a Spanish-appearing headdress, complete with a coy veil. "La Farosa" alone is attired in a dress

5.4 and 5.5 | "Flor De Claro"; "Irma," 1897

with no headgear, and yet even this image shows a decorative outfit that only a middle-class woman could afford. All of these women could easily be identified as Spanish, Portuguese, or Turkish, given the popular imagery that abounded about such countries as producers of tobacco.

5.6 | "La Farosa,"
1915

Given the vague national origins and the iconography developed around racialized non-white women in this industry, it is striking that none of these women has other than a fair complexion. The cues of their exoticism are entirely telegraphed by clothing and decorative features in their hair. Their costumes work to connote the strange and the exotic without the apparent need to have skin of colour. The exotic imagery common for tobacco is blended with representations of the women of the Canadian nation, shown to be diverse in costume but nonetheless racialized white. As well, the imagery encircling the women is safely geographic in nature, with no hint of the steamy working conditions or life experiences of the smoker or cigarette-maker from such climates. As a comparison of exotic types, these images are far less threatening than the Turkish cigarette girl presented in the school textbook in figure 5.1.

5.7 and 5.8 |
"Arabela,"; "Union
Star," 1897

A second category of the cigar-box label girl was that of the sexually enticing woman, echoing again the Turkish cigarette girl. Some cigar labels,
as with "Arabela" (figure 5.7), mix messages of sexual availability and exoticism. Arabela sits with one leg crooked, barefooted and bare-armed in
some generically temperate location that looks far from Canada. Her low-
cut dress, loosely arranged about her curvaceous body, and with a simple
band to hold back her hair, bespeaks a woman composed as "natural"

5.9 | "You Know," c. 1907–15

with little means or desire to "dress up." Exotic and sexualized women on cigar boxes are portrayed as exceedingly casual, rejecting formality or conventional modesty. The woman pictured on the Union Star tobacco box (figure 5.8) also has an unconventional stance. She leans with her leg propped on a decorative chair while she sits on the table. If she is meant to represent a typical American nineteenth-century woman, she is far from the image of the dutiful daughter pictured in contemporary popular culture. This woman is a rebel. Here, the class position of the woman seems considerably above that of "Arabela." She is surrounded by statuary, urns, and other indications of a comfortable, even elevated status. Taken together, Arabela and Union Star seem to suggest that rebellion, even a mild version of it, is sexy.

Other lithographs are more frankly sexualized, as with figure 5.9, which was possibly made for the Ottawa Cigar Factory about 1897. The buxom model reclines in a tousled chaise with her skirt drawn up above her knees in classic boudoir style. Her dark stockings and skimpy top are reminiscent of a dancer's outfit. Alternatively, she might be portraying a partly undressed woman waiting for her lover. The sly title of the tobacco is "You Know," redolent of an unspoken, forbidden secret. Was cigar-smoking being forced into a "forbidden secret" before the turn of the century? The

5.10 and 5.11 |
"Magnet," 1897;
"Pebble," 1915

historical record belies this, but perhaps advertisers derived an advantage in representing male cigar-smoking as embattled, the indulging in a forbidden habit.

When tobacconists William Ward of London, Ontario, and J. Bruce Payne of Granby, Quebec, chose lithographs for their signature cigars, they decided on pretty young women marked by their sexuality (figures 5.10 and 5.11). The young women have a holiday spirit about them. One young woman stands in shorts before a giant magnet, perhaps at a country fair, offering a variety of meanings to the gaze of the tobacco con-

5.12 | First Miss Toronto Contest, 1926

sumer and to women in these men's households. "The magnet" referred to here has a denoted meaning as a title for the cigars on sale. Beyond this, there are several connoted meanings: one as a spectacle before an audience and another – and very importantly – as a metaphor for the young woman's nature and her power to draw attention and admiration. This metaphoric meaning of the woman's sexual power is given special resonance by her very scanty costume and by her stance, which is relaxed, using the giant magnet as a prop. In "Pebble," the young woman plays at the beach in the sand. She is dressed suitably enough in a swimming costume with a protective hat. Still, the image-maker ensures that her décolletage is fully in view, emphasizing her sexuality. Her figure, her solitary game in the sand, and her absorption all signal sexual tension.

To assess how intentionally sexualized the women in both "Magnet" and "Pebble" are, we can compare their portrayal to that of women being celebrated for their beauty, such as the young women competing in the first Miss Toronto contest in 1926 seen in figure 5.12. The women engaged in this beauty contest were doing so almost thirty years after the bathing beauties of "Magnet" and "Pebble" appeared. Despite the loosening of moral strictures in the "Roaring Twenties," the Toronto women are far

5.13 | "Pharaoh," 1897

more modestly attired, even wearing sensible shoes with their suits, than the (by comparison) hyper-sexualized girls on the cigar boxes. It need hardly be noted that cigarettes are nowhere in sight for the contestants.

How is the "gaze" used with the "Magnet" and "Pebble" images? In the case of the "Magnet," the young woman appears to play to the observer, posturing before the prop, showing off her youth and glorying in her sexual allure. The "Pebble" lithograph, on the other hand, presents a young woman so absorbed in her own game and world that she seems not to notice the gaze cast upon her. This does not suggest that she is less sexualized for her disregard; in fact, she presents a distinct approach by pretty young women being ogled by observers: to seemingly ignore them while still attracting them. In both cases, however, the gaze is manipulated to draw the observer into the composition and to cast admiration on the charms of the young women.

"Pharaoh" (figure 5.13) again mixes sexuality with the exotic. A pharaoh and his "queen" lounge on a double throne in full embrace. Even though the decorations on the throne appear to be Egyptian, the pharaoh is more a Victorian gentleman than an eastern potentate. The woman's main identifier is her scanty clothing, meant to be sexually enticing. Her pose is also

5.14 | "Ideal," 1897

intended to support her sexuality: she appears to have run to her lover's arms, perhaps guiltily. The larger composition is intended to be exotic in tone, with the characters drenched in sexual attraction for each other. Here too the models are racialized white with the whiteness of their skin colour appropriating exotic "Otherness" through their costumes. Here again, the advertisement supported by "Pharaoh" is extremely revealing for its era in late nineteenth-century Canada. This degree of overt sexuality was still anathema in the cinema of the 1920s, a full three decades later. While hard to appreciate today, it would have represented an unprecedented degree of sexuality and lascivious innuendo.

The theme of sexual availability and expression runs through so many cigar-box lithographs that the selection is enormous. Nevertheless, in

5.15 | "Varsity," 1897

addition to scenes emphasizing the exotic and the sexually available, many images also idealized women and presented them as refined and delicate on a classic Victorian model.

Nap. E. Grodin, a tobacconist in Trois-Rivières, Quebec, commissioned the label shown in figure 5.14. It offers his clientele an image with which many Canadian men would have been familiar. A woman with her hair piled high looks away from the gaze. She has netting covering her hair and neck to signal her modest purity. The fact that this woman is presented as a chaste example of womanhood does not detract from her sexual capital; in fact, through the contrasts of form and function, it enhances it. That a very proper and demure example of womanhood is peddling cigars would not be lost on M. Grodin's Victorian consumers. It is interesting as well that M. Grodin has chosen English text for his francophone region. Did the English terminology speak to a cosmopolitan sensibility that the tobacconist wished to nurture? Had M. Grodin borrowed a label developed for some other purpose and had his name affixed to it? We will never know, but we can guess that the text was less important in the sales than the graphic and that the female "ideal" – racialized white, middle-class, advertising her virtue, but contrarily, while also advertising tobacco – travelled across linguistic and national boundaries with ease.

Figure 5.15 is one final example of the range of idealized female types pictured on cigar-box lithographs. The university-educated woman as smoker and as magnet to other, male smokers makes her appearance here, as she did later in other forms of advertising, in literature, and in the press. While images advertising the "New Woman" were not unusual in Canada, generally they appeared about twenty years later than this 1897 example. This image is unusual as well because it appears to be directed to the woman smoker of the period. In most instances of advertising, academic women were not targeted until the late 1920s in print or cinematic representations.[13] Alternatively, the image of a cultured, hard-working woman of letters might well have been intended to attract similarly directed male smokers. The "Varsity" woman had been ordered by S. Davis & Sons of Montreal, cigar manufacturers. She is pictured with mortarboard, academic sash across her bosom, and encircled by the icons of academic life, both of her present and the distinguished past. Papyrus scrolls are strewn to her left, while books with the midnight oil are arranged to the right. Despite the unclear intended audience, the "Varsity" woman in turn-of-the-century Quebec could only have been an urban icon and unusual for its period. Almost four decades later, in the interwar period, tobacco manufacturers often pictured the scholarly woman as a smoker. See, for example, the billboard advertisement for Grads Cigarettes shown in figure 9.8.

Canadian cigar-box lithographs from the late nineteenth and early twentieth centuries show that their sexualized symbolism seems to have been less than that in American tobacco art during the same period. In Canada, for example, there were no suggestive brand names to match the incendiary White Slave Tobacco brand sold in the United States.[14] Cigar-box lithographs favoured by Canadian urban cigar-store merchants were different from the choice of the small-town tobacco entrepreneurs. Even if the merchant in small-town Canada had himself wanted a more sexualized image of women, he would likely have had concerns that his customers would object to such representations of women on the cigar boxes in his shop. Nevertheless, the women pictured on the Canadian cigar-box labels were far more sexualized than other representations of women in Canada at this time.

The aesthetic and commercial power of cigar-box labels speak to the importance of packaging of tobacco products as an enticement to consumers. The packaging had been recognized for its authority long before the twentieth century, as these artistic products show. Predictably, they had also enraged some anti-tobacco activists. Frances Willard of the American WCTU deplored the suggestive pictures of women on cigar boxes, noting that "if we were as self-respectful as we ought to be, [they] couldn't stay there overnight."[15] And yet both cigar boxes and cigarette packages have remained a battleground for pro- and anti-cigarette advocates well into the twenty-first century precisely because of the visual power of the images. The decision of the federal government in January 2011 to insist on more graphic images and slogans on cigarette packages is testament to the importance of the wrapper and of visual cues in helping to regulate behaviours.

Linking Smoking and Sexuality in Other Advertising

From the interwar period, the connection between smoking and women as sexualized creatures was strengthened in cigarette advertising and in selling other products as well. This process in Canada appears to have been muted in comparison to that in the United States where the acceptance of sexualized models was well advanced by 1910.[16] In Canada, exploiting women's sexuality in cigarette advertising was contained in two ways: first, although young, pretty, and sexualized, women in cigarette advertising were rarely shown smoking themselves. Second, the women were "types," not definable women.[17] In other words, the women appearing in these advertising images were intended to stand in for any woman, or at least a racialized white, middle-class, pretty woman. Later, advertising would be focused on recognizable stars, but in this period, the smoking models were anonymous. This had the effect of containing women's expression, since the viewer could not identify a specific personality with the advertisements, as would be possible later. Starting in the 1930s when women's smoking had become more integrated into polite popular culture, cigarette advertisers accentuated their women models' authority and sexuality. The two examples of billboard advertisements shown in figures 5.16 and 5.17, both dating from between 1937 and 1939, are typical of the kinds of messages being presented through visual culture in this period. These billboards were mounted in the Toronto area and present the woman smoker as sexually charged and even boundary-breaking. The Winchester Cigarettes model smiles out from her billboard perch, staring directly and provocatively at the passersby. Her hair is suggestively tousled, and she reclines on a cover of some kind but not on a chair. With no other details than these, we can ascertain that this is a woman well aware of her sexuality and willing to be photographed sitting on the ground. Moreover, her beach outfit is explicit for the period: a tightly wrapped halter top accentuates her bosom, a skirt wrap is thrown back to expose undergarments to match the top, and both legs are extended in a luxurious pose. We might again contrast this explicitly sexual outfit with the modest misses competing in the first Miss Toronto contest (figure 5.12). But there is much more to suggest her sexual availability: she

5.16 and 5.17 | Billboard for Winchester Cigarettes, Toronto, 1937–39; Billboard for Buckingham Cigarettes, Toronto, 1937–39

actually smokes the product she is flogging, with cigarette in one hand, package in the other.

The Buckingham Cigarettes placard is less overtly sexual, with the model adopting an athletic pose. And yet this example too is an advertisement with a surprising edge for its time, particularly with regard to the racialization demonstrated. It shows a woman archer, very improbably without a cover for her bathing suit. The background indicates that she is at the seaside and "shooting" Buckingham cigarettes as part of her sport. Her companion, who smokes and smiles appreciatively, stands to the side while the woman is the central active agent. He is heavily muscled and appears to be a man of colour. The denotated message is that the woman who smokes is a healthy athlete. There is an underlying connotated message as well: that the woman smoker is prepared to engage in sexual relationships and activities that fall at the margin of propriety. The man in this advertisement has taken the place of the exotic costumes and other accoutrements on the labels of the cigar boxes from an earlier era, which appropriated racialized Otherness to exotify the female image. Here, the dangers of engaging in a sport like archery are made to parallel the dangers of racialized white women engaging in relationships with men of colour. The trope of the dangers of mixed-race relationships is well documented in the literature and in Canadian history.[18]

We have a further advantage in reading the context for this advertisement, since the name of the sponsoring firm is detectable: a Refreshment and Billiard Parlor. To what degree does the billboard's placement in the cityscape make this placard with its sexual and racial overtones less shocking? One thing is certain: such advertisements are not to be found for that period in other common advertising venues such as women's or family magazines. The explicit nature of both billboards suggests that a certain licence was given to advertising on city streets or in certain establishments rather than in the more conservative setting of the magazine. Studies of the development of the popularity of women's smoking in other countries show that these trends in Canada are quite typical of the general pattern well advanced by this time in the United States[19] and Britain.[20]

The suggestive implications of women smokers' sexuality and the sexual allure of smoking itself was further reinforced by government-sponsored campaigns mounted during the Second World War to combat venereal disease.[21] One government-produced pamphlet produced in 1944, entitled "Three Queens but I'll pass" (figure 5.18), shows in cartoon form "the story of a couple of gals who'd love to meet you!" The "Three Queens" are syphilis, gonorrhoea, presented as a smoker, and all "easy" women: "Where you find one of these babies you'll usually find the other ... They're the VD sisters, chum – Venereal Disease Sisters (if you want it spelled out) and they're pushovers to meet!" All of these "easy" women are presumably also easy to detect. They wear short, sexy skirts and lots of makeup, they smoke, and they prey on soldiers. Except for the latter quality, one would have difficulty distinguishing between the Three Queens and the Winchester Cigarette smoker or the Buckingham Cigarette archer. The Three Queens are presented as sexually rapacious and dangerous. That message is underscored in the bottom left slide of the cartoon where the fighting men appear as startled, naive, and frightened but never themselves a danger to anyone. As Ruth Roach Pierson notes in her study of women in the Canadian Women's Army Corps, "[i]n vain one looks in the official sources for a world of women in need of protection against sexually demanding, aggressive, or overpowering men. Neither the word 'rapist' nor the notion of VD spread by rape occurs."[22]

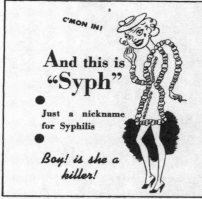

5.18 | "Three Queens but I'll pass," pamphlet, 1944

Sexualizing Women and Tobacco in Literature

Popular literature has long traced the link between smoking and misbehaviours. In the nineteenth century, youthful male smokers were condemned for being intellectually dull, dishonest and lazy, crude, and unprincipled. This is discussed at greater length in chapters 2, 3, and 4. During the Second World War, for example, Gehman's alarmist *Smoke over America* admiringly quoted a range of authorities, including President Coolidge, on the view that "no agency in the world today" had more directly affected the "health, efficiency, education and character of boys and girls as the cigarette habit."[23] "The relationship between cigarette smoking and juvenile delinquency is intimate beyond a shadow of a doubt,"[24] he concluded. According to many authorities of the period, female juvenile delinquents broke sexual codes by being promiscuous; smoking was an indication of this code-breaking.

By the 1940s, community groups such as the Big Brothers and Big Sisters attacked smoking as part of a long list of worrisome habits engaged in by youth, including "street dawdling," or frequenting "cheap dance halls, hamburger joints or seedy cafes," among other adolescent thrills. Jeff Keshen documents one of several scares in this period around rising delinquency rates among both boys and girls and the inevitable use of the cigarette to signify these rebellious ways.[25]

Pulp literature in the same period described women as uncontrollably sexualized and smoking as promoting flagrant sexuality. Sane women kept their sexual impulses in balance, articles pointed out, while "insane" (and bad) women were "love-starved" with their "raving lusts" and "unconquerable ferocious life impulses" unchecked. Lara Jefferson's article, "These Are My Sisters" in the Toronto-produced pulp pamphlets *Sisters of the Damned* sets out the horror awaiting inmates of insane asylums. The image accompanying her description shows a woman smoking nervously as she beholds this terrifying world, retracing an intimate association between smoking, sexuality, and madness.

> The screaming, writhing, fearful horror of life behind the grim, cold walls of a mental institution gripped the writer from the first numb day when she was incarcerated and adjudged insane. From that moment on she lived in the twi-lit half-world of the women doomed by their unconquerably ferocious life impulses that drove them to frothing madness and worse! In the ward, where sadistic nurses gleefully tortured the patients, she saw scenes of sheer horror that have never been duplicated in human experience and lived through

5.19 and 5.20 | Roy Langdale, *Hot Number*, March 1950; "She Was My Girl," *Sensational Love Experiences*, 1949

a seemingly unending nightmare of throat-clutching insanity without hope for the future or a prayer for the hereafter. There she saw the tragedy of women without men, of creatures whose raving lusts drove them to the brink of despair, of love-starved souls seeking that last final fling of the only madness denied them – the madness of love.[26]

Women depicted as lesbian, dangerous, and even crazy in the pulp press were often represented as smokers. Nor did they disappear with the Second World War. In the 1950s, the link between women smokers, overt sexuality, and instability was also made explicit. The cover of Roy Langdale's pocketbook, *Hot Number: Burning Passion Was Her Plaything* (figure 5.19), leaves little to the reader's imagination, even without any supportive text. A beautiful, languorous woman reclines on an easy chair in a filmy, semi-transparent outfit. She smokes expansively, one leg thrown carelessly across the arm, and is absorbed in her reading rather than in the man who sits awkwardly and attentively next to her. The woman's leg takes up part of the space the man would expect to occupy as he sits constrained in a straight-back chair. He looks dishevelled and also smokes, eyes averted, absorbed in his own thoughts. Beside the figures is a table with liquor and cigarettes strewn across the top. Clearly, this woman smoker is fully in charge of the scene, even if acting oddly, and is possibly a threat to the nervous man beside her. She is a smoker, and her indulgence seems to extend to more than cigarettes.

Another pulp magazine of the era, *Sensational Love Experiences*, frequently pictured sexually experienced women or those actively seeking sexual liaisons as smokers. In "She Was My Girl," a man of nineteen falls in love with Nora, his junior by a year. The caption that accompanies figure 5.20 reads: "Nora's hands were large and tanned with long, blood-red fingernails. I had never seen such hands before ... I watched her fascinatedly [sic] when she lighted a cigarette."[27] Despite her youth, it is made clear that Nora is a "fast" girl, hungering for male regard and a relationship built on her sexual attractiveness. Nora tells Tommy, the narrator, "One day, Tommy, I'll have real things – rings, bracelets, earrings, and nice clothes – and a car." "How will you get all those things?" he asks. "A girl doesn't have to learn much to make her way in the world if she's young and pretty," she points out to him, "and if she is, men are only too glad to show her a nice time and give her everything she wants." Nora is fully aware that men will give her what she wants only if she holds up her end of the bargain by giving them something they want, and she seems fully ready for this reciprocity to begin, cigarette already lit. A second character in the same short story, Lena, is also portrayed as a smoker, although a more refined one. Blonde, sexy Lena sits reading, cigarette hanging from her mouth and with her legs tucked under her. Smoking by young women is almost ubiquitous in such pulp magazines.

When women were written into "police procedurals" or "true crime" magazines, report Carolyn Strange and Tina Loo, the male-line stories wove "a thread of sexual temptation into tales of greed."[28] Very often too, the sexualized, criminal, and otherwise hardened women were pictured as inveterate smokers. The woman in the "Women behind Bars" issue (figure 5.21) is both sexually enticing and a tough girl. Her level stare, dishevelled hair, and sculptured blouse, especially with the background of the prison bars, all define her as a loose and criminal woman. Most important of all as a marker of her identify is the set of her cigarette as it dangles from the corner of her mouth. Long a masculinized cigarette pose later popularized on the screen by James Dean, here it defines a tough and criminal femininity. The result is a visual marker for the female criminal, at once knowing, sexualized, determined to get what she wants, and inclined to smoke.

5.21 | "Women behind Bars," *Daring Crime Cases*, November 1943

Sexualizing Women and Tobacco at the Movies

Consumers of pulp and popular fiction were likely also movie-goers. Actresses had been one of the earliest groups of public women to take up smoking. Certainly, they were the first "models" of smoking for many men and women, as oral testimony from women who learned to smoke after the Second World War makes clear.[29] Only rarely were movie stars shown as actively smoking in the pre-war period. Mary Astor's *White Shoulders*, shown in figure 5.22, was an early and exceptional example of an actress smoking on screen. A remake of the 1924 film *Recoil*, *White Shoulders* was released in 1931 and promoted as a thoroughly modern story, with the leading actress, bare-backed and smiling provocatively, posed with a cigarette prominently displayed within a narrow frame. The advertising poster was in itself a charged "window" on the film, and it is significant that the producers chose to have Astor introduced with her cigarette fully visible and lit, along with her sexual availability, her enticing attire, and her posture, which thrusts the cigarette to the foreground.

By the 1930s, Hollywood starlets were supported by fan clubs, which distributed photographs of the most popular actresses and actors. A network

5.22 | Movie poster for *White Shoulders*, 1931

of movie magazines, much like today's tabloids, also acted as conduits for studio-approved biographies of the stars to be widely disseminated. Official posters were issued by the Hollywood studios. Mae West was but one of many stars who were photographed with cigarette and holder in full view. In figure 5.23, West dreamily props her head up, with one hand extending a cigarette and holder. The other hand rests on a satin pillow, which reflects the opulence of her extravagantly jewelled dress. Her bleached-blonde hair, rosebud lips, and heavily made-up eyes all emphasize her sexuality.

It has been argued that in the movies, a woman smoker telegraphed sexual desire without there needing to be any further demonstration of her interest.[30] Partly because of the studios' strict self-imposed morality code of the 1930s, smoking became imbued with even stronger sexual connotations in movies, since it was one of few allowable markings. This studio-produced image of West is so stylized and sexually provocative that even in its day it must have shaded into camp. Many of these carefully com-

5.23 | Mae West with cigarette holder, c. 1930–40. © John Springer Collection/ Corbis image JS825

posed studio images also found their way onto cigarette cards, available in cigarette packages for collecting and expressly enticing young men (see chapter 3).

Readers of screen magazines would also discover a close elision between sexual allure and smoking. The extraordinarily popular Bette Davis is profiled in a December 1948 fan magazine photo spread. She smokes in several of these "candid" shots. In one, she sits relaxed and cross-legged on a couch. Dressed in trousers, a vest, and a low-buttoned blouse, she holds her cigarette, resting it on one knee while her other arm is thrown back over the couch. Behind the couch is a fully stocked bookshelf, with more books piled on the cabinet. Made-up, with carefully styled hair, she is the image of the modern, sexy, and serious woman. In a promotional feature for her latest movie with Gregory Peck, "June Bride," Davis is portrayed as consistent with her film role as if the screen mirrored her real life. In other images, she is shown with her adorable baby daughter, in discussion with the movie's producer, and out on the town with her mother. All of these pastimes bespeak an actress of the modern age, one who can "try on" a series of identities to adapt to or fit changing circumstances. In most of these identities, the cigarette is a helpful and supportive prop.

With the dawning of the conservative 1950s in Canada, the imagery of the woman smoker took a decided turn away from overt displays of sexuality. Not until the late 1960s would advertisers again test community tolerance for displays of the sexually alluring female smoker. But when it finally reappeared, the tone for this sexuality was changed from that of the explicitly sensual vamp to the socially aware second-wave feminist, as famously portrayed by the various extra-long "Slim" cigarettes. That story is taken up in chapter 10.

The tradition of imbuing advertising of the smoking woman with sexual overtones was reborn in the 1970s and remained a Canadian staple until magazine and billboard advertising was disallowed by legislation in 1988. Often, sexuality was presented as a natural accompaniment to the physically active and healthy young woman.

Research with adolescent women who currently smoke indicates that one reason they offer for smoking's appeal is the pleasure it gives them after sex or alone.[31] They report that the act of smoking is itself pleasurable, and when combined with food, alcohol, conversation, and socializing, it is especially so.[32] It cannot be denied that one strong motive to smoke is the pleasure it confers on the smoker, just as tobacco enthusiasts have long insisted. Internal studies by tobacco manufacturers researched the particular interests of young women in the 1980s. Termed "Project Young Women," their research showed that mild-tasting cigarettes with less side-stream smoke, pleasant aromas, and reduced aftertaste with flavoured additives all appealed more to young women than to males.[33]

From the earliest cigarette advertisements about and for women smokers, smoking has been promoted as a sexually alluring act by women. Women were shaped as erotic subjects, and many themselves promoted this image. Whether the promotions are found on cigar boxes, in print, on billboards, or at the cinema, the message has remained the same: the woman who smokes is sexy – and powerful. If the pious young women of the Young Woman's Christian Temperance Union (profiled in chapter 2) were empowered in the nineteenth century by their harnessing of and leading anti-tobacco campaigns, women smokers of the twentieth century were frequently profiled as empowered by smoking, whatever their station in life. Further, women themselves have presented their smoking as empowering. Defined by tobacco advertisers as well as by the women who shaped smoking practices, this association of smoking, sexuality, and women was welcomed and further nurtured by popular culture, resulting in a powerful amalgam. At the same time that these insinuations of women as erotic subjects were broadcast, smoking gave otherwise respectable women licence to develop and exercise a sexually charged and independent persona in ways that probably would not have been possible for them, given the restrictive societal norms that governed women's behaviour.

6

Sophistication

The spectre of the independent woman smoker had haunted Canadian societal leaders since the nineteenth century. Women of this persuasion had rejected marriage and taken up work that interested and sustained them, were sure of their own minds and willing to share their opinions freely, and tested the boundaries of decorum by such acts as public smoking. Labelled a "New Woman" at the beginning of this period and a "Modern Girl"[1] by the 1920s and 1930s, the independent woman was frequently portrayed as a smoker. She was often an early entrant to the new professions like nursing or social work or to the skilled labour force or an active member of the arts, and her image made larger statements about equal rights for women by asserting women's rights to brandish cigarettes in public. This profile of the New Woman grew into a "type of female personality,"[2] which developed into the Modern Girl. In Canada, as in the United States and Britain, women who subscribed to modernity were identified as well-educated, independent-spirited, and insistent on the vote and a public role in society, while at the same time often wanting a fulfilling domestic life, either in conventional companionate marriages or in same-sex households. Hence, in this construction smoking carried with it a symbolic claim to many of the pleasures now taken for granted by privileged women in our society

In Britain, the New Woman was also often a suffragette, demanding the right to vote. British journals carried advertisements for cigarettes ("Vallora" by name) and even launched "Votes for Women" cigarettes in 1910. They were sold alongside "Votes for Women" soap, marmalade, chocolate,

6.1 | Magazine advertisement for Buckingham Cigarettes, *Chatelaine*, 1936

and sweet pea seeds.[3] Partly because of the Canadian suffrage movement's close ties to temperance, no such products were sold in this country, but the image of the independent-minded New Woman/Modern Girl as suffragist otherwise thrived in this country as well.

In addition to representations of independent-mindedness, the intellectual and often artistic New Woman might also have been considered sexually experienced. However, unlike her sisters who had been forced into this nether world through economic straits, the sophisticate was generally from a privileged background. She was often a recognizable figure in society. Indeed, across generations many path-breaking Canadian "stars" of the intelligentsia and arts have opted to embellish their public personae with the cigarette, or, as with k.d. lang (profiled in chapter 11), have played off its counter-cultural messages by adopting it as a personal signifier.

In almost all instances, the sophisticate was presented as an older, more serious figure than early representations of the woman smoker. Middle- or even upper-class, talented, and an active member of "society," the sophisticate had far greater choice in her adoption of visual identities. The sophisticate-as-smoker was well entrenched in popular culture by the 1920s. The first advertising campaign in Canada to invoke the image of the sophisticated smoker was that of the "Diva" brand in 1905.[4] Advertised widely throughout Quebec, the brand ceased to be actively promoted within the year. Thereafter until the 1920s, tobacco manufacturers in Canada encouraged women to purchase brands already pitched to men. By the late 1920s, and again in the 1980s through to the end of the 1990s, advertisers again targeted the woman smoker with imagery and packaging[5] specifically designed to appeal to women.[6] The sophisticate-as-smoker remains with us today, firing the imagination of many teenage girls as they light up. Representations of the sophisticated woman smoker in advertising celebrated her skills, many of which were once popularly represented as exclusively masculine traits and contrary to emphasized femininity. The woman in figure 6.1, a full-page 1936 advertisement, has all the markings of wealth, ability, and confidence. She sits casually, one leg drawn up, displaying her smartly cut pleated culottes (with a special pocket for the tees). Her hat both shades her eyes and matches her outfit, and her gloves are professionally fitted, with a cigarette poised easily in the hand closest to the camera. This golfer might well have been a recognizable star of the 1930s no longer in the public eye. But even if she were not, we could not miss her confident stance and becoming smile. Clearly too, this is a woman with athletic interest and skill, further validating the confidence she displays here. Advertisements aplenty in women's magazines of the 1930s show women smokers as steeple-chase jumpers, as society hostesses, and as graduating students.

This chapter explores a compelling identity sought by many women who smoke: that of the accomplished woman who chose to smoke as a marker of her sophistication rather than the sexualized good-time girl profiled in chapter 5. The chapter investigates the developing profile of the sophisticated smoker through advertisers' imagery in magazines, on billboards, and in the cinema and through women's active construction of that profile as shown in diary accounts and published biographies. It argues that women early recognized the value of developing a sophisticated identity and that smoking allowed them to become active agents by harnessing smoking as a visual means to that end. In the process, women developed a much expanded range of performative and visual identities. The woman smoker could aspire to more complicated and useful identities that took her far beyond the sexualized woman of chapter 5 to include mature and upper-class women as well. From the point of view of advertisers, these extended possibilities allowed more women to imagine themselves as smokers. From the point of view of women smokers, women seeking an identity of sophisticated charm had another powerful symbol at their disposal.

Constructing the Sophisticated Woman Smoker

The choice to make smoking part of a prominent woman's visual autograph was and is based on complex considerations. First, smoking for women had been a risqué act from the nineteenth century when it was strongly associated with the fulfillment of personal pleasure. In that period, women who smoked were at either end of the social spectrum: either so debased as to have nothing further to lose (and perhaps something to gain by drawing attention to themselves) or so elitist and celebrated as to be able to get away with behaviours that were discredited in the less privileged. By the Victorian era, smoking further added to its counter-cultural status by challenging long-standing middle-class male control of public spaces – for example, smoking rooms in rail cars. Women's smoking called into question the spatial gender divisions in households whereby men retreated to smoking rooms after dinner. Smoking spaces claimed by men were prized not only for the opportunity to smoke in the company of gentlemen but for the associated rights of discussion topics, games of chance, and other male-preserved privileges. Women were not welcome when the pleasurable tobacco was broken out.

Thus, women's smoking spaces became an early and irritating demand, forcing a renegotiation of public gender prescriptions. When women gained entrance to their own colleges, they often requested rooms where they could smoke. In public spaces like hotels and restaurants,[7] women demanded the right to exercise control over their own areas, for smoking or not. Public smoking spaces validated women's right to engage in this activity and provided a forum for female socializing and for engaging in serious discussions of all kinds, including discussions of equal rights.

Smoking by women called into question more than control of domestic and public space, however. Fundamental definitions of gender roles were destabilized by tobacco and by the powerful challenge presented by the sophisticated woman smoker. As noted in the introduction, the argument had been made since the days of Havelock Ellis that smoking masculinized women and feminized men.[8] When that female smoker was a declassé woman of shady reputation, any assertion of this kind could be credible. But when women of considerable social standing and accomplishment took up smoking, the destabilization was more jarring. As reported in *The Globe and Mail* in 1929, the Rev. Dr W.H. Riley deplored women's smoking because, he pointed out regretfully, "[t]he desire for thrills was serving to replace home life with hotel life."[9] This charge that smoking lured women away from their rightful domestic duties and besmirched their feminin-ity was an old one, voiced by both male and female opponents of smok-ing. Canadian temperance advocates condemned women who chose to "lay aside their flannels for an evening, bare the upper part of their chests and the greater part of their arms, leave their own warm apartments and promenade in cold banqueting rooms" as profligate, self-centred, and un-feminine.[10] But when a silly society woman was replaced by a substantial and talented sophisticated woman who smoked, the danger to her femin-ine purity was more evident.

Public smoking by women of renown and/or recognized status and sub-stance foretold the demand for a panoply of public rights and responsibil-ities that gave heart to many and terrified others. From women finding a place in the House of Commons immediately after the First World War to membership in the Senate in 1931 and women demanding the right to professionalize in the 1920s, smoking meant demanding far more than the right to engage in this one act in a space of their own. In short, a woman who smoked visually claimed the right to satisfy her own desires and hopes rather than serving others, as the prevailing ideology of the so-called "angel in the house" required.

Critics of the independent woman as smoker took up this theme of her selfishness and her insistence on pleasing only herself. It was noted time and again in popular literature that smoking tended to limit or destroy the "fecundating power," or women's fertility.[11] But even when such mod-ern women agreed to have children, it was alleged that they had fewer of them and that there were more stillbirths with smoking mothers.[12] (We now know the latter to be true.) Children of mothers who smoked who did survive were said to suffer far poorer health than children with non-smoking mothers.[13] Many thought that children raised in such conditions were more vulnerable to contracting tuberculosis.[14]

The narcissistic face of the sophisticated woman who chose to smoke despite the moral and health risks to herself and her children was also "painted." A smoker was very likely to use cosmetics – "both habits or styles are intermingled and associated with the modern woman in the most inextricable manner."[15] Smokers were assumed to favour high heels[16] as well as drinking and swearing.[17] Smoking was said to destroy "natural" beauty[18] and prematurely age a woman, giving her a sickly pallor.[19] A "nonagenarian" interviewed in a 1935 issue of *The Globe and Mail* offered her view that female smokers were "disgusting" and said that she feared for the longevity of modern women.[20] Ultimately, the case against the woman smoker by many in the interwar period was a revulsion against that aspect of modernity that encouraged women to reject the "sacred responsibility of motherhood."[21]

About the product itself there was also much distrust. How could women of substance put such things to their lips? There were reports that cigarettes contained the sweepings from cinemas. It was alleged that these sweepings "consist of a number of exceedingly filthy articles – cigarette ends, match ends, bits of chocolate and chocolate paper, pieces of string, and every conceivable form of filth … It was then distributed among girls who sorted out the cigarette ends as far as possible from the other refuse, cut off the burned portions, and removed the tobacco. This was next treated in the 'secret' room. The cigarettes were sold in boxes inscribed 'Seal of Quality.'"[22] Cigarette tobacco was said to be treated with arsenic,[23] the wrappers were said to be impregnated with opium. Countless classroom or clinical experiments showed that distilled nicotine placed on the skin or tongues of mice, cats, dogs, rabbits, and many other animals caused them to die almost immediately.[24] It is entirely possible that a number of these claims about the adulteration of cigarettes were true in whole or in part. The central importance of such claims, however, when juxtaposed with the criticisms of the New Woman or the Modern Girl who smoked these products, was that they succeeded in re-incriminating women who had denied their most "sacred" role, that of selfless motherhood. Such claims were not generally made about men who chose to smoke as if the adulteration of the products somehow did not effect them.

While the New Woman presented an enormous challenge to Victorian conventions, she also shared much ground with the earlier model of the religious public woman described in chapters 2 and 3. It should not be assumed that this new definition of womanhood was a sharp break from the older prescription of respectability and against which the New Woman was contrasted. Public-spirited religious and temperance women in the nineteenth century had demanded many of these same rights. The temperance woman of the late nineteenth century was certainly not a smoker, but she was independent in her opinions, famously breaking with male views on many subjects. She cultivated a public role and in Canada at least politely requested the right to vote in order to bring a new moral code to politics. Above all, these women had been middle-class in their sensibilities, and they frequently contrasted their own goals with those of elite women who seemed unproductive and narcissistic. Commitment to the many campaigns championed by nineteenth-century public women made them feel needed, important, and capable.

To conclude that the older model of female piety and purity was pushed aside by the New Woman is to misunderstand both the proto-feminist demands of groups like the WCTU and the endurance of those ideals well into the twentieth century. Canadian women's clubs and associations, like the WCTU, the Young Women's Christian Association (YWCA), the Imperial Order of the Daughters of the Empire (IODE), and the National Council of Women of Canada (NCWC), to mention just a few, had demanded the right to vote for women and lobbied for an otherwise meaningful public life through leadership in educational, artistic, and social welfare fields. A profile of one such woman, Bernice Robb, is offered at the end of this chapter. She was at once a woman who valued religion and duty and a sophisticate.

One of the women's temperance movement's most identifiable leaders and a clear transitional figure into the era of the New Woman was Nellie McClung. Public speaker extraordinaire, author, member of the Legislature, McClung did not hold to all of the prescriptive elements of the New Woman, but she did insist on the right to a career alongside motherhood. Like her WCTU sisters, she was implacably opposed to tobacco. McClung understood the anxiety about what was just around the corner in women's changing roles. "The world has never been partial to the thinking woman – the wise ones have always foreseen danger … That seems to be the haunting fear of mankind – that the advancement of women will sometime, someway, someplace, interfere with some man's comfort … Ideas do not break up homes, but lack of ideas."[25]

By the interwar period, smoking was often associated with the Modern Girl or "flapper" image, the boyishly stylish girl in a short shift, heeled shoes, and cloche hat atop bobbed hair. The cigarette acted as a symbolic assertion and display of her right to take full advantage of society, culture, and entertainment. Of course, not all women could identify with the Modern Girl prototype, and tobacco manufacturers were aware that new markets needed to be opened up among female smokers. This awareness arose in part from women themselves. Demanding more diverse representations of femininity, including greater range in how the smoking woman was represented, women placed pressure on the market. The challenge for tobacco advertisers would be to make smoking by several classes of women seem natural. These categories included both elite and middle-class women, for whom smoking was a clear abridgement of the norms of respectability. When advertisers argued that smoking was a sign of sophistication and implied that sophistication was an attainable and visible goal, middle-class women might be brought into smoking's fold in a way that would serve advertisers' quest for an expanded market. At the same time, women's active pursuit of multiple ways of defining themselves would also be served. The image of the sophisticate as smoker was one with

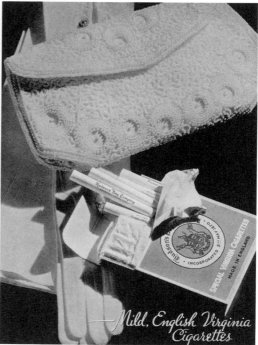

6.2 and 6.3 | Magazine advertisement for Sweet Caporal Cigarettes, *Canadian Home Journal*, 1938; Magazine advertisement for English Virginia Cigarettes, *The Beaver*, 1933

which advertisers experimented in the interwar period, as with the advertisement for Sweet Caporal in 1938 shown in figure 6.2.

Here, two friends walk an Afghan dog, a classic pure breed. The dog is leashed, an unusual practice in urban centres at the time and possibly underscoring the women's willingness to contest restrictions. Dressed almost identically in conservative suits, perched hats, and corsages, the women step down an elegant stairway. The cigarette, not shown in this case, promises happiness, further explicated in the copy as that "something" that so many smokers want, "taste" – a carefully constructed double-denotated message for upscale female consumers who demand the best. Imagining the sophisticated woman as smoker only began to receive advertisers' treatment in the 1930s and 1940s in Canada. The same was true in the United States. Canadian readers of American journals would have seen reports of cosmopolitan women smokers visiting from Britain and Europe being shunned by American audiences in the 1920s.[26] By the 1930s, however, the smart woman smoker was more clearly defined and separated from her "good-time" younger sisters, the flappers. The Modern Girl succeeded in welding the sophisticate to an elitist image that had existed long before. The sophisticate/cultural maven came to be marked as self-confident, experienced, and talented.

Rebranding a tobacco product became a common practice as new social trends demanded different messages.[27] Canadian tobacco brands, which had made their reputation with men's pipe tobacco such as the Hudson's Bay Company brand, redefined themselves as appropriate for the female sophisticate, as in the advertisement shown in figure 6.3 from *The Beaver*. To reconfigure the Hudson's Bay Company tobacco as a woman's product, the accoutrements of a woman's evening bag, gloves, and cigarettes are displayed with the phrase, "Mild, English Virginia Cigarettes." The lack of verbal text in this advertisement suggests the advertiser's confidence that the Hudson's Bay Company brand was already well known to male smokers and something of a Canadian icon through the company's long history. Women were to be added to the pantheon of nationalistic smokers.

John Burnham has argued that the fundamental change to occur after the First World War in the prescriptive behavioural code for Americans was a movement away from "respectability" toward "pleasure-seeking."[28] While the distinction he draws seems too sharp, there is evidence to support this contention in its application to Canadian women as they took up smoking in ever greater numbers. In Canada, the interwar revised definition for respectability included pleasure as well as duty, self-gratification as well as personal salvation. Judging from prescriptive literature and popular culture in this period, the new behavioural code constructed around the modern Canadian girl was one that reconfigured respectability further by adding to it a component of sophistication as represented by elite women's images being merged with middle-class interests. The act of smoking placed a version of this embodied sophistication, and thereby elevated status, within the reach of many aspiring middle-class women. Thus, the new prescription included pleasure-seeking but did not abandon respectability. It especially emphasized the elite and middle-class status of women smokers to reduce the still significant risk of women smokers being considered racy and declassé.

If the image of the sophisticated woman smoker were to bring profits to tobacco manufacturers, the imagery of the woman smoker would need to be extended. The relatively less privileged models would allow middle-class Canadian women to identify more easily with cigarettes and the lifestyle they promised. Thus, in this period there was a clear attempt to reposition smoking as a natural pastime of both the middle-class woman and her more privileged sister, the sophisticate. Ironically, this process

6.4 | Billboard advertisement for Ira-Berg Clothes, Toronto, 1931–33

was launched just as the size of the Canadian elite was reduced through the Great Depression. In figure 6.4, a billboard sign for Ira-Berg "character clothes," two women are outfitted in smart, off-the-rack clothes. One wears a riding outfit, complete with crop, and holds a cigarette in her hand. The other, in a smart day suit with long jacket and three-quarter-length skirt, appears to ask her friend for something, possibly a cigarette. The billboard dates from between 1931 and 1933, and in those Depression years in the Toronto area, very few women could hope to own their own horse for competitions in the ring or even dress the part. We can reasonably assume that the woman in the riding outfit is meant to speak for sophisticates everywhere, women who apparently smoked to complete their "look." The woman attired in the day suit could be any middle-class woman or indeed a waged woman dressed up for her job. Assuming she is asking for a cigarette, and the lack of text cleverly keeps us guessing about this, these two women represent the dream of sophistication for the working woman and the more prosperous woman. Given the context of the Great Depression and the over-determined optimism of the billboard, one could also read this image as an individualistic assertion that one can "dress" herself out of privation. Picking oneself up and carrying on after a reversal is possible, the image seems to say. Even sophistication is achievable, especially if one enhances upward mobility by smoking. Such a reading would appeal not only to women caught in the economic downturn but also to those who were smokers as they explored how the cigarette could enhance their identity.

Canadian advertisers in the postwar period began inserting biographical sketches of admirable women in many advertisements. This testimonial approach had been honed in American cigarette advertisements from the 1930s.[29] As magazines charted the reaction to their advertising copy very carefully, the biographical advertisement must have found favour with the readership. The idea was to make the cigarette an expression of the woman's personality and, in the process, show how useful cigarettes could be in visually representing a woman's best qualities. The Canadian society florist, Judith Garden, was profiled this way in a 1948 issue of the Canadian *Ladies' Home Journal*. As a character, Judith Garden has been lost to history, but her expressive magazine presence lives on. She is shown, polished and glamorous, with a sketch biography as part of a larger advertisement. Instructive in many rules of the art of smoking, Garden demonstrates the appropriate stance for a woman smoker: bent arm, cigarette in "flag" position held mid-neck. Judith Garden's lesson was that cigarettes belonged naturally with other skills of the sophisticated middle-class woman, like flower-arranging, in which Ms Garden specialized. Like many advertisements in which society hostesses were presented as models of (smoking) sophistication,[30] the improbably named Ms Garden also offered readers of the *Ladies' Home Journal* the testimonial that she had "tried and compared many brands – and I learned that cool, mild Camels are the cigarette for me!"[31] "It's experience and taste that counts," whether in flowers or cigarettes, she advises. As powerful as the denotated message is, the connotation is that smoking is a route to sophistication. Power, beauty, and professional status for women are also all closely aligned with smoking in this biographical profile.

Metaphoric devices are also used in the Judith Garden advertisement. Ms Garden is posed in the centre of a picture collage, holding her cigarette reflectively while she contemplates the beauty of her craft. The central textual message invites the observer to construct a "parallel implication complex" between Judith Garden and "you," the real subject of this advertisement and actually pictured (as a kind of Everywoman) in the lower corner. Judith Garden functions as the culturally relevant and recognizable reference point, but most of the text is addressed explicitly to the subject, "you": "Let your own 'T-Zone' – T for Taste and T for Throat – tell you about Camels. Let your taste tell you about Camel's marvelous flavor. Let your throat discover that wonderful Camel mildness and coolness. See how your own experience tells you why more people are smoking Camels than ever before!" The cut-out subject box with "Everywoman's" image rephrases the same message in a different format, reminiscent of techniques used in catechism or temperance lessons:

Let your "T-Zone tell you

T for Taste...
T for Throat...
that's your proving ground for any cigarette.
See if <u>Camels</u> don't
suit <u>your</u> "T-Zone"
To a "T."

The emphasis in this advertisement/profile on corporeal matters that embody the product and the women who consume that product shows the importance of this feature in modernist advertising. The observer is invited to use all of her senses in imagining the pleasure to be received from this cigarette through her "T-Zone," her "T for Taste" and her "T for throat."

The advertisement also summons other authorities to make its case to the reader. In the event that the observer missed the message, the advertisement ends by invoking the popular eminence of medical doctors and their commitment to Camels: "According to a Nationwide survey: More Doctors Smoke Camels than any other Cigarette."

Advertisements like this one, which appealed to cigarettes' taste as the main determinant of value as opposed to, for example, the satisfaction of a nicotine hit, known to attract men more than women, had been carefully researched by cigarette manufacturers after the Second World War. By the late 1960s, research had confirmed to tobacco manufacturers that women were drawn to smoking more by the taste, particular kinds of packaging, the promise of social engagement, and weight control.[32]

Advertisements stressing the sophistication of smokers appeared in most women's and family magazines in the postwar period. American tobacco manufacturer Philip Morris regularly ran advertisements for its Virginia Oval Cigarettes in Canadian magazines, with images of modestly hatted and demure women portrayed in line drawings. Some of these hearkened back to Wedgewood graphics, making the connection between the refinement of smoking and expensive china. The distinguished magazine *Saturday Night* ran advertisements for upmarket Pall Mall in which well-dressed and older women were shown taking tea in elegant hotels while they smoked.[33]

By the late 1940s, the more common representation of the sophisticated woman smoker was through photographs in which the realistic setting and other figures would lend credence to mature middle-class women imagining themselves as part of modern smoking society. The Canadian

6.5 and 6.6 | Publicity photographs, CPR, 1949 and 1954

Pacific Railway advertised its chain of lodges through photographs such as figure 6.5 in which a middle-aged woman reads in the rustic but comfortable lounge at the Devil's Lake Lodge in Kenora, Ontario. Considering its remote location and the focus on hunting, the women's dresses and dainty shoes, as well as the formal wear by the men, denotes a particular clientele: prosperous, older, and married. The woman smoker's casual posture, with the cigarette prominently displayed, also speaks to her ease and unapologetic choice of smoking. The Canadian Pacific Railway also profiled its new Princess Lounge in the elegant Royal York Hotel in Toronto, connected to Union Station. The CPR had been one of the first railways to respond to its male customers' concerns about women joining them in the male "smokers." It added women's smoking compartments to its trains and lounges like this one to its hotels in Canada in the 1940s.[34] The women shown in figure 6.6 from 1954 are hatless but dressed in a variety of stylish yet sexy gowns. All of the women are older and suitably escorted by at least one male for each female grouping. Several of the patrons sip a drink and smoke in the prescribed way, repeatedly demonstrated, of crooked arm, holding the cigarette aloft. The elegance of the furniture, the recessed ceiling, the flower arrangements, the liveried waiter, the pleasant social gathering all privilege connotative meanings of the smokers as sophisticated and sociable. With this visual offering of a variety of presumably achievable identities for otherwise respectable women (and men) of the middle class, all of which were closely associated with smoking, we can anticipate that many women adopted one or more of these "looks" as a way to actively make and remake their identities.

Women's diary accounts from the late 1940s allow us to test that hypothesis. Edith Archibald "Polly" Dobson was a well-known Halifax philanthropist and upper-middle-class matron who created an identity for herself that seems to have been informed by the popular smoking culture of her day. Born in 1897 to Professor and Mrs MacMechan of Halifax, Polly was educated at Halifax Ladies' College and later, along with her sisters, at the Wakefield Girls' High School in Yorkshire, England. Polly was in Halifax during the 1917 explosion, where she helped by nursing an injured naval cadet. As a young woman, she became social secretary to Mrs Alexander Graham Bell, living with the Bells at their Cape Breton estate and becoming more like a member of the extended Bell family than an employee. She was there when she met her future husband, Commander C.C. (Tommy) Dobson, who was a member of the Admiralty Commission sent to evaluate Bell's invention of the hydrofoil. They married in 1920 in England, and twin daughters were born in 1923. Her husband died in 1940, after which she returned to Canada. In 1947, she resettled in Nova Scotia, founding the Red Cross Lodge at Camp Hill Hospital, which she ran until her retirement in 1972. Polly died in 1990.[35]

Well-born with a good education and also well-married, Polly provides for us a profile of a woman aware of her authority and class advantage over three decades. From the 1940s to the 1970s, Polly recorded her activities and her thoughts in her diary, showing that she remained a dutiful woman throughout her life, working hard for the Red Cross Lodge. In that project, however, she did not pitch in with manual labour. Indeed, a woman of Polly's means in this era would not have been expected to work at a conventional salaried job. Instead, she busied herself with finding resources to finance the project, making Halifax's well-heeled patrons aware of it and supportive of its goals, and supervising the less elite women volunteers and staff. She was the manager; they were the workers. The relational part of her role was intensely pleasurable for her. Polly loved to travel and often took the train on Red Cross business and to visit her friends. She played bridge as often as possible, and in that company, she liked to smoke.

As a thoroughly modern and sophisticated woman, she monitored her appearance and especially her weight rigorously, smoking to help control it.[36] Her life was intensely social in the years of her widowhood. Many days reported in her diary feature a late breakfast, lunch out with drinks, tea, then drinks, dinner, then more drinks. Gifts from friends often included cigarettes: "Sheila Mappin met me at the station; went out to their

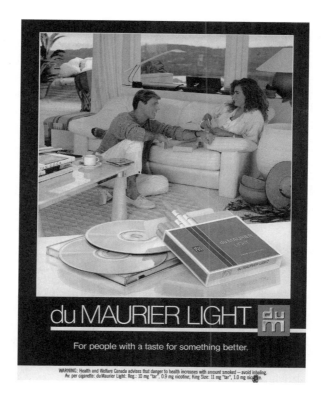

6.7 | Magazine advertisement for du Maurier Cigarettes, *Chatelaine*, 1988

house had a lovely bath & dinner played family bridge afterwards; won .45. Sheila took me to train showered with books cigs etc."[37] As Polly was presumably recording these gifts for her own eyes only, her special noting of the cigarettes is significant.

Polly Dobson was the very image of the sophisticated and prosperous woman whom Judith Guest and other advertising authorities were referencing in their definition of the modern middle-class woman smoker. We have no images of Polly's home or of Polly herself, but we can assume that it would not have been markedly different from Judith Guest's prescription for the sophisticated woman smoker. Polly's diary shows that the aesthetic being defined for women smokers – both in terms of personal behaviours and public image – found their mark with women of her type. Polly used smoking to add to the general image of sophistication she had already achieved and to maintain that aesthetic through weight control.

The strategy of associating smoking with allowable sophistication of both the elite and middle class has carried on into our own era. To take just one example, one might consider an advertisement from *Chatelaine* magazine in 1988 (figure 6.7), which aligns smoking with consumer intelligence and prescience.

In this advertisement, a handsome couple recline companionably in some tropical paradise. The living area gives onto an outside deck with a spectacular view. Inside, they listen to newly introduced compact disks and smoke, clad in comfortable beach clothing, each sporting a deep tan. The props in the room speak of sophistication and wealth: a picture folio of Van Gogh sits atop a coffee table, pottery bowls are arranged about the room, and a matching lamp sits on a shelf. The clothing chosen for the models is understated but expensive, and each happily smokes. The advertisement's connotated message is simple: smoking is a natural accompaniment to a sophisticated lifestyle. That this could still be presented as an argument for smoking twenty-four years after the damning surgeon general's report connecting smoking to cancer is an indication of how securely established smoking had become for those seeking sophistication in our society.

Thus, the marketing strategies to promote smoking as a means to sophistication and the illusion of wealth if not the real thing contrasted with earlier campaigns intended to associate smoking with youth and rebellion, as described in chapter 5. First, rather than presenting the woman smoker only as a young and often edgy character, as had been common in the 1920s and early 1930s (an approach that did not disappear in succeeding decades), the sophisticated woman smoker is profiled as older, elegant, prosperous, and professional in bearing. Sophisticated smokers are often developed as full personalities in advertising, with achievements and opinions presented as wholly their own. Part of the popularity of this strategy might have been the large group of media icons who were known smokers and who were pleased to receive this free advertising for their own purposes, depicting their choices in a positive light. This can be seen as indirectly resulting from middle-class women's efforts to free themselves from the shackles of public censure for their decision to smoke.

Certainly, the combined effect of this new approach to advertising and mature women using smoking to buttress their claims of sophistication was to further normalize and naturalize smoking. It all helped to persuade younger women by providing a range of visual identities that they could try on, much like an outfit. It seems clear that the campaign to associate smoking by both men and women with such qualities as maturity, professionalism, sophistication, and especially social cohesion resulted in increased rates of smoking for all sectors of society. The statistics for smoking rates in the postwar period, which saw Canadian women's rates continuing to climb until the mid-1970s, confirms this assumption.

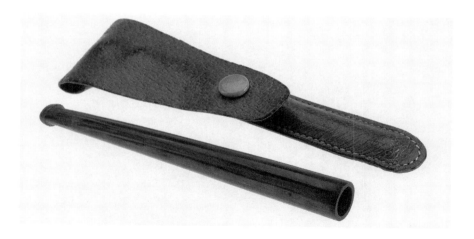

6.8 | Cigarette holder and leather case, c. 1920–30

Accessorizing the Sophisticate

One of the ways that the cosmopolitanism of smoking could be telegraphed was through the production of high-end accessories for the female smoker. In this, the products marketed to women followed the same pattern as those developed for the pipe-, cigar-, and cigarette-smoking older, middle-class male. The male market of smokers had supported an extensive range of smoking paraphernalia, including, for example, such objects as the cigarette holder shown in figure 6.8. Hand-made of fine turned wood with its own leather carrying-case, this cigarette holder could have been ostentatiously pulled out of a breast pocket for use at a moment's notice. The object dates from the interwar period, but ones like it were produced until after the Second World War.

Accessories for women could also be expensive or modest, as with those intended for the working girl (see chapter 8). Most of those that have been preserved in museums and galleries, understandably, are smoking accessories that were at the same time art forms intended for the sophisticated smoker, and most date from the early nineteenth century through the 1950s, the heyday of elitist smoking.

As discussed in chapter 1, snuff was one of the earliest forms whereby women consumed tobacco. Boxes to hold the powdered snuff had been made for elite women from the seventeenth century, but most Canadian examples preserved in museums date from the nineteenth century, as with the one shown in figure 6.9. Decorative boxes were fashioned for

6.9 | Snuff box of "yellow wood" with spattered exterior design, early nineteenth century

women to secret the snuff away in a skirt pocket or satchel or on a table. The first example is a fine snuff box, a delicate wooden object from the early nineteenth century.

Made of "yellow wood" with a spattered exterior design in red and blue, the box was originally owned by Montreal's Lady Dawson. A second example of a finely wrought snuff box is figure 6.10, black papier-maché and wood box, decorated with mother-of-pearl. This beautifully made and very feminine artifact might have been intended for a widow or older woman because of the choice of black colouring. It dates from the late nineteenth century, indicating that by that time, fine pieces continued to be made for elegant snuff-taking by women of means. Both of these snuff boxes are delicately designed as would befit a ladies' outfit and trappings, with feminine decorative flourishes, and each is individually detailed. Owning a specially designed, made, and decorated snuff box marked the user as part of the elite and as predating modernism in the twentieth century. Not long after this, however, snuff fell out of fashion with most Canadian women as more tobacco-users adopted cigarettes.

The triumph of cigarettes as the popular choice of tobacco for many Canadian women after the First World War offered even more scope for fine objets d'art to be produced for the sophisticated smoker. They often

6.10 and 6.11 | Snuff box of black papier maché, wood, and mother-of-pearl; Mother-of-pearl and metal cigarette case, c. 1940–50

served as models for less expensive pieces acquired by women of more modest means. For example, cigarette cases from exquisite to pedestrian in terms of design, materials, and quality were a very popular accessory for both men and women. Figure 6.11 shows a mother-of-pearl and metal cigarette case that dates from between 1940 and 1950. It is very traditional in appearance and probably was owned by a woman of means. The gold and inlay bands of mother-of-pearl suggest delicate feminized decorative

6.12 | Monogrammed woman's cigarette case, c. 1920–30

features. This case had been designed to hold longer cigarettes than had many cases in museum collections.

Figure 6.12 shows a dramatic cigarette case in brown and silver ceramic with a monogrammed insert of black marcasite that belonged to Mrs John J.A. Murphy, a Montreal artist specializing in woodcuts. The case is a beautiful example of art nouveau style. It has a textured cover, indicating that it could only have been owned and used by a woman of the elite, as the provenance of the object confirms. Dating from 1920 to 1930, the cigarette case suggests that its owner would have expected to take her case into society and use it freely.

Sometimes, cases were made in the shape of the cigarette itself. Tubes made of fine metals could collapse and fold into tiny cases "to be dangled from neck chains when not in use."[38] In producing such accessories for the elite, Canadian makers were following British and American examples. An article from 1922 in the *Ladies' Home Journal* noted that tobacco suppliers in New York City were ready to provide "the most exquisite and expensive cigarette accessories their designers can conceive ... They have on display dainty jeweled holders ranging in price from fifty dollars to five hundred dollars and cigarette cases from fifty dollars to one thousand dollars."[39]

6.13 | Silver match case (or safe), c. 1890–1900

The increasing popularity of cigarettes among women encouraged the production of other accoutrements. Decorative match cases were a very popular item for women to carry with their cigarette cases. They were often made in ingenious designs and materials. The example in figure 6.13 has a striking band on the bottom of the case. Smaller than the cigarette case, the match case could draw attention through its fine detail and materials. This one was produced in sterling silver by the Henry Birks and Sons Company, possibly of wrought silver, and might have originally been a set with a silver cigarette case. This match case dates from between 1890 and 1900, an early example of the tasteful carrying of the self-striking match, which had been introduced in the 1890s. The embossed silver case with delicate scrolled edges shows exceptional workmanship.

At about the same time that self-striking matches appeared, early lighters were introduced. The "Ladies' Lighter" shown in figures 6.14 and 6.15 was produced in Austria between 1875 and 1900, making it a very early example of the mechanical lighter, especially in terms of lighters for women.

6.14 and 6.15 | Ladies' lighter, c. 1875–1900

A gift from the Baron and Baronesse de Rothchilde to Montreal socialite Mrs Laurent Perreault, the lighter features a romantic eighteenth-century scene on one face and a silver arabesque decoration on royal blue enamel on the other. The complexity of the construction also sets it apart from other more common examples of mechanical lighters introduced in the early twentieth century. The lighter has enamelled, engraved, and printed scenes on enamel, glass, sterling silver, and other metals in a neo-roccoco style. It has a heavier mechanism than would later be featured for women's use in lighters, also marking its pre-modern status as a unique objet d'art.

By far the most popular accessory for the woman smoker of all stations in life, however, was the holder. According to one authority, cigarette holders held only 10 per cent of the "accessories" market for American smokers before 1914 but 60 per cent by 1920.[40] Most holders were used by women. The holder was intended to serve several purposes. It could slim the profile of the smoker through lengthening the cigarette. It allowed the woman smoker to avoid staining her fingers with nicotine. And very importantly, it allowed for more dramatic gestures by adding a demonstrative object to the woman's arsenal of everyday smoking paraphernalia. The first, shown in figure 6.16, is a delicate gold holder from about 1930. The woman using this holder would insert the cigarette in the small circle, and hold it at right angles by the larger circle. The unusual angle at which the cigarette

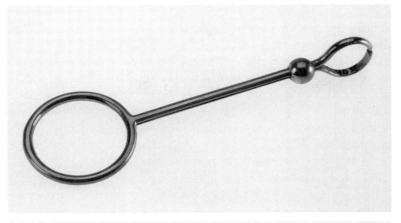

6.16 and 6.17 | Woman's gold cigarette holder, c. 1930; Woman's bone cigarette holder and leather case, c. 1920–30

would be held is evidence that this holder is intended to draw attention to the smoker rather than merely to protect her fingers from staining.

A second example of a woman's cigarette holder, and a far more conventional one, is figure 6.17, also dating from the interwar period. Probably made of bone and ivory, the holder has a gently fluted end where the cigarette would be inserted and a detailed stripe. Reminiscent of the man's cigarette holder shown earlier in figure 6.8, the holder and its leather case bespeak the wealth of the owner and care of the prized cigarette extension. Both of these cigarette holders point to their having been treasured and used, given their condition. Often, expensive holders came with their own cases, as in these examples, generally made from leather. The varied materials used for these holders is representative of the range available.

Here we have seen gold, wood, ivory, and bone used, but in addition one could find cigarette holders in many other materials, such as jade, amber, mother-of-pearl, and tortoise shell.

The colours used not only elevate the holders to art forms, they would also allow colour-matching with outfits, nail enamel, and lipstick. Media reports made much of the co-ordination of cigarette paraphernalia and costumes in women's magazines. The essence of these cigarette holders, lighters, and cases was that all were designed to be used in public spaces and social gatherings where women put on their best attire to see and be seen. As an example of commercial opportunities using these accessories, a report circulated in 1922 of a combination shop and lounging room for women. The female manager explained the many attractive features for women smokers in such a space:

> We have everything here a woman requires in the way of an acces-
> sory to her smoking, and we offer in addition a lounge, where they
> can smoke their favorite brands in repose. Even our cigarettes are
> in harmony with the costumes our patrons wear. If a woman comes
> in wearing a black costume we give her a black holder with a black
> silk-tipped cigarette. You know nowadays dinner favors are usually
> cigarette accessories. We are prepared on forty-eight hours' notice
> to supply hostesses. The holders are in ten colors and are made
> either of hand-blown glass or tortoise shell, and the cigarettes are
> silk tipped and in ten different colors. They are passed among the
> women on a silver tray and each selects the color harmonizing with
> her costume of the evening.[41]

It is very unlikely that many women had the opportunity to indulge in their cigarettes in settings like this, and yet reports of this kind circulated widely, adding to the reputation of cigarette smoking as the sophisticated woman's accessory.

Canadian smoking accessories of fine quality were modelled on American and European examples. Canadians abroad were struck by the range of smoking accoutrements that could be purchased for women and by the delicacy of the work. The celebrated artist Emily Carr, a smoker, observed and adopted European habits during her frequent trips to the continent during the 1920s and 1930s. Of Russian smoking habits, she noted, "I don't like the Russian idea much, even if their leather does smell so delicious and their little ladies' cigarettes do come in the most intriguing boxes."[42]

Of all of the products for the sophisticated woman smoker, cigarette holders maintained their fashion far longer than any of the other articles. By the 1920s, it was considered declassé in the United States for a woman to smoke without a holder if she were in evening wear.[43] Audrey Hepburn's iconic character, Holly Golightly, used a long black cigarette holder in the 1961 film *Breakfast at Tiffany's*, briefly rekindling interest in the holder for all who wished to appear as sophisticated as Hepburn. For her tour of Australia in 2007, Beyoncé Knowles came under criticism from anti-smoking advocates for including a cigarette in a holder on billboards and in advertisements featuring her. In this case, as in others, a young woman of colour like Beyoncé is permitted far less expressive range as far as smoking is concerned than are mature stars like Audrey Hepburn or k.d. lang, profiled in chapter 11.

The Woman Artist as Smoker: Doris McCarthy

One of Canada's most celebrated and productive artists, as well as a writer and educator, Doris McCarthy embodies many of the qualities defined by advertisers and actively incorporated into the identity of sophisticated, independent women. McCarthy has become well known for her luminescent oil paintings, many produced on her trips into the Far North. She produced her art from the mid-twentieth century until well into the twenty-first century.

In her autobiography,[44] McCarthy does not tell us when she took up smoking, but by 1950, she had comfortably incorporated smoking into her public persona. In one iconic image of the artist-as-smoker, McCarthy gazes steadily at a painting, with cigarette in crooked arm folded over the chair back. Despite her brush and cleaning rag, McCarthy's appearance lacks any other indication of her work. She is not wearing protective covering but a smart sweater with a brooch and a finely tailored skirt. Her hair is braided and pinned in place. The mess of paint rags and a palette before her belie her studied and carefully constructed image. This is not a photograph of a working artist so much as one of a skilled and serious woman, gazing at the results of her own labours. It is also one that underlines her embodiment as a woman in control of both the process and the product.

Doris McCarthy was no bohemian; she was raised in privilege in Toronto, the dutiful daughter of a demanding mother and emotionally distant father. She was a member of long-standing of the Canadian Girls' in Training (CGIT) as well as a devoted Sunday school teacher, and she tried hard to get on with the other teachers at Central Tech. Here she taught art after attending the Ontario College of Art (OCA). As she describes herself, in most respects she was a spirited but conventional young woman, mirroring the norms of her age. Given much freedom by her own family, she travelled with both female and male friends on sketching trips, camping for long periods in the Maritimes and Quebec. When confronted with her mother's frustrated rants at domestic crises, she sat obediently, listening silently. At the same time, Doris was prepared to follow her heart, bridging conventions that might have alienated her from polite society had she not also forged loyal friendships. She admits in her writings to two serious affairs with married men. A friend "rationalized our 'affair' as good for me, because it enlarged my experience as a woman and therefore as an artist,"[45] she writes. She repeatedly points to the importance of the relational in her writing and work.

In Doris's diary accounts and memoirs, smoking is so naturalized that she does not think to disclose what drew her to it in the first place. In this, she is not unusual. The decision to begin smoking, then as now, relates to social and emotional needs, and these are often not easily or comfortably expressed. Her description of smoking is always incidental to other, more momentous events. In 1935, for example, Doris and a friend decided to take a year off from teaching and study in England. They travelled by freighter from New York to London and while on board heard of Mussolini's bombing of Abyssinia. The degree to which the party was stunned by this news is described through the metaphor of the forgotten cigarette: "There was a queer minute or two in the lounge after dinner, when I came in and found a group of perhaps ten people in front of the radio, all standing, all watching and listening with hushed attention, cigarettes forgotten, and only the man's voice, English and cold, telling us that the League was meeting in committee at that moment to consider steps in Abyssinia."[46]

Doris was a confirmed smoker by 1939 when, returning from a sketching trip on Georgian Bay where there was no radio, "we stopped at a little roadside stand to buy cigarettes and heard that war had been declared."[47] When Doris begins the second affair of her adult life and the relationship that would remain the most significant of all of her male friendships, she describes it through the cigarette: "One late afternoon we had been working on a job that was taxing, concentrated and creative. When the meeting wound up and the others took off, we were ready to find a retreat under the trees, to talk it over and share a sociable cigarette before we also went our ways."[48]

Doris travelled in circles where smoking was common. As both an artist and a teacher, she spent happy times in the school staff lounge with her colleagues and friends. Artists had been associated with smoking since the nineteenth century, along with other avant-garde intellectuals, and it is entirely possible that it was through her friendships with other artists at the OCA and at shows where they displayed their work that she first chose to smoke. However, secondary school teachers have long been committed smokers as well. This seems not to have been the case to the same degree with elementary school teachers, however. The oral accounts I have gathered and those provided to me by other historians offer very few examples of elementary school teachers smoking. Framing her identity through smoking would have been an easy association for Doris McCarthy as both a secondary school teacher and an artist.

Smoking and Teachers

Oral testimony from teachers in postwar Canada confirms the popularity of smoking[49] and the intense same-sex socializing that characterized women teachers' leisure activities.[50] This continued long after the Second World War. Sadie Chow,[51] who taught in Vancouver schools from 1956 to the mid-1980s, recalls male and female teachers congregating at one end of the lunch room/lounge to smoke in her school during the 1950s or 1960s. She describes a companionable setting where smoking seems to have been quite acceptable, as long as it occurred indoors and away from students. My own memories of teaching in the 1970s and 1980s confirm this same pattern in the secondary school staff room. Similarly, Catherine Darby recalls meetings at school where (mainly) male teachers turned the air blue with their smoking: "as soon as men went into the room to sit down and start discussing these things, out would come pipes, cigars, cigarettes and soon the air was just thick." Catherine does not recall women smoking during those meetings, but since she taught in Vancouver from 1947 to 1978, it is very likely that women figured among the smokers.[52] Many other colleagues and friends recount similar memories of staff rooms in secondary schools during the 1960s and 1970s where the air seemed permanently blue from smoke.

These collective recollections remind us of the importance of public space for female secondary school teachers who wanted to smoke. In Sadie's case, her memory is of the space being equitably shared; in Catherine's, male teachers asserted their right to discuss matters of union policy by taking over the space through their cigarette smoke and discouraging any non-smokers. My own memories include both women and men smoking in the same space, and I well recall the shock that rippled through the staff room when a male teacher asked if the smokers would kindly desist from smoking in the dining area of the room in the late 1970s. After much complaining, the smokers agreed to this space division.

Yet another secondary school teacher who taught between 1947 and 1968 in Toronto,[53] Muriel Fraser, has a different memory of how smokers occupied the public space of schools. Muriel recalls smoking as forbidden in the teachers' lounge of her school: "there was a teacher's lounge and then there was a horrible little room down in the basement where they all went down to smoke ... you know. That was a great spot to smoke because you know a lot of people smoked in those days. You didn't smoke in the lounge." In describing the teachers being forced to retreat, Muriel both denigrates the space – "a horrible little room" – but then suggests that it was valued – "that was a great spot to smoke," suggesting both the popularity of the habit and its control through denying space. While none of these female teachers admitted to being smokers themselves, all wove stories of their colleagues' heavy smoking into their accounts of teaching, demonstrating that at least in the schools where these women spent their working lives, smoking was a common pastime.

Other oral histories with teachers who taught in the 1970s report the freedom to smoke in the staff room or preparation rooms, including science labs. But in the early 1980s in Ontario, the locations where teachers could smoke were restricted to the staff room. One respondent notes that this was enough of a disincentive for her to quit.[54] Those who smoked in the 1980s and 1990s report hiding their smoking. One teacher noted that she smoked in the car on the way to and from school but never in the building. "I was not proud that I smoked and would have avoided revealing it – the tide was turning in society by then."[55] This teacher was in an urban setting, but in rural areas of the same period, smoking seemed to remain acceptable in the staff room throughout the 1970s. "When teaching high school in Red Lake, we could still smoke in the staff room, so it became associated with taking a break from classes."[56]

None of these accounts sound particularly glamorous or befitting a sophisticate, and yet outside the school setting in adult company, a cigarette-wielding teacher could add assurance and a tone of modernity to her public pose, just as Doris McCarthy managed to do in her studio. As one respondent said in her oral history, smoking "meant being grown up, being a sophisticated, free woman."[57]

It would be less than accurate to conclude this brief survey of the sophisticated woman smoker in the twentieth century by suggesting that smoking always went hand-in-glove with sophistication. Sophisticated women came in various forms and from various backgrounds, including single women who had been born into the middle class and maintained that class orientation while working for a salary. This class orientation would have applied to many female teachers in mid-century Canada and later. Such women were indeed independent but were also helped by their education, networks, and family privilege. Often, they were not rebellious but dutiful and conservative in their personal and public lives.

One woman in this category was Bernice Robb of Halifax. Descended from a very prominent family, Bernice attended Halifax Academy until 1928 when she decided on a career in business.[58] She graduated from business college and in 1929 began working in the Dalhousie University Business Office as the "joe girl," earning $50 a month. Dalhousie was familiar territory to her, since one of her grandfathers had helped found the college. Bernice went on to become the cashier supervisor in the Dalhousie Office, responsible as well for convocation arrangements for forty-nine years. Her years at Dalhousie made her both feared and revered. In many respects, she was treated by students and faculty as if she were an academic. She retired in 1978 and travelled widely, continuing her life as an accomplished, sophisticated, and well-educated single woman.

Bernice was not a smoker, a drinker, or even a card-player. Even though she was well-born, intelligent, and independent, her "sophistication index" would very likely have been lowered by her failure to smoke. However, like so many women of her age, she held to the older prescription of the respectable and community-minded woman, engaged as she was throughout her life in girlhood leadership through the Canadian Girls in Training, just as Doris McCarthy was. Many of Bernice's passions were transformed into programs for various CGIT groups throughout the Maritimes and in Ontario. The photograph albums she contributed to the Dalhousie University Archives speak not only of a woman of enormous energy and commitment to the CGIT movement but also one aware of her historical significance and prepared to contribute to the record.

The page shown in figure 6.18 from one of Robb's many photograph albums illustrates the depth of her commitment to young women's leadership, particularly through the CGIT. During the summer camp profiled on this page, the young women enjoyed swimming, Bible study, hiking, and boating. Her friendships with the other leaders were intense and lifelong.

In her views, Robb hearkens back to the women of the YWCTU profiled in chapter 2. Bernice had attended both the CGIT and the local young people's group at her church in her youth, noting in her diary her interest in lectures by visiting missionaries. She took music lessons and attended the cinema but was drawn to worthy pictures like *Clive of India*. As a modern woman, however, she was concerned about her appearance, sewing her own clothes and coats. She immortalized a great number of these home-sewn outfits in her enormous photograph collection. She taught at the Halifax North End Mission for girls and believed in the

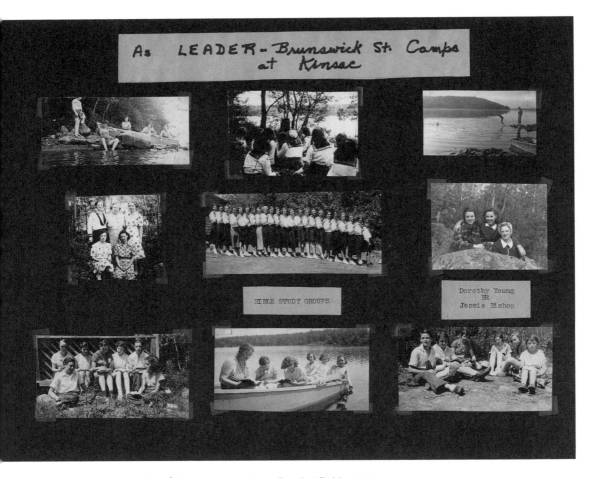

6.18 | Photograph album, Bernice Robb, 1920s

saving power of education. "Probably good stuff in girls but no training – certainly good stuff in a few of them," she allowed at the height of the Depression in 1935.[59] To make extra money and help out the students around her, she typed their essays.

Part of the independence of mind of a Bernice Robb, and of the many women like her, was her ability to reject advertising promoting smoking throughout her life. This is not to suggest that Bernice was immune to the many consumer-based messages presented by advertising; she was clearly a modern figure in her appreciation for fashion. Her story gives evidence that the prescription presented to women related to cigarette smoking was accepted by many women holding to the modernist aesthetic but rejected by many as well. Of particular importance in the life view of Bernice Robb was her religiosity. This ingredient seems to have been very important in protecting women against the dreams spun by cigarette advertisers and offering other routes to attain a form of "social magic," as other profiles of women who rejected smoking will show.

Through advertising, personal examples of women smokers, and up-scale accessories, smoking promised the prospective woman consumer the means to create an identity that bespoke cosmopolitanism. Smoking helped women to exercise a technology of the self by aligning smoking with sophistication. Other women, like Bernice Robb, found the means to generate a different technology of the self without cigarettes but rather by manipulating other sources of social power. Not all women had the financial means to be considered wealthy, but with the judicious use of cigarettes, all had the potential to add a certain "gloss" to their identity and to be considered a sophisticate through their polished gestures rather than their pocketbooks. Research with young women of our own era shows that smoking is still considered one of those factors that can add lustre to a young woman's image, injecting an element of glamour and conferring an element of "social power."[60]

The sophisticated woman, smoker or not, combined many of the features of her serious-minded predecessors with the new modernist aesthetic. These women followed the fashions of the day in personal adornment and accessories, consciously fashioning a personal identity reflected through visual features. It is striking that when advertisers promoted the sophisticated woman smoker, all of the representations are of emphasized femininity: women are flower arrangers or society matrons or hyper-feminine workers. From the advertisers' views, only certain representations of the sophisticate as smoker were allowable. But when the sophisticated woman smoker presented herself, emphasized femininity was but one of many identities forged by women through smoking.

All of the women profiled in this chapter were acutely aware of how they "looked" to others. In several cases too, these women took an active part in memorializing their visual choices by becoming photographers and then mounting the photographs, using particular themes. Even in instances when the women did not take their own photographs or preserve others, women like Polly Dobson wrote diary accounts in vivid "word pictures" offering the "observer" a picture-like rendering of their activities, including their smoking. The power of visual representations for the sophisticated modern woman is undeniable.

7

Thinness

The 1920s was both the first decade when sizable numbers of women took up public smoking and when the ideal aesthetic for women first glorified youth and slimness. This was not a coincidence. In 1928, the American Tobacco Company's advertisements for Lucky Strike made the claim that tobacco was an appetite suppressor through its slogan: "Reach for a Lucky, Instead of a Sweet." By the 1930s, Lucky Strike was the best-selling brand of any cigarette in the United States.[1] It had been recognized for decades that smoking suppressed the appetite. This was one of the reasons why smoking was thought to be so dangerous for growing boys. When women were first drawn to slimming diets in the 1920s, this characteristic of smoking was celebrated rather than deplored.

This chapter explores the origins of the notion that cigarette smoking is a means to control the body, particularly the body's weight and its fleeting youth. Women's desire to control their own bodies through smoking held enormous appeal from the 1920s. Recent research shows that it remains a primary reason why women choose to smoke and why they continue in the face of well-publicized health dangers.[2] This modernist trend is explored through advertisements found in the pages of leading Canadian women's and family magazines, in fiction, and in movies in which women found the argument that a self-respecting woman was by definition devoted to improving her visual appearance. Women were alerted that a "visual identity" was crucial to a woman's success or failure and that without a great deal of work, women could easily become disgusting to everyone around them.

7.1 | Billboard advertisement for Winchester Cigarettes, Toronto, 1931–33

The young woman on the Winchester billboard advertisement (figure 7.1) is a classic example of these ideals. She is youthful, pretty, and of an undetermined class because she is shown at leisure, not at school or work or in her domestic space. Winchester Cigarettes displayed this billboard in Toronto from the mid-1930s with only a two-word descriptor: "Blended Right," as if the woman smoker were an amalgam of qualities just as the cigarette had blended tobacco. The young model with her casual, fresh-faced beauty is also a prototype of sexual attractiveness.[3] She exudes confidence, her slenderness profiled with her cigarette. At the same time, the model has a familiar girl-next-door quality to her, making her a template and an attainable "look" that would be well within range of most style-conscious young women. She is undeniably sexy as she sits with her cigarette resting on a carelessly poised knee, arm thrown across the chair back in an expansive posture that would have worried her WCTU grandmother deeply. She says nothing, simply posing with a frank, open look. Very importantly, she is not a recognizable screen star; she could be any young middle-class or working girl, eager to show her readiness for fun and pleasure.

The phenomenon of the "Modern Girl" – of which this image is an example – placed the youthful woman in the limelight: pleasure-seeking party-girls, drinking bootlegged alcohol, dancing at unchaperoned evening events far from home, or "joy riding" to escape the stultifying strictures of home. All fed the public appetite for pictures of pretty girls and showed young women themselves the many advantages of taking on the flapper persona. Advertising and popular fiction featured the Modern Girl. Slender, athletic, and sporting perfect skin, the Modern Girl was profiled as always having a very good time. Meanwhile, older women were offered products to reverse the ravages of time and enable them to reclaim youth, slimness, and unblemished features. The regularity with which these messages were broadcast and the different media used to reinforce the message meant that whether or not female consumers were smokers, they encountered these ideas, creating a positive climate for smoking.

This is not to say that the "thin ideal" was uncontested, however. Particularly by the 1940s and 1950s, the voluptuous female was still regarded as the sexual gold standard. Marilyn Monroe's weight, as a case in point, fluctuated between 115 and 140 pounds over her career.[4] By the 1960s, the wraith-like Twiggy and the Barbie-doll thin waist, as well as other unrealistic depictions of women as unhealthily thin, further redefined women's acceptable body weight downward. These very restrictive standards have placed even more pressure on young women's thin shoulders in the current age, convincing many that they can never be thin enough and forcing them into yo-yo dieting and smoking. Thus, the origins of what today is called the "supergirl" as part of girl culture are clear. Young women have been expected to be smart and responsible and to demonstrate leadership while being thin, pretty, and smartly dressed in the latest fashions. The stress endured by virtually all young women along with their older sisters, mothers, and aunts cries out for relief. For many, that relief has been found in the cigarette.

The anti-sweet Lucky Strike campaign in the United States is credited as having been revolutionary in cigarette advertising because it "created consumers" rather than simply luring patrons from another cigarette brand.[5] It serves as a prime example of advertising having generated a new market in response to a perceived need. "Whereas earlier models of markets focused on the interrelationship between supply and demand, modern advertising in the consumer culture emphasized the creation of both need and desire," writes Allan Brandt.[6] One of these desires was to be thin.

In addition to messages that weight must be controlled, Canadian women in the interwar period were alerted to the many imperfections of their bodies as advertisements bombarded potential customers walking down streets or glancing through newspapers or magazines. Women's idealized representations were just that: idealized but presented through advertising as everyday reality. The message from advertisers was that women's fate was a horrible one without unrelenting work and the appropriate consumer products. Cigarettes were one of the products that kept women appearing slender and modern, they argued. In other words, a woman could scarcely afford *not* to smoke. At the same time, women welcomed a good deal of the new aesthetic, weaving it into a redefined modernist "look." In contrast to the often-stated and oversimplified position implying that women were duped into smoking by tobacco companies and advertising firms, I am arguing that women subjugated and shaped themselves as empowered subjects (in relation to patriarchal hegemony, among other forces) through using the cigarette.

Joan Jacobs Brumberg has asserted that during the 1920s, cultural prescriptions for young women were moving from an emphasis on "good works," as had prevailed in the nineteenth century, to "good looks" in the twentieth.[7] The hallmark of this "first modern generation,"[8] as Cynthia Comacchio terms youths of the 1920s, was an emphasis on visual bodily features, including unpocked, clear skin, shiny hair, and importantly, a slender profile. Nancy Bowman notes that the uncoupling of appearance and moral worth during and after the First World War permitted new definitions of beauty to emerge in North American society. Best of all, this beauty could be purchased if the young woman were a sophisticated enough consumer of the new products. Henceforth, beauty was marketed as truly only skin-deep but also as attainable by any woman prepared to work hard on her most important project, herself.[9]

Smoking helped women to control their appearance and the image they projected in a number of ways. In addition to weight control, the act of lighting up and holding the cigarette aloft drew public attention to the carefully made-up face and manicured hands, with the exhaled smoke softening the facial contour and making it appear younger. In the crowded and noisy public arena of the classroom or workplace, attention could be captured through wordless performance, telegraphing as well sexual allure or worldly sophistication without the need to "find the right words." Thus, women's appearance was important not only to demonstrate a personal station in life, and implicitly that of one's family as well, but as a visual marker for women's very identity.

Visual identity formation was closely associated with the broader set of social values born in the interwar period. Smoking advertisements promoted the "cult of personality" of celebrities, portraying stars as if they were personal friends of the observer.[10] Personal appearance, a woman's home, her personal space in the workplace, and any other controlled environment allowed women to telegraph a given identity, altering it as she chose through visual details. By controlling her environment and herself, the woman could hope to produce the "social magic" that would help constitute that nascent identity. A cigarette was but one of many objects a woman might adopt to support her visual identity. It was one imbued with powerful symbolic referents because of its shady past and its present possibilities.

The "woman as consumer" identity was set out in didactic visual panels, such as the Winchester Girl shown in figure 7.1, and also through entertaining self-help articles in women's magazines and in fiction from the 1920s. Susan Ertz's best-selling novel *Madame Claire*, published in 1923, is a case in point.[11] As Mary Vipond notes in her survey of popular novels in English Canada during the 1920s, the book industry helped to spread mass culture through reprints of popular American and British works, such as Ertz's and the many books written by Frances Hodgson Burnett. Rental or lending libraries in bookstores and American institutions like the Book-of-the-Month Club placed novels of this type fairly readily in the hands of women, especially those with modest means.[12]

Ertz's central character, Madame Claire, is the elderly, gracious, and improbably wise matriarch of a large upper-middle-class English family. The widow of a former ambassador, she lives well in a London hotel suite, attended by a loyal maid and by a large, troubled family intended to represent many of the new century's flashpoints. Most problematic by far is Madame Claire's daughter, Connie, a faded beauty fatally attracted to abusive, charming, and glossy men who woo her, take her money, and leave her for a younger version of herself.

Of all the women in Ertz's novel, Connie alone smokes, and she smokes a great deal: perfumed cigarettes in public places. Despite the difficulties Connie causes for her family and indeed for herself, she has lived an undeniably exciting life as a "New Woman" in which she has purchased happiness, or as close as she can come to it. Connie is introduced to the reader through her visual qualities: "She had the prettiest and weakest mouth, and the most irresistible blue eyes that ever gave delight to a painter of pretty women ... She had a very small share of wit, but with women like Connie, a little wit goes a long way."[13] She values "allure" and "magnetism" in all of her relationships, dresses beyond her means, and spends most of her time seeking happiness. "[A]t any rate, I have lived," she notes reflectively to her brother, who has come yet again to rescue her. "Lived!" he retorts. "You surely don't call that living? Junketing around Europe with a lot of bounders!"[14] But Connie favours this upscale life to the one lived by her mother, holding to the old code of maternal order and duty.

Connie is not the only model for young womanhood provided by Ertz in her novel, however. Madame Claire's granddaughter, Judy, offers another and presumably even more modern image of independent womanhood. She "sometimes wakes at night in a sort of fever, hagridden by the thought that she may have made a mess of her life by not marrying this man or that, fearful that she may never meet the right one at all, hating the thought of spinsterhood, and, she says, seeing nothing else for it."[15] Judy has a mind of her own and refuses to conform in many ways: "I shall begin signing myself, 'Judy Pendleton, V.F.C. Virgin From Choice.' Doesn't it sound charming?"[16] Still, Judy eschews smoking. Her independence is telegraphed through a variety of activities that just border on the "unrespectable" but are made acceptable by her good heart, stability, and generosity. Needless to say, Judy is young, pretty, and thin. However, she rejects the consumer code of buying her way to prominence.

The cigarette in this fiction not only supported the new code for women, it also telegraphed a certain danger to the user. Before the Second World War, smoking could mark a woman as superficial and vain, just as it did poor Connie. At the same time, the cigarette could help a woman of substance fashion a modern image if it were employed carefully. In Ertz's study, Judy is presented as a tentative character, wracked by doubts and insecurities, treading that fine line of respectability. Many women reading Ertz's novel would have found it easier to identify with Connie, the "good-time girl," than with her more sturdy niece. They would likely have worried that the natural flaws and aging of the body would gain ascendancy unless they actively fought the process. This was a new interpretation of the work ethic: to "manage" the body and face by manipulating perceptions of the visual or to face dire consequences.

The code of bodily management was also an expression of how the urbanized woman should be distinguished from her country cousin, because since 1921 more than half the Canadian population lived in urban settings. The urban woman was abjured to deny the "natural" processes of aging, processes that rural women were thought to be content with because of their closer proximity to the land. The city woman, more often in the paid workforce, was expected to remake her appearance as a statement about the changing and managed "public face" of women. It was the urban woman who represented modernity in her role as the discerning consumer of products and as one who took her pleasures where she made them. One such pleasure was smoking.

The Flawed Body

Women were repeatedly warned about their bodies' multiple imperfections through the magazines they consulted, the fiction they read, and the movies they watched. The female consumer was informed that virtually every part of the typical woman's body needed expert intervention if she were not to be shunned by friends and sweethearts, lose jobs, and be

7.2 | *Chatelaine* Service Bulletins on Beauty Culture, 1936

ashamed of herself for her slovenly appearance. The 1930s solution to deal with the body's many shortcomings was found in the "Beauty Culture" movement.

A variety of Canadian social arbiters offered advice and instruction on Beauty Culture. For example, *Chatelaine* magazine produced a series of booklets, all authored by the mysterious "beauty editor" (see figure 7.2). The message in them was that maintaining an acceptable standard of beauty required hard work and discipline. This was said to be particularly so with the challenges of aging. Women were warned that once the body had been "let go," all manner of serious and sometimes permanent maladies resulted, with the woman's appearance serving as a barometer of her general health. The complexion was said to be naturally "muddy," and hands were unsightly without the proper cream; nails could easily become jagged unless professionally manicured. Drab hair was an embarrassment, and most important of all, faces required the right cosmetic enhancements, expertly applied. Cosmetics from such firms as Helena Rubenstein and Max Factor proliferated in the interwar period.[17] They, and others, developed formulations for women with different skin types and of varying ages, selling them in department stores and beauty parlours.

"Beauty Culture" has been defined by Kathy Peiss as "a system of meaning that helped women navigate the changing conditions of modern social experience."[18] One modern experience that women needed to learn in order to survive in the workplace, domestic zone, or social world was the newly ascribed importance of a woman's appearance. From her choice and condition of clothing, the degree and kind of makeup, and her choice of other personal adornments, a woman was to fashion her identity through her appearance. Part of this system of meaning of beauty culture involved when, how, and with whom a woman should smoke, how she was to negotiate the paraphernalia that accompanied smoking, and what she said by way of explanation to her friends, family, and employers about this practice. Beauty culture was eventually formally taught through the curriculum by the 1930s (albeit without any instruction on smoking), but for women beyond their school years, informal instruction was necessary. It might be offered at the workplace, as was the case for employees of the Maidenform Undergarment Company,[19] or through popular literature.

Magazine advertisements alleged that women's bodily flaws arose through lack of cleanliness. A dizzying range of products were offered so that women would not suffer the humiliation of losing their natural beauty through careless disregard for teeth; for an example, see figure 7.3. A full-page advertisement for Forhan tooth powder in 1932 shows a man too distraught to draw on his pipe. Impeccably turned out himself, this man would naturally favour a beautiful partner with flawless teeth. It seems that this was the case before pyorrhea loosened her teeth, causing them to fall out. The cause? Sloppy teeth-cleaning. "Lost teeth are a source of mental anguish. Even after they are skilfully replaced, the experience leaves a scar on the memory" as it seems certain will be the case with this man, suffering so visibly. We never see the woman. Is she too frightening to be pictured, or is the aim that every woman "see" herself in that position, bringing pain and sadness to her husband through this shameful neglect of her mouth?

Short of falling out, teeth might cause distress because of their less than sparkling colour, directly denoting poor oral practices. Keeping one's teeth for life was still a rather new notion in many parts of Canada in the interwar period. It had only been a few decades earlier that children's oral health became part of public health campaigns waged in schools and in the community, especially among the poor (see figure 4.2). Convincing women that one essential mark of beauty was to maintain white teeth, thereby reducing rot and gum problems, was accomplished largely

7.3 | Magazine advertisement for Forhan tooth powder, *Chatelaine*, 1932

through women's and family magazines. Discolouration was the simplest problem for a woman to solve. An advertisement in *Maclean's* in 1926 assured women that "the social handicap of 'off-color teeth'" need not worry them, since Pepsodent was "different in formula action and effect from any other known." Both a male and a female figure are shown in the advertisement, and yet the tag-line of "She has overcome the social handicap of 'off-color' teeth" clearly refers only to the woman, and a young woman at that. Of course, one way by which teeth become discoloured is smoking. Thus, the appeal could easily be to smokers, but it need not have this referent to bring terror to any woman's heart.

But producers like Pepsodent did not confine their advertising claims to new and improved scientific formulae to capture their share of the teeth-cleaning public. Pepsodent also made the older formula tooth powder, claiming the same miraculous effects, and promising that romance would be assured through the "come-closer smile" that was the product's chief reward. To imbue this product with the same impressive scientific claims, the tooth powder is said to contain an ingredient called "Irium." In the late 1930s advertisement shown in figure 7.4, one young woman catches our attention by using a new, slightly abrasive colloquialism that seems out of place in a discussion of tooth powders. The challenging "Oh yeah?" is meant to attract the attention of youths who had adopted the phrase as their own even if they had not also adopted the tooth powder. The text belies the easy and casual visual camaraderie of the two women; it lays bare the intense competition many women were meant to feel, socially and in the workplace. "Have you ever envied some one who has a 'Come-Closer' smile?" it asks suggestively. "You know, that sort of irresistible, sparkling smile that just naturally *zooms up* a person's rating right to the top." Apparently, whether women realized it not, they are being compared to every other woman and rated. Those without sparkling teeth, polished "to dazzling natural brilliance in record time!" stood little chance in the race for acceptance. In this context, the initial aggressive catch-line of "Oh yeah?" takes on new meaning.

Of all cosmetics produced to "improve" women's appearances in the interwar period, none matched the advertising rates or sales figures of facial creams. Facial creams existed long before the 1920s but as medicinal formulations that drew on traditional recipes of rendered products. They occupied much the same field as toiletries and other over-the-counter remedies in the pre-war period. Estée Lauder's

7.4 | Magazine advertisement for Pepsodent tooth powder, *The Star Weekly*, 1939

uncle, from whom she learned the basic formulations for her creams, sold a "six-in-one cold cream, Dr. Schlotz Viennese Cream, Flory Anna's Eczema Ointment, poultry lice killer, dog mange cure, embalming fluid, and Hungarian Moustache Wax"[20] before the First World War. The new facial products were promoted on placards, in women's and family magazines, and by word of mouth, and they were meant only for a woman's delicate face, not to kill poultry lice as well.

99 *out of* "DIRTY FACE"
100 *have*

Think of it! Only one face in a hundred as lovely as nature intended it should be. Only one skin in a hundred is really clean. And that skin is the one which stays young. Entrancing. Winning in its beauty.

Avoid 'Dirty Face' with Daggett & Ramsdell's two creams. Every store carries them. They are made of the finest ingredients that money can buy. And they don't cost a fortune, either. Just a few cents a day to keep your skin naturally smooth, soft and fresh. Surely a youthful skin is worth that, isn't it?

● EVERY NIGHT use Perfect Cold Cream liberally to get rid of below-the-surface dirt. This marvelous cream provides the essentials every skin must have—lubrication, moisture, protection. Three groups of special ingredients supply them, all balanced properly of course. Famous for more than 40 years.

● DURING THE DAY whenever your skin needs freshening, cleanse it quickly with the new Perfect Cleansing Cream (liquefying). Melts instantly upon application, its fine oils cleanse in half the usual time.

DAGGETT & RAMSDELL
Daggett & Ramsdell (Canada) Limited

7.5 | Magazine advertisement for Daggett & Ramsdell, *Canadian Home Journal*, 1932

With the far greater emphasis on a woman's appearance after the First World War and the possibility of visual reinvention, facial creams came to share more common ground with facial colourings like rouge, lipstick, eye shadow, facial bleaches, and mascara than with medicinal products. The new-age purveyors of "improved" creams in stylish bottles also vastly expanded the advertising range for these products. Magazine advertisements were maintained, but added to them were billboards, handbills, radio ads, and beauty shop and department-store displays. New strategies were developed to market the creams, including the personal consultation and, later, the gift-with-purchase.

In Canadian women's magazines, facial cream was presented as one way to keep the face "clean" by using "cold cream" formulations. For instance, Daggett and Ramsdell produced two creams to avoid the horrifying condition of "Dirty Face," as decried in figure 7.5. Whether or not consumers actually believed this statistic, for which no reference is offered, they would not miss the significance of having facial skin that is "really clean," for clean skin is "the one which stays young. Entrancing. Winning in its beauty." Women would not have missed the promise that creamed skin stays "naturally smooth, soft and fresh." It seems that in order for either skin or teeth to be "natural," they must receive a great deal of attention, especially if the woman in question was also a smoker. The premature aging of the skin would have worried the woman smoker with the advertising emphasis on unlined and youthful skin. As with most facial cream advertisements of the era, science is invoked to prove the claims. "Three groups of special ingredients supply them, all balanced properly of course." It thus demands a formal regime to maintain it: one cold cream at night, another during the day. Without this, the woman faces the possibility of presenting a dirty face to the world, sealing her own failure.

The greatest failing of women's unclean bodies, it was suggested through advertisements, were the odours they emitted. And bad odours drove men away. This threat of repelling others, especially desirable men, with unpleasant smells could be corrected with cleaning products. Women who smoked probably feared this shortcoming of their body and the consequent need to mask stale tobacco smells with something more feminine and pleasing. Women who didn't launder their clothing often enough were unacceptable wives, sentenced to the unhappiness of solitude. Joan (shown in figure 7.6) had not taken due care to "Avoid Offending" with her body odour, even though she seems obsessively concerned about meeting men. Once given clear directions by a kind girlfriend about the necessary nightly laundering of her "underthings," Joan is able to abandon her plan to snag a man by taking dancing lessons and works her magic on a former suitor. In this advertisement-strip, Joan is strongly supported by her nameless friend who educates her and then ensures that the man she lost by offending his sense of smell is re-invited to some social event so that Joan has a chance to win him back. We might conclude that the competition with other women is not woven into this advertisement were it not for the poisonous leading line, "– and I used to think she was a born old maid" and the catty and insidious whispering of the two women as they fix the now happy Joan in their gaze. There is no celebration of her good fortune, only a nasty reminder of the unacceptable woman she once was and the consensus that she had been considered unmarriageable material. Here we have a visual "collective gaze," personified by the two women in the image, to add credence to the enormity of Joan's failing before being saved by Lux soap.

7.6 | Magazine advertisement for Lux soap, *Chatelaine*, 1935

7.7 | Magazine advertisement for Lysol disinfectant, *The Star Weekly*, 1939

In the advertisement shown in figure 7.7, told from the point of view of the offending woman, we learn that body odours are so serious that they can undo a marriage. A dutiful wife, "a perfect housekeeper," "wonderful cook," and "ideal mother" finds her husband "indifferent" to her obvious pain and fears that another woman has come between them. Here, the odours seem to require a hygiene product to correct, a situation that remains in effect with women today, with their fear supporting a huge feminine hygiene industry. This advertisement from the popular *Star Weekly* from 1939 uses a technique similar to that of the previous one as the various phases of the woman's happy life and growing anxiety are presented to us visually and in chronological order. The difference here is that the artist's gaze is focused directly on the worried woman as if it were following her everywhere in her home. As the frames roll past, we can see her growing realization of the problem reflected in the woman's expression.

The "perfect housekeeper" is above reproach, we are shown, keeping her home tidy and "fragrantly clean." Even though the woman herself in this frame looks acceptable, we are alerted to some hidden failing to explain the screaming headline of "Another Woman" and "One Neglect" immediately above it on the larger frame. What could the error be, we wonder? Could it be her sloppy cooking? No, she is a "wonderful cook," serving meals which are "tempting," "dainty," and "piping hot." We might wonder for an instant at the value of a "dainty" meal for her growing son in the third frame and her hearty husband, whom we see in the fourth. That word seems out of place, usually associated with women's physical condition, and often cleanliness. We are encouraged to wonder if she is "dainty" in all of her hygiene habits. The "ideal mother" is defined mainly in terms of cleanliness, and here she passes the test. Her son is "always clean," "sweet," and "immaculately cared for," never "unkempt." By the fourth frame, our mother looks increasingly distraught, as does her husband. Perhaps he is the problem? The "neglect was on his side," we are told. She blames "another woman," apparently the "first and natural thought." This might have come as something of a surprise to *Star Weekly*'s family readers. A man's neglect is necessarily rooted in womanizing rather than in career problems, illness, depression? But even this "first and natural thought" turns out to be wrong. Our perfect housekeeper, cook, and mother fails as a perfect wife because she smells bad. The advertisement allows a bit of tolerance for our hapless wife, acknowledging in the bold left column that while this lapse is likely due to carelessness, it might be rooted in lack of information. Happily, Lysol will save her future and her self-respect. To bump up her knowledge on body odours, the conscientious woman should send for the free booklet produced by Lysol, *What Every Woman Should Know*.

The advertisements in family and women's magazines in the interwar period warned women about foul odours from their underarms, from their feet, and even from their skin generally, all of which could be remedied by anti-perspirants, foot powders, and perfumes. A woman's body was to be feared and distrusted, especially by its owner. To avoid the dreadful fates as set out for the reader in full visual horror, women were abjured to manage their bodies, to work hard on their appearance, and to beat out the female competition. Much of this could be accomplished by learning to smoke so as to improve a woman's visual capital. If in the process she fell victim to lined skin or tobacco odours, other consumer products would save the day.

The greatest fear of all lay ahead, however. Advertisements told women that aging accentuated all of the natural failings of a woman's body. To be smelly and old was almost too much to bear, requiring significant energy and consumer products by any woman trying to hold back the sands of time.

The Cult of Youth

Starting in the 1920s and continuing into the twenty-first century, advertisements, fiction, and movies all made it clear that old age was to be avoided or tricked through more consumer products. Women in their forties were thought to suffer morbidly from menopause and other ailments that drained energy from the system, making them prone to mysterious crying fits and depression. Lydia Pinkham's vegetable compound was offered, as was Fleischmann's Yeast and a range of other products to keep women looking younger longer. Most of these advertisements advised women that with aging, they would likely feel unwell. Suggestions were offered on how women could keep themselves "fit" to slow the degeneration. Becoming older was the equivalent of becoming ill, unless some advertised intervention saved the woman.[21]

Youthfulness was so important in a woman's personal and work life because it symbolized progress in a period of rapid change. One advertisement for the Dominion Life Assurance Company has office girls witnessing an older colleague, Miss Armour, fired purely for her advancing age. "Sorry, Miss Armour – but we must make way for younger girls." The text adds to the reader's anxiety about aging by having the young women locked in fearful, gossipy discussion (another example of a "collective gaze") just as their workmate must be in true distress with this heartless firing. The girls are brought to speculate on their own future by being asked in the text, "Will you be independent in later life? It will be time well spent if you send for our booklet."[22]

Anxiety about aging is explored in fiction of the period as well. Constance Kerr Sissons's short story "When a Girl's Thirty," which appeared in the New Year's Day 1926 issue of *MacLean's* magazine, examined the stunted expectations and relative unhappiness of both single men and women as they aged. Charlotte Glendon, a matronly and interfering busybody, regularly deplores the numbers of unmarried men and women in her town. In fact, talking about this problem constitutes Charlotte's "hobby." For some unfathomable reason, Charlotte is able to convince her weak-minded childhood friend, Hamilton Sanders (familiarly known as Ham Sandwich) to ask another long-standing single friend, a woman he has always greatly admired, to marry him. Neither Charlotte nor Ham expect Mabel Findlay to accept, but Charlotte argues that in this way, Mabel would be able to say to others that she had been asked at least once to marry but had refused. Ham is presented as a man without ambition or knowledge, a drifter through life, but as decent and kind. Given Charlotte's malicious suggestion, he is obviously also a man with little com-

"We have
our secrets
my perfume and I"
says JOAN BENNETT

"At first you think it's so naive . . . so
dryad-shy . . . discreet . . . my new perfume, Seventeen.

"But what that perfume knows of life. It
tells me the strangest things . . . hints at magic
. . . sings of Youth and its own allure . . .
invites me, dares me, lures me . . . on and on
. . . to lighter moods, to gayer talk, to thrilling living.

"My perfume asks so much of me! I just
can't disappoint it . . . I MUST be young
. . . and gay . . . forever!"

Seventeen Youth-
tone Rouge brings
elusive color tones
to your com-
plexion . . . Seven-
teen Face Powder
blends shades to
simulate the radi-
ance of youthful
skin . . . Also:
Seventeen Per-
fume, Dusting
Powder, Com-
pact, Brillantine,
Sachet, Toilet
Water.

Seventeen

1761

7.8 | Magazine advertisement for
Seventeen perfume, *Chatelaine*, 1931

mon sense or social awareness. Nevertheless, for this silly plot to make any sense at all, one must assume that an unmarried woman, even one of substance like Mabel Findlay, would be grateful for an excuse for her singlehood, especially as she reaches the advanced age of thirty. Mabel is presented as intellectually capable, community-minded, and active in sports. She also seems quite happy as she pursues graduate work in economics with a professor who becomes a mentor to both her and Ham. She is clearly the stronger of the two, and yet we are invited to worry about her future when she will stand old and alone.

Ham proposes, clumsily as one would expect; Mabel senses the game and unexpectedly accepts. Their mismatched relationship becomes the object of gossip, and yet the longer they spend in each other's presence, the better and happier each of them becomes. Ham is promoted as he studies to impress Mabel; she takes on less strident positions and is more patient with her inferiors, Ham included. Of course, they decide in the end to marry, having fallen in love through friendship and common interests. The message is clear: singlehood is fine for the young because they have so many other advantages on which to draw; however, it is to be avoided for women beyond thirty or for men beyond forty, such as Ham. The closer one moves to old age, this source argues, the weaker one becomes, and the more a marriage means to the partners. Becoming a couple requires accommodation on the part of both, and each is improved by the relationship. Neither Ham nor Mabel are presented as smart in a modern way, and neither participate in any of the new lifestyle options open to their generation – cars, nightclubs, drinking, or smoking. Those choices seem reserved for the young, single, and slender young folks around them.

The horrible fate of aging is discussed in such banal advertisements as one for Seventeen perfume (figure 7.8). This perfume is apparently imbued with magical qualities that hold back the aging process. It "sings of Youth and its own allure ... invites me, dares me, lures me ... on and on ... to lighter moods, to gayer talk, to thrilling living ... I MUST be young ... and gay ... forever!" Rarely does one find such a transparent fear of getting older.

The valorization of perpetual youth remains very much a characteristic of our current culture, with all of the demands placed on women in particular to hold back the effects of natural aging. As Rothman and Rothman set out for us in their analysis of the history of "medical enhancement," the ultimate promise to force time to stand still lay with cosmetic surgery whereby the body is literally resculpted to the owner's specifications.[23] Before such interventions were available, however, the bid to appear young, modern, and slender was often made in the form of becoming a smoker.

Women in the interwar period were pressured by popular culture into distrusting and even loathing their bodies. At the same time, however, they were active agents in this form of self-improvement. They accepted some products and rejected others. One product that they accepted with increasing enthusiasm was the cigarette, likely because of the range of uses to which it could be put to contest this restricted definition of modernist beauty. By smoking and posturing with the cigarette, cigarette holder, or any other smoking paraphernalia, women took back a measure of their agency in deciding how they would present themselves as modern actors.

Slenderizing the Feminine

Part of the control that women imposed on their bodies involved the body's weight. The pressure to be slender became one standard of acceptability among many for the public woman, as is still the case,[24] and it was a standard that could be more easily reached through smoking. If women could not hold back time and avoid wrinkles and grey hair, they could at least remain thin, or become thin if they had put on weight through negligence. "Every woman's ideal figure is slim, with curves in proper places," began an article on "Those Pampered Bulges" in *Chatelaine*. "Romantic poets, sweet tenors, and smart illustrators sing the slender, rightly proportioned model: the middle age spread is immortalized only in the funny pages; even the corset company publishes booklets on how to avoid unlovely sagging and pampered bulges after thirty." *Even* the corset company?

as GOOD . .
as it is
Beautiful

QUALITY
CONTROLLED

"UTTERLY lovely!" You'll say when you
look at "Quality Controlled" Rayon.
"Such softness of texture, such delicate colouring, such richness of fabric."

And, what a joy to know that with this love-
liness goes complete assurance of quality and
satisfaction.

For, Courtaulds, Canada's largest manufacturers
of rayon yarns, have now combined with Canada's leading underwear houses to give you
exquisite rayon knit underthings, lovely and
durable as to fabric, perfect as to garment cut,
fit and wear. Each dainty garment clearly
marked, for your protection, with Courtaulds
"Quality Controlled" label. Look for this
label and you can buy with confidence.

**Courtaulds "Quality Controlled"
Label Means**

1 That every detail from yarn to finished garment con-
forms to rigid quality specifications established for
your protection by the Ontario Research Foundation.

2 That the yarn is Courtaulds Mattesozu, the finest and
strongest viscose rayon known, assuring fabrics
soft in texture and permanently lustrous in colouring.

3 That fabrics are strength tested . . firmly and evenly
knit . . . will wash perfectly with ordinary precau-
tions and iron at ordinary temperatures without marking.

4 That each garment is correctly sized . . . cut to
full standard measurements . . . expertly tailored
and finished.

COURTAULDS (CANADA) LIMITED; Head Office and
Plant, Cornwall, Ontario; Sales Offices, 159 Bay St., Toronto; Trade Service Offices, University Tower, Montreal.

COURTAULDS
Quality Controlled
RAYON

7.9 | Magazine advertisement for
Courtaulds Rayon, *Canadian Home
Journal*, 1934

According to popular magazines of the time, what caused this weight gain? "[S]itting, sitting, sitting, too much food of the wrong kind at the wrong time, lack of complete exercise, shallow breathing, labor saving devices" were all to blame. In other words, laziness and prosperity were at the root of the problem.[25] In fact, the young women used in advertisements generally were remarkably thin, even boyish, as in the one for Courtaulds Rayon shown in figure 7.9. Should a prospective customer not look like the very thin woman in the illustration, she would be comforted to know that "each garment is correctly sized ... cut to the full standard measurements ... expertly tailored and finished." Thus, a full-figured woman could expect to be fitted properly with a Courtaulds garment. Alternatively, she could lose weight through smoking or dieting or both.

Styles of the interwar period did not help the full-figured woman. Diaphanous fabrics and undergarments were less restrictive than their counterparts in the pre-war era but also less helpful in camouflaging a plump figure. Thus, starting in the 1920s, weight control took on a new urgency for all women, especially for those in the public gaze. Images of feminine beauty presented to consumers during this period all emphasize thin waists and often straight-line "flapper" thinness for the whole physique, as can be seen with the Courtaulds model.

The prescriptive codes for women to remain forever young, with a perfectly maintained and slender body, were embodied in the interwar period by screen starlets. In women's magazines, screen magazines, and in the movies themselves, women could watch, and re-watch repeatedly if they chose, the stars on whom they could model their own visual identities. They might choose as visual mentor a pol-

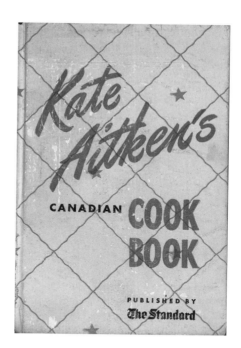

7.10 | *Kate Aitken's Canadian Cook Book*, 1945

ished, aristocratic pose such as offered by the English actress Anne Grey. If something racier was sought, a Greta Garbo or a Carole Lombard might be mimicked, or Rita Hayward after the Second World War. Readers of movie magazines would have learned that Greta Garbo, fresh from her triumph in *The Torrent* (1925) was reportedly warned by Louis B. Mayer on her introduction to the American cinema business that "American men don't like fat women." Preparing for her new role in *Flesh and the Devil* (1927), Garbo, a heavy smoker, promptly lost weight,[26] partly by replacing food with cigarettes.

Of course, the aesthetic of slimness did not end with the Second World War. Despite the "hourglass" figure celebrated during the 1950s, the demand to be thin remained. Canada's broadcasting maven of the 1950s, Kate Aitken, could counsel her huge female listening audience for "Your Good Neighbour" program on CFRB Radio to cook healthy meals for the family using her sponsor's product, Good Luck Margarine.[27] She offered women a double message: construct elaborate and fattening desserts, using recipes from her own cookbook (figure 7.10), while at the same time remaining slender and attending to just the right makeup for their colouring in her other book of the 1950s, *Lovely You: A Blueprint for Beauty*. Importantly, Aitken was selling her fans the prescription of "illusion," not reality.

Despite Aitken's middle age and less than glamorous appearance, the models for her advice were young, beautiful, and slender. In their off-hours, one would not be surprised to see them smoking. Certainly, Kate Aitken was never shown as a smoker, nor did she suggest that women do so, but she did support the slenderizing of Canadian women. Those who found it difficult to take off those pesky pounds or who needed instruction in the latest cosmetics and inspired primping could go to Kate Aitken's personal spa, opened in the early 1950s.[28]

By that time, however, the connection between smoking and cancers of various types was more widely accepted, and convincing new clients to take up smoking was more and more challenging. In 1953, *Business Week* reported a "widespread fear" about the effects of smoking, profiling an advertisement by Philip Morris with the header, "The cigarette that takes the *FEAR* out of smoking!"[29] Without actually using the word "cancer," the advertisement claimed that the cigarettes used an ingredient called "Di-GI," or di-ethylene glycol, because it "does not produce irritating vapors present in every other leading cigarette." The US Federal Trade Commission had contested this claim in 1952 when it ordered Philip Morris to stop making the unfounded claims and to desist in disparaging other cigarettes. However, since the order had not been finalized, Philip Morris continued to advertise with the spurious product claims. By 1955, there were enough reports linking "excessive smoking" to lung and other cancers to have a clear effect on American smoking rates. The Canadian *Monetary Times* reported that American smoking figures had fallen 10 per cent in 1954 over their 1953 rates, while Canadian consumption had jumped 7.2 per cent in the same period. At least some of this increase was ascribed to women smoking more heavily during the 1950s.[30]

In the 1960s, movie stars continued to be prime models for Canadian women in their search for youthfulness, slenderness, and air-brushed beauty. One of the top-grossing movies of 1961, *Breakfast at Tiffany's*, featured all of these characteristics in Audrey Hepburn's Holly Golightly. In figure 7.11 we see the sheet music cover for "Moon River," the song by Johnny Mercer and Henry Mancini that came to orally identify *Breakfast at Tiffany's.* Holly's slender profile, as displayed here, is further exaggerated by the outlandish length of the cigarette holder. Her form-fitting black dress and long black gloves further slenderize her figure. In case we have missed Holly's attractive characteristics, these are helpfully listed on the cover: "extraordinary" and "glamorous. The image was not sold as attainable only by gorgeous film stars, playing as she was at being a call-girl. It was worked and reworked by advertisers to make it appear accessible to young women everywhere, with smoking seeming to slenderize them.

7.11 | "Moon River"
sheet music cover, 1961.
© Redferns/Getty Image
89740662

Cigarette advertisements told young women that extreme thinness could be obtained through smoking. The fresh-faced beauties presented as smokers promised social acceptability whereby handsome young men, themselves smokers, would also be theirs.

Thus, the cigarette became popular for women at a time when consumer culture first trumpeted the necessity of remaining ever young, slender as a pre-adolescent, and without any bodily flaws. As the twentieth century progressed, this unforgiving standard for women did not relax. The literature on "girl culture" suggests that if anything, the bar for young women has been raised. Mitchell and Reid-Walsh argue that even women in their thirties now struggle to be considered "girls," embarking on unrealistic and demanding programs of fitness/slenderness, personal style choices, and language use. They name this pilgrimage for all things youthful a "reconstruction of youth."[31] Unless we are able to address such disabling imagery in the society at large, one cannot reasonably blame young women for finding substances like cigarettes to help them achieve this aesthetic.

8

In the Workplace

Women who spent a good deal of their time in public spaces were the first to be documented as smokers. From the nineteenth century, this included women of the demimonde who lived much of their lives on the street, some labourers, and elite women searching for rituals to set them apart. By the twentieth century, the group of women smokers had been expanded through significant numbers of women engaging in waged work. As described in this chapter, some waged women before the Second World War could not legally smoke on the job. However, war work bestowed respect on the woman worker, and the opportunities to share a cigarette with co-workers and friends were greatly extended. Because of this, women had access to a broader range of visual identities, many of which involved smoking. The freedom to smoke remained a feature of the workplace until the 1980s, when public space for smokers of either sex was again restricted. In the nineteenth century, smoking had been defined as a moral issue through the temperance movement; by the last decades of the twentieth century, it was again moralized, this time by health and anti-smoking advocates.

Canadian women first worked for wages outside the home in any numbers during the period of industrial capitalism, starting in the 1880s. The period of a woman's life when she was most likely to be a waged labourer was after she had completed formal schooling, if she were lucky enough to have had schooling at all, and before she married. Girls joined brothers and fathers in bringing home wages, which were commonly pooled. Women were offered the least skilled jobs, were paid about half as much

8.1 | Dr Mary Percy Jackson feeding bear cub, Alberta, 1929

as similarly skilled males, and were neither welcomed nor protected by their male co-workers.[1] The justification for underpaying women was the ideal of the "family wage," the notion that working-class men should be able to support families on their wages alone. As a middle-class model, it eventually became the societal standard. The vulnerability of women who were not supported by their families – "women adrift" – and who depended on their own meagre wages as they aged must have been terrifying. Unions in this period had little interest in women's particular needs or plight. Such women would have been constrained in any barely respectable habits, such as smoking.

By the 1920s, the archetypal public woman smoker was one who was employed with enough freedom to act as she chose. Dr Mary Percy Jackson, a British immigrant and adventurer, was part of the elite group of salaried women who smoked openly. Women medical doctors were often portrayed as smokers in fiction, representing one of the few acknowledged elite groups in Canadian society.[2] In figure 8.1, a photograph of Dr Jackson with a cigarette propped in her mouth while feeding a bear cub on the Alberta frontier in 1929, one can immediately detect a fiercely independent woman who was conscious of the effect of her behaviour on those around her. Even in these early days of women's public smoking, Dr Jackson chose an unconventional pose for her cigarette. Instead of poising the cigarette daintily between her fore and third fingers, she holds it between her lips in a classic masculine manner. What statement is she making in this seemingly candid photograph? As the local "can-do" woman doctor in the masculine space of the frontier, Mary Jackson might be emulating male smoking norms in order to reinforce her authority in that community. The feeding of the bear cub – an admittedly dangerous act – might have encouraged this display of bravado with the cigarette. In any case, Dr Jackson is visually announcing her control of the scene.

A 1927 graduate of the University of Birmingham with degrees in surgery and medicine, Mary Percy Jackson answered an advertisement urging women doctors to emigrate to Alberta.[3] She was assigned to the Battle River area and travelled on horseback to provide medical care to five generations of Peace River residents – First Nations, Métis, and racialized whites – for more than 45 years. Her duties typically included setting broken bones, delivering babies, treating dysentery, pneumonia, smallpox, scarlet fever, and tuberculosis, as well as extracting teeth, since there was no dentist in the area. On occasion, she also acted as a veterinarian. In the winter of 1952–53, for example, she helped combat an outbreak of rabies, spread from foxes and wolves to sled dogs in the northern community of Keg River. This was the community where she settled after marrying a widower with three children in 1931. The area was terrorized all through the winter by rabid wolves and foxes. The disease then moved on to domestic animals. Hundreds of cows, horses, pigs, dogs, and cats died or were put down.[4] Since she was a lover of animals of all kinds, the outbreak was upsetting for "Doc," as she was known throughout the district.

Dr Jackson was undoubtedly a privileged citizen with considerable personal freedom, but she was also a salaried government employee and then an independent general practitioner and rancher. She remained in the same region for the rest of her life, raising her family and continuing to provide medical services. Dr Jackson was like many women workers of her era, announcing her strength of personality partly through her use of the cigarette as prop. In these respects, she is representative of the working women who smoked and who are profiled in this chapter.

The courting and representation of female waged and salaried workers is one focus of this chapter. In many jobs, evidence of smoking would have resulted in firing. Women working as domestic servants are therefore not included here, nor are those working directly with young children as teachers. These occupations either specifically forbade women from smoking or strongly discouraged it through workplace norms, since they were grounded in nineteenth-century notions of purity, which smoking or drinking compromised.[5] On the other hand, secondary school teaching harboured enough smokers in the later period to command rooms specially for this purpose in schools.

It is not coincidental that women's smoking paralleled their gaining the federal vote at the start of this period, their greater social independence, and the continued opportunity for all-women groupings through membership in clubs. In some urban areas, night clubs beckoned the working woman. Women played team sports from the 1920s, giving them more scope for social interaction.[6] The affordability of cars allowed women an even greater range of social events beyond the prying eyes of chaperones. Far from being the simple dupes of tobacco advertisers, women used smoking – and use it still – as a means of social facilitation and social exchange. Moreover, the act of smoking and the settings in which it occurred signalled growing public autonomy and power.

By the interwar period, women engaged in clerical or service occupations were also constructing a public persona for the workplace in ways never required for more cloistered paid work in the past. In the early 1920s, most of these women were single, since postwar legislation in 1921 dramatically narrowed the possibilities of waged work for married women.[7] In 1931, the first year that statistics were kept, only 3 per cent of married women were engaged in paid labour.[8] Apart from during the exceptional period of the Second World War, work for married women was frowned upon and in some places disallowed. This remained the case in some professions after the war.[9] However, married women's participation in paid work increased rapidly after 1951.[10] By 1991, married women represented 61.4 per cent of the women's sector of the labour force.[11] The majority of the married women who worked were young in the period before the Second World War but older after 1970.[12] Not until the 1960s, with the effects of second-wave feminism, did the female workforce begin to age.

By no means all waged or salaried women smoked. In fact, from the scanty data available to us, it seems that many waged women rejected public smoking in Canada before the Second World War, and for good reason. The act of smoking in public could endanger the waged and personal position of a woman who needed to please her employer but lacked the privileged position of a medical doctor like Mary Percy Jackson or that of a middle-class woman who did not depend on her wages. The cultural framework within which women's long romance with smoking was born suggests that while smoking did telegraph women's growing assertiveness from the 1920s, the act also placed a woman in social jeopardy, hinting at ruin if smoking were not used in the right places and in the right ways. As the working woman became a fixture in offices across Canada, she was subject to an increasingly restrictive social code.

Smoking was long known to carry health risks, as discussed in chapters 1 and 2. The assumption that smoking caused damage to both physical and moral health held even greater fears for the young woman smoker than for the male. Since women were assumed to be more delicate of nature and bodily constitution than men, as well as more pure of nature (but with a disturbing tendency to "fall" into sin and addictions very easily),[13] there was much worry about the woman smoker's moral peril and the ruinous effect her fall would have on society.

For the working woman, then, smoking offered both pleasure *and* danger.[14] It presented a means for young women to act out their fantasies around new consumer-based norms of overt sexuality,[15] sophistication, and slimness,[16] as shown to such women on the wide screen of the cinema. Despite the many concerns associated with smoking, the waged woman seemed an ideal host for the development of the new daring social ritual. The waged female worker was a growing sector of the female population; she had disposable cash and a need to develop her own customs for a new age. Encompassed within this demographic group of smokers were both line workers and the newly minted professionals of such rising occupations as social work and dietetics.

Waged Women Smokers in the Interwar Period

Between the wars, Canadian waged women often took pains to hide their smoking. Penny Tinkler confirms that the same concern governed female smokers in Britain in this period, with rare displays of public smoking confined to upper- and middle-class women.[17] Tinkler notes that in this period, factory girls favoured small cigarettes called "brownies," sold in packages of three, and that domestic servants were also known to smoke.[18] In Canada, the influence of temperance remained strong longer than it did in Britain. Smoking would have been more than adequate as a reason for the dismissal of a domestic servant. There is also no evidence that any particular types of cigarettes, "brownies" or otherwise, were marketed to working women in Canada. Until the introduction of the various extra-long "slim" cigarettes in the 1960s, tobacco marketers did not introduce cigarettes for the woman's market only.[19]

Beyond this, however, there is much about the experience of smoking for waged, salaried, or professional women in the past that we still do not know.[20] We have only general estimates of how much tobacco the typical female smoker consumed before formal records were maintained in the mid-1960s. And yet the cultural depiction of the working woman smoker is rich in this period, providing evidence of great public interest in and general support for the woman smoker.

The woman worker who smoked was often represented in the interwar period in family and women's magazines, in newspapers, in advice literature and medical commentary, on billboard advertising, on street-level advertisements, and in material culture, including clothing, accessories, and decorative objects. She was also found in the newly developing film industry through American and European film stars and watched avidly by Canadian women. Smoking was portrayed in the pages of popular novels and in the pulp fiction industry. Diary accounts give us insights into how working women lived their lives and of the role of smoking and drinking within that developing culture. Oral histories collected with women who came to maturity during this period demonstrate that powerful messages found their way through popular culture into waged women's consciousness.

Norms that increasingly accepted women's smoking were all developing against a backdrop of the negative nineteenth-century anti-smoking advice literature for serious young women, as described in chapter 2. Despite widespread assumptions in the literature then and since that the anti-cigarette message had been blown away by the Roaring Twenties and the image of the Modern Girl, arguments from this older prescriptive code remained very much in the public mind, especially as they applied to waged women.[21]

We must make some educated guesses about what waged women read for instruction and leisure between the wars and later. There were no labelled "working women's magazines" in Canada; in fact, the two most popular women's magazines of the era were *Chatelaine*, introduced in March 1928, and the *Canadian Home Journal*, founded in 1910.[22] Both have been used here intensively because of their low subscription and counter costs (among the lowest of Canadian subscription rates at no more than $1 yearly through to the end of the 1930s) and their large circulation numbers. These figures suggest that waged women in both line jobs and professional positions, along with middle-class women, read these magazines for pleasure and instruction. Certainly, both magazines aimed to capture waged women in their readership.[23] In postwar Canada, waged women seem to have read many of the same magazines as their middle-class sisters, with the important inclusion of movie star and "true confessions" magazines.[24] Cigarette advertisements first appeared in both of these women's periodicals in the 1920s.

The Business and Professional Woman also existed from 1930, the official journal of the Canadian Federation of Business and Professional Women.[25] Offering reports from its local organizations in such places as Brandon, Saint John, and Ottawa, from its national executive, and from its annual conventions, the journal aimed to place political pressure on legislators on behalf of employed professional women and provide diverting and instructive activities for the working woman's leisure hours. From April 1932 onwards, it carried the advertisements of life insurance dealers, suitcase manufacturers, vacation sites and respectable hotels for business travel, "gasolene stations," and beauty products, including slimming corsets. At once conservative in social policy and radical in its support for the international peace process and disarmament, The Business and Professional Woman began to carry cigarette advertising in March 1933.[26] Pulp fiction such as detective stories were also probably enjoyed by waged women in households where men had subscriptions.[27] They featured cigarette advertisements from the late 1920s.

To be a waged woman before the Second World War did not necessarily place one in the working class in cultural terms, although this would usually have been the case. Dr Jackson exemplified the exception. In 1921, about 19 per cent of salaried women were classified as professionals and about 15.3 per cent by 1941.[28] About half of women engaged in waged labour between 1921 and 1941 worked in clerical, trade, transportation, and manufacturing jobs.

In contrast to women's paid work experience in the 1880s and 1890s, far larger percentages of the workforce in the interwar years were machine operators of some kind.[29] Thus, throughout this period line workers and professionals between them constituted approximately 61 to 68 per cent of female waged workers. Armed with disposable income, however scanty, they were the waged and salaried women who were targeted by cigarette advertisers, and they figure prominently in popular representations of smoking.

Many female waged workers were particularly vulnerable between the wars. Commentary from the period, including a 1926 column in MacLean's by the temperance activist and author Nellie McClung, testifies to the many biases that kept the working woman alert to being undermined. She noted that "[t]he emancipations of women came with the typewriter and the introduction of electricity to the home, and to-day the trade winds have carried her a long way on the road to self-determination. But these same winds, strong as they are, have not entirely blown away all the prejudices that have grown up around women during the long years of their economic dependence."[30]

Another important prescriptive source for women searching for modern personae was short fiction in women's magazines. In 1930, *Chatelaine* offered a profile of Jacqueline Dent in "You Can't Love the Boss."[31] Miss Dent represents both the line worker through her past and the professional or employer sector in her current position. She could easily have been a subscriber to *The Business and Professional Woman*. She is portrayed as coldly efficient, cutthroat in her negotiations with suppliers for her perfume distribution firm, and dismissive of her male underlings, who occupy all the positions in her office from secretary to salesmen. "[H]ow simple were men," she muses. "All day long in the secluded sanctum of her office Jacqueline Dent talked with them, outwitted them, struggled with them, and almost always overcame them." That Harvey Stewart, sales manager, acknowledges that there "was something unnatural about having a girl for a boss" indicates the knife-edge on which Miss Dent is poised as a female employer. But Harvey has a problem too as far as Jacqueline Dent is concerned: he is too much the gentleman, too reserved for modern commerce. For some unexplained reason, Jacqueline sets out to lure Harvey to kiss her. She invites him to dinner, then brings him back to her grand residence, slipping into something "a little less formal" soon afterwards, and encourages him to join her in smoking. Miss Dent's breaking of conventions in which she courts her underling, bringing him to her residence in a display of sexual availability, and completes the performance by inviting him to join her in smoking, clearly unhinges the victim. "He fumbled with a match, and gave her a light. Over the top of the flame her eyes met his. They were assured, confident, unembarrassed."[32] Or so they seemed at least. The profile drawn here could be illustrated by Marlene Dietrich, Mae West, or any of a number of other cinema stars. They dance, they embrace, and then suddenly Jacqueline becomes enraged. Jacqueline is drawn as a conflicted personality who has confused unbridled sexuality with power. Ignoring the still-intact requirements of respectability, she is made to appear hysterical, manipulative, and cruel. Her negative signification is made most apparent by the fact that Jacqueline smokes privately, and with a mission, but never in the workplace she controls. Jacqueline Dent is presented as a failed personality, if a successful waged woman. In the end, Harvey saves Jacqueline from her prosperous but personally unsatisfying career by marrying her and sharing the leadership of the firm. Thus, the unnaturalness of "having a girl as a boss" was reasserted.

Representations of the women smoker such as this one signalled sexual availability via smoking. Truly successful women smokers were said to constrain that sexuality and their smoking. The acceptable limits of sexual expression were still being defined, but in studies such as the Jacqueline Dent fiction profile, sexuality as recklessly flaunted seems intended to warn the reader against an assumption that all of the old rules had disappeared. They had not, and the new code of sophistication carried with it the possibility of ruin if not carefully managed. Film stars like Marlene Dietrich were constructed as sexy, tough, and knowing. Yet a Dietrich was presented as in control of her fate, already having succeeded in the modern world of entertainment.

Magazine articles about the real working woman present no hint of her sexuality or her smoking. Even when successful working women were profiled, as in the pages of *The Business and Professional Woman*, readers were abjured that "The Trend for the Mannish Casual" was the best fashion route. The C.H. Smith Company of Windsor, Ontario, recommended that "[t]he most feminine thing to do is to 'go masculine' in your suits and coats – copy the casual, comfortable mannish styles, so admirably suited to a busy day – a silhouette. Broad shouldered, Square, Courageous; built of mannish fabrics."[33] No mention is made of accessorizing office fashion with cigarette cases.

Many women had so little disposable cash in the interwar period as to make even small pleasures like smoking out of reach. Helen Gregory MacGill's heart-rending article on "The Jobless Woman" in the September 1930 issue of *Chatelaine* shows a young woman with a deeply worried expression, conservative clothing in muted colours, and a cloche hat (see figure 8.2). The description MacGill gives of the few employment opportunities in business for women is bleak. Despite the increased numbers of wage-earning Canadian women, in 1930 estimated at 200,000, most were underpaid, employed only during "rush" seasons with long and exhausting hours and then dismissed during slack periods. MacGill points to the persistent bias and even hostility toward the waged woman, concluding that unless "there is a quickening of social conscience and an awakening of responsibility for the welfare of the worker" in business and industry, little will change. By 1937, the situation was even worse, as would be expected. Mary Sutherland, chairman of the Advisory Committee for the National Employment Commission, noted in *The Business and Professional Woman* that young rural women seeking employment in the cities magni-

The Chatelaine, September, 1930

The Jobless Woman

by
Helen Gregory MacGill, M.A
Judge, Juvenile Court
Member B.C. Minimum Wage Board

The hardest and most pitiful cases are usually those of the women with children

8.2 | Magazine feature, *Chatelaine*, 1930

fied the problems faced by unemployed or underemployed women there.[34] The unemployment problem was further worsened by a parallel process of de-skilling in many trades where women were concentrated, such as dressmaking.[35] There can be little doubt that in periods of instability, an office worker who smoked could endanger her future.

Waged women workers in newly defined fields would have experienced high levels of stress, little control over their workplace lives, and a clear need to develop discipline over emotions and mood in order to present a calm demeanour. Graham Lowe's study of the changing conditions and feminization of the Canadian office between 1891 and 1931 shows that managerial controls were regularly used to maintain a compliant female workforce, leading to a deterioration in work culture.[36] Susan Gelman shows that in this period, secondary schools were also feminizing and squeezing that workforce.[37] There is evidence too in the primary literature of women workers feeling isolated. "A Professional Woman," in a letter to an advice columnist of *The Canadian Home Journal*, bemoans the lack of male

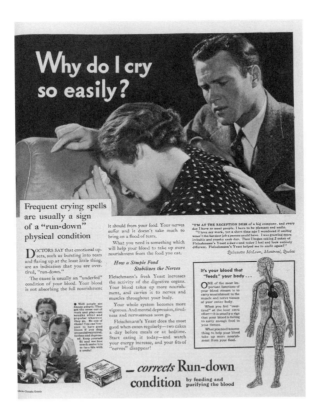

8.3 | Magazine advertisement for Fleischmann's yeast, *Chatelaine*, 1935

friends for women between thirty and forty because males feared that they would be pressed into marriage when they could not afford it during the Great Depression. "We have our professions, or our 'jobs', and we want to make good in them. But there is no denying that men-friends are jolly and stimulating, and that, in spite of all our modern ways, there are times and occasions when a male escort is both necessary and entertaining."[38] Then, as today, high stress levels and the desire to control appetite are given as important reasons why women were and are drawn to smoking.[39] Chapter 7 provides a number of examples of magazine advertisements in this period that promised to control stress.[40] Paid work required that workers suppress negative emotions and control mood swings, other justifications that modern women give for smoking.[41] Women workers reported exhaustion and depression from the exacting standards imposed on them.[42] Smoking would have assuaged this as well.

The fear of expressing emotions openly in the workplace was fed by terrorizing magazine advertising, like figure 8.3 from *Chatelaine* in 1935. The man in this full-page ad looks utterly distraught at the sight of the woman crying. While we might take her to be his wife, the caption under the picture suggests otherwise. The man is likely this woman's boss. "Quinetta McLean" from Montreal writes, "I'm at the reception desk of a big company, and every day I have to meet people. I have to be pleasant and smile. I love my work, yet a short time ago I wondered if smiling wasn't the hardest job a person could have. I was growing more irritable and cranky each day." Happily, Fleishmann's Yeast is said to have saved the day. If only it had been that easy for most working women. What is being described here – fatigue, depression, and tearfulness – is likely the result of stress that comes from close monitoring of work. Instead of acknowledging the unforgiving pressure that most women experienced in the workplace, however, the problem is presented as one of "tired blood" or an inefficient digestive system. The woman worker's condition is pathologized by locating it in the essential functioning of the blood, needing to be both fed and purified. Ultimately, the sickness is important because of the social isolation it can produce, as is made clear in the text next to the three happy people, only one of whom is a (very young) woman. Here, the nub of the issue is defined in bolded text: "Well people are happy people. They get the most out of work and play – are sought after and popular wherever they go … Keep yourself fit and see how much easier it is to face life with a smile!" Not all waged or salaried women controlled their emotions with Fleishmann's Yeast. Increasing numbers took up smoking to achieve the same effect.

Advice columns ran letters from professional salaried women that speak as well to the woman worker's lack of control and tenuous hold on her job.[43] In addition to showing too much emotion, a woman's advancing age presented another threat. An advertisement by the Dominion Life Assurance Company begins with the commentary, "Poor Miss Armour. What will she do now – fifty years old – no position – nothing saved – no family to help her?" The solution it offers is of a self-saving plan, but the implicit message of the women worker's lack of security would not have been lost on any reader, especially a waged woman reader. Indeed, photographs of workplaces for women, such as figure 8.4 from the London Life Insurance Company in London, Ontario, show a salaried workforce of young women.

The tensions between the rigours of the workplace and smoking were explicitly drawn in a series of films produced by the Ontario government in 1921. Silent with English inter-titles, one film is titled "Her Own Fault."[44] It traces the lives of two factory girls. One employee takes care of her health by getting enough sleep, eating wisely, and staying with re-

8.4 | Workplace of London Life Insurance Company, London, Ontario, 1950

spectable friends in her after-work life. She prospers and is promoted. The second parties at nightclubs in the evening, is chronically tired, and, predictably, smokes. She becomes ill, not because her workday is exhausting and her working conditions grim but because she undermines her own health. Eventually, she is admitted to a sanatorium. The fault of young working women spending too much time in hotels, rather than in their own homes, was a frequent theme in the press as well.[45] The audience for these films is unclear, but they are part of a collection commissioned by the various provincial governments in 1921 for a variety of audiences: teachers, schoolchildren, parents, and workers.

To facilitate the social exchange working women understandably craved and to control stress, moods, and anxiety, some waged women chose to smoke. Easy discussions in the press further normalized smoking.[46] To women who had accepted some of the advantages of smoking, then repeated the performance with friends or co-workers, tobacco offered a rare, comforting treat in a potentially hostile work environment.

Two Women Speak for Themselves: Ella Liscombe and Ethel Fry

Life as a salaried worker is set out for us in the expressive diaries and personal letters of two women from this period: Ella Muriel Liscombe of Sydney, Nova Scotia, and (Harriet) Ethel Fry of Vineland, Ontario. Neither

8.5 | Canadian National Railways switchboard at Montreal, 1929

of these women smoked, but both had that option and had friends who did. The recorded life experiences of two women who lived in small-town Canada help us to unravel workplace culture, inducements to smoke, and factors deterring women before the Second World War. They confirm claims made earlier in the chapter.

Ella Liscombe maintained her diary from 1913 until 1938.[47] She was born in 1902 and raised in relative comfort, with a maid to help around the house and an education from Mount Allison College, but her family slid quietly into genteel poverty after the death of her father. Liscombe spent much of her work life at the Bank of Montreal in Sydney where she was regularly frustrated by the male hierarchy and her co-workers jockeying for power in a stifling climate of small-minded bureaucracy.[48] The women pictured in figure 8.5 at the telephone switchboard represent a work culture similar to the one described by Ella through her years in Cape Breton during the Great Depression. Despite her exemplary work, when she was regularly scolded for working too hard and for too many hours at a stretch, Ella's position was unstable, and she feared dismissal for the slightest of errors or infractions. She watched as young men whom she had trained were promoted to become her supervisor, with higher pay, and moved to bigger offices. After years of loyal work, she was crushed when she received a paltry $25-a-year raise as her Christmas gift in 1935.

8.6 | Claudette Colbert, 1941. © Gene Lester/Getty Image 3233619

As the historical literature suggests, Ella admits to very high levels of stress in her workplace. She was also lonely much of the time, feeling that she was in competition with both her male and female co-workers for the few rewards available. In May of 1934, she fumes to her diary: "Hated the Bank today, disliked Miss Rigby, who made remarks about my hair, and disliked Nauss who is getting too pompous."[49] And Ella was not alone in these hard feelings. She reports that every other woman working with her in the bank was burdened with nervous exhaustion. One of her close co-workers was forced to take an extended unpaid leave during the worst of the Depression. Their workplace was not a setting of jolly conviviality. She does not indicate which of her female co-workers smoked and which did not, but she does set out the conditions that would both encourage and discourage smoking by women.

Liscombe provides us with a full accounting of her busy life both at and outside of her paid employment. Part of a warm and loving family comprised of her mother and sister, assorted relatives, and a very wide collection of friends, Ella tells us about her skating parties, the Sunday school and CGIT groups she led, her young people's group, what she read, and who she watched at the movies, which she attended at various stages of her life at least weekly. Cinema icons like Claudette Colbert in the 1941 photograph shown in figure 8.6 were presented to avid viewers as edgy models but acting in ways that could be emulated and identified as middle-class through their wardrobes, speech, and behaviours.[50] In this photograph, Colbert lightly grasps a man's wrist as he lights her cigarette. She leans forward, with eyes downcast. We see only the man's arm, and it denotes good taste. He wears a suit and finely tailored shirt with cufflinks; his little finger sports a ring. Colbert herself dresses modestly and in the style that any working woman could emulate: a suit and matching hat is "dressed up" with an enormous corsage that could be real or silk. Film stars' performances, both in still photographs like this one and on the big screen, literally taught audiences how the new woman should pose with cigarette as stage prop, how she might speak, dress, and move.[51] Ella freely commented on cinema stars, both male and female, critiquing those she found believable and those lacking credibility. She noticed the small and large details of these performances: actors' accents, clothing, the sets, story lines.

On 10 January 1934, Ella writes, "Just home from the movies after seeing 'Good Companions.' Took Mamma. Dare I say I was a little disappointed? A little too slow and the dialect intense." Ella's social life, the romances of her friends, and the movies frequently shade into each other. When she was just 17, Ella noted in her diary that "[i]n the evening, Alex Morrison and Rolley Lewis came. Neither of them are very exciting but I like Alex pretty well. Haven't met my ideal yet. He must look like Wallace Reed or Miles Welch [movie stars]."[52] Life frequently seemed to mirror and inform her understanding of the movies she watched so avidly and vice versa.[53]

Ella's fascination with the movies was matched by tobacco advertisers'. Edward Bernays, the master manipulator of cigarette promotions, recognized the power of the cinema in transmitting wordless emotions, especially by using smoking. "Everything from the gayest comedy, to the most sinister tragedy can be expressed by a cigarette, in the hands or mouth of a skillful actor," he observed.[54]

Through all of the twists and turns of her friends' romances, Ella had the "pictures" to console and interest her: "Ollie and I to see Janet Gaynor in 'Carolina.' Nice picture but slushy. Lionel Barrymore was good."[55] Going to the movies also offered an excuse for a brief treat at the local café: "Saw a lovely picture tonight. 'Stage Door' with Katherine Hepburn, Ginger Rogers, Andrea Leeds, and Adolph Menjou. Very interesting and different. Mickey Mouse was good too. To the Diana afterwards with Ollie and Dorothy. Ollie and Doris had toast, Dorothy a soda, and I a 'Bugg About' piled high with whipped cream."[56] Clearly, movies were deeply important to Ella. As a young woman, she had collected pictures of her favourite actors and actresses, pasting them into scrapbooks. The final entry in Ella's last diary is a list of twenty-three women film stars, made without comment, a telling inventory of Ella's enduring fascination with the big screen.

Ella Liscombe lived much of her social life in single-sex groupings, from book clubs to church groups, from shopping trips to parties. She herself neither smoked nor drank. A serious woman, closely akin to the YWCTU girls profiled in chapter 2, she had a religiosity and family-oriented lifestyle that seems to have given her little sympathy for smoking. Her friend Gertrude was of a faster type, however. At 17, Ella records that "Gertrude called and wanted me to go over there. She was going to wash her hair. Went over and read ... She has some rouge hidden in her top drawer. I tried it. She used to have cigarettes but doesn't do that now. She doesn't approve of it for girls."[57]

As she aged, Ella indulged in criticism of those who did drink or smoke. This was influenced in part by the struggles with drinking experienced by her brother, Bob, who was frequently incapacitated. He had difficulty holding a job or even interacting with the family, and by the 1930s, Bob had dropped out of her diary accounts entirely.

Official reports of women's unstable employment are also reflected in letters of the era. By 1936, when her letters begin, (Harriet) Ethel Fry had been a registered nurse for two years. Unable to find work during the Great Depression in Hamilton where she had trained, she joined her friends in finding work in Albany and then Buffalo, New York. Ethel made about $70 a month in both of these positions between 1937 and 1940, at which point she married and stopped paid employment. She received room and board as part of her pay package. We know from Ethel's letters to her brother and family how she spent her spare cash, meagre though it was. Her younger brother had begun studies at the University of Toronto, and she tried to send him a money order each payday of between $10 and $25. However, her aim was often frustrated by other claims on her small paycheque.

On 3 February 1938, for example, she tallies her expenses that month, which "seem to have been heavy." She is delighted to have been asked to be a bridesmaid for a friend, but this necessitates a new dress, which she cannot easily afford. She "lays down" $1 to have the right to buy it on instalments and adds an undisclosed amount to begin the payments. She finds a "lovely lace tablecloth" for $6 as the wedding gift, intending to share the gift with her brother who cannot yet pay his half of the cost. She attempts to spend as little on herself as possible, allowing herself one movie a week, the only entertainment she acknowledges. She frequently borrows items of clothing from other nurses. For instance, when she decided to accept an invitation to a tobogganing party, she realized that she

8.7 and 8.8 | Ethel Fry with her brother, John; Ethel Fry with other nursing graduates

had nothing warm enough or otherwise appropriate to wear, forcing her into more borrowing.[58]

She regularly bemoans her limited ability to support her brother, even declaring that she could not act as a guarantor if he decided to borrow money to continue his education.[59] She avoids having surgery for appendicitis attacks until her financial condition improves.[60] In another letter, she notes that the money she had intended to send her brother is needed instead by her parents to prevent foreclosure of the family farm through failure to pay the taxes.[61]

Ethel seems to have been a conscientious worker, but she was also a Canadian working in Depression-ravaged American hospitals. In March 1938, she was dismissed, exactly as she had long feared, sharing this experience with scores of other women colleagues in tenuous employment. Prior to the firing, she and her nursing colleagues had endured a long period when salaries were reduced by 10 per cent. As an alternative, there was ample work for private-duty nurses. Here the nurse "lived in," providing meals as well as light cleaning for ill family members. Ethel had worked at this before her time in hospital service. Her own mother worked as a private-duty nurse for neighbours and friends in the same period that these letters were written, as did her aunt.[62] As impoverished as the family became during this period, they were forced to call on the services of such a nurse when everyone fell ill with pneumonia.[63] Such positions could not have paid very well.

Ethel was descended from evangelical Mennonites. Like Ella's, Ethel's religiosity, as well as a family deeply invested in temperance, pride at having descended from Lincoln County's earliest Loyalist settlers, the small-town orientation, and probably also the family's poverty, deterred her from ever taking up smoking. Yet she was surrounded by equally straitened nursing colleagues who did smoke. Of one friend who had dated her brother, Ethel writes, "Audrey is the same old girl she ever was. She inquires about you quite often. She has become quite a smoker. Marg and Min also do occasionally."[64] In fact, it was widely accepted that smoking in the workplace forced a certain discipline on the woman smoker that she lost once her paid work came to an end. Dr Jennie Smillie from the Toronto Social Hygiene Club observed in *The Globe and Mail* in 1937 that once women began smoking in the privacy of their own homes rather than in the workplace, their health often deteriorated.[65]

These two profiles of working women who eschewed smoking do not deny that many young working women had became "quite the smoker[s]" before the Second World War. More would follow suit with the onset of war.

Waged Women Smokers during the Second World War

Women were offered well-paying employment in industries normally staffed by men during the Second World War. In providing this highly valued service during a time of national crisis, women had greater freedom than ever before to engage in male leisured activities such as smoking. Visual evidence shows that many women smoked in public during the war without fear of censure. As an example of the confident wartime woman smoker, consider the famous image of a Second World War employee of Toronto's John Inglis Company (figure 8.9). Veronica Foster, known as the "Bren Gun Girl,"[66] poses with a Bren Gun. Her hair is coiled in the mandatory wrap, and a cigarette is in her hand. Neither the originator of the still photograph, the National Film Board, nor Library and Archives Canada, which now holds the photograph in its collection, notes that Veronica takes this opportunity to have a quiet smoke on the job, partly obscuring her face as she exhales just as the photograph is snapped. Apparently, Veronica's machinist work utterly normalizes her smoking and her smoke-wreathed appearance. Caught in the photographer's gaze while working at the most patriotic of tasks, Veronica *seems* oblivious to the camera. In fact, given the photograph's official origins and status, this is impossible, suggesting that this naturalized use of the cigarette has been chosen by Veronica, the photographer, *and her employer* as a fully staged act to dem-

8.9 | Bren Gun Girl, John Inglis plant, 1941

onstrate her comfort and freedom in that workplace. Women producing war materiel did not typically smoke at their stations. The photograph is an important one because it demonstrates official approval for the smoking woman as war worker.

The photograph is also noteworthy for presenting a war-munitions working woman as a sexual being, a most unusual representation. Veronica strikes a devil-may-care pose that is in direct contrast to her serious role as a munitions worker. The playfulness and ambivalence of this image shows one of the enduring attractions of smoking for women in the war era and today: sexual attractiveness.

Veronica's apparent nonchalance about her smoking might well have emerged from her confidence as a Canadian skilled worker. She was part of a wave of women employed during the war with dramatically increased wages. Canadian women's overall labour force participation had been only 24.2 per cent in 1939, but by 1944 it was 33.5 per cent. In 1939, Veronica and her working sisters had earned on average $12.78 a week, while in 1944 average wages had increased to $20.89 weekly for women.[67] Some of this discretionary income would surely have been spent on cigarettes.

During the war, when the percentages of waged women had dramatically increased and when wages were far higher than had ever been the case, working women succeeded in making smoking both accepted and even expected in many quarters. Nevertheless, it is unlikely that working women smoked without sanction in the 'open' except in purpose-built locations like cafés. Smoking on the street, for example, was still regarded as rude. More accepted was smoking in the semi-seclusion of the workplace at break time, as can be seen in figure 8.10 in which Joyce Jones, shipyard rivet passer, takes a smoke break with Len Christianson on the work site in 1943. Joyce Jones offers another image of the woman worker as smoker during wartime. As a shipyard labourer engaged in heavy work heretofore associated with men, she reasonably enough also has adopted male habits of leisure. Her stance as she smokes companionably with her workmate bespeaks male norms as well. Instead of the coquettish "flag" stance in which the hand with the cigarette is elevated above chin level to frame the face, Joyce Jones seems to smoke absent-mindedly, seeming to concentrate instead on her conversation. There is almost no sexual charge with Joyce Jones, as we saw in the image of the Bren Gun Girl. Joyce smokes in full protective gear of hardhat and coveralls, staring reflectively over her cigarette.

Joyce Jones might well not have had any exposure to heavy industry prior to the war, although her cigarette makes her seem fully in her element. The caption on this photograph notes that the photograph was intended to show that if women were prepared to re-skill during this emergency, they could move from such professions as beauticians or nursing into war work. Hence, Joyce Jones's taking on of approved male behaviours like smoking is carefully staged in this image.

At breaks, lunch, and after-work socializing, women workers were very likely to relax with friends by smoking in same-sex and heterogeneous groupings. Smoking is one of those rituals that bonded women with women, and women with men, depending on the situation, as we see with Joyce Jones. We have documentation of groups of women smoking at the clubhouse lounge at the Montreal Business and Professional Women's Club.[68] Women sought out cigar stores as places for smoking where some proprietors had tried to feminize their surroundings by equipping them with soda fountains, stationery, lending libraries, and smoking spaces.[69] Smoking became so common that newspapers featured debates about the "gentility" of women's smoking habits: at what point during the meal could a woman light up and still be considered polite?[70]

Women engaged in war work and serving in uniform seemed to feel an even greater freedom to smoke alongside their male colleagues. In doing so, they broke many of the behavioural limits that had applied to women before the war.

8.10 and 8.11 | Joyce Jones, shipyard rivet passer, NFB, 1943; Juliet Chisholm, Oakville, Ontario, 1944

In figure 8.11, WREN Juliet Chisholm stands in full uniform, casually holding her cigarette openly in a decorative garden. Had she not been so clearly identified as a servicewoman, she might have been subject to criticism for smoking outdoors. Juliet Chisholm betrays no concern about her propriety, however. She stares evenly into the camera with a slight smile, holding her cigarette at hip level. Her stance is casual as well, with one leg slightly crooked.

Grace Juliet Chisholm Turney (1902–1964) was the granddaughter of the founder of Oakville and a very cosmopolitan woman. Born in Oakville but raised in the United States and Paris, Juliet had long been an artist by the time this photograph was taken. She married playwright Robert M. Turney in Paris in 1926, and although the marriage failed, they never bothered divorcing. Juliet graduated from McGill University in medicine in 1940, serving overseas with the Royal Canadian Army Medical Corps

8.12 | Evelyn Pepper's lipstick tube lighter, Ottawa

during the Second World War, where she was made a captain. She also served with the United Nations in China. For some years, she maintained a medical practice in Oakville. Juliet Chisholm, like many other women in this book, displayed sophistication and style in her demeanour, setting off her smart appearance with her cigarette.

Autobiographies and personal accounts attest to professional and middle-class women taking up both paid employment and smoking during the war. The range of accessories developed in this period illustrate the degree to which smoking was valorized during the Second World War, even by women who chose not to smoke. In figure 8.12 a cigarette lighter is disguised within a far more common article for women – the lipstick tube. If smoking were so common among servicewomen, one of whom owned this artifact, why would it be necessary to disguise it at all? Or is this simply a conversation piece, a cleverly designed joke for a woman to pull out of her pocket and delight her male friends and servicemen, whose cigarettes she could now light in an inversion of the usual gallantry?

As for the origins of the lighter, the Red Cross on the top of the tube suggests that it was given by one of the Red Cross organizations (Canadian, American, or British) to its nurses or to a volunteer who then gifted the item to this nurse. The Red Cross specialized in giving supplementary comforts and supplies – including tobacco and tobacco accoutrements – to army personnel as well as sick, wounded, and POW servicemen and women during the Second World War.[71] In this regard, the Red Cross was similar to many charitable organizations (including the YWCA and the IODE) that supported the war effort by giving tobacco and other gifts to servicemen and women. For example, the Ottawa Women's Canadian Club reported proudly that it had provided about 500,000 cigarettes to Canada's fighting men and women over the course of the Second World War.[72]

There is no evidence that the owner of this "lipstick lighter" ever herself smoked, showing how deeply smoking culture had penetrated polite society. The owner was Nursing Sister Evelyn Pepper. Her long-time friend, Hallie Sloan, another Second World War nursing sister, speculates that the lipstick tube lighter might have been used by Ms Pepper to light the cigarettes of wounded servicemen. She notes that uniforms of the era had a "slip pocket" on the uniform's left breast where such an article could easily have been kept.[73] Sarah Glassford speculates that masking the lighter as a lipstick tube and secreting it in a specially designed pocket in the nurse's uniform might have been attempts to feminize otherwise severe and masculine military uniforms.[74]

The fact that the lighter may have been owned by a non-smoking nurse and that she carried it with her regularly, giving it a well-worn sheen, indicates that even if it were intended as a sly joke, smoking in the nursing stations of the Second World War was common and condoned. This is not surprising, given information we have about the war.[75] Nursing sisters often actively smoked alongside servicemen.

About the owner of the lipstick lighter we know a good deal. Evelyn Pepper, who eventually rose to the rank of major, became known as the "Florence Nightingale of disaster planning."[76] Pepper used her wartime experiences with the Royal Canadian Army Medical Corps in Europe to guide her development of a wound-simulation training manual, illustrated with full-colour pictures. The manual became a resource for instruction in both the Canadian and American military.[77]

Pepper was born in Ottawa in 1905. She graduated from the Ottawa Civic Hospital School of Nursing in 1928, serving in the hospital's Radiology Department until she enlisted in 1939 in the Royal Canadian Army Medical Corps. Her career as a nursing sister took her into the heart of the combat zone in England, Italy, Holland, and France.[78] She was principal matron of the No. 1 Canadian General Hospital during the Second Battle of Arnheim. Here her staff treated more than 2,800 casualties.[79] Living and working in such circumstances, Evelyn Pepper would surely have had reason to take up smoking.

Whether or not Nursing Sister Evelyn Pepper ever used the lighter for her own cigarettes, she fit the image of the sophisticated middle-class woman worker as smoker. "Tall, immaculately elegant and soft-spoken, with an occasional saucy social side, she was the epitome of class and grace. She spoke in measured words, though she never shrank from speaking her mind."[80] She was thoroughly modern but also kept up her guard to protect her public image as a professional and responsible single woman. And she did this for good reason, for there would still have been critics of a woman of her social standing smoking or encouraging others to smoke while engaged in nursing administration.

The demands of war did succeed in dissolving many pre-war standards of propriety, with smoking often mentioned as a means to calm jagged nerves. This is demonstrated in an anonymous diary from 1943. It recounts an emotional event for a servicewoman as she waited to hear of her posting: "I went in [to see her commanding officer] and she seemed pleased to see me ... Capt. Ritchie offered me a cigarette and when I went to light hers for her my hand shook so that she noticed it and said, 'Morrison, it's all right.' I said 'It's just the strain leaving me. I have been under great strain, you know.' 'Yes,' she said, 'and I am sorry that this had to happen.' We got into conversation ... During the time I was in her office, the cadets started to come down but she put them off and offered me another cigarette."[81] Such accounts give us some insight into the use of sharing cigarettes in female company during a period of reported anxiety. It is also obvious that these practices mirrored male norms. The junior officer waits until she is offered a cigarette before indulging. The invitation from her superior carries with it the implication that she too will smoke, and the protocol is that the junior officer offers her superior a light. Her emotions are betrayed by this act, and her ensuing explanation is graciously accepted. Finally, the taking of another cigarette is meant to extend and deepen their meeting, justifying the delaying of the superior's other duties. It clearly validates the junior officer's experience and includes her in this warm and accepting environment. That the anonymous servicewoman in her account connects her superior's generosity to shared smoking indicates the power of the entire tableau she recounts.

The reported anecdote about shared smoking by two women in a private setting also demonstrates that smoking became a vehicle for the more powerful woman to invite her subordinate into a "culture of power," just as men had often done throughout the nineteenth and twentieth centuries. The interpretation placed on the simple act of a more powerful woman offering a cigarette to someone under her authority – releasing stress, encouraging camaraderie, giving evidence of respect and kindness extended during an official meeting – all show how deeply meaningful the shared smoking was to the diarist. It is further evidence for Foucault's notion of governmentality. The account also shows how actively women used these shared rituals for their own purposes, demonstrating that smoking's significance extended far beyond advertisers' prescriptions for the woman smoker. By the Second World War, women had made the act of smoking their own, imbuing it with deep social importance.

Waged Women and Smoking after the Second World War

The expected depression following the Second World War did not materialize. While women were shifted out of their industrial work by returning servicemen, many were offered jobs in traditional "pink ghetto" service industries with lower pay.[82] Smoking was largely accepted by women on the job in this period of phenomenal commercial growth. From 1945 into the 1970s, smoking rates for Canadian working women climbed steadily. By the mid-1970s, the apex for smoking among Canadian women generally, the waged or salaried woman who smoked was so common that imagery of them was ubiquitous and commentary about this taken-for-granted behaviour almost nonexistent.

The two women stenographers shown in figure 8.13 in the foreground of this typical office interior in 1950 Montreal both have ashtrays prominently displayed at the front of their desks. These women were on the front-line of the service industry as receptionists, and their propriety would have been closely monitored. Hence, to have desks equipped with ashtrays indicates a high level of public acceptance for everyone smoking, women included. The assumption that a client would wish to smoke as he waited with the receptionist or visited with her speaks too about the norms of postwar Canada. By this period, ashtrays were common in office settings, and oral testimony from women employed and smoking in that period confirms the invitation to workers to smoke as they worked.[83]

In postwar Canada, the preoccupations of the workplace were much more with social reconstruction than with social norms around smoking. The reincorporation of a million returning servicemen and women into the economy,[84] and the consequent squeezing out of many women wage-earners, made concerns over social practices like smoking seem unimportant. The renewed cult of consumerism, early marriages for many women, and a soaring birthrate created a new code of domesticity for women.

Nevertheless, a sizable proportion of Canadian women continued to be employed outside the home. From a high point in 1944 of 33.5 per cent of women engaged in the workforce, the rate declined to 25.3 per cent in

8.13 | Typical office interior, W.J. Bush & Co., 1950

1946, remaining between 23 and 24 per cent until the mid-1950s when it began to increase again.[85] During the 1950s, the main concern surrounding women workers was the unionization of white-collar and female-dominated industries and workplaces. The massive though unsuccessful effort to unionize the 15,000 employees of the T. Eaton Company between 1948 and 1951 became the hallmark of this process. Desmond Morton has called it "the closest thing to a crusade in the English-speaking union movement."[86] New Canadian female labourers, many of whom were employed in the low-paying textile and needle trades, were exploited and vulnerable, with unions making few inroads.[87]

In the 1960s, increasing numbers of women returned to the workforce and many into the public sector, which became increasingly militant. Public-sector unions came to dominate the Canadian labour movement[88] in the 1970s, with the industrial/manufacturing sector further shrinking. Many women also obtained jobs as service workers in the private sector. These jobs were characterized by low wages, and they too had difficulty in organizing to improve their working conditions.[89] Issues of paid maternity leave and equal pay for work of equal value topped the agenda of labour issues. The old battles about the propriety of women smoking faded in the face of these momentous issues.

On a personal level, using smoking as a means of controlling negative emotions and eliciting pleasant ones continued to be identified by women as prime reasons for smoking.[90] Smoking has long been perceived as helping women to cope with stress and promoting relaxation. One explanation for this salutary effect is thought to be the repetitive actions by the smoker in selecting, lighting, and smoking, helping to calm the overwrought. Another is the "permission" to take a break from stressful activities, such as those found in the workplace, and thereby to distract oneself from unpleasant circumstances, either alone or with a supportive group. Whether or not smoking has the properties to support these claims, the belief that it has these effects is significant in itself. The social value of smoking for women engaged in waged labour is enormous.

Other Cultural Incentives for Smoking by Waged and Salaried Women

If smoking resulted in both dangers and pleasures for the working woman, what other features drew women to it? Clearly, the greatest physical danger associated with smoking was the risk of heart disease and cancer. But the link between tobacco and cancer was not confirmed in the public mind until the 1960s and was contested for much longer in the public press.[91] Hence, in the period before 1963 women and men lived in a simpler age as far as smoking was concerned when the many attractions of smoking and a few confirmed dangers were publicly acknowledged.

As was true for the middle-class academic woman (see chapter 9), cigarettes allowed women to add dramatic gestures to their personal repertoire and thus focus attention on their face and hands. And as with Evelyn Pepper's lipstick lighter, accessories could be added to the wardrobe at little expense. In his study of the nineteenth-century British male smoker's "paraphernalia of smoking consumption," Matthew Hilton argues that smokers aimed to construct a "distinctive picture of themselves as smokers."[92] And so it was for the woman smoker. For example, to match a particular costume, cigarette cases or matchboxes could be carried in a variety of colours. As discussed in chapter 6, the refinement of the self-striking match in the early twentieth century meant that lighting the cigarette was a fairly reliable act. The case in which the matches were kept could be personalized and used as a decorative prop to set off a woman's costume. By the early twentieth century, personal mechanical lighters offered even more scope for a show of lighting the cigarette. Henceforth,

8.14 | Three cigarette cases owned by salaried women, 1930s

the lit cigarette could act as a prop to aid discussion without damaging clothing. Marketers helped in this process as well by making cigarettes' natural companions coffee and sweets, thereby further normalizing the previously sinful activity when opium had been the main accompaniment to tobacco in many peoples' minds. Cigarette holders were especially dramatic and popular additions to any wardrobe because they extended the length of the cigarette, protected the fingers from nicotine stains, and had the potential to add or accent a particular colour in clothing, nail enamel, or lipstick. Holders were available for the well-heeled in fine materials like wood, glass, and ivory or in cheaply produced materials like brass for the working girl. Cigarettes might be purchased with perfumed and tinted cigarette ends to match a woman's lipstick or nails. These accoutrements, together with the waged woman's carefully constructed visual representation, helped the woman smoker to shape a distinctive identity.

An additional array of inexpensive products were produced to grace the working girl's home, although they are harder to find in museum collections. Decorative cigarette containers were manufactured for the coffee table or desk, such as the cigarette cases shown in figure 8.14. The introduction of the cheap, mass-produced cigarette in the 1880s had standardized the shape so containers could house them. Cigarettes were made even more affordable by James Bonsack's cigarette-rolling machine in the same decade. The articles shown in figure 8.14 date from the 1930s and

1940s, but similar objects would have been produced in every decade for women smokers. The cigarette case on the left is made of plastic and designed with a spring mechanism so that the cigarette sitting in its chamber could be popped up smartly, allowing it to be gripped by a delicate glove-encased hand. The cigarette chamber would be filled from a package or box and held approximately six cigarettes, enough for an evening's outing or work breaks. The case would fit neatly into a small purse or a coat or skirt pocket. The object in the middle, in a delicate blue thistle design, is intended to display cigarettes on a table or work-space top. Here too, cigarettes purchased in bulk would be decanted and set out for guests or co-workers to indulge in socially. The thistle design might well have had an ethnic significance to the owner, reminding her of her Scottish origins or associations. The third cigarette dish would have been an accompaniment to a tea set, in this case one by Royal Crown Derby, "Blue Mikado." Among other patterns, the Blue Mikado was popular with upwardly mobile women in most parts of Canada from the interwar period to the 1970s. This one was owned by a secondary school teacher. A tea set consisted of cups, saucers, tea plates, a serving plate, creamer, sugar bowl, and teapot. In many cases, the tea service included a covered dish for cigarettes to be left on the table for the visitors to smoke with their drink, as was the case here. Cigarette dishes and ashtrays were also produced to match simple crockery sets and meant to be left permanently on the table. Ashtrays from vacation spots were a popular souvenir. Aside from the Blue Mikado dish, many of these products were to be had for modest sums, bringing them well within the reach of the working woman. Thus, products ranged from modest to expensive to support the woman smoker in accessorizing her rented room, apartment, or work space.

When a woman went out during the evening to socialize, she often took a small bag for her cosmetics and cigarettes, and one can well imagine her slipping in the delicate compact shown in figures 8.15 and 8.16. Alternatively, it might have been carried in a shirt or suit pocket by a gallant companion. Inexpensively produced around the time of the Second World War, the compact was likely designed to be hooked over the wearer's wrist with a strong chain soldered to the frame. It might have been modelled on a popular combination vanity/cigarette case developed in the 1920s by a Chicago company.[93] Probably made of a brass alloy, the compact is light and probably cost a modest amount. The decorative details of roses on the cover are stamps and partly worn, suggesting that the compact was well used by the owner. Yet it would meet all of the needs for a woman out on the town. One compartment has room for cake-foundation powder, a puff, and a mirror; a second would hold perhaps a half-dozen of the shorter

8.15 and 8.16 | Salaried woman's brass alloy compact/cigarette and lipstick case, 1940s

cigarettes produced before the longer "Slim" cigarettes of the 1970s. The ring would hold a liptstick tube. The associations of smoking with lipstick and powder remind us that for most women, smoking was a social act, offering pleasure with friends and co-workers.

Once a working girl's wardrobe had been organized and the home decorated, the use of the cigarette itself could serve several purposes. For one, cigarettes were more practical for the waged woman than smoking any other form of tobacco. Cigarettes had the advantage of being small enough to allow consumption over a short break, such as working women took on the job. Sharing a cigarette with workmates in the semi-seclusion of the workplace became a bonding ritual for women, as we have seen with Joyce Jones earlier in this chapter. Cigarettes also gave a woman something to do with her hands during after-hours socializing in other protected leisure settings, such as cafés, where the holding and displaying of cigarettes made even eating and drinking a theatrical feminine performance.

The combination of cheap prices, reliable and theatrical possibilities as a wardrobe prop, the short time required to light and finish a cigarette, and workplace norms of peer associations help to explain cigarettes' growing popularity for working women by the Second World War and thereafter to the 1970s. While pipe-smoking had been constructed as an independent masculine act, cigarettes were from the start a social experience and strongly favoured by women. The smaller size of the cigarette was also thought to complement the smaller female frame and the aesthetic of a woman's decoratively filed and coloured fingernails.[94]

Waged women who relaxed with magazines would have found many representations of the smoking woman in those pages. The racy *Daring Confessions* often teamed pictures of starlets, looking fresh and relaxed, with cigarettes. For instance, Alexis Smith, a minor screen star, is shown in a fetching blouse and skirt that could be worn by any working woman. We are told that she has "many blouses and skirts in her summer wardrobe. By mixing them up, she is able to make her stock of clothes go much farther." Alexis Smith is slender and pretty and holds a cigarette. Profiles like this one typically pictured the woman smoker as relaxed, with upscale accoutrements relating more to a sedate middle-class life than the one the working woman actually lived. Certainly, a relaxed pace would have been a contrast to the experience of office workers, who regularly endured periods of speed-up, unpaid overtime, long hours, and fines.[95] Furthermore, they were routinely very closely monitored, as described by Ella Liscombe in her diary. Hence, smoking supported the fantasy of repose for the working woman and helped her to endure the most challenging of stressors.

The pose struck by Alexis Smith was reproduced time and again in cinema productions, on posters, in magazine advertisements, and elsewhere. Used in tandem with expressive fingernails, shaped, buffed, and polished, cigarettes allowed for expansive gestures, wordless expression of emotion, and calculated framing of the face with softening exhaled smoke. The very act of placing the cigarette on the lips, a titillating and much-discussed feature of life in the 1920s, caressing the tip before inhaling, which in turn swelled the chest and contracted the stomach through the movement of the diaphragm, allowed women to use their bodies as means of communication in a calculated and effective manner. For the learner to fully absorb the message, as in any pedagogical setting, repeated lessons were necessary. Movies were ideal for this purpose. It has been argued that in movies of the 1920s, women were presented as smokers more often even than were male villains.[96] Therefore, while viewers could potentially take multiple meanings from these representations of smoking, both still and moving, a preferred meaning of "smoking woman as sexy and authoritative" was repeatedly reproduced and gained hegemonic ascendancy. A normative understanding of the empowering possibilities for the smoking woman was thus established.

The crucible for waged and salaried women's smoking in Canada occurred between the world wars. Still, many women in the labour market chose not to smoke, holding to an older prescription of women's respectability and often one rooted in a religious sensibility and close familial and community ties. Those who did take up smoking were courted by tobacco manufacturers through advertising and by the many obvious benefits of smoking. The Second World War employed many women in jobs that had been defined as male preserves, and in that way, the norms associated with smoking were broadened.

Evidence from this period is convincing that smoking was widely used to defuse the enormous stresses of wartime service or domestic work, binding women, and sometimes men and women, together in much the same way that all-male groupings had experienced long before. Smoking could also blunt the most unpleasant features of an unforgiving workplace that took advantage of "imperfect" women. The working woman who chose smoking could fortify her social and work life with accessories that both normalized smoking and added to her social capital in new circumstances, helping to construct a new type of waged woman on the Canadian landscape. Smoking could help control weight and add glamour. Working women in particular, therefore, negotiated the spaces between modernity's workplace culture, with its concomitant values of independence, suppressed negative emotions, and cool sophistication, and an older prescription of the respectable woman based on Christian duty, selflessness, and purity. The advantages of smoking for the waged woman were many, with the decision to smoke a rational response to the rigours of workplace culture.

9

Status

Convincing the Canadian middle-class woman to smoke was not easy. While rebels, self-styled sophisticates, sexually provocative women, and some working women were drawn to cigarettes for their performative possibilities before the Second World War, most other women in Canada were less willing to experiment with smoking in public. The task for cigarette marketers and for smoking enthusiasts was to reduce the social danger presented by smoking by making the product broadly acceptable across class, age, and gender lines. For this to occur, smoking needed to be reconfigured from being considered a drug in its own right, a gateway drug to "harder" products, or the natural choice of drinkers, prostitutes, and disreputable artists to a benign product chosen by middle-class men and women of all ages. For more women to be attracted, the market needed to be extended to the female middle and elite classes. Further, this new set of associations needed to be *visually* traced for onlookers, as was now necessary in a modernist world. The aesthetic constructed around the woman smoker needed to be associated with polish, or what is commonly called "class," sophistication, allowable sexuality, pleasure, and a sense of worldliness. This process was a collaborative one between marketers and consumers, who developed socially acceptable uses for smoking by middle-class women.

By the time the advertisement shown in figure 9.1 appeared in a 1987 issue of *Chatelaine*, that process had long since been completed. The young woman who graces this advertisement has nothing in common with women of the demimonde: she is the very picture of health, easy sophisti-

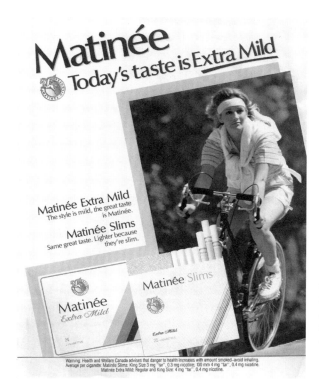

9.1 | Magazine advertisement for Matinée Extra Mild and Matinée Slims, *Chatelaine*, 1987

cation, and financial comfort. Holding her long, shiny hair back with a fashionable sweatband, with her sweatshirt slung carelessly around her shoulders and her no-nonsense shirt and shorts, sweat socks and sneakers, the young woman rides an expensive bicycle through the greenery of a glorious day. For the era, she cuts an apt image of a "classy" woman, one who is at the same time serious about her health and insistent on natural pleasures. This woman is symbolic of the many Canadian women who had by this time adopted the so-called 'extra-mild' and extra-long 'slim' cigarettes, thought to be healthier than conventional cigarettes.

If middle-class Canadian women were to accept smoking and make the act their own through repeated visual demonstrations, wholesome women like this one needed to be seen embracing it. Cigarettes and smoking needed to be indicative of status and as elided with other healthy pastimes like cycling. In the nineteenth century, a high-status woman might have been a debutante or a privileged daughter of a founding family, but in Canada before the Second World War, university women were the largest female elite available in one place and time, a captive audience with much opportunity to learn and enact new social norms within a protected space. Other young women engaged in professional training, such as nursing, were a further market. By the postwar period, these young women's female professors were yet another part of the demographic of the woman student smoker. In chapter 4, I explored the world of the high school girl smoker through the silences of official curriculum and community-based resources; here, we investigate the world of post-secondary women's education as a site where smoking culture developed and was practised as a route to sophistication and status.

How and when did Canadian middle-class women engaged in post-secondary education as students and instructors first adopt smoking as a common pastime? What features of professional training or university culture either discouraged or promoted the practice? What functions has smoking served for the intellectually elite woman in the twentieth century? In other words, how did smoking serve the status-conscious post-secondary woman student as she developed a technology of the self in her search for an enhanced visual identity?

This chapter will argue that while smoking was slow at first to catch on with this group of women, the decision to smoke supported a variety of modernist notions related to status-rich visual identities. Women's social capital became deeply invested in their bodily qualities from the interwar period onwards, including their ability to command and maintain attention through dramatic gestures associated with smoking. Smoking offered women the means to make, and possibly remake, a visually based identity to suit the time and circumstance. As in the case of the working woman discussed in chapter 8, the many powerful and enduring disincentives that operated until the 1940s were largely removed in the patriotic iconography of the Second World War, ushering in an era in which smoking became increasingly common for both men and women. By the 1970s, yearbooks and other records of university life show that undergraduate women and their female professors frequently smoked on Canadian campuses, partly through smoking's close identification with Canadian feminism, as will be discussed in chapter 10. The data available from Health Canada charting smoking rates supports this visual evidence.

The process by which smoking by privileged and conformist middle-class Canadian women moved from a potentially exciting act indulged in by a minority to one that was normalized in the 1970s was gradual, specific to region and ethnicity, and intimately connected to class. Through a close reading of both textual and visual evidence, the smorgasbord of visual identities on offer to middle-class Canadian women through popular culture can easily be seen. To understand what meanings young middle-class women attached to these identity choices, I have investigated visual products as well as personal testimony from those involved in university and professional training culture. Young women engaged in professional training or who attended university on a number of Canadian campuses have participated in helping me uncover the process of smoking's normalization from the interwar years to the 1990s. Some have offered commentaries, others have been interviewed; I have studied as well many sources generated by women while they were students. University yearbooks, photograph albums, and other memorabilia for women who attended Queen's University in Kingston, the University of Ottawa, Wilfrid Laurier University and the University of Waterloo in Kitchener-Waterloo, the University of Toronto, McGill University in Montreal, the University of Manitoba in Winnipeg, the University of Saskatchewan in Saskatoon, the University of Alberta in Edmonton, the University of Calgary, the University of British Columbia in Vancouver, and Dalhousie University in Halifax have all been important. Faculty members from Carleton University, Queen's University, the Royal Military College, and the University of Ottawa have also offered commentaries on their smoking experiences. I have also studied behavioural codes to chart the official policy on smoking on campuses. Through these sources, the valuing of smoking in two periods has been explored: first, the interwar years, the presumed first era of large-scale public smoking by women, and second, from about 1940 to 1990. In each period, samples of the prescriptive code constructed by advertisers are presented and compared with photographic evidence produced by university authorities and women undergraduates. In this way, I seek to understand both the message broadcast by advertisers and the ways in which women themselves took up this prescription, bending it to their own purposes.

From available records, it appears that smoking as part of a liberated lifestyle of "flaming youth" during the 1920s and 1930s was too weak a motivation to convince many Canadian women students to smoke. Likewise, there is little evidence of female faculty members smoking in public in this first period. Rather, it was not until the Second World War when the range of visual identities had been extended through screen and media icons as well as peer examples and many more middle-class women were engaged in post-secondary education that smoking came to be normative for the Canadian woman post-secondary student. By the 1950s, smoking had become a common prop for both young and mature women on many Canadian university campuses, in residences, and in the halls of professional schools.

Smoking's Attractions for the Woman Student before 1950

Smoking's eventual popularity suggests that young women students were attracted to it for a number of reasons. Movies, billboards, periodical advertisements, and much else refined the image of the woman smoker. As modernism privileged visual markers such as changing fashion and new sites and rituals associated with cigarette smoking,[1] the range of identifiable "smoking types" broadened, inviting the consumer to find at least one with which to identify. Especially beguiling for the young woman who was actively "finding herself" was the understanding that she need not choose only a single identity. With smoking, she was free to "test drive" one or more by adopting the characteristic gestures associated with one type of public female smoker. Perhaps a reflective and sophisticated (smoker) intellectual or professional by day, she could experiment with the visual orders associated with the sexualized and playful (smoker) "vamp" for evenings or the friendly and pretty (smoker) "girl next door." All of these identity models were developed in visual detail and through repetition in the popular media, and most were within reach of the young middle-class woman. She had only to choose, for this was a period when women lacked as many role models on whom to pattern their developing modern identities as later would be the case and when formal curricular materials were virtually silent on the woman smoker. The woman smoker as represented in popular culture taught many young women how to explore new visual identities while remaining on the socially sanctioned side of this very thin line.

Of course, what was true for racialized white women was far less possible for racialized non-white women and for non-heterosexual women. Here, the range of allowable visual identities for the woman who chose to smoke remained more narrow. Such women saw few examples in the popular press with which they could easily identify, and the danger of being considered unrespectable or abnormal was a much more pressing concern for them. Aside from the racialized non-white women presented as models of sexuality on cigar-box lids, as described in chapter 5, advertising for cigarettes in Canada adopted only racialized white models through most of the twentieth century.

A woman moving into the public sphere, as most university co-eds and professionals-in-training were required to some degree to do, needed to develop strategies by which she could announce her presence. She had few historical models to guide her in this, because her mother's and grandmother's generations were encouraged to be self-effacing and modest, rarely even speaking in public. One of the groundbreaking characteristics of women's temperance groups had been to encourage them to find their public voices, a skill still contested by the twentieth century.

Careful attention to the details of smoking through popular cultural representations allowed respectable women to learn how, when, and with whom to smoke. The focus of visual attention that smoking made possible must have been an incentive as well for the mature academic woman, greatly outnumbered by her male colleagues and until the 1970s mainly employed at universities as service personnel, deans of women, or instructors in home economics or modern languages. More serious than a debutante, more stylish than her blue-stocking or temperance-oriented grandmother, the first generation of Canadian female faculty members found themselves in privileged and yet unfamiliar public roles within the academy. This generation of collegians needed to cut a distinctive figure if they were to be taken seriously in the male-dominated academic environment.

Smoking offered social facilitation that was casual, democratic, and genial. Unlike the cigars and pipes favoured by men who engaged in a languorous process of stuffing the tobacco into the pipe, lighting, and drawing the smoke through in an extended performance that seemed to create its own gravitas, cigarettes had the advantage of being small enough to be carried in the smart new handbags, to be consumed as a break between classes, and to offer their own distinctive support to a woman intent on proving her intellectual abilities.

Cigarettes also welded academic peer groups. Sharing a cigarette and coffee with friends or classmates created a social exchange that was inexpensive, much more socially acceptable than drinking alcohol, and as short-term a social act as one chose. With the introduction of decorative lighters, the process of lighting up a cigarette could command attention on even more levels. The lit cigarette could then act as a prop to aid discussion and focus attention on the speaker, as well as on her expressive face and hands.[2]

Factors Discouraging Smoking before 1950

From the 1920s, smoking had held the potential of both danger and a sense of exciting liberation for any woman smoker. The forces holding women back from smoking included the traditional temperance message, which, while on the wane after the First World War, could still muster enough social sanction to make public smoking by women an act that few would hazard. As well, smoking's long-standing negative associations with the demimonde of the theatre, petty crime, and noisy intellectuals and the remaining positive associations of non-smoking women with social purity, maternal feminism and the Victorian doctrine of the 'angel in the house' meant that despite inducements to smoke, most respectable women resisted. Undergraduates at universities with a strong religious identity, such as the University of Ottawa or Waterloo Lutheran College/University, took up public smoking later than those at more secularized institutions like Queen's. Similarly, those in faculties that remained aligned with notions of maternalism, such as home economics, also adopted smoking more slowly than did women in faculties that were less freighted with connotations of female purity, such as political science.

Living arrangements in academia could also present barriers for women smokers. Middle-class women in formal education often lived in residence, and female faculty, like deans of women, always did. In these settings, smoking was difficult to mask. Until the 1970s, smoking was expressly forbidden in most Canadian university residences and classrooms. Tantalizing hints that women students tested the boundaries of decorum and safety by smoking on the sly comes to us through codes of behaviour and records of punishments for breaches as early as the nineteenth century. One institution to record infractions was the famous women's college in St Thomas, Ontario, Alma College, recently destroyed by fire. There, the minutes of the Alma College Council record that a young woman was censured in 1896 for "burning cigarettes in her room."[3] The offending student received four censure marks for this infraction, on a par with "creating a disturbance after retiring hour," "clandestine correspondence," or "injuring the furnishings," all of which one could imagine in association with smoking. Accounts of European women students who smoked were sprinkled throughout educational treatises on the fallacy of educating young women.[4] At the same time, living in close quarters with other smoking students might well have encouraged women who were unfamiliar with the practice.

As a comparison, the young men at the Evangelical Lutheran Seminary of Canada in Waterloo were permitted to smoke in particular areas of the dormitories and grounds at the turn of the twentieth century. They were reminded, however, that smoking was "forbidden upon the streets or outside the Institution."[5] The same code of discouraging public smoking applied to women, likely because it was seen as a badge of the streetwalker. As public smoking called young women's purity into question, so too it could besmirch a young seminarian.

Advertising campaigns in the interwar period promoting women's smoking were in their infancy and had yet to find the convincing formula that would develop by the Second World War. By that time, large numbers of middle-class women were in the workforce along with their working-class sisters, creating ideal conditions for smoking to facilitate the same type of social bonding that men experienced in combat. Popular culture had also embraced women's smoking with vigour, making varied images of the woman smoker a normalized part of the visual map. Not surprisingly then, this was the era when many Canadian female university students and collegians took up smoking, continuing in the long tradition stretching back to the nineteenth century of the female intellectual as rebel-smoker.

Selling Cigarettes to the Canadian Woman Student in the Interwar Years

Both the primary and some secondary literature of the 1920s confirms the belief that smoking was common as an expression of women's rejection of conventional norms expecting them to become young wives, then mothers, or compliant labourers.[6] Such forces as postwar urbanization, waged labour for the middle- as well as the working-class woman, secularization, gaining the vote, and the quiet death of maternal feminism, which undid Victorian notions of respectability for women, are all cited as reasons why public smoking by women became common. Young women were expected to act differently from members of their mothers' generation, and to a degree they did by learning new codes presented through the prescriptive images found in tobacco advertising. I will argue that there were more reasons for women to accept smoking than simply as a consequence of liberating norms, however. I begin that argument by asserting that to assume that social norms changed rapidly in the two decades of the interwar period is incorrect. The evidence suggests that with some exceptions, pre-war standards of feminine respectability remained intact for much of this period on most Canadian university campuses. Consider the image shown in figure 9.2 from a United Cigar Stores advertisement in the new Canadian women's magazine, *Chatelaine*, in 1928. The ad appears to convince young women that the respectable middle-class girl could not only safely smoke outside her home but also shop for her tobacco supplies while maintaining decorum.[7] It accompanied a rash of ads directed to the woman smoker in the late 1920s, including Lucky Strike's ad line to "Reach for a Lucky Instead of a Sweet," which helped to associate smoking with slenderness and contemporary norms of beauty.[8] In 1928, the Lucky Strike campaign cost $7,000,000, second only to General Motors' advertising campaigns.[9]

Ladies Welcome!

In every United Cigar Store courteous salesmen pay special attention to the purchases of ladies. The moment you enter you will find attentive, helpful service. And the merchandise you buy will be *fresh*.

United Cigar Stores
Limited
Canadian Owned and Controlled

9.2 | Magazine advertisement for United Cigar Stores, *Chatelaine*, 1928

This advertisement is noteworthy on several levels. First, the denotated messages are unusually full. The visual arrangement shows three young and attractive women in their stylish wool coats, wide fur collars, pumps, and cloche hats framing the middle-aged male merchant. While the women seem delighted with their purchases, hailing each other in the shop seemingly reserved for women, the merchant appears as a passive agent, staring downward as he offers other tobacco products to the women. (Other versions of this advertisement cast a young man as the clerk, with him staring directly at the women and their purchases.) Immediately before the women are the stock-in-trade of the United Cigar Stores: box after box of ornately decorated cigar boxes, which beckon to the middle-class (and middle-aged) male clientele. Within such an alien masculine space, women would justifiably feel some anxiety about their place. (See chapter 5 for an analysis of the cigar-box labels found in these stores.)

To answer their reasonable fear that they might feel uncomfortable, the ad devotes considerable copy to address "Ladies" and their worries directly. Smoking at home is one thing, but buying tobacco products in public spaces would put the young middle-class woman at the mercy of a working-class male clerk who could easily insult her, intentionally or not. The popular literature of the period is replete with snide jokes about women venturing into cigar stores to purchase tobacco products. A popular cartoon, of which several versions exist, had a woman presenting one of her husband's cigar butts to the agent and saying, "Here is the colour of my husband's cigars. Please match that." There was so much ridicule of women being out of their "place" in the cigar shop that the occasional columnist came to their defence.[10] Thus, the anxiety implied here was not unjustified.

The advertisement is interesting in that it confronts this anxiety and the young woman tobacco purchaser's obvious vulnerability through a carefully phrased statement. The potential woman customer is assured that her shopping experience will be pleasurable rather than an affront to her respectability, that the clerk will act appropriately by taking sufficient notice of her so that she will not feel rebuffed, and that he will provide superior products, since her novice status as a tobacco consumer might make her an easy mark to being sold inferior goods. Thus, rather than the denotative message telegraphing happiness and security, instead the image recognizes the connotations of the many social barriers for the young middle-class female buyer of tobacco.

Included in these barriers was the implication that the smoking woman was overtly sexual, an exceedingly dangerous suggestion for any woman, particularly one who was already on a modernist track by claiming post-secondary education. The implication of sexuality is countered both by the visual arrangement and by the text. The clerk makes no eye contact with his female customers, fixing his gaze instead on his product. The text addresses "ladies" respectfully and frankly. Interestingly, the advertisement underscores its naturalized depiction by presenting women smokers through a photographic image rather than through line drawings, the more common device for the period. At the same time, the young woman in search of an updated visual identity would find in these three similarly garbed customers the visual cues of friendly confidence and the smart, stylish woman as consumer. Is our young consumer a middle-class student, one of the newly salaried workers in Canada's burgeoning service sector, or perhaps a helpful purchaser of tobacco for a male relative? We are left to draw our own conclusions about this, with the manufacturers conveniently casting the audience as widely as possible. Other versions of this advertisement feature younger women without fur collars on their more modest coats and women in pairs but never women alone. The emphasis in both the text and visual imagery is on the question of respectability, whatever the woman's class and whatever her status as a smoker.

Chatelaine ran three very similar advertisements for United Cigar Stores in its March, April, and May issues of 1928. After this brave start, it stopped advertising cigarettes specifically for women until December of 1929 and only spottily until the 1930s. The secondary literature shows that female-targeted advertising of specific brands was revived in the late 1960s, continuing through to the 1990s.[11] This interrupted campaign causes us to wonder whether *Chatelaine's* editors feared they had misidentified and possibly offended their clientele.

The message we are intended to take from this advertisement and several others on its model is that cigarette smoking is a naturalized habit of women of all ages and that respectability and even prosperity could be claimed by the woman smoker. Very likely, advertisements like this one directed to the woman smoker were among the first to be placed in any Canadian magazine. A survey of American magazine advertisements reveals that none were directed to women before 1926.[12]

In fact, advertisers in the 1920s operated in a hostile climate. Potential women smokers, their anxious parents, and university authorities all would have encountered the long-standing message in educational textbooks of tobacco's dangers for young people, said to be both physical and moral.[13] Textbooks typically grounded discussions of smoking as physiologically dangerous to all parts of the body.[14] More troubling yet, the textbook reader was told, was both the alcohol- and tobacco-user's "powerlessness to improve the character," since "it is a habit which *grows*; and constant indulgence renders the person powerless to resist the desire."[15] A woman with a blemished character caused by smoking would be one whose future would be in jeopardy, according to these accounts.

In popular literature as well, the dangers for women smokers were said to be far greater than those for men. Considering her essential reproductive role, the woman smoker was accused of placing her body as well as her morals in peril. Readers of Mac Levy's popular 1916 book, *Tobacco Habit Easily Conquered*, learned that smoking "devitalizes and debilitates even the sturdiest and healthiest of women. It retards the normal functioning of the delicate organs. It has a harmful effect upon offspring before and after birth. It is even a potential cause of sterility itself."[16] Consistent with this view, John Harvey Kellogg's *Tobaccoism or How Tobacco Kills* argued that tobacco "destroys the sex glands and hinders reproduction" in men, women, and animals, the latter shown in clinical studies.[17] The "family press" such as *MacLean's* magazine also put the case that women were particularly at risk from smoking. Thus, any campaign to convince the educated young woman to smoke somehow had to contend with the weight of educational and popular literature, of which this is but a small sample, which stated outright that smoking was dangerous for young women and that it should be avoided.[18] Even with clear social change, behavioural norms actually changed much more slowly, especially with regard to liminal activities like public drinking and smoking for the middle-class woman. Furthermore, what might have been acceptable in large Canadian cities took much longer to be accepted in small-town and rural Canada.

Searching for the Canadian Woman Undergraduate Smoker between the Wars

Despite the claims of advertisers and the evidence of the secondary literature about smoking by university women in the 1920s, what do self-produced documents show us about that life? Raised in Winnipeg, Charlotte Scott Black graduated with a Bachelor of Science degree in home economics from the Manitoba Agricultural College at the University of Manitoba in 1925. In this Charlotte was something of a pioneer. Established in 1906, the Agricultural College had been transformed into the Faculty of Agriculture in 1924, with responsibility for the new degree program in home economics.[19]

One of the convocation gifts received by Charlotte was a scrapbook sent to her by her Auntie Maude in Los Angeles. Redolent with pride in her niece's achievements, the card carries the hope that this "little gift" will do its part in helping Charlotte to transport "memories of [her] college life into the larger and fuller life" she was about to enter.[20] The scrapbook became the frame for a wide variety of documents and memorabilia for this exciting milestone in Charlotte's life: postcards, letters, invitations, notations of social outings and receptions, and many photographs of the graduation itself as well as of events over her undergraduate years. It offers what Susan Close calls a "representational discourse" in her study of photographic albums.[21] From her carefully planned scrapbook, we learn that in honour of their graduation, Charlotte and her classmates were invited to a reception at Government House hosted by Lieutenant Governor and Lady Aikins, to dinners hosted by the Manitoba Agricultural College faculty and the dean of science, and to a luncheon at the lavish Fort Garry Hotel hosted by the University of Manitoba Alumni Association, among other events.

Clearly, Charlotte Black and her classmates occupied a position of some status in this agricultural society; in their era, they would have been acknowledged as part of the intellectual elite of the city of Winnipeg. Women entered university in Manitoba in increasing numbers after the First World War, but by the 1950s they still occupied only one-quarter of the undergraduate places at the University of Manitoba.[22] This placed Charlotte in a select group.[23] Further, as a student in the "science" program, Charlotte and her classmates had a higher status than prospective teachers of home economics, who spent only one year on campus. There is some evidence that Charlotte, or "Blackie" to her chums, was quite aware of her social entitlement. Included in the scrapbook, for example, is the invitation to a banquet in June of 1924 at the Fort Garry Hotel. The sponsor was her father's fraternal lodge, the Order of the Royal Purple Supreme Lodge. Charlotte notes that she "attended with Daddy because Mother was ill. The most awful banquet ever experienced. Danced with such things as gas-meter-men after dinner – a scorching night," she sniffed. Because she was raised in a comfortable urban middle-class family, feted by the university and its families, and armed with a relatively rare university degree, we might assume that Charlotte Black and/or her friends might have adopted a common marker of modernity and feminine authority, cigarette-smoking.

The many photographs and descriptions kept by Charlotte Black to memorialize the best of her undergraduate experience suggest otherwise, however. Leaving aside the obviously posed pictures of the happy graduates, the "candid" photographs show a tight group of eleven young women at work and play but with no evidence at all of smokers in the group. At leisure in a lounge, taking tea "in Isobel's room," lounging on the building's steps after their last lecture, shopping as a foursome, camping with the same eleven classmates or enjoying a bonfire meal with men friends too, hiking, studying, strolling – they perch, sit with feet drawn up, hang companionably on each other, laugh helplessly at their own antics, but never, ever smoke. Some of the men sport pipes, but none of the women even play-act at smoking. It is entirely absent from this female visual space.

The denotative meanings of these photographs are clear through repeated patterns and spatial locations: university life is comfortably co-educational, for the young, and within a select number of private and public spaces. Appropriate leisured activities included studying, amiable conversations with tea, camping, or elegant dinners, always in groups of varying sizes but apparently never with women faculty members, of whom there were only two during Charlotte's university years, one each in arts

Class '25,
3rd year

Jessie Fraser. Mac. Kirk
Strat,

Blackie. Mac. Kirk. Strat,

Mac., Merle C. Stra
Lena,

9.3 | Charlotte Black's graduation scrapbook, Winnipeg, 1925

and home economics.[24] Charlotte's socializing appears to have been done almost exclusively with her peers. The connotative meanings are limited but suggestive: the undergraduates tended not to "date" one partner but rather socialized in groups, female graduates dressed in a virginal white "uniform"; both leisured and academic activities remained closely tied to the natural environment of the western prairies rather than to a built landscape; and the code of respectability for the university-educated middle-class woman seemingly offered little opportunity for personal expression. In the images selected by Charlotte Black (figure 9.3), one young undergraduate looks very much like the next: short hair swept off the face, mid-calf skirts, shapeless tops and coats, a profusion of hats for any social event. Charlotte's supportive and non-smoking peer group helps to explain the absence of cigarettes in these frames, just as smoking peers might have influenced her decision to "light up." No one could reasonably argue that because Charlotte Black's personal scrapbook contains no references to women smoking, no women in her social group did so or that other women on her campus or others did not smoke. It should be noted as well that a thorough investigation of yearbooks for a number of Canadian universities during the 1920s and 1930s turned up not a single photograph of a woman smoker in either official or candid images.

However, there is considerable evidence that undergraduate women were smoking in this period, both on Canadian campuses and elsewhere. Phyllis Lee Peterson, a student at McGill in the 1920s, remembers her "rush down to Murray's for five or six cups of coffee on an original ten cent investment because women are not allowed to smoke at McGill and the management of Murray's is more understanding."[25] This situation was eased in 1927 when 39 women living in the McGill University residence for women petitioned the women's warden for a separate smoking room. One was established for senior students.[26] In the mid-1920s, the authorities at Bryn Mawr, the exclusive ladies' college, had lifted the ban on smoking for students.[27] The diary of Yvonne Blue, a freshman at the University of Chicago in 1927, suggests that sorority sisters often smoked together. Yvonne became a member of the Acoth Club and reported that the members "talked of nothing but boys, smoked incessantly, and scattered 'O my Gods!' quite liberally through their conversation." In response, Yvonne also took to smoking, cut her hair in a severe bob, and dressed exclusively in black.[28] A survey at Vassar College in the 1920s revealed that almost half of the students claimed to be smokers.[29] Women at Girton College, Oxford, had been permitted to smoke in their rooms since the end of the First World War.[30] Even in Saskatchewan, oral testimony from undergraduates indicates that many smokers indulged on the sly, smoking while hanging out of windows or finding secure areas on campus out of the public gaze.[31]

We can only guess at Charlotte's own opinions about the woman smoker or her intentions as she set about creating her keepsake document. Furthermore, we cannot know whether one of Charlotte's friends might have smoked but not for the camera or in this crowd. Evidence of female undergraduates' vocational intentions in the 1920s at Queen's University shows that the majority sought positions in teaching, one of the few professions open to women in this era for which a university degree would be advantageous.[32] It is possible that the spotless visual record kept by Charlotte and her friends was motivated in part by their vague intentions to one day teach and therefore to be a "moral exemplar" for children.[33] Whatever the reasons for Charlotte's and her friends' rejection of

9.4 | Toronto General Hospital School of Nursing yearbook, 1929

smoking, this window into a young Canadian undergraduate's life through her photograph album shows that the much-discussed smoking practices of university women did not pertain to this student on this campus and in this era. Furthermore, Charlotte and her friends were not alone in eschewing smoking. Just a few years later, however, the story would be different.

In addition to the woman teacher, Canadian nurses in training would have been discouraged from smoking in any public area where the nurse wore her pure white uniform. Conversely, women who trained as nurses in the interwar period remember "smoking rooms" set aside for them in the student residence – for example, at Vancouver General Hospital.[34] The same nurse reporting this, Hallie Sloan, recalls a curious enabling of nurse-smokers by the owner of a café where the young women escaped to listen to music and socialize. She remembers the owner "keeping" the young women's cigarettes at the café for their smoking pleasure rather than sending them back to the residence with the cigarettes. Ms Sloan credits this to convenience for the young women, who worked long hours and had too little time to socialize. An alternative conclusion might relate to the discouragement of or outright ban on smoking in the residence. The saucy line drawing (figure 9.4) from a 1929 yearbook of the Toronto General Hospital School of Nursing contrasts the nursing-student-as-smoker with the official prescription. Under the young nursing student's caricature, in which she poses with one leg crooked and her arms akimbo, is the hand-written phrase, "The right attitude." Immediately below is the official and ironic "voice" – "Things We Could Never Imagine." We do not need to use our own imagination to determine which label is the more accurate.

Regardless of how and when women students chose to smoke in this period, the textual record of this era suggests that smoking by women students commanded a great deal of attention and generated anxiety in the general population. Hollywood films like the 1920s *Confessions of a*

Co-ed: A Flaming Diary of Flaming College Youth played in theatres across the Canadian west and doubtless would have added to public worries about smoking youths.[35] The American *Ladies' Home Journal* in 1922, for example, ran a long article, "Women Cigarette Fiends."[36] In it, Harry Burke told the (mythical) story of a certain Eleanor Smith, who had been sent to an exclusive finishing school in New York City, far from her home in the midwest. On visiting Eleanor, her parents discover that she "knew how" to smoke when she deftly lights her father's cigarette. To her mother's distress, Eleanor and the other girls are provided with a separate smoking room in their school, and it is patronized by most of the girls. The author bemoans this trend, pointing out that these schoolgirls take up the habit to emulate "their so-called smarter sisters."[37] In *The Truth about Tobacco*, Bernarr MacFadden, the so-called "Father of Physical Culture," credits the "tremendous increase" in women smokers in the 1920s to a desire to be "smart" and cosmopolitan rather than Puritan or provincial.[38]

To capitalize on the belief that the American college woman typically smoked, marketing authority Edward Bernays sent out the following press release to the American college market: "Seven out of every 10 coeds at Northwestern Like to Smoke. Those figures were computed on the basis of a petition signed by the women students living in houses on the women's quadrangle. The petition, in protest against the established ban on smoking, asked the right to smoke."[39] Undoubtedly, some university-educated women did smoke in this era, as the evidence shows, but visual and textual sources suggest that smoking in public during the 1920s on Canadian campuses might have been less typical than has been claimed, calling into question the amount of smoking generally. Certainly, in Canadian universities located in denominational or otherwise conservative settings, the rate of smoking uptake was far slower than that in major urban centres.

Joan Jacobs Brumberg has argued that in the United States, smoking was common among college women because it supported the new "flexible personal image"[40] of the era. In Canada, Cynthia Comacchio has documented the many destabilizing forces during the 1920s that caused authorities to be anxious about the "problem of modern youth" with their presumed rejection of their parents' generational authority.[41] But Canadian historians generally agree that these anxieties exaggerated "flaming youths'" level of rebellion,[42] certainly the female version. As with many other social changes, the promise of rebellion outpaced the practice.

This assessment of smoking by many young university women was beginning to change by the eve of the Second World War on many Canadian campuses. As a case in point, McGill University packaged its own brand of

ENDERS for the construction of the "Sir Arthur Currie Memorial Gymnasium-Armoury" are being called as this issue of the "McGill News" goes to press. Before another year has passed it is expected that the first units of the new building will be completed ready for use. ¶ Because of lack of funds it has been necessary to omit the swimming pool, hockey rink and other units that form a part of the complete scheme. ¶ The contribution made by McGill Cigarettes has added an appreciable sum to the building fund and your continued purchases of these cigarettes will do much to make possible the building of McGill's gymnasium in its entirety.

McGILL CIGARETTES

9.5 and 9.6 | Advertisements for McGill Cigarettes, Montreal, 1939

Virginia Cigarettes, as did other large urban universities across the country,[43] including Queen's. From the mid-1930s, McGill used the proceeds from the branded cigarette sales as part of its fundraising campaign for a new gymnasium and armoury.

By 1939, when advertisements (figures 9.5 and 9.6) appeared in the *McGill News*, the campaign was drawing to a close. Despite the "appreciable sum" contributed from the cigarette sales, readers were informed that significant components to the original plans, including the swimming pool, hockey rink, and other unnamed areas, would have to be omitted due to lack of money. Perhaps McGill University authorities had also overestimated the number of smokers, including women, on campus.

To reinforce the university undergraduate's decision to take up smoking – for her university's welfare, after all – the *McGill News* regularly ran an advertisement of a very modern undergraduate woman and a dashing male companion carrying ski gear. Had the reader forgotten the significance of the fundraising project, the advertisement reminds us that "Every Package Sold Adds to the Building Fund." The same image of snow-laden hills and spruce trees ran in all seasons of the *McGill News*, possibly

9.7 | Wood and papier maché match case

to link this "cool" university-season sport with smoking in readers' minds, just as it had previously been linked with golf, cycling, and other healthy sports. The woman is modestly attired and, unlike her companion, does not hold a cigarette, bespeaking the uncertain status of the undergraduate woman smoker.

We have evidence too that McGill University women faculty members either smoked or celebrated smoking through their objets d'art. The match case shown in figure 9.7 from the late nineteenth century features a painted lid showing a hunting scene. It was owned and used by Gladys Bean, who taught physical education at McGill University. But universities were not alone in pre-war Canada in defining the woman scholar as a smoker. Cigarette manufacturers, possibly influenced by universities' initiatives in targeting the women smoker, had diversified their market before the Second World War to include the woman student. The billboard advertisement for Grads Cigarettes (figure 9.8) is one example of advertising likely directed to the academic woman. A fresh-faced and attractive graduate holds all the symbols of academia: roses held high at graduation, mortar board atop her carefully coiffed hair, diploma clutched in her hand with beautifully manicured nails. The smart university graduate is encouraged on this billboard to smoke a brand offering "the height of good

9.8 and 9.9 | Billboard advertisement for Grads Cigarettes, Toronto, 1937–39;
Bette Davis, lounging with cigarette, c. 1945. © Moviepix/Getty Image 75038010

taste" just in case she might debase herself with a more common choice.
Many advertisements made the case that women who smoked were discriminating in dress and makeup, happily coupled, and confident. Thus,
even if prospective smokers were not themselves students, this brand assures women that a woman seeking an identity that defined her as intelligent and discriminating could achieve it by adopting this cigarette brand.

Cinema star Bette Davis is shown in figure 9.9, a studio photograph, as
a woman of beauty and culture. She could easily represent in the public
mind the image of a woman privileged through wealth and formal education. In this photograph, Davis reclines on a couch, with her cigarette
held high. She is wearing a satin blouse or dress as well as tasteful ear

rings, and her hair is upswept in a sophisticated style. She holds a script before her, denoting her status as a movie actress. Women of substance, or women who hoped to be perceived in this way and wanted to look the part, needed only model their purchases and gestures on Bette Davis in photographs like this one or on the representations of women found on brands like Grads. Women could easily emulate the hairstyle, clothing, and feminine flourishes with their cigarettes.

These images and many others accompanying them on billboards, in magazines, on wall signs of buildings, or in the movies made the case that intelligent, middle-class, and happy women smoked and were *themselves* "blended right" in mixing sophistication, good taste, and of course, smoking. Not surprisingly, such women were presented as racialized white.

Convincing the Undergraduate Woman to Smoke: Popular Media, 1940–60

By the time of the Second World War, Canadians were exposed to many more images of women as smokers in a variety of types: glamorous, demure, serious, playful, sexy, and sophisticated. This is not to say, however, that public smoking by women was accepted in all social quarters. In many places, including, as described by Donald F. Davis and Barbara Lorenzkowski, on buses and trams, public smoking remained a male activity. For many, the woman smoker still summoned a constellation of loose and otherwise unseemly connotations, as in this letter to the editor of the *Ottawa Morning Citizen*: "Smoking, drinking, wearing slacks and shorts (the latter so brief) a loose kind of conversation, yes and all this ... on street-cars."[44] In fact, Nancy Kiefer and Ruth Roach Pierson argue that in comparison to earlier periods, the liberated status of the female undergraduate eroded somewhat during the war years.[45] Reflective of the still robust conservatism, piety, and moral leadership in Ottawa, the yearbooks of the École Normale at l'Université d'Ottawa feature young women standing demurely, surrounded by the Oblate Fathers, who still administered the university in those years.[46] A cigarette in this landscape would have been unthinkable, and they are nowhere. Likewise, at the University of British Columbia in 1944, the "Frosh Smoker" was understood to be only for male students: the student manual for that year, *The Tillicum*, noted that this event was "an evening with pipes, tobacco, cider and masculine entertainment." [47]

If there still was little evidence of women smoking on Canadian university campuses in the interwar period, it was much more evident both in public and popular culture. The means invoked to "sell" this message to women by the 1940s had also become more refined. Cigarette advertising before the Second World War often represented the woman smoker as a very young woman primarily in search of pleasure. By the 1940s, the image was more often of an older woman who sought pleasure and sexuality, to be sure, but also represented such qualities as mature accomplishment and prosperity with her glamour. In the array of images by advertisers, the consumer could easily find many models to emulate. In this period too, more women academics were moving into scholarly posts at universities. One of them was Pauline Jewett, a lecturer at Queen's University during the 1940s, then engaged at Carleton University from 1955.[48] It was during this period that Pauline became a smoker.

Canadian Women Undergraduate Smokers and Universities Represent Themselves, 1940–80

Textual and photographic evidence as well as oral testimony from the postwar period indicates that both male and female students' smoking rates climbed steeply in this period. In addition to the reasons already noted for this trend was the apparent blessing of university authorities. Traditional academic strictures against women smoking at campus events became so eroded that authorities not only tolerated young women smoking but celebrated it in staged scenes. In an earlier period, after the First World War, former servicemen returning to Canadian campuses brought with them a culture that supported smoking. Indeed, a major student strike in 1928 had occurred at Queen's when university authorities attempted to reduce leisure activities such as drinking and smoking on campus.[49] Shenanigans by rambunctious students, especially males, were common, as presented in figures 9.10 and 9.11 of postwar images of campus life.

Following the Second World War, this landscape changed significantly. University authorities were now keen to demonstrate the university's modern face. Images of the female smoker were thought to be an important way to accomplish this goal. Official university photographers snapped pictures of both undergraduate and faculty members enjoying smoking in social settings. In this innocent period before the link with cancer was confirmed, cigarette smoking still seemed to most a harmless, inexpensive way to spend time with others; it also appeared nationalistic, since Canada had developed into one of the major producers of tobacco. Among other inducements for the university woman to take up smoking, the visual record produced by undergraduates themselves shows the presumably harmless fun of social smoking, indicating that more peer examples of smokers were available.

9.10 and 9.11 | Campus life

Two photograph albums from Queen's University in Kingston, Ontario, both from the 1940s, offer evidence of this. Despite historian Frederick Gibson's assertion that in its early days, Queen's had a reputation for being a poor man's institution, by the 1930s it was drawing from a solid middle-class base for its students, with women students' families showing higher class status than men's.[50] The proportion of female graduate students peaked there in 1929–30 when 28 per cent of graduate students were women.[51] As with the Charlotte Black scrapbook, the candid photograph allows us to peek into the world of undergraduate life at a given place and time. The camera's owner chooses what to photograph, but the person being photographed also has agency in deciding whether she will allow herself to be photographed, how she will pose herself, and what props she will choose to share the frame. Both albums contain photographs along with other artifacts of university life: invitations to events, dance cards for formal proms, and so on. However, unlike the 1920s album from Winnipeg, cigarettes are photographed in these albums from the 1940s and almost always playfully. It would seem that the edge had been taken off the act of women's smoking at this university through class entitlement and repeated viewings in the media and on campus by that date.

9.12 and 9.13 | Woman in park, reading, photograph album, Kingston, Ontario, 1940s; Woman in park, holding puppy, photograph album, Kingston, Ontario, 1940s

In one album, a group of six young dorm-mates pile onto a bed, hair in "rag rollers" in their nightgowns.[52] One of the women "smokes" a cigarette, which appears suspiciously oversize, as if it too were constructed from one of the rag rollers. Real or not, however, it is included in the photograph as a marker of innocent good times, relaxation, and especially, social conviviality in the style of undergraduate pranks pictured in most keepsake albums. This photograph has been mounted on heavy paper with the intention of using it as a postcard. It was to be sent to "R.R.I. – 117 East Ave, Brantford." Whether or not it was ever sent, the photograph's intended use as a public document advertises the owner's pride in the image, its public acceptability, and its denotative and connotative meanings. Two photographs from a second Queen's album (figures 9.12 and 9.13) show two young women relaxing in a park or in some other public space. Despite the lack of captions, we can see that both are attractive and modestly clothed for outdoor cool weather. One holds a book, the other a new puppy, and both casually smoke. Interestingly, the stance

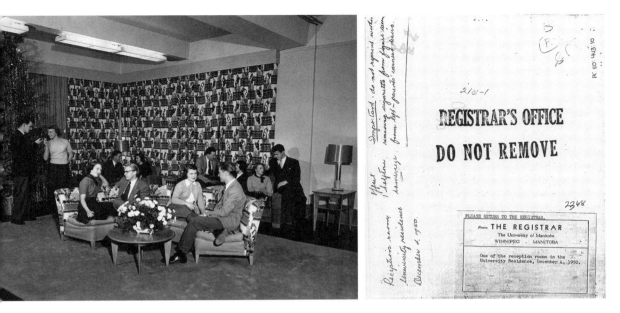

9.14 and 9.15 | Photograph produced by Registrar's Office, University of Manitoba, 1950; Image on back of photograph produced by Registrar's Office, 1950

adopted by the young women does not mimic the screen idols with the "flag" display of crooked arm, cigarette at mid-neck level. In both cases, the cigarette is held away from the body in one hand, with the alternate hand holding another object. The denotative meanings in all three album pictures concern young women undergraduates' leisured activities. But the connotative meanings are quite different when compared: in the first photograph, "smoking" is presented as a light-hearted prank, along with piling many into a bed; in the second two photographs, smoking has lost much of its surplus meaning as an act of rebellion. "Two friends smoke while relaxing in a park": there is little edge to this act. The cigarette is such a normalized part of the women's appearance that it has also lost its central framing power. The cigarette is merely one of several objects of interest in the second two photographs. Apparently, the rules of how to smoke at Queen's had been loosened with the war, allowing for a broader range of expressive poses for women.

A similar message of sophisticated sociability appears in a publicity photograph for the new reception room at the University of Manitoba residence in December 1950 (figure 9.14). The Registrar's Office had arranged for posed photographs to be used to promote the university's new facility. In this image, however, the photographer chose to have one couple, on

9.16 | Football game at Queen's University, Kingston, Ontario, 1950s

the extreme left, staged as smokers. The woman evinces the typical "flag" posture with her partner offering a light. The controlled respectability of the event is underlined by the placement of the furniture and by the students arranged in strict pairs. Although smoking had become increasingly common by this date, the back of the photograph reminds us that the decision to pose a woman undergraduate smoking in 1950 in one of Canada's conservative urban centres would be noticed and unfavourably by some. It bears the Registrar's Office stamp and this note: "Important – do not reprint without removing cigaretts [sic] from figure second from left – parents' earnest desire."

But even if parents did not want to admit that their university-attending daughters were smoking comfortably at the University of Manitoba or at Waterloo Lutheran, other institutions embraced the woman student smoker.

Staged photographs were employed by the Queen's University administration. A photographic collage purports to show the range of student activities during the 1950s at that university. The collage provides pride of place in the middle to a photogenic couple at some university event, possibly a football game (figure 9.16). In only one of the photos included in this set is anyone clearly smoking, and that is the beautiful, well-dressed woman with her hair tied back by a scarf and a double strand of pearls at her neck. She clings winsomely to her escort while lifting her cigarette

9.17 | Open house reception, University of Manitoba, 1953

in the prescribed stance. As a photographic collage, we do not know how this set of photographs was actually utilized by the authorities at Queen's; what we do know, however, is that by this time, smoking by young women was not just tolerated, it was celebrated as normal and even glamorous behaviour typically engaged in by the undergraduate woman at this modern university.

Beyond the official photographs, how did student yearbook editors choose to represent smoking in student life? By the 1950s, smoking had become associated with dating, allowing a woman to develop new uses for the attention-focusing cigarette. One of my respondents notes that she was a committed smoker as a university student in the early 1950s. "It was normal behaviour, as I recall."[53] The potential for serious young women to show off their hands to good effect or contrive to gently frame the face in softening smoke, like the iconic Bette Davis, telegraphed important social messages, often saturated with sexual content. The same conclusion must be drawn with more formal events associated with student clubs, such as sororities. In figure 9.17, Pi Beta Phi is shown with its open house reception and the sorority executive committee at the University of Manitoba. The photo is interesting both in itself and for its placement on the page with other artifacts of the sorority. The denotative meaning of the images is similar: smiling young women clad in matched sweater sets, curled hair and strings of pearls. However, the connotation of the upper photograph includes new features to explain the young woman casually smoking in the centre of the image. It shows a social occasion, calling for crowds of

9.18 and 9.19 | Scene at UBC, 1959; Formal event at Queen's University, 1957

young men and women as well as older members of the community, refreshments, and conviviality.

Women in sororities of the 1950s and 1960s on Canadian campuses often chose to have their members shown smoking. While this might not seem such a momentous decision, recall that it had been only since the Second World War, a scant decade before, that conventional women had decided to represent themselves as public smokers. By this self-representation, women were in fact claiming a right that they had not demanded only a few years before. In figure 9.18 from the UBC *Totem*, a student-run campus newspaper, four young women try the can-can without even bothering to rest their cigarettes. In the sorority house or private home, well-groomed, conservative, middle-class young women could expect a semi-private setting where one could smoke without censure. At formal social engagements too, particularly when young women controlled the agenda, they were very likely to be found smoking. In figure 9.19, two couples, with the women dressed in tulle and lace, enjoy each other's company, a refreshing drink, and a cigarette. From the Queen's University yearbook of 1957, it shows the central female subject holding liquor glass and cigarette in one hand, a feat of both dexterity and modernism. Other evidence indicates that considerable numbers of university undergraduates were smoking by this time. A report from the University of Alberta revealed that of first-

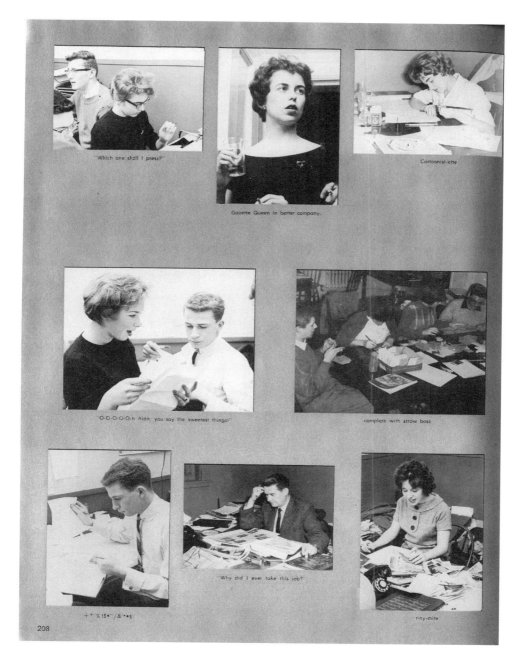

"Which one shall I press?"

Gazette Queen in better company.

Cartoonist-ette

"O-O-O-O-h Alan, you say the sweetest things!"

complete with straw boss

+ * ' % !$•" /& ••s

"Why did I ever take this job?"

tiny-mite

9.20 | Yearbook staff at Dalhousie University, Halifax, 1961 year education students in 1960–61, 18.5 per cent of the women and 32.4 per cent of the men admitted to being regular smokers.[54] A pan-Canadian study of Canadian university students in the same year showed much higher rates for women smokers, higher than their male colleagues. A total of 46.3 per cent of women university students in British Columbia claimed to be smokers, as compared with 45.8 per cent of men.[55] These figures are consistent with oral interviews of women who were university students in the 1960s. Several indicated that smoking occurred at most social events and very often to calm nerves when assignments were being completed.[56]

Frayed nerves seem to have been uppermost in the minds of the year-book staffers at Dalhousie University in 1961 shown in figure 9.20. Of the eight hard-working staff workers portrayed in this collage, three hold cigarettes, including a woman centrally placed. Smoking and stressful work seemed to go together.

Faculty members and support staff were also commonly presented as smokers in the 1960s. At the University of Waterloo, private scrapbooks[57] and the official yearbook[58] all show faculty members smoking in social settings. The same was true at the University of British Columbia, with female faculty members and wives of faculty shown both drinking and smoking in photographs.[59] In fact, so naturalized had smoking become within the academy by this decade that the official rules were often broken. Like most university institutions of postwar Canada, Waterloo College had rules for smoking, as set out in its handbook for 1961–62: "Smoking is not allowed in the University classrooms, problems rooms, libraries or laboratories, but is only permitted in those areas where ash trays are provided. This includes corridors, coffee rooms, common rooms and the cafeteria."[60] In that same year, however, a major debate was held, and photographs of it show that most of the participants smoked in the classrooms. Eventually, the regulations seemed to catch up with practice. By 1966–67, the *University of Waterloo Student Village Handbook* had reduced its statements on smoking to this bland, single sentence: "Residents are not to smoke in bed because of the fire hazard."[61] Tellingly, any statement at all related to smoking was omitted from handbooks for 1967 through 1972.

By the early 1970s, candid photographs of women undergraduates often showed them smoking. This was true even in universities with a strong religious base, such as the University of Ottawa.[62] The young women shown in figure 9.21, with briefcases in view, could easily be in a classroom. They seem to be listening intently to someone, possibly a professor, both smoking the extra long cigarettes popular in that period. On the year-

9.21 | Two women smoking, University of Ottawa, 1971

book page from which this image is drawn, almost every picture shows students smoking. The smoking rate was also possibly a reflection of the franco-ontarien population base at the University of Ottawa, a sector of the population with higher rates of smoking among both men and women than in anglophone quarters.[63] In addition, by choosing such images for their yearbook, the staff had further normalized a practice that had been officially and normatively forbidden only a few years earlier.

University Academics and Smoking, 1945 to 1980

With the end of the Second World War, more female academics began to move into Canadian universities. The returning servicemen who were now students brought with them smoking habits and presented significant challenges to their female professors. In 1946, Pauline Jewett was engaged as a lecturer in political science at Queen's University. This is the approximate period when the glamorous photograph shown in figure 9.22 was taken of her. With her dissertation uncompleted and with only the most rudimentary pedagogical skills, Pauline faced daunting challenges to her authority from the returned soldiers. She recounts them rolling marbles down the steps of the amphitheatre where she lectured, the men cat-calling and whistling at her, and other attempts to undercut her authority whenever possible.

9.22 and 9.23 | Pauline Jewett, 1940s; Pauline Jewett, 1950s

I did have some trouble in the first couple of weeks in one of those large classes. There was a tendency for them to shoot craps at the back of the class and push each other around and laugh and go to sleep and what not. One day, when I was beginning to think that this class would never be disciplined, I got quite annoyed because this chap in the sixth row had gone to sleep and was snoring loudly and his mouth was wide open. And I reached behind me to the ledge of the blackboard and picked up a piece of chalk – and, by the way, at one time I had been centre-forward on the basketball team – and threw it, and it went right into his mouth. And he gagged and woke up and everyone looked at me with some admiration, I must say, and they behaved better after that chalk episode.[64]

Shortly after this event, Pauline would lose a tenure-track position at Queen's to a less qualified male colleague. Academic women in the post-war period were tolerated but not welcomed in the academy. One response to this discrimination was to adopt male models of leisure and comportment. Many academic women became smokers to indicate that they belonged in the "club."

Life in the academy was lonely and stressful for women like Pauline Jewett. This is not to say that women pioneers like Jewett did not have friends and mentors. One of Pauline's was Jean Royce, registrar at Queen's between 1933 and 1968. In her role as a university administrator and as convener of the Canadian Federation of University Women and of the Standards Committee of the International Federation of University Women, Jean Royce exercised almost unparalleled authority on campus. She resolved to support women students. Her particular mentoring of Pauline Jewett along with other women was enormously important to them.[65] As Pauline reports: "Then I got a call to go and see Miss Royce. She asked if I were interested in going to graduate school. The idea had simply never occurred to me. Going on in mathematics was not the normal thing it became later … I was completely taken aback, said that I was definitely not interested and went off. However, she had planted the thought in my mind."[66]

Regardless of such mentors as Royce, however, most academic women of the era felt isolated. Many took up smoking, including Pauline Jewett.[67] "She liked her smokes, loved her scotch," summarized Pete McMartin in Jewett's obituary in 1992.[68] The attraction was undoubtedly what it had always been for the academic woman: the projection of a sense of world-liness in this male-dominated setting of intellectual one-upmanship as well as a stress release. Photographs such as figure 9.23 showing Pauline Jewett after she had joined the staff at Carleton in the 1950s help to explain her particular brand of magnetism: pictured in full laugh, showing her infectious energy, her lithe figure and beauty. But brave photographs do not negate the frustrating and difficult times she often experienced in that role.

Similar accounts of the problems in academia emerge from testimony given to me by female academics who are, or were, also smokers. One notes that "initially, what was pleasurable was the social aspect – sitting talking, drinking, laughing, discussing and of course solving or at the very least identifying the world's problems … When I went back to school and eventually began teaching … we could smoke in our offices. It was then, I think, that I really began to associate smoking with my work – not consciously, but part of that coffee, cigarette, writing process (and it is still the case)."[69] Judy Rebick, a student at McGill in the 1960s, recalls starting smoking then because she "wanted to be one of the boys."[70]

By the mid and later 1970s, however, there is less evidence of casual smoking on campuses by either women students or faculty. Always a

9.24 and 9.25 | Dalhousie University scoreboard, 1962; Young women smoking in library stacks, Dalhousie University, 1973

popular companion to alcohol, smoking remained a regular pub activity. It is striking that in the same period, alcohol consumption seems to have increased and was certainly celebrated in the "campus life" sections of university yearbooks. Smoking was so omnipresent at such universities as Dalhousie University in Halifax that Players' Cigarettes were fea-

9.26 | Plant with sign, Dalhousie University yearbook, 1976–77

tured on the basketball scoreboard (figure 9.24). Students smoked even while using the library stacks (see figure 9.25). By the late 1970s, there was an attempt to better control smoking in public spaces on campus (see figure 9.26). During the next decade, the tide against smoking on Canadian campuses would turn inexorably. Taking Dalhousie as an example, while social events seemed to justify copious amounts of beer, more and more rarely was the alcohol pictured with cigarettes, at least in women's hands. At the same time, there was increased consciousness about "working out" and the need to exercise away study-pounds.[71] By that period too, student editors of Canadian university newsletters and yearbooks took up the anti-smoking call. Nevertheless, the pace of rooting out smoking on Canadian campuses was slowed, because many student productions were supported by tobacco advertising. In addition, the lag in targeting smoking as a health issue seems to have been partly due to the degree to which smoking had been incorporated into university culture as a marker for sophistication and intellectual aspiration.

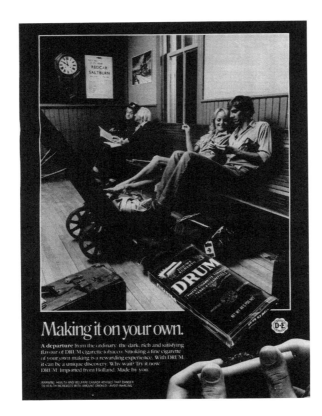

Making it on your own.

A departure from the ordinary: the dark, rich and satisfying
flavour of DRUM cigarette tobacco. Smoking a fine cigarette
of your own making is a rewarding experience. With DRUM,
it can be a unique discovery. Why wait? Try it now.
DRUM. Imported from Holland. Made by you.

WARNING: HEALTH AND WELFARE CANADA ADVISES THAT DANGER
TO HEALTH INCREASES WITH AMOUNT SMOKED—AVOID INHALING.

9.27 | Student news-
paper advertisement for
Drum Cigarette Tobacco,
University of Waterloo,
1982

The advertisement in figure 9.27 points to other components of university culture that were supported by advertising: the ideal of a simple and
self-made product, the appeal of "a departure from the ordinary," and the
desire to "discover" something new. Evoking a practice from the past, the
attractive and extremely thin young couple rest their feet on an old bag-
gage cart placed in the station; an elderly couple sit on the same wooden
bench, providing a contrast to the modern pair. Despite the young man's
act of rolling his cigarette, it is likely that the young woman could also
perfect this skill; thus, the connotative meaning of the advertisement is
also one of levelling and democracy. The advertisement also promotes the
heteronormative standard: the young couple is mirrored by the older example (of themselves in coming years?). One objective frequently noted
for young women to attend university was to find a suitable "match," as
this woman seems to have done. Yet even such a clever advertisement as
this could not hold back the aversion to smoking on campuses across the
country in the 1980s.

9.28 | Pauline Jewett and the NDP sisterhood, 1980s

As the federal government was mustering its energies to pass Bills C-51 and C-204 in the late 1980s, most university authorities passed policies again strictly limiting locations for smoking on campus. The campus pubs remained acceptable smoking territory until after the turn of the century, however, further reinforcing the link between smoking and leisured enjoyment for university students and faculty. It would take federal legislation to remove this last bastion.

To say that university campuses no long permitted smoking on their premises by the 1980s does not suggest that faculty and students had quit by that time. Confirmed smokers continued to find out-of-the-way spots to suck back a cigarette, including, of course, professors' own offices. Detecting the smell of smoke from behind closed doors became a common game in university hallways. And those who had learned to smoke on campus carried right on, including Pauline Jewett. Dawn Black, the NDP member of Parliament for New Westminster, recounts an event from election day in 1983 when Pauline arrived at Dawn's election headquarters: "So suddenly Pauline appeared with her handbag and her strand of pearls [her classic trademarks] and Pauline always had a presence about her – there has never been a question about that. And at this point, people were still allowed to smoke at campaign offices, and there was Pauline with her handbag and smoking a cigarette and she said, 'Well dear, I'm here. What would you like me to do?'"[72] Pauline Jewett died of lung cancer in 1992, but she remains an icon in her own right as the brainy, forthright, and intensely social academic and politician of the last half of the twentieth century. The first woman university president in Canada, she oversaw the increasing network of restrictions on smokers, female or male, on her own campus at Simon Fraser University before her retirement from academic life. She took care never to be photographed smoking.[73]

Canadian middle-class women students and professors eschewed cigarettes longer than their American cousins, but by the 1940s many women in academia experimented with smoking. They did so for reasons different from those that motivated their working sisters. Needing a means to control stress in this male-controlled space, to exert their right to be a respected part of the academy, and to signal the sophistication and "cool" that drew many to academic life, women students and faculty accepted the claims of advertisers and used smoking for their own performative purposes. Although there were marked differences in the uptake rate of smoking on different university campuses, mainly because of religious orientation but also ethnicity, most academic women did not take up smoking on Canadian campuses until after the Second World War. By the 1970s, smoking was increasingly common on all Canadian university campuses and other post-secondary training sites. Not coincidentally, this was also the period when smoking became closely identified with feminists, of which there were many on Canadian university campuses. This alignment will be discussed in chapter 10. Only in the late 1980s was smoking re-moralized and pushed back by restricting the spaces in which one could publicly smoke.

10

Feminism

This chapter explores the intersections of smoking culture and second-wave feminism as it developed in Canada from 1970 to about 1990. In particular, I explore the overlapping histories of second-wave feminism and women's smoking as an act of identity formation. I contrast samples of representations of Canadian women smokers before 1970, and therefore before the rise of the Canadian women's movement, with those associated with second-wave feminism after 1970. I do so to demonstrate the further expansion of visual imagery made possible by feminism's adoption of smoking as a symbol of liberation. Images of women smokers in the earlier period fell into two main types: the young, attractive, sexualized good-time girl and sometime criminal smoker, teetering on the brink of immorality, and a parallel representation of the woman smoker as sophisticated, prosperous, intelligent, and well-groomed. In the post-1970 period, I argue that the welding together of these tropes with second-wave feminism resulted in a powerful amalgam: the feminist smoker as mature, talented, and demanding of her pleasures, while also sexy and intelligent. This is very close to the definitive type of woman drawn into second-wave feminism. I contend that between 1970 and about 1990, the adoption of smoking as a "feminist act" was encouraged by a number of factors. They include the social and performative advantages conferred by smoking and the control smoking gave women over their bodies, principally the control of weight, mood, and pleasure. In addition, an alliance of women's magazine interests, advertisers, and popular culture was able to successfully claim that the truly liberated woman smoked. I argue this through a survey of the role of three women's magazines and of feminists themselves in promoting this construction of the modern feminist smoker: in Canada, the premier women's monthly, *Chatelaine*, its francophone counterpart, *Châtelaine*, and in the United States, the definitive feminist periodical, *Ms Magazine*. I show that these three magazines and the self-defined feminists who ran them had a direct hand in defining perceptions around smoking and feminism by shaping advertising and also by failing to report the medical evidence about smoking's many health risks. In this assessment, and while all three magazines eventually represented anti-tobacco positions, I find the Canadian women's periodicals to have taken the more responsible stance.

The apex for women's smoking in Canada was 1974 when about 40 per cent of Canadian women admitted to being active smokers. That this significant percentage of Canadian women adopted smoking in an era when the health dangers were fully known and advertised in this country demonstrates the power of linking smoking to other important ideological positions. Second-wave feminism was one of them.

Joni Mitchell: Cultural Icon for Smoking

The immense influence of trend-setters in movies and music, with stars like Joni Mitchell, helped to popularize smoking during second-wave feminism's heyday. It was not by chance that Joni Mitchell adopted cigarettes as integral to her artistic identity. Hailed as one of the most important and influential female recording artists of the late twentieth century, Joni Mitchell helped to symbolize second-wave feminism in late twentieth-century Canada. Independent-minded, multi-talented as a singer, songwriter, artist, and poet, Joni Mitchell seemed to have it all. After she had been recording for more than a decade, she recorded *Hejira* in 1976. It was widely regarded as a masterpiece. The image Joni chose for her record album cover was fully in keeping with this time of liberation, including women's right to be pictured as a smoker. In the studio photograph pictured here, she listens intently, holding her iconic cigarette in the "flag" position.

In fact, Joni Mitchell became a committed smoker earlier than she had become a feminist. Born Roberta Joan Anderson in Fort Macleod, Alberta, in 1943, and raised in Saskatoon, Saskatchewan, Joni Mitchell first took up smoking as a nine-year-old. Mitchell proudly admitted this on national television, noting that she had maintained the habit for her entire life.[1] "I took one puff and felt really smart," she reported of this first experience. "I thought, 'Whoa!' I seemed to see better and think better."[2] She may have

10.1 | Joni Mitchell in Amsterdam, 1972. © Redferns/Getty

been very young, but since the average onset age for girls today is around fourteen, Joni was well within statistical norms for taking up smoking. Mitchell ranks among the many young women who took up smoking before adolescence and long before the modern women's movement had begun. Despite many attempts throughout her life to quit, she has so far failed to do so and instead has celebrated her smoking by incorporating it into her public image.

A folksinger beginning in 1962, Mitchell has repeatedly underlined her greater interest in the graphic arts. She frequently describes herself as a painter derailed by circumstance. Those circumstances were largely associated with the era in which she came to maturity, the rising popularity of the folk scene, and her romantic liaisons, as well as her own interests. Yet it has been in song-writing and performing that this enormously talented woman has gained her greatest recognition.

Joni Mitchell began her post-secondary education in 1964 at the Alberta Southern Institute of Technology (SAIT) College of Art in Calgary. During her time there, she also played her guitar and sang her haunting songs at a variety of Calgary coffee houses, such as the Yardbird Suite and the Depression, as well as at similar coffee houses in Edmonton. In that period, she was a typical young female folksinger: tall, slender, with chiselled face and ironed blonde hair, often with a cigarette placed enticingly as she concentrated on her craft. She is remembered by classmates of the 1960s as having a "presence" and a "strength" about her, appearing "driven" to compose and perform.[3]

The culture of Joni's youth, including her time at SAIT's College of Art, was rife with patriarchal entitlement. One of Joni's classmates remembers that soon after she arrived at SAIT with Joni, she was advised by a guidance counsellor to abandon serious art and to "go into crafts. My wife did that and she always had fun, teaching children."[4] While Joni was not overtly politicized during her time at SAIT, she undoubtedly reacted against its male-centred culture, expressed as it was in restricted social codes for women, a male-centric curriculum – which another classmate recalled as including not a single female artist[5] – and traditional life expectations.

When Joni became pregnant in the mid-1960s, she and her lover parted, and Joni moved to Yorkville in Toronto. With the other hippies of the era, she continued her writing and performing away from the critical gaze of her family and community. She recalled long afterwards that she hoped her daughter's bones and teeth were strong, since she had smoked throughout the pregnancy.[6] Her baby was first placed in foster care in 1965 and then adopted. Her grief resulted in a flood of original and wrenching songs, including "Crow on the Cradle" and "Little Green," which she and many others have recorded. She began a period of prolific production, having thirty-eight published songs to her credit by the time she was twenty-four.[7]

On three of Joni Mitchell's album covers, all of which she oversaw, she ensures that the cigarette is prominently featured. Consciously and expertly, she has incorporated the cigarette into her visual map in a central position, paying it homage as an important component of her artistic identity. Using it on stage as well, the cigarette has become closely identified in the public gaze with her artistic production.

Second-Wave Feminism and the Woman Smoker

Like all broad and deep social changes, second-wave feminism, the so-called "women's movement," was complex. The "second wave" of organized feminist activity is said to have occurred between the late 1960s and the early 1990s. This "wave" of feminist activity had been preceded by a "first" wave that occurred from the late nineteenth century until about the First World War. The first wave was characterized by women's demands for a significant public role, including the right to vote and, eventually, to be considered "persons" under the British North America Act. The women profiled in chapters 1 and 2 have often been identified as proto-feminists in the first wave. The right to a public life was situated by many first-wave feminists in their moral superiority, what has come to be known as "maternal feminism." Some noted first-wave feminists, particularly American women, smoked and used the cigarette as a symbol of liberation. But the roots of first-wave Canadian feminism were deeply informed and sustained by evangelicalism in the nineteenth century and by the social gospel in the twentieth, particularly in English Canada. Neither movement imbued smoking with any significance for the women's movement except to give them a cause for moral reform by stamping it out. Hence, Canadian first-wave feminists generally eschewed smoking. This was not true with advocates of the second wave.

The second-wave feminist movement was first and foremost educational, with consciousness-raising and study groups, primarily for middle-class and racialized white women, and included materials for informal, school, and post-secondary curricula as well as for research centres and publishing houses. Second, second-wave feminism championed women's health, pressed to have women's illnesses included within officially funded research, and demanded better dissemination of health-related information. Closely related to this, social services specifically directed to women's needs resulted in more women's shelters, resource centres, halfway houses, and addiction research centres. Finally, but by no means exhaustively, the women's movement featured political activism and direct action to right political wrongs. This included creating women's caucuses, organizing marches, direct-action initiatives, and research into and encouragement of women's increased involvement at all levels in the legal, political, educational, business, medical, and health systems. In the latter days of the second wave, it also meant women's increased participation in global initiatives against the abrogation of civil rights and violence against and harassment of women and girls, particularly in developing countries where political regimes exploit and profit from women's unpaid or poorly paid labour and their sexuality.[8] In Canada, the second-wave women's movement first received formal recognition with the appointment of the Royal Commission on the Status of Women. Appointed in 1969, the commission submitted its report in 1970.[9]

The Royal Commission on the Status of Women acknowledged the growing influence of the "Women's Liberation Movement" and called for a thorough examination of women's treatment in the unpaid and paid workforce and in education, taxation, immigration, and the law.[10] By the 1970s, the women's movement had touched most institutions in Canadian society, the music industry included, and popular culture was under sustained pressure from young, talented, and confident women who insisted on having the same rights, visibility, and rewards as their male counterparts.[11]

Joni Mitchell and Feminism

By no means did Joni Mitchell throw her support behind all of the causes associated with second-wave feminism, and yet the movement was so broad and multi-faceted that many women chose components from the entire canon of beliefs and practices. In Mitchell's case, the particular inequities of the music industry frustrated and challenged her. We have much evidence of feminism in her responses to patriarchal and restrictive practices in that setting. In an interview with *Rolling Stone*, she described the music industry as a "cesspool" and even threatened to curb label controls over her artistic freedom by releasing her music on the Internet,[12] at that time a revolutionary threat. The democratic spirit heralded by Joni's anthem "Woodstock" was belied by much that she found as a musician and songwriter in this stridently patriarchal industry.[13]

Joni identified as feminist in a number of other respects as well. For example, her increasingly strong identification with leftwing politics and feminist action found her supporting Native Americans in their resistance to the FBI. She criticized rightwing religious intolerance, opposed the wars in Iraq, and exposed the vicious moral code applied to poor single mothers. Her leftwing social commentary also helped to draw many young people to her music, a demographic that remains committed to her art forms.

Joni Mitchell also represented the era in her refusal to remain within a conventional marriage and family. Her first marriage, to Chuck Mitchell, did not survive long, partly because Mitchell was jealous of Joni's greater success as a folk performer. After leaving the marriage, Joni established passionate relationships with some of the most successful of folk's pantheon of artists: Leonard Cohen, James Taylor, Graham Nash, and Larry Klein among them. She rejected conventional marriage with all of them. "We don't need no piece of paper from the city hall, keeping us tied and true," she wrote of her relationship with Graham Nash. Joni rejected marriage and took lovers as she chose, supported by the sisterhood of other aspiring women musicians. Joan Baez, Judy Collins, Carly Simon, and others all figured among her friends and had similar life histories in this regard.

In forging her feminist identity as a talented, independent artist, Joni Mitchell was treading well-worked ground. As noted in earlier chapters, many such women had adopted the cigarette as a symbol. While we have no overt statements by Joni Mitchell of the performative uses she found in smoking, we do have a wealth of visual evidence – some of it created by Joni herself – in which she celebrates the cigarette: in publicity photographs, on her album covers, in filmed interviews and performances, and in personal appearances. She even drew on cigarette imagery to denote her sense of exposure in her early career. "At that period of my life, I had no personal defenses. I felt like a cellophane wrapper on a pack of cigarettes. I felt like I had absolutely no secrets from the world and I couldn't pretend in my life to be strong."[14]

Representations of the Woman Smoker before 1970

The Canadian woman smoker from the 1920s was presented, as in the iconic Winchester cigarette girl in chapter 7, as young, pretty, slender, and sexy. Her sexual allure was rarely offered as menacing; rather, given all of the features of a "good-time girl" emphasized by advertisers, she was presented as a thoroughly modern girl interested in fashion, consumer products, and pleasure. There was another trope of the woman smoker that was firmly grounded in history as well: the woman smoker as avant-garde. In 1929, Edward Bernays had staged a protest at the New York City Easter Parade, defending women's right to smoke "torches of freedom," as he called them. Feminists of the era staunchly backed his demands, making smoking their own.[15] "Women! Light another torch of freedom! Fight another sex taboo!" urged American feminist Ruth Hale.[16]

In the 1930s, this winsome and sexy girl smoker was joined by the image of a more experienced and older woman. As the woman smoker was sketched in pulp and popular fiction, women's magazine columns and articles, as well as advertisements, this woman smoker often took on more sinister features. Women involved in prostitution and crime and those with mental health problems or living in poverty were often featured as smokers. Furthermore, the smoking style these women evinced did not conform to feminine norms of holding the cigarette in the "flag" position, as demonstrated by screen stars and other prominent women. More often, these hardened and knowing women allowed the cigarette to dangle from their lips, or they held it carelessly while engaging in some other activity. Both of these heavily ritualized ways of "performing" smoking were based on masculine models, showing that through their deviant behaviours, the woman smoker's femininity was compromised.

Smoking rates for women climbed steeply and quickly during the Second World War when women took over many of the jobs vacated by servicemen. In so doing, they had more opportunity to smoke in public spaces while engaging in legitimate tasks and while socializing with their co-workers. Many women took up smoking at this time, developing rituals that men had initiated long before. With the increase in smoking rates, the range of allowable identities of the woman smoker expanded, partly because of the agency exerted by women themselves in finding new ways to "do smoking." Representations of the woman smoker in this period showed women who were more serious, more skilled, and older. The image of the woman smoker did not exclude the possibility of sexiness, however, and female models like the Bren Gun Girl discussed in chapter 8 traded on their sexuality while also displaying valued skills and patriotism.

By the 1950s and 1960s, smoking by the typical woman made her seem sophisticated. As demonstrated by the smartly dressed women at the new Princess Lounge in the Royal York Hotel in Toronto in figure 6.6 or by the demure young undergraduate with her beau in figure 9.19, a cigarette was considered to add glamour to a special outfit. With the dawn of second-wave feminism in the late 1960s, yet another layer was added to the imagery of the woman smoker.

Second-Wave Feminism, *Ms Magazine*, *Chatelaine*, *Châtelaine*, and the Image of the Woman Smoker

Second-wave feminism again altered prescriptive codes, especially those related to middle-class, "liberated" women. In the "Age of Aquarius," smoking offered the modern woman the visual means to telegraph her personal authority. The elision of smoking with the women's movement became a staple of visual culture. Produced *about* and *by* feminists, it took hold so firmly in popular cultural products like women's magazines, advertisements, television, and films that the dangers of smoking were masked by the powerful and positive cultural messages. Because of feminism's deep investment in education and other serious-minded social projects, its advocates were naturally drawn to representations of women smokers as forthright, introspective, and cultured. But it added to those qualities the earlier-defined ones of the youthful, assertive woman intent on receiving her rights. The young woman, caught in two candid photographs (figures 10.2 and 10.3) in 1969 for the University of Alberta's yearbook, *The Evergreen and Gold*, demonstrates the interplay of smoking and feminist activism. Participating in a protest, the woman carries a hand-

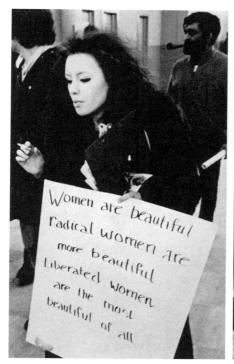

10.2 and 10.3 | Feminist protester, University of Alberta yearbook, 1969

made placard with this statement: "Women are beautiful. Radical women are more beautiful. Liberated women are the most beautiful of all." Later, she speaks into the microphone, still with her cigarette held high in the prescribed fashion. She is the very image of the feminist activist smoker in Canada.

Judy Rebick, academic, media personality, and noted feminist, reports that she began smoking on the advice of friends to "calm her nerves" while she was a student at McGill in the 1960s. "Everyone smoked," she asserts, noting that her life in that decade and beyond was lived largely in cosmopolitan centres like Montreal and Toronto. Having successfully quit once, she began smoking again when she became president of the National Action Committee (NAC) and Canada's most visible feminist in the 1990s. Rebick sees a link between feminists' rebellion against behavioural strictures such as "good girls don't smoke or drink" and their heavy representation as smokers in the 1970s and 1980s. She points out that the practice was so ubiquitous that feminists were considered "weirdos" if they did not smoke.[17]

We must question why the intelligent and socially conscious woman drawn to second-wave feminism and the many projects associated with it – including health issues and services for women – did not question the practice of smoking for women. In a bygone era, as described in chapters 1 and 2, first-wave feminists had *fought* tobacco, not embraced it. Moreover, the medical evidence linking smoking and cancer was far stronger by the 1970s than it had been in the nineteenth century. How can we account for the obvious blindness of feminists taking up smoking in this context? The answer to this conundrum will be addressed in the next section. Through a complex nexus of feminist magazines – for example, *Chatelaine* and *Châtelaine* in Canada and *Ms Magazine* in the United States – the women who directed the editorial processes at these magazines, and tobacco advertisers, a new prototype of the feminist smoker was constructed in the face of clear medical danger.

Chatelaine and *Châtelaine* Magazines

Chatelaine

Chatelaine was one of a number of women's magazines that courted Canadian women readers in waged and salaried positions and in the ranks of stay-at-home middle-class wives from the late 1920s. Three of these magazines – *The Chatelaine*, which by the 1930s had become *Chatelaine,* the *Canadian Home Journal*, and *the Business and Professional Woman* – had broad readerships through to the Second World War. From its launch in 1928, *Chatelaine* set its mandate to inform Canadian women about current events and new movements and to mobilize women in support of events that united them. In the inaugural issue, the editor, Anne Elizabeth Wilson, set this goal for her new magazine: "If the light of *The Chatelaine*'s lamp, when it shall have fallen your way, has brought more meaning into the every-day world about you, shown you an unexpected beauty, helped you to find better methods in any activity of your home or life, then she will have accomplished the purpose for which she came into being – to serve the Canadian woman in her every interest and need."[18]

Early issues of *Chatelaine* debated the same conservative questions preoccupying the women's club movement and the later echoes of first-wave feminism: companionate marriage, the new field of child psychology, music, poetry, uplifting art, and fashion. Vogue patterns were given free of charge. The fiction profiled in *Chatelaine* in these years also explored the world of courtship and early marriage, maintaining the home, and fostering healthy relationships, all issues that affected women of varying

10.4 | *Chatelaine* masthead, 1980s

circumstances. The magazine, as with the other national journals, was cluttered with advertisements for face cream, deodorants, cars, watches, baking powder, home cleansers, floor wax, cheese, toothpaste, fabric dye, Jell-O, light bulbs, tea, Kellogg's All Bran, and much, much more. While the first few issues did not include alcohol-related advertisements, they did feature tobacco advertising. In fact, and as illustrated in chapter 9, the first issues ran three advertisements from the United Cigar Stores. The women's outfits, their ladylike stance, and the carefully worded copy of the advertisement, which ambiguously skirted whether ladies would be purchasing tobacco for a male family member or for themselves, all tried to appeal to women consumers of various social classes and financial standings (see figure 9.2). Mysteriously, the tobacco advertisements disappeared almost immediately from succeeding issues, making a weak return with sketchy advertisements in 1936 when Byrne Hope Saunders was named to the editorship. By this time too, alcohol figured frequently in fiction but often negatively. The working-class lout who drank too much beer and then brutalized his wife was criticized,[19] while his wife was an object of pity who deserved sympathy and help.[20]

By the 1960s, *Chatelaine* had positioned itself as a middle-class Canadian woman's magazine, still supporting tobacco advertising and promoting a variety of images of the woman smoker, all of them fully respectable and sophisticated. Liquor advertising had also become a staple. Advertisements, feature articles, and columns profiled capital punishment, how to update the appearance of the family home to conform to middle-class norms, and the current thinking on the institution of marriage. The appeal was clearly for a middle-class readership. *Chatelaine*'s women were shown as living with smokers and often were themselves presented as both smokers and drinkers. We can also see a growing willingness by the magazine to engage modern topics of sexuality through its advertising. Consider the following two examples. In the first one (figure 10.5) from 1960, we see a stylized drawing of a middle-class woman

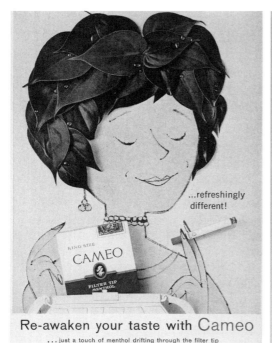

...refreshingly different!

Re-awaken your taste with Cameo
...just a touch of menthol drifting through the filter tip

looking for lightness?
(but loving that lift!)

Then Matinée is best for you

the lighter smoke

10.5 and 10.6 | Magazine advertisement for Cameo Cigarettes, *Chatelaine*, 1962; Magazine advertisement for Matinée Cigarettes, *Chatelaine*, 1967

smoking Cameo King Size cigarettes. The copy for this advertisement is short and to the point. The image shows a "King Size Cameo" package of cigarettes peeking out of the woman's fashionable purse. The longer length is emphasized by the cigarettes only partly fitting into the purse. The information that this cigarette is a "Filter Tip Menthol" is still visible above the purse top. The presence of a menthol blend is picked up again in the final line in which the consumer is invited to "re-awaken [her] taste with Cameo," which offered "just a touch of menthol drifting through the filter tip." The full denoted message of Cameo's greater volume, the filter tip, and the menthol addition is summarized immediately next to the woman's satisfied smile, as if she were passing judgment: "refreshingly different!" (By this date, the longer cigarettes were just being introduced. By the late 1960s, women had declared their support for longer cigarettes, filter tips, and menthol flavouring.[21]) The woman's middle-class orientation is displayed through the ad's connotative elements with her modern haircut, her dangly earrings, her choker necklace, and filed and lacquered fingernails. The connotative message is simple but focused: to complete the well-groomed image of a middle-class woman smoker, one needs a Cameo cigarette with all the "trimmings."

The connotative message from an advertisement in a 1967 issue of *Chatelaine* (figure 10.6) is very different. A full page is devoted to a collage of "light" images: the woman sits with head upturned, lightly blowing smoke at soap bubbles while an adoring man looks on. The care of the woman's hair and makeup confuses the composition: where are those soap bubbles coming from? Is she in the bath? Or doing the dishes? In either case, or neither, she playfully challenges huge bubbles, failing to burst her target, presumably because of the light smoke she blows. Are the bubbles meant to suggest a childlike game of "burst the bubble" or a sexualized fantasy? Without the text anchoring the images, we cannot ascertain this. In this case, the image appears to be the dominant connotative messenger. The woman is centrally placed and with her suggestive bubbles occupies about four-fifths of the space. The text introduces a new element of sexualization ("loving that lift"), making the man's gaze more meaningful. Combining the sexualized text of male sexual arousal (slyly "hidden" by the parentheses) with the man's patriarchal gaze as the object for her sexually charged image changes the advertisement's meaning. At first the message seems to be directed to the woman – "looking for lightness?" it asks, pairing the question with the woman's playing with the bubbles. This could be interpreted as a liberating offer to all women smokers. But before an answer can be given, the predominant "last word" is marshalled ("but loving that lift!") as if to "answer" the woman's question with *the man's* sexualized concern.

The whole composition could also be read as a study in subversion. While the woman occupies much of the frame, the patriarchal gaze dominates. While she is asked a seemingly important question, the affirmative statement following belongs to him. Insofar as the woman is given the right to "lift" the man she desires, however, this is a liberating message, consistent with the developing feminist norms of the time. This woman's sexual identity is not only a sexualized subjectivity shaped by proto-feminist discourse but also constructed in relation to the subjectivizing forces of patriarchy.[22] Readers interested in seeing the francophone version of this advertisement might look ahead to figure 10.7.

As the magazine moved into the 1970s, it became increasingly radicalized under the editorship of June Callwood. While continuing to run articles and advertisements speaking to middle-class women's consumer interests, their worries and hopes for their children and husbands, *Chatelaine* opened up new avenues of journalistic investigation. Features ran on the challenge of balancing paid employment with domestic responsibilities, on the abortion debate, and on women's sexual expression, alongside the older interests. By the 1980s, despite continuing to accept tobacco advertising, *Chatelaine* introduced more features about the health risks associated with smoking. Much of this evidence had been available since the mid-1960s. As with *Ms Magazine*, however, the combined effect of the value of tobacco advertising, the interests of its readership, and the popular cultural images of liberated women smoking discouraged an early critique of smoking.

Châtelaine

Founded in 1960 by Maclean-Hunter, the sister magazine of *Chatelaine* was from its inception pitched to the middle-class francophone Canadian woman. With visual effects very similar to those of the anglophone version of the magazine, and sometimes direct translations of English advertisements, *Châtelaine* positioned itself as an arbiter of good taste in all respects: housing styles, interior decoration, cuisine, women's rights, and most particularly, personal fashion. It offered Canadian women a translation to a North American context of the latest in European styles, making its anglophone counterpart magazine look provincial in comparison. Even a cursory survey of *Châtelaine* demonstrates its stronger aesthetic elements.

Châtelaine's first editor, Fernanda Saint-Martin, adopted a frankly feminist position, running feature articles on the inequitable status of women in Quebec, questioning social policy that permitted abandoned women to live in poverty while trying to support children, and celebrating women's leadership in societal change. Launched in the early days of the Quiet Revolution, *Châtelaine* prodded the assumptions underlying women's appropriate role in francophone culture. Its early issues featured first-ranked fiction for its readers, running short stories by Gabrielle Roy,[23] Anne Hébert,[24] and André Laurendeau.[25] Articles ran on a wide variety of women of substance and authority, many of whom were shown smoking in accompanying images.

Throughout the 1960s, Saint-Martin continued to represent the accomplished and stylish woman as a smoker in *Châtelaine*. A feature article on one of Quebec's power couples, the Pelletiers, ran in 1962, for example. In the photograph accompanying the feature, Alec Pelletier is shown looking reflectively at her husband, who in turn frowns into his documents. She holds a cigarette in quiet repose. In this same issue, a familiar advertisement for Matinée Cigarettes ran. As a companion advertisement to figure 10.6, the Matinée image speaks to the international nature of much ad-

10.7 | Magazine advertisement for Matinée Cigarettes, *Châtelaine*, 1962

vertising. The caption on the francophone version reads, "*fumez 'plus léger' ... fumez 'satisfait,' Fumez Matinée*" ("smoke 'lighter' ... smoke with 'satisfaction,' Smoke Matinée"). Despite the earlier publication date of the francophone version – 1962 as opposed to 1967 – the advertisement appearing in *Châtelaine* is much more cautious than the anglophone product of some years later. The lack of any sexualized innuendo in the francophone copy is striking when one compares the two. Otherwise, the model is identical: the woman is well made up, engaging in her bubble-popping, and with an adoring man smiling close at hand.

How can we explain the difference? Is it simply a matter of the sexual revolution having loosened advertising strictures by the later 1960s, of a more conservative society for francophone women in the perceptions of their roles, or a decision by advertisers to be cautious in an area less well understood than, say, interior design? Likely, all of these considerations played some role in the substantive revisions.

The women's movement in the 1970s also received extensive treatment in *Châtelaine*. A report on the situation of women in Quebec was accompanied by a series of photographs in which women wrestled with weighty questions bedevilling Quebec society.[26] Of the five women shown as involved in one set of roundtable discussions, at least one smokes reflectively while drinking coffee or tea. Two other women have their cigarette packages open before them, and a filled ashtray sits in the middle of the table. Features like this one lead one to conclude that by this date, smoking had been deeply integrated into francophone female culture, particularly among women of the intelligentsia. Such illustrations help to catalogue just how the cigarette was used by Quebec women in their social lives.

In the mid-1970s, Saint-Martin was replaced as editor by Francine Montpetit, and by 1985, Montpetit in turn gave way to Pauline Thornton. Thornton continued to take an approach that kept feminism in the public eye through *Châtelaine*. In December 1985, *Châtelaine* ran an article on the current flagging position of feminism entitled *"La feminisme n'est pas hereditaire!"*[27] It told of a generation of feminists who had married, had daughters, and who found themselves incapable of dissuading their daughters from playing with and idealizing Barbie dolls.

The strength of support for women's causes, including feminism, might help to explain why markedly less tobacco advertising appeared in *Châtelaine* beyond 1970. Many issues from the 1970s have none at all, while a select few advertisements were included in the early 1980s. By 1985, they had disappeared completely, largely replaced by heavy alcohol advertising. Fiction pieces continued to show women smoking, however.

The explanation for the light tobacco advertising in *Châtelaine*, despite its representation in magazine art, is not available in the records. However, we can hypothesize that *Châtelaine*'s editorial board and publishers made the connection between women and the dangers of smoking or that they thought it unnecessary to continue to advertise in a demographic already strongly committed to smoking. In any case, the public record of both *Châtelaine* and *Chatelaine* is much stronger in terms of curbing tobacco advertising than that of their American counterpart.

Ms Magazine

The background of *Ms Magazine* is very different from *Chatelaine*'s, reflecting the period and culture in which it was founded. *Ms Magazine* became the unrivalled channel for disseminating feminism in its various forms across North America. Such feminists included the academic, the political activist, and the woman worker, straight and gay. In so doing, it did not need to be as concerned about the interests of a broadly based readership as general women's magazines such as *Chatelaine* or *Châtelaine* were required to do.

Ms Magazine began in 1971 as an insert in the *New York Magazine* and published its first stand-alone issue in 1972. From its inception to 1987, it maintained a monthly publication schedule, profiling many feminist issues that received little or no treatment in other mainstream periodicals: sweatshops, sex trafficking, the wage gap, the glass ceiling, and date rape among them. In 1976, it did a cover story on battered women, becoming the first American national magazine to deal with domestic violence. Much of *Ms Magazine*'s early energy and feminist focus came from its founding editor, Gloria Steinem, who remained with the magazine through to 1989, when it began publishing without advertisements. Until that date, *Ms Magazine* used its advertisements as well as its feature stories to give a face to second-wave feminism. That face often had an extralong cigarette in the featured woman's hand.

In an article on high-achieving women from a 1977 issue of *Ms*, every woman shown in this double-page spread is smoking. Shown in quiet solitude, in conversation, and in laughter, all of the women incorporate the cigarette into their sophisticated appearance. Each woman's name is identified at the bottom of the photograph in apparently handwritten script to simulate a photograph album or some other intimate picture collection. Because they are being celebrated for their achievements, the symbolic power of real women smoking would have been greater than that of a model in an advertisement. There were many of those as well, of course.[28]

Ms Magazine's editors and publishers depended heavily on advertising for survival. One of its path-breaking decisions was to force advertisers to pay much more for advertising space than was common for women's magazines. In 1972, for example, it negotiated a price of $11 per thousand issues for each advertising item when the going rate for traditional women's magazines was $2.17. The $11 benchmark had been set by such magazines as *Esquire* and *Psychology Today*.[29] This success had a double edge, however. That rate locked *Ms* into "a kind of prison,"[30] as Gloria Steinem wrote, with the magazine heavily reliant on its tobacco and liquor advertisements.

At the same time as forcing up the payment for advertising copy, *Ms Magazine* very consciously chose the kinds of ads it wanted to represent the blossoming feminist movement. Instead of personal product advertisements, the editors sought Panasonic, AT&T, and new-wave representations of women labourers, showing female telephone-line installers and the like. Fully consistent with this blueprint of what constituted feminist interests and aspirations, *Ms* was filled almost from the beginning with cigarette and liquor advertisements. Not surprisingly, even when the readership objected to the heavy tobacco and liquor advertising, the editorial staff continued to accept the trade because of its ideological and practical value.[31]

Women's Magazines, Tobacco Sponsors, and Representations of Smoking

Lest it be thought that *Ms* relinquished all effective control over its advertising policy, consider the case of Philip Morris's Virginia Slims campaign and the devastating effect on the magazine of adopting what it considered to be a principled stand. According to Mary Thoms, a long-time *Ms* editor, when Philip Morris tried to introduce the first Virginia Slims advertisements, the *Ms Magazine* editorial team objected on several counts. The campaign phrase, "You've come a long way, baby," offended the team for infantilizing women and for its claim that smoking in itself was an indication of women's progress. It argued that the readership would react negatively and agreed to run only a small sample advertisement. The expected readership backlash occurred, and *Ms* took the position that it would not accept any more.

In refusing to run the Virginia Slims ad, *Ms* courted the wrath not only of one of its sustaining sponsors, Philip Morris, but also the women's professional golf and tennis circuits, both of which were sponsored by Philip Morris. Billy Jean King made repeated personal pleas to *Ms* staff to reverse a position that she considered ideological. King, along with other professional athletes, used smoking to her own advantage by accepting personal sponsorships from cigarette producers.

In response to *Ms Magazine*'s continued refusal to run Virginia Slim advertisements, Philip Morris withdrew advertising copy for every one of its products, not just Virginia Slims. This decision is estimated to have cost the magazine somewhere around $250,000 over the course of one fiscal year,[32] with lesser reductions in succeeding years. The shattering result almost closed the periodical and was ample demonstration of the "prison" that Steinem had earlier articulated.

Even though *Ms Magazine* took this difficult position on Virginia Slims advertisements, it did not eschew the fashion of "slim" cigarettes that were extra long and emphasized a woman's slender figure. These cigarettes were a hit with women smokers. The Salem campaign in the mid-1970s teamed the Salem Premium Lengths with designer clothes, including fashions by Rena Rowan of Jones New York, Ralph Lauren, and Diane Von Furstenberg.[33] The Salem Premium Lengths series did not claim that smoking alone accounted for women's progress, nor did it infantilize women in any apparent way. What it did do was link a lifestyle defined by designers, with a sample outfit and a prominently displayed cigarette, to the act of smoking. It made no attempt to explain women's progress, but it took great pains to argue that a result of smoking was to lay claim to an elite lifestyle admired by millions.

One advertisement forging this link will be described. Unfortunately, it cannot be shown. The advertisement's denotative meaning was achieved by projecting a very thin woman dressed in a dramatic striped top and bias-cut skirt standing laughing before a marquee in an elegant room. The connotative – and even mythic – meaning here is clear: greater length of the cigarette creates greater pleasure and refreshment for the smoker. "FOR MORE OF A WOMAN – A study in stripes from CALVIN KLEIN. And it's downright refreshing. As refreshing as you. And the way you live. And your Salem Premium Lengths. MORE OF A SALEM – Salem Premium Lengths. Designed a little longer to refresh a little longer." The truncated sentences add drama to the copy, mimicking spoken rather than written language. Salem also offered a "Long and Natural dress pattern" that emphasized the slenderness of the wearer (or the less-than-slender profile of the woman desperately trying to lose weight by smoking) for 50 cents and one empty Salem Super King pack. "It'll look great in just about any knit fabric. And you'll look pretty special, too. All the way from your Salem Super King down to your toes."[34] This giving of "prizes" is reminiscent of the coupons offered to male smokers, including children, in cigarette and pipe-tobacco packages and described in chapter 3. *Ms Magazine*'s refusal to run the Virginia Slims advertisements appears rather less revolutionary or moral, given this campaign and others that mirrored it.

Chatelaine too participated enthusiastically in the promotion of a thin aesthetic for women. In the 1980s, for example, it freely ran advertising for Matinée Slims ("Milder because they're slim"). Figure 10.8 shows a very thin young woman in sneakers and leg-warmers sitting with her back to a mirror, inviting us to speculate about the connection between smoking and high culture, good health, and slender beauty. The emphasis in this image is apparently on the "mild" feature of Matinée Slims, and yet everything else about the image draws our attention to the "slim" woman and her reflection, as well as her cigarettes, scrolling out of their package because of their extra length.

The *Ms Magazine* editors were also slow to acknowledge either the short- or long-term physical dangers presented by smoking to women. This is both significant and perplexing considering their courageous and timely interventions in social problems like violence against women. Former *Ms*

10.8 | Magazine advertisement for Matinée Slims, *Chatelaine*, 1986

editor Thoms admits that throughout the 1980s, the evidence accumulated and became increasingly more difficult to ignore. The effects of second-hand smoke were becoming clearer, lower birth weights in babies of mothers who smoked had been recorded, and it was well known that more young women were taking up smoking during that period and having more difficulty in stopping the habit. Still, "tobacco advertising was such a large category for *Ms*, and for magazines in general once television banned them, no one on the staff thought the magazine could survive without the income from cigarette ads."[35] It was not until February 1987 that *Ms* published an in-depth article on smoking as an addiction as part of an issue on cross-addictions. The article had been preceded by a questionnaire to *Ms* readers the previous summer, collecting data about women's overlapping addictions and offering valuable data for others to mine in the coming years. The article was supported by an editorial preface and this particular issue contained no cigarette or liquor advertising, creating a challenge to the magazine's bottom line. To a reader's plea that she could not "help but wish *Ms* would let go of *its dependency* on revenue from liquor and cigarette advertising ... *Ms* is in a position to model something different," an editor responded: "Actually, *Ms* is *not* in a good position to model something different. As a nonprofit feminist magazine, we can't rely on traditional economic support; we have no corporate publisher and our editorial policy limits our appeal to traditional advertising directed to women ... Nonetheless, we're the only women's magazine to do a cover story on women and addiction, and to sacrifice advertising revenue to do so. We're proud of this fact and of the thousands of reader donations that made it possible."[36] *Ms Magazine* as a corporate personality, through the "voice" of this editor, responded to the ambiguous assessment of cigarette smoking for women and its clear need to have tobacco sponsorship in order to survive with a policy that regretfully continued to accept tobacco advertising.

However, the contention by Thoms that *Ms* stood alone among women's magazines in uncovering the addictive features of smoking by 1987 is quite inaccurate. By this time, smoking's hold on women had been addressed at some length and depth in magazines like *Chatelaine*, which was much more active in pointing to the many risks associated with smoking, drawing heavily on the available medical evidence. In 1982 alone, the magazine ran three major features in its "Medical News" health column. It reported that Canadian researchers had established that women's lungs were more damaged by cigarette smoking than men's[37]; it reviewed the National Cancer Institute of Canada's assessment of the recent American surgeon general's report and concluded that "[s]moking is Canada's number-one cause of preventable death," and it supported a new federal anti-smoking program aimed at women of childbearing years, adolescents, and their parents.[38] It reported new evidence that women smokers who had experienced breast cancer had a higher recurrence rate than non-smokers.[39] In 1984, *Chatelaine* ran a feature on cancer as well as an article on smoking and its dangers. For this issue, it accepted no tobacco advertising.[40] Later that same year, *Chatelaine* ran a feature article on weight issues and smoking, again documenting the numerous health concerns associated with women smoking. This feature acknowledged the difficulty many women faced in stopping smoking and the likelihood that weight would be gained in this period. It noted that the 1980 American surgeon general's report had shown that weight gain was in direct proportion to the heaviness of the smoking, with smokers who consumed more than 41 cigarettes a day gaining up to thirty pounds while light smokers (one to ten cigarettes daily) gaining around four pounds. This information encouraged cutting back on smoking before the final cessation. Such discussions in *Chatelaine*

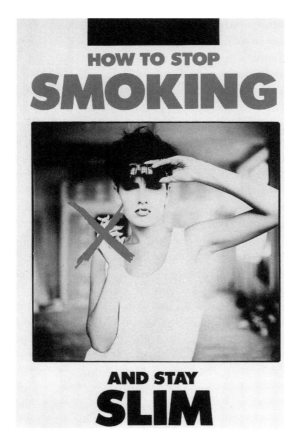

HOW TO STOP SMOKING AND STAY SLIM

10.9 | Magazine feature article, *Chatelaine*, 1986

placed it far ahead of *Ms Magazine* in its public recognition of smoking's special dangers for women and the allure of slenderness that kept many women trapped as smokers. Furthermore, it reported research that spoke of the experience of smoking for *average* women, normalizing the difficulties faced by women from all stations of life in quitting. The *Ms Magazine* feature of 1987 of which it was so proud presented smoking as a feature of life for those women who were prone to addictions of many types. This likely would have had the effect of distancing the dangers of smoking for women with only *this one* addiction. Women smokers could easily rationalize their position, given that smoking's dangers were presented exclusively as part of a constellation of interdependent addictions.

Thus, the *Ms Magazine* contention that it alone of women's magazines had explored difficult issues, including smoking addiction, is exposed for the fabrication it was. Undoubtedly, it was in a difficult position in which it had to justify its ongoing acceptance of tobacco advertising, but such a rationale is not credible.

Furthermore, *Ms Magazine* gave tacit approval to women's smoking and even celebrated it in many feature articles, giving more fodder to the image of the feminist woman as smoker. It did so with a legion of committed women feminist smokers, many of whom read and supported *Ms Magazine*. When cigarettes were placed in the hands of characters in fiction pieces, smoking was even further normalized. In one article on sisters in the sisterhood, for example, which addressed the responsibility of older sisters mentoring younger ones, the *Ms* artist chose to place the younger teenaged girl in a room laden with telephone, stereo, rock star posters, study notes – and a cigarette poised expertly and prominently. The younger sister rolls her eyes dismissively at her older sister perched companionably on her bed. The implication of the graphic is that the hallmark of the teenage woman is the creation of her own space with uncompromising modernity – in her decorations, her appearance, and her insistence on smoking. The young woman's worldly appearance and her active re-making of her environment as part of the "culture of the bedroom" reminds us too that adolescent women have limited access to their own spaces and that the decorative devices applied to these spaces are important indicators of values.[41] Apparently, that is one more thing that the older woman cannot teach her sister: she knows it all already. In presenting it playfully, *Ms Magazine* appears to condone the young woman's choices. Not surprisingly, most of the editorial team, including the powerhouse editor Gloria Steinem, were all heavy smokers, holding to the longstanding tradition of journalists with their cigarettes dangling from their lips as they pounded out stories on their upright typewriters.

Regardless of which women's magazine is consulted throughout the 1970s and 1980s, however, it is clear that all had an important role in welding together images of sophistication, liberated lifestyles, apparent happiness, prosperity, and success with smoking by women. This was accomplished through advertisements, fiction, and feature articles that offered profiles of women who had achieved all of this, including smoking. It was only in the 1980s, almost two decades after the link between cancer and smoking had been medically proven, that these magazines took seriously the medical dangers of smoking for women.

Canadian Television, Movies, Feminism, and the Woman Smoker

During the women's movement, feminist issues were aired on Canadian television, including the public affairs programs of the time, "This Hour

Has Seven Days" and the redoubtable "Front Page Challenge." On both of these programs, guests or hosts smoked freely until the CBC's voluntary ban of tobacco advertising in 1988. Other networks and smoking locations thereafter rapidly followed this lead. With very few exceptions, the smokers were male. Even known feminists generally did not smoke on air, possibly indicating that the revolution welcoming the woman smoker was not as complete as has often been claimed. Beyond the public affairs programs, however, situation comedies, dramas, and especially soap operas showed much smoking by both men and women. The effect of this on social norms is debatable: the women who were visible as smokers in these fictional television productions played at being "regular people," presenting a model of normalized behaviour, which in turn was added to many other models in print, on billboards, and in the cinema. These many representations of the woman smoker likely would have had a fortifying effect for the prospective or active woman smoker. On the other hand, if it were noticed that the most authoritative of women on Canadian television did not smoke in public, that too would have sent a message to women.

Meanwhile, on the big screen through the 1970s and 1980s and indeed well into the 1990s, female actors were often presented as smokers. This was particularly true when women emphasized their authority, liberation, toughness, or intelligence. Here, young women in particular could find a cigarette-smoking actress to represent almost every visual identity imaginable. Without any doubt, films were and are deeply important in the instruction of those seeking to construct new identities. By the 1930s, Edward Bernays understood the immense potential of cigarette use in films to telegraph intense emotion and other features of identity. Bernays wrote:

> There is many a psychological need for a cigarette in the movies. The bashful hero lights a cigarette, the better to gain a hold of himself in the trying interview with his future father-in-law. The villain smokes hasty puffs to hide his nervousness or to ease his conscience. But perhaps the most dramatic scenes are those where the cigarette is not smoked. How much can be expressed by the habitual smoker, when he is too perturbed to smoke? The gambler in the Casino, who has staked his last thousand on one card, and has lost – his cigarette falls unlighted from his trembling hands, and tells us worlds of chagrin. The deceived husband, deserted by the heartless wife, reaches for a cigarette, but lets the package drop, to signify his utter loss, his absolute defeat.[42]

And the power of film as a site for smoking continues to thrill young women. Those engaged in the study of contemporary girl culture through film argue that films of the 1990s represent a kind of post-feminist response to second-wave feminism in their representation of girls' and women's culture. Some argue that the message of 1990s film and television for girls is that young women need to recognize the merits of deploying their sexuality to gain an advantage over other competitive females. Smoking helps to telegraph this sexual knowing better than most other symbols.[43]

The alignment of smoking with the women's movement in the late 1960s to 1990 was the culmination of a long-standing association between women in the middle class, the intelligentsia, and the entertainment industries through which cigarettes were constructed as a symbol for the sophisticated, intelligent, artistic, and socially conscious woman. Through icons like Joni Mitchell, that symbolic meaning continues to receive wide dissemination. And yet, precisely because cigarettes are not much in evidence with the public woman in our own era and have literally been pushed to the marginalized exterior with the public more generally, brandishing the cigarette has even greater power when wielded by an established star who is practised in using counter-cultural messages for her own purposes.

Joni Mitchell self-represented as a smoker and as a feminist from the 1970s, when the female smoker was a common sight, through to the twenty-first century, when her picture appeared on the cover of *CARP* magazine, Canada's national periodical for the comfortably retired. Picturing herself with cigarette poised, whether on album or magazine covers, in press shots, or in her art, was fortifying for Joni Mitchell, just as it has been for generations of groundbreaking, artistic women before and after her youth. In the decades of the 1970s to the 1990s, when smoking became so ubiquitous through the influence of women's popular and feminist culture as a symbol of female liberation, empowerment, and modernity, women who self-defined as feminists but who did *not* smoke were seen as odd. By the early twenty-first century, third-wave feminism had been articulated and enacted by a new generation of young women. The cigarette took on different representational significance through that system of meanings. This will be explored in the next chapter.

11

At the Margins

The preceding chapters have argued that in the twentieth century, women have had access to and the means to deploy a wide range of representational identities, many of which have been enriched by the performative use of the cigarette. Despite being subject to a variety of constraints – discursive, economic, political, and social – women have found the means to enact complex and compelling identities through smoking. Particularly for marginalized women, some of these identities would be termed "alternate" or "counter-hegemonic." This study has taken as one of its goals the investigation of how the cigarette has added to the identity construction of women in various stations in life and in different periods. The following chapter explores the particular utility of performing smoking for women living on the margins of Canadian society. It frames the discussion in terms of what has come to be called third-wave feminism, which formally arose in the 1990s.

Third-wave feminism was built on second-wave feminism's successes and blind-spots. Feminists associated with the second wave were preoccupied with issues of equal access to community and academic resources – in health, child care, entertainment, and education – issues mainly of concern to middle-class, racialized white, heterosexual women. Throughout the 1980s and early 1990s in Canada, a critique of this movement gathered energy. It was increasingly seen as a movement of interest to an exclusive club: one that was middle-class and even elite, heterosexual, physically and mentally able, racialized white, and Western in outlook.[1] Often as a way to distance themselves from the second-wave movement and particularly from what were perceived as essentialist notions of gender inherent in second-wave feminism, young women who took up this new variation of feminism have rejected the term itself, disparaging the "F" word. They have championed the causes of women outside the second-wave club, insisting that issues of importance to women who are racialized non-white, bisexual, lesbian, and trans-gendered women, those with disabilities, those subject to the abrogation of their civil and humanitarian rights, sexual violence, harassment, or those trapped in poverty in Canada and transnationally be recognized and supported.[2]

In no sense does this chapter argue that women marginalized by life's circumstances or through conscious choice are by definition third-wave feminists. Nor is there an assertion that all such women smoke, although statistics note that far more than the norm do, as many as 90 per cent of women experiencing some forms of marginalization. Rather, this chapter explores how selected women in this loose category have made use of smoking as a constituent of identity and alternatively, why some marginalized women have chosen not to smoke. Inasmuch as third-wave feminists have a singular view of anything in society beyond their common critiques of the assumed legitimacy and primacy of masculinity and of the pervasiveness and persistence of patriarchy, I am not aware that there is any official third-wave feminist prescription on smoking, women's or otherwise.

The fundamental feature of many marginalized women's lives is their fragile economic status. This in turn gives rise to other characteristics of marginalization. "Women's economic reality is a significant source of stress ... one might assume that when an individual does not foresee the ability to raise her standard of living by finding a better job, it would engender a state of hopelessness and despair. Consequently, it is easy to see how such a person could become increasingly dependent on drugs, gambling or some other 'quick fix' in order to escape a feeling of helplessness, despair and powerlessness."[3] Nevertheless, not all women living with financial need succumb to problem gambling, alcohol, drugs, or even smoking. Many women demonstrate resilience in the face of powerfully discouraging life conditions, some of which are explored in this chapter. Other women living in such circumstances embrace the cigarette as part of a highly stylized visual performance, exercising agency otherwise denied to them. We can speculate that the point of this performance in which smoking is celebrated rather than hidden is to draw on smoking's power to constitute a defiant identity and to bring pleasure to a life burdened with cares, anxieties, and material and symbolic exclusions.

As with previous chapters, this one casts its net widely, taking as examples women who chose to smoke and those who did not. All of the women profiled here would have been regarded by societal arbiters as marginalized. Given a very limited record on which to draw, we can assume that many of these women also regarded themselves as marginalized, as unfairly denied mainstream advantages. The decision by a marginalized woman of whether or not to smoke was made because of her life view, because of those with whom she socialized, because of the meanings she attributed to smoking, and because some women could more easily afford this indulgence, financially and socially.

The chapter begins with an examination of two historically situated displaced women, one who lived in the county jail and a second who found work as a domestic servant. The first woman, for whom we have only visual evidence, could easily have smoked when living independently; the second, for whom we have only diary accounts, consciously eschewed the comforts of smoking. These two women demonstrate the experience of lived privation at the root of marginalization, which helps to explain the choices women have always made about smoking. The chapter follows with several modern profiles of disadvantaged women who have incorporated the cigarette into their public identities: women jailed, those engaged in the hard-drug street culture, those assuming a "butch" gay identity, or "tough" girls in adolescent groups. It ends with an analysis of a privileged woman but one who understands the isolation created by lifestyle choices: k.d. lang. Lang has used the symbolism of smoking to powerful effect in her own life performance.

Most of the women profiled in this chapter were or are real, while some are creations of the media, defined both positively and negatively. The visual culture underpinning the analyses of these women all draw on codes about race, sexuality, and poverty that are often grounded in clumsy stereotypes. It is not by chance that the largest collection of women smokers who are racialized non-white appear in this chapter. Nonetheless, it should always be remembered that the profiles provided here are constructed both by the image-makers and by the women themselves.

Two Displaced Women

To be marginal is often to live outside a protected domestic space, possibly in someone else's home, on the streets, or in a public institution, and to do so with unstable resources. "Polly" whose image appears in figure 11.1, was living at the time the photograph was taken in the Carleton County Jail in Ottawa. Women of the underclass were known to be smokers, and it is likely that Polly indulged when she could. Dr L.J. Lemieux asserted that

11.1 | "Polly" at the Carleton County Jail, 1886

90 per cent of the inmates of the Montreal Women's Jail were smokers during this period.[4]

This photograph is likely an "official" one, since it appears in the records now housed at Library and Archives Canada rather than being part of a private collection. It was probably taken by an administrator on Polly's admission. We know nothing about her apart from this image, but it is clear that at the time the photograph was taken, Polly was confused, or perhaps drunk, causing her to choose not to sit on the chair at hand but on the floor. She is dressed reasonably tidily, although a tear appears in the front of her long dress. And yet some elements of her appearance also mark her as marginalized.

While it was cool enough for her to need a shawl around her shoulders, she is barefoot, and the wrap is soiled. In a period when virtually all women wore their hair long, Polly has hers close-cropped, possibly as a result of lice treatments, which called for the hair to be shorn and the head bundled in coal-oil rags. Alternatively, her hair length might have been a choice she made for easy maintenance. Polly sits with her eyes closed and her head wearily propped by one arm on a chair. Behind her, another chair is upturned as if a struggle had preceded the taking of the photograph. The room in which Polly finds herself is bare, with little furniture other than straight-backed chairs and a wall scuffed by the chair rails.

How are we to "read" this photograph, taking into account the *real* woman documented by it as well as the intentions of the photographer or administrator who has placed Polly so blindingly in the gaze of the photographic lens? Clearly, Polly is meant to represent more than only her own sad circumstances: in this photograph, she has been coded as a poor, a possibly intemperate and certainly an incompetent member of society. Her debasement is presented literally in the nineteenth-century context by her position on the floor, by her silly facial expression, and by her tattered clothing. There can be little doubt that Polly was marginalized in several ways – at least socially, with no family to care for her; economically, with too little money to buy shoes or proper clothing; but very likely in other ways as well that we cannot tell 130 years after the photograph was taken and in the absence of other corroborating evidence. At the same time, Polly has been intentionally defined as a woman who *belonged* in the county jail, as one of the jail's appropriate inmates. Her photograph would likely have been used to justify the existence of this institution and its care of poor intemperate women like Polly. Polly is the face of poverty in late nineteenth-century Ottawa. It must be remembered that Polly was much more than this sad photograph shows, even when she was poor and unable to live independently. The image robs her of any agency to assert her own version of "Polly." In so doing, while it offers important information about women in the nineteenth century, it also obscures and misleads, rigidifying the category of "poverty" and possibly also "intemperance" and erasing markers that might have shown Polly in a more balanced perspective.

Polly was a vulnerable woman of the Canadian underclass. She *looks* defeated and very tired, and we are intended to note these characteristics. If she were a smoker, she would never have been permitted to light up in such demeaning circumstances, as would a woman in her own home. "Private" behaviours and habits, those that are normally exercised in protected spaces, in the case of the marginalized woman are often acted out in public. This in part signals the outlier nature of these women's lives as codes are integrated into such women's representations and then reified.

When Lauretta Sluenwhite's husband died of cancer in 1930, she had no visible means of support.[5] She was without a home and had no skills or interest in working in industry. While she had lots of friends and kin-folk, they too were living close to the margins as the Great Depression took hold in her home in Lunenberg County, Nova Scotia. Both of her sons were by then away from home eking out a sparse living as occasional labourers, and Lauretta longed for a home where they could visit her and stay awhile. Lauretta chose to do what countless women before and after her have done: she let it be known that she would provide domestic services with her room and board as part, and possibly all, of her payment. Lauretta seemed never to formally advertise for work; her job offers came to her by word of mouth within the county where she had lived for many years, although she had to occasionally move away from her small town of Pine Grove in order to take up suitable domestic positions.

Lauretta's diary gives us insight into the life of a marginalized woman of the mid-twentieth century. From her faithful diary notations, we have some idea of the hard physical labour she shouldered, scrubbing and haul-ing and preparing huge meals, day in and day out. She kept house and nursed the elderly; she did housekeeping and provided companionship for elderly widows much like herself; she offered to stay with neighbours when the household was stricken with illness, making her work similar to that of Nurse Ethel Fry in chapter 8. She found the means to feed her charges when there was little available. Clearly, she was a talented woman who could "make something out of nothing" in the old style of house-wifery, and these talents had real value in her survival and in her justi-fied pride in providing for herself and in helping others in the process. Her skills and hard work allowed her to edge away from the most danger-ous marginal position for a woman in her time – being without shelter or the basic means of survival – into something resembling stability as she moved within a fairly small circle of households year after year, main-taining her familial and neighbourly networks with apparent ease.

Lauretta was marginalized through her poverty; at the same time, she was privileged in being a woman who was racialized white (we assume), in having intact social relationships that protected and nourished her in her time of need, and in having developed skills that were valued in her time and place. She was also healthy. In sustaining herself, Lauretta's great-est fear was that she would become ill or too frail to carry out her daily duties. Her diary is filled with anxious notes about the state of her health and that of her kinfolk and of her nursing her own maladies to make a speedy recovery. As far as her own embodiment is concerned, she holds to a pre-modernist script, never mentioning any component of her personal appearance – her figure, her clothing, her hair, anything. It is no surprise that no picture of Lauretta survives. We don't even know whether Lauretta often looked in the mirror. She seems unconscious of what she wears or how she looks, aside from the daily necessity to be "respectable," which seems to have translated into wearing *enough* clothing rather than any particular type.

This seeming disinterest in her appearance and clothing had the effect of adding to her personal satisfaction and even happiness at the same time that she was penurious. Since her employers generally provided her with the foodstuffs she needed to lay a meal on the table, feeding herself in the process, her needs were very few. She liked to have "stamp money" to correspond with family and friends, although letters were often carried by hand to their destination by someone travelling in that direction. Lauretta often purchased or was given wool to knit gifts for others and warm shawls for herself. She used wool for hooked rugs and hoarded scraps of fabric for her quilting. Beyond these few products, she seems to have ignored the consumer revolution well advanced all around her.

Lauretta tells us that she had kept a diary through much of her adult life, as was common in early twentieth-century Canada. Sadly, only her 1936 diary has been saved, but even it gives us insight into the daily life of a woman with few resources at her disposal. In a delightful twist on the presumed privacy of diaries, Lauretta shared her diary with relatives as she was offered theirs: "Got a letter from Florence and her Feb. Diary which I read and enjoyed very much. Its lots nicer than just a letter."[6] In her own life record, using a quirky system of capitalization to indicate pauses in the text, Lauretta describes her pleasures as well as her labours, although most of them also involved group work of some kind. She participated in a women's sewing circle, she hooked rugs alone and in company, and she regularly quilted with the women in her community, "I've finished our quilt. It is only a common one so quilted it in squares and it went quickly. Mrs. Hartley Marshall and Mabel . Was here to dinner and helped quilt a while."[7] Hence, as has been so for millennia, Lauretta's work shaded into her leisure activities and was done in the company of other women.[8]

Lauretta's position as a domestic servant was reliant on her neighbours' needs, her "good name," and her abilities. Through hard work and careful management, Lauretta did make a comfortable home for herself, with a bedroom of her own, a parlour where she could entertain her friends and relatives, and a kitchen where she could make meals for guests. "Willa S. Was in a while and before supper Charlie Sluenwhite from down Pine Grove blew in. Stayed over night. I got lots of home news."[9] With good cause, Lauretta had a strong sense of pride in her accomplishments and in her position in the community. She knew her place in the social hierarchy and protected herself against criticism by any appearance of reaching beyond her station. She recounts being invited to an afternoon tea in one of the town's wealthier households. She declined, claiming poor health, with the comment, "Too much classy folks for me."[10] Had Lauretta still been in her own home, with a healthy husband and the energy of her youth, it is likely that she still would have rejected the invitation to take tea with these "too much classy folks."

If we were to compare Lauretta's interests and general bearing to those of the other women in this book, she would be closest to the proto-feminist temperance women profiled in chapter 2. While never bothering to note this in her diary, she had a pro-temperance frame of mind. In Butler's terms, she performed as a church-attending, ethical, and serious woman whose ideals were rooted in the assumption of women's moral virtue. She was rarely verbally judgmental of others, and there is no indication that she accepted alcohol or smoked tobacco. From her comments, it is likely that her husband did smoke, however, especially since he died from cancer. To have indulged in either alcohol or smoking while living under someone else's roof, even if the owners were themselves infirm and dependent on her and themselves smoked and drank, could easily have ended her employment. It would certainly have besmirched the "good name" on which she was dependent for survival and on which she had pinned so much of her personal identity.

Inasmuch as Lauretta might impress the reader as having had few choices in her life, in fact she shows a good deal of agency in fashioning a satisfying life for herself by making consistent and careful decisions, duly recorded in her diary. Like the many temperance women who came before her and like first-wave feminists who shared much ideological ground with their temperance sisters, Lauretta held firm beliefs about her duties, her rights, and the many sources of pleasure in her life. Her story is a hopeful one of a woman without any visible means of survival making her way in the world during a period of international depression. It is an indication that by no means did all marginalized, indeed, destitute women take up smoking or take to living on the street. Further, it shows how her daily round of common activities, strongly supported by her religiosity, constituted her feminine subjectivity, allowing her to speak for herself and to be known to others as a strong and admirable woman whose life as a domestic servant did not likely differ radically from her life as a wife and mother before she fell into poverty. As with the several other women profiled in this book who chose not to smoke, Lauretta was religious and tried to live according to Christian principle.

Lauretta is one of many women who was almost totally invisible in her community and yet found a way to contribute and to make an independent way through life. Such women were not regarded as "historically relevant" even in second-wave feminist writing, and yet they constitute an important part of Canada's social history in the twentieth century. Lauretta Sluenwhite was by no means alone in her plight, and her experiences too deserve to be regarded as historically relevant. Lauretta's experiences also caution the reader to avoid easy assumptions that marginalization through poverty almost inevitably led to smoking among women.

Poor Woman Engaged in Illicit Activities

Very often, women on the margins of society were associated in some way with socially illicit or illegal behaviours like prostitution, drinking alcohol, criminality, smoking, or all of these. Joan Sangster observes that one common theme of all "delinquency narratives" for Canadian girls over the nineteenth and much of the twentieth centuries has been "the threat of sexual corruption and downfall."[11] One of the many contributions of third-wave feminism has been its insistence that normative standards of morality be closely scrutinized to ferret out hidden power disparities, all of which contribute to marginalized women's position being even more precarious. Velma Demerson's story demonstrates several of these principles.

Velma Demerson had a troubled youth punctuated by physical and psychological violence. She became pregnant by her racialized Chinese boyfriend, Harry Yipp, during the Second World War. In retaliation, Demerson's mother had her admitted to the dreaded Mercer Reformatory in Toronto. There, she gave birth to a son. Of her time at the Mercer, she recounts such searing and brutal mistreatment that one could imagine young women being lead astray *by* this experience rather than being reformed.

Velma had been incarcerated under Ontario's Training School Act of 1939, which allowed children to be sent to one of the training schools if they were considered to be "incorrigible and unmanageable."[12] This covered a wide span of infractions, with "non-conforming sexuality" considered one of the most serious.[13] The roots of her behaviours would have been enumerated: a "broken home," with inadequate and promiscuous mothering, poverty, and encouragement into transgressive behaviours.[14] Under this system of thought and with the overt racism of the era,[15] Velma's response of developing a partnership with a racialized Chinese man would have been considered a social pathology, redeemable only

11.2 | Velma Demerson, 1950

through incarceration where new and acceptable social patterns would be introduced and supported. Driven largely by Freudian psychology in this period,[16] Velma would have been considered a danger to others, particularly with the evidence of her immorality shown by the birth of her son. In the opinion of the courts and many Canadians, illicit sexuality, venereal disease, "feeble-mindedness," and racialized non-white status were closely linked.[17]

Velma's smoking would have been considered to be one material indication of her delinquency. It had begun long before her incarceration at the Mercer, and she was in good company with the other girls, many of whom she describes in her autobiography as smokers as well. One wonders where the smoking would have occurred for such closely monitored inmates.

Plans of the institution during the time when Velma was an inmate show no lounges.[18] There was an exercise yard, however, with an open pavilion, and this might have served as a smoking space. In 1941, a classroom was converted into a recreational centre with basketball boards, but it is doubtful that smoking would have been allowed in a space of this type either. Hence, even if the inmates were not given a special place to smoke, Velma Demerson's autobiography indicates that they managed to smoke anyway.

Despite her difficult start in life, Velma's own record of her life demonstrates a good measure of agency used throughout her life. With the help of others, she raised her son, travelled widely, and worked at a variety of interesting jobs in Canada and abroad. Relations with others were frequently disappointing for her, from her earliest family interactions through to her romantic partnerships and even extending to her relationship with her son.[19] In the tradition of modernity, Demerson describes herself as intensely aware of her body and its needs but also of the possibilities created by it to navigate the world. Through it all, she constructed an identity of the survivor living on the margins of her society, wielding her cigarette as a badge of independence. On the cover of her autobiography, *Incorrigible*,[20] she chooses an image of herself sitting by the water in a conservative suit and white blouse, with a cigarette nestled in her hands.

In fiction too, the trope of the unconventional spirit and fiercely independent woman as smoker is epitomized by the enchanting Carmen, discussed in chapter 3. Such women were presented as fetchingly lovely, usually racialized non-white, sexually charged, and fun-loving. In the nineteenth century, women caught in poverty were often assumed to also be immoral and to be drawn to earthy and bawdy activities at the best of times. In the twentieth century, poverty remained sexualized, and "fast" women were often thought to be "gold-digging" or willing to exchange their youth and beauty for pleasures in life, including sexual favours.[21] In advertising, images of slightly shady "good-time girls" associated with tobacco are legion. Take, for example, the advertisement for Sweet Caporals in 1940 shown in figure 11.3. Two men stand before a lightly clad woman who extends one hand. One man opines, "What an appealing pose." The other says, "Yes, appealing for a Sweet Cap." Whatever the woman's reason for standing in what seems to be her underwear on an elevated dais, she is assumed to be begging the onlookers for a cigarette. Viewed from the twenty-first century, the message of this ad, and the series of which it was a part, is strikingly sexist and denigrating, portraying as it does a nearly naked woman under a censorious male gaze. Clearly, the young woman is presented as an object of masculine pleasure, and yet, as a woman who

$1.00 will send 300 Sweet Caps or 1 lb. Old Virginia pipe tobacco to Canadians serving in United Kingdom

Address—"Sweet Caps"
P.O Box 6000, Montreal, Que.

11.3 | Magazine advertisement for Sweet Caporals, *The Canadian Unionist*, 1940

"What an appealing pose."
"Yes, appealing for a Sweet Cap."

smokes and asks others for cigarettes, she is also portrayed as a rebellious and even defiant woman smoker, claiming equality with the two fully clothed men who stand and stare at her. The message is further supported by the monochromatic line drawing in its severity. For its period, the cartoon was a slightly risqué but unremarkable comment on young women who smoked and who were assumed to be boundary-breaking in one regard or another.

Female cigarette sellers were commonly shown as underdressed, while male venders in cigar shops never were: the young male tobacco entrepreneur was typically presented in a neat suit, polished shoes, and slicked-back hair. An example of the typical male tobacco sellers can be found in figure 9.2. Of course, the female salesperson was never assumed to own her own stock as her male counterpart might; hers was a declassé version of a reputable man's job. In summary, examples of women smokers or venders from literature, opera, or advertising often represented women associated with tobacco as disrespectable, lusty, and shameless. Thus, the elision of smoking with marginality in women's condition was a long-standing one.

Women Smokers, Hard Drugs, and Trauma

Drug addiction has a particularly high correlation with smoking. A subset of this group of women who have been exposed to personal violence will be found later in life to be homeless and/or working in the sex trades[22] as well as battling drug addictions. A recent study of young women living on the street in Toronto indicated that 91 per cent smoked,[23] while 87 per cent used alcohol and 60 per cent took hallucinogens.[24] Other research shows that childhood or adolescence experience with physical or sexual abuse is associated with a greater likelihood of early-onset smoking, drinking, illegal drug use, and self-medication during adulthood.[25] Higher rates and heavier use of smoking as well as greater difficulty in quitting later in adulthood have been linked in women with major childhood stressors and adversity, including a history of abuse, violence, and trauma.[26] Finally, the coincidence between mental illness and smoking is very high, although the debate continues as to the exact relationship.[27]

Women needing to find street customers to survive and possibly feed drug dependence typically do so by visual displays of particular kinds that involve wearing enticing clothing and accessories, displaying skin and "attitude." All are intended to demonstrate something particular and identifiable about the woman in a process of self-constituting her version of femininity. But while women living on the street seem ubiquitous in some areas, the limitations of the documentary record have made it difficult to record their motivations in the construction of an identity around street life.[28]

Since the 1980s, many women trying to survive while living with addictions have clustered in Vancouver's Lower Eastside. Long known as "skid row," before the 1980s this neighbourhood had been the home of former seamen, loggers, miners, railway workers, and veterans down on their luck. Accommodation was mainly single-room-occupancy hotels scattered around East Hastings.[29] First catapulted into public awareness in the 1970s by a campaign by the federal Central Mortgage and Housing Corporation to renew inner-city urban housing and by an early documentary by Alan King, *Skid Row*, the area was soon again forgotten. The trial of Robert Picton in 2007 after five years of investigation and his eventual conviction of first-degree murder in the deaths of six women from the

Lower Eastside re-ignited interest in the occupants of this neighbourhood. Further, the fact that many of the women who disappeared, both by Picton's hand and by others, were from First Nations has fed a growing movement to recognize this district as racialized non-white.[30] The final galvanizing force in "rediscovering" the Lower Eastside was the preparations for the 2010 Winter Olympics in Vancouver. The need to "clean up" such areas for the expected influx of visitors was suddenly a major public concern.

In this context, Lincoln Clarkes, a Vancouver photojournalist, took more than 400 portraits of the women of the Lower Eastside over a period of five years. Situating his work in the long tradition of Lewis Hine and Jacob Riis, who used photography as a form of social commentary, Clarkes profiled the conditions of the neighbourhood as much as he sought to document the women who lived within it, because the area was his home as well. Through a long and respectful process of inviting each woman to choose her location as well as her stance, gestures, clothing, and props, Clarkes sought to create a forum in which these women, many of whom were addicted to heroin, could express themselves freely. Many of the women chose to pose with a cigarette. The collection has appeared as a photo display, a documentary (2001),[31] and a book. At the same time, Clarkes carefully preserved the anonymity of each woman by recording only the location and date of the photo shoot. In so doing, he provided a public identity for these women, encouraging them as well to use agency in how they preferred to be presented. The difference between them and Polly, discussed earlier in this chapter, is vast.

In figure 11.4, a young woman stands before the heavily barred door of the Hastings Medical and Dental Clinic. Her features suggest that she might be a First Nations or racialized non-white woman. Wrapped in a raincoat and jaunty straw Stetson, she holds her cigarette in the time-honoured "flag" position with her other arm wrapped around her waist and supporting the outstretched one. She chooses to face away from the camera, but her thin frame and pale face speak of exhaustion and illness. In holding her cigarette as she does, she hearkens back to an earlier, glamorous age of the woman smoker (see figure 11.5). A cinema star from the 1930s to the 1970s, Rosalind Russell was known for playing character roles of exceptionally wealthy, dignified, and ladylike women.[32] She often set off these characterizations with her cigarette and holder, as we see in this photograph of Russell in 1953. Russell stands smiling before us, in a fur stole and an elegant long dress with heavy appliqué. She radiates confidence and sophistication, with her cigarette and holder held high. Clearly imitating such cinema stars, the young woman in figure 11.4 brandishes

11.4 and 11.5 | "The Worldly Traveler," 2002; Rosalind Russell, 1953. © Vandamm/
Getty Image 3227306

the cigarette in a similar coquettish style. Were this in a different place
and time, we could imagine her as anyone's daughter or sister, standing
in front of a public building somewhere, enjoying her cigarette and flirting with her boyfriend. And yet, standing where she is in the twenty-first
century, bearing indications of marginalization through her race and
status, we can detect the struggle of her life. Recalling Judith Butler's insights into the importance of ritualized performance in the constitution
of identity, one can perceive the "social magic" created by the cigarette in
this image as the woman invokes an easier time and age than the one in
which she now lives.

A second photograph in which another woman averts her eyes from the
camera is figure 11.6. This woman perches atop a graffiti-covered public
porch, which has been further defaced. A feathery chalk drawing graces
the building wall immediately behind her head, adding a softening effect
to her hair, which seems to blend with the drawing. Official architecture
and counter-cultural graffiti act as a frame and backdrop for a mixture of

11.6 | "The Combatant," 2000

sadness and politicized irony, reminding the observer of the woman's tenuous position in society. The woman is ambiguously clothed: shorts bare her legs while she wears mittens and a sweater under her leather jacket. She is also ambiguously raced. Skin tone and hair colour suggest whiteness, but her hair has been streaked and likely coloured, and her features leave open the possibility of First Nations identity, a possibility supported by the context for the photograph. The day must be cold, since she wears warm socks in her tasselled boots. She appears older than many of the women in this collection, judging from her musculature, her face, and her neck. Her streaked hair suggests care about her appearance and the possibility that she has manufactured or enhanced a racialized white identity. Her necklace, barely peeking out from her shirt-front, adds further to that impression of a carefully constructed image. The cigarette hangs from the

11.7 | "The Flirt," 2001

corner of her closed mouth as she stares off into middle space. Interestingly too, she holds drug paraphernalia in her hands, moving it enough that the camera blurs the image. Is she nervous, or drug-addled, or just seeking a prop for this photographic session? This is beyond our capacity to know. One thing is certain, however: this woman is fully conscious of the identity she is projecting; she has co-ordinated her wardrobe and projects an image of control. And the cigarette she holds with such practice in her mouth adds to that general image of worldliness.

The young woman in figure 11.7 dressed in a delicate voile top stares directly into the camera but with her face slightly averted, eyeing the camera with a hint of rebellion, just a bit of a scowl. Accessorized very carefully with matching silver bracelet, rings, and necklace, this young woman projects a conventional, even conservative image back to the camera. Her face is made up heavily and carefully with enhancements to her eye-brows, her eyes, and her lips. Her sunglasses sit atop her head as would any high school girl's as she stands casually chatting with others. Her outfit is hyper-feminine, and she is thin in the prescription of the modern girl. She has loosely wrapped around her a leather jacket in the way of young women. And yet she isn't just any girl in any setting. She stands in front of a site locally called "the old Buddha" with a tangle of pipes and bars framing the photograph. Her cigarette is central in the photograph, positioned like a pointer between her index and second fingers. Taken with her hostile expression, the cigarette looks almost like a weapon. The young woman's angry expression telegraphs the truth that she is engaged in a zero-sum game in her life, that her chances of ever escaping it are limited, and that every day requires a hard scrabble to continue on at all. Her cigarette punctuates the stark realism that she faces daily.

Again, this young woman's appearance is racially ambiguous. She does not present as stereotypically white, and thus there is some probability that she would be identified, or that she would self-identify, as racialized non-white or as ethnicized white. Third-wave feminists have insisted that race matters deeply in determining one's life conditions, even in our utopian hopes that it should not.

There are many reference points from popular culture from at least the First World War to explain why this young woman chooses this look and this stance with her cigarette and her jacket. She situates herself in a long tradition of the female vamp as smoker, as described in chapter 3. Who is caught in this gaze? Is she the one controlling it, or does the photographer determine her "look," despite his protestations about the agency he offered the women? Is being immortalized by the photographer an empowering act or a diminishing one?

A final image of a woman in the Lower Eastside is figure 11.8, of an apparently butch dyke sex worker. Of the four photographs, this woman stares most directly, unflinchingly, into the camera, her head slightly raised so that eyes stare in a downcast. The power of her gaze contrasts with the other women's, and one immediately takes the connotative privileged or preferred message: "don't mess with me!" There is a regal and almost haughty turn of her head's position, belied by the provocative set of her legs. Even more provocative is her vest, unlaced as far as she can manage if the top is to actually stay on her extraordinarily thin, even emaciated body. As if to further draw attention to her thin arms, she sports several tattoos. Her boots, a cultural code for her butch status, are placed by the woman in the centre of the frame. Her hair is short and swept away from her severe and unmade-up face. Her cigarette completes the composition:

11.8 | "The Provocateur," 1998

unlit, it is poised between her fingers in a relaxed grip. But one would misunderstand this pose as one of leisure. With her alert, knowing stare, she seems ready to spring on anyone who might threaten her. Her maturity lends dramatic effect to the photograph, as does her conscious performance as a butch sex worker. Here, the unlit cigarette advertises who she is; the cigarette is left to be smoked at her wont. As with the first image, she creates her own "social magic" through the brandishing of her cigarette, in this case to add to her social authority and power rather than to create a vision of the "gal next door" as with the first photograph.

What can these photographs add to the search for meanings made of smoking? The "text" for these women's self-presentation is consistent with most prescriptive norms for all women in society. The women are thin – in fact, painfully thin – and some look ill. In an ironic twist on one of the most powerful reasons for women smoking – weight control – we see women who have achieved the societal prescription for slenderness but apparently little else. Most of these women have an ambiguous racial or ethnic identity, and most have altered their appearance through careful cosmetic use. We must not lose sight of the women's racialized status and their marginalization. These women demonstrate through their identity construction both their normality and their exceptional status. Cigarette-smoking is the least of their worries in terms of a shortened life span. Of course, in addition to their smoking keeping them thin, their drugs almost guarantee it, but at a great cost.

In every case, the cigarette is used as an expressive instrument by the woman being photographed. We see here the cigarette used in a wide variety of ways to support the identity performance of the woman using it as a prop: smoker as worldly traveler, smoker as combatant, smoker as flirt, and smoker as provocateur. In every instance before us, the women evince pride, finding ways to add to a wide range of identity styles with the creative use of the cigarette.

Gay Women and Smoking

There is a long tradition of gay women being considered naturally drawn to smoking. In *The Psychology of Sex*, Havelock Ellis identified smoking as a male practice, as indeed it still was in some places when he wrote in the early 1940s. He also defined smoking as "mannish," especially favoured by women engaged in some form of "transvestism." Although by no means did he identify all such individuals as representing a sexual "inversion" or gayness, he did hold that smoking imbued women with male-like characteristics.[33] He also named cigar-smoking as a common lesbian practice.[34]

For butch women, the cigar does seem to have offered a particularly powerful visual code for appropriating masculine privilege, with the cigar or cigarette operating as a phallic symbol. In heterosexual as well as homoerotic culture, the cigarette can often be used to telegraph isolating difference and loneliness. Carellin Brooks in her study of the masculinized woman, *Every Inch a Woman*, invokes Radclyffe Hall's description of the sad mannish lesbian in *The Well of Loneliness*. Brooks describes as well the character of Ed in Terry Castle's *The Apparitional Lesbian* as another character marked by isolation: "She spoke to no one, smoked a cigarette, and seemed, despite her great beauty, consumed by sadness."[35] The power of the cigarette to suggest alienation and loneliness is not distinctive to the lesbian community, although this portrayal has become iconic for that community. One could refer back to any of the young women in Vancouver's Lower Eastside to find similar studies in frustration and loneliness.

The association between a lesbian way of being, enjoying, and cultivating "drag" and cigarette smoking has been explored by k.d. lang through her music and imagery. Lang has mined the margins of society in her own life and career. Beginning in mainstream country music, she courageously risked alienation from it by her declaration of vegetarianism, enraging large sectors of the Albertan beef-producing community in which she had been raised. She had come out as a lesbian before releasing her fourth album, *Ingenue*, which also departed from the country rock category she had helped to define. The album's first single, "Constant Craving," became a top 40 American hit, won the Grammy Award for best pop vocal performance for a female artist, and pushed into double platinum status in Canada, with strong sales internationally. With the 1997 release of her album *Drag*, lang further pushed the boundaries of acceptability in the still-conservative music industry. Ambiguously titled to refer both to the allure of smoking and cross-dressing, lang's album reinforced the image she had been steadily building since the mid 1980s. The very titles of the songs she chose for the album, including "Don't Smoke in Bed," "Smoke Dreams," and "Love Is Like a Cigarette," speak to the sexually charged nature of cigarettes in both gay and straight culture. Lang herself is not a smoker and reports that she was drawn to the imagery of the cigarette "as a visual stimulant, as a prop initiating all this imagery and commentary."[36] Demonstrating a nuanced understanding of the cigarette's significance for identity construction, lang notes that it "has been viewed as an extension of the personality in art so much, and it's so topical in our consciousness with the war between smokers and nonsmokers"[37] that she regarded it as an ideal vehicle for her work. Furthermore, the resonance of the cigarette as a symbol for powerful emotions, both positive and negative, is well understood by her: "The cigarette is an elaborate metaphor for love and relationships, for addiction and release."[38]

As a piece of art, the *Drag* album cover is in itself a study in ambiguity and authority. Dressed in splendid drag, lang presents a costumed image of a male dandy, complete with cravat, diamond stick-pin and pin-striped suit. The colouration is dramatic, with splashes of red on black and white in the style of the "siren" postwar period when gender roles were at their most inflexible and visually sexualized. Had lang posed as a screen starlet, we would expect to find her lips coloured in the same deep red with matching rouge. Lang continues the siren theme with her pose, as if holding a cigarette. The actual cigarette is missing from where one would expect to find it, between her fingers, further playing off and confusing the romantic stance she adopts here. She stares almost belligerently at the camera, at least unsmilingly, with her head tilted down and eyes up-cast, in a stance

11.9 | k.d. lang's *Drag*

opposite to that most glamorous women's smoking imagery. Even if k.d. lang had recorded nothing that spoke to the boundary-bridging of her sexuality or her life choices, such as vegetarianism, an image like this one with the (absent) cigarette reinforces her boundary-bridging and signals to us her intention to break with convention.

Insofar as k.d. lang has contributed to women's empowerment in their own cultures and communities where they can discover and use their own voices, she can be identified as representative of and sympathetic to third-wave feminism. As such, she has fashioned an identity that draws strength from many of the injustices that third-wave feminists have contested. Rooting her public identity in a range of counter-cultural expressions – including, for example, pacifism, vegetarianism, gayness, and Buddhism – lang has bridged national and gender boundaries in a consciously post-modern approach to her artistic expression. Sensitive to the enduring power of symbols, she has made good use of the performative possibilities of smoking by gay women while never actually smoking.

'Tough' Girls and Cigarettes

Rebecca Haines's research into young women's narrative and visual explanations for smoking illuminates the world of the tough adolescent girl smoker. A number of her respondents, all young women between sixteen and nineteen, described themselves as having survived lives of disruption, abuse, and neglect. While a few were middle-class in origin, most came from working-class families where smoking was common. The young women also testified to the various self-management functions of smoking, including creating pleasure for themselves and controlling their bodies. They recognized smoking's many social functions, such as meeting others through "bumming" cigarettes, sustaining friendships, claiming adolescent space, and initiating adult practices. Beyond these reasons for smoking, girls in such circumstances pointed to smoking for its survival functions whereby adversity of various forms was made more tolerable through smoking.[39] Such instrumental uses make smoking a logical choice for young women living in privation of one type or another.

The girls in Haines's research project were offered a digital camera to record circumstances associated with their smoking and the people with whom they smoked.[40] The goal was to engage the young women in self-examination of their behaviour as well as to add to a greater understanding of what factors encourage smoking among young women. In the images and captions they produced, the teenaged photographers refer to cigarettes' ability to calm those who are agitated or stressed. Participants demonstrated the appropriate stance for holding the cigarette in adolescent street culture, commenting on the options available to the smoker. None of the young women's commentaries or images are groundbreaking in the information provided. Yet they are rare in providing insight into the thoughts of young women, especially marginalized young women smokers. Their testimony and analysis adds depth to our knowledge of the "tough" adolescent female smoker.

Two decades ago, Hilary Graham pointed to the gendered functions of smoking and its salutary effects for women living in disadvantaged circumstances, where she found women "surviving by smoking."[41] In their investigation of girls' social hierarchies, Mitchell and Amos argue that adolescent smokers are part of a distinct social hierarchy and that any understanding of the social exchange implicit in that subculture must take the "pecking order" into account.[42] Anything, smoking included, that helps girls and women who have experienced trauma or crisis to survive has a clear and obvious value. Some adolescent girls report that smoking is used as a conscious harm-reduction strategy when the desire to "cut" becomes too strong.[43] Others report that smoking began while they were in treatment for mental health issues where the majority smoke as a bonding technique.[44] The value of much of the research investigating the reasons why women begin and persist in smoking demonstrates that women consciously use smoking as a coping mechanism rather than witlessly or recklessly engaging in risky behaviours. Smoking's benefits, and sometimes its costs, are obvious to those who use it in this way and very particularly for women whose lives are fraught with stress and danger.

Posing with a cigarette has been a supportive theatrical device chosen by many women living on the margins of society, surviving without the usual supports conferred by a protective family or peer group. Often, girls and women who find themselves living in such circumstances by choice or fate seek the pleasure conferred by smoking – a pleasure that has a documented physiological effect on women along with a strong social impulse.[45] Such women frequently trade cigarettes as an act of friendship and support, they use the cigarette to meet and sustain relationships through conversation, they practise the theatrical possibilities of holding and smoking the cigarette for visual effect. By no means do all such women smoke, now or in the past, but those who do report having found an empowering force to counter the many other undermining features of otherwise difficult lives. They have adopted the cigarette for good reason.

Conclusion

THE WAY FORWARD

Smoking still holds a powerful attraction for Canadian women in the twenty-first century. Approximately one in five women currently smoke in this country, and for younger women between eighteen and twenty-four, the rate is higher yet at about 24 per cent. Women marginalized by race, poverty, or addictions remain particularly heavy smokers, and cessation programs seem to have limited success with them. Pre-teen and teen smoking rates by both girls and boys are again on the rise. The latest Canadian Youth Smoking Survey found that the number of young people who identify themselves as current daily smokers is increasing in all adolescent age groups.[1] The substantial decline in youth smoking between 2006 and 2009 has "stalled."[2] By 2020, women's life expectancy will be roughly equivalent to men's in Canada, bringing to an end the historic health advantage women have enjoyed. Female mortality rates are closely tied to women's continuing romance with cigarettes, the early uptake of smoking by girls, and the slower reduction rates for women as smokers compared with those of men.[3]

Internationally, the statistics are equally disturbing. The World Health Organization (WHO) recently forecast that "the epidemic of tobacco-related disease and death has just begun." By 2030, the annual death toll could easily reach eight million, it noted. The WHO's Framework Convention on Tobacco Control had 172 signatories by 2011, obliging governments to take steps to cut smoking rates, limit exposure to second-hand smoke, and curb tobacco advertising and promotion. In encouraging stronger measures, Margaret Chan, WHO director-general, observed that tobacco kills up to half of all users, to say nothing of causing cancer, chronic respiratory ailments, and cardiovascular diseases. These non-communicable, chronic diseases account for 63 per cent of all deaths worldwide and nearly 80 per cent of deaths in poorer countries.[4]

What does the history of women and smoking contribute to our understanding of why so many women still choose to smoke? I have argued that without a recognition of the combined effects of such forces as consumerism, the need for women to control their bodies and emotions, allowable displays of sexuality, status, and sophistication from smoking, the pleasure of social exchange, and the unrelenting gaze on the idealized female figure as slender and forever young, we cannot appreciate the depth of the cigarette's hold on women. All of these factors developed as part of or were exacerbated by modernism after the First World War in Canada. All contributed to women's increasing public roles, as well as to their insecurity with their bodies, and encouraged women to seek modern visual identities that marked them as in control. The demands on women to conform to the merciless ideal of physical perfection have not slackened with the intervening years, just as North Americans become ever fatter. Many argue that the pressures on girls and young women who struggle to find a place in the social order are increasing as well. In response, girls and women turn to smoking.

This book has traced the relationship between women and smoking through a wide range of historical documents as well as visual culture. It has relied on the products of visual culture for several reasons. First, modernism's revolutionary notions of commodification, sexual expression, and aesthetics have been represented mainly through the visual. Tobacco manufacturers' marketing of cigarettes, women's interpretations of what the modern woman smoker looked like, female-led attacks on tobacco, and debates about how best to dissuade youths from smoking all have made use of the visual in creative and often startling ways. Second, the uses women have made of smoking, in particular those relating to bodily and identity performance, have generally been expressed visually. As one example, photographs taken by and of women have shown this repeatedly. Third, the popular cultural response to smoking, including its promotion of smoking culture, has resulted in a rich resource of visual artifacts, from cheaply produced cigarette compacts to museum-quality matchboxes, cigar-box labels, and fine china. All of these smoking paraphernalia and cultural products were meant to impress by their visual qualities. They remain an important means of understanding the attraction of smoking for women.

Visual culture reminds the historian, who usually relies on words and numbers, that to fully appreciate long-standing social phenomena such as smoking, the visual truly is worth "a thousand words." The recent decision by Health Canada to force tobacco manufacturers to place disturbing pictures on at least 75 per cent of each cigarette package is evidence that even government departments have come to realize the power of the visual. Heather Crowe's success (and that of Health Canada) in underlining the danger of second-hand smoke to non-smokers resulted from her moving, quiet television advertisements and posters featuring her, both of which *showed* an unremarkable everywoman, someone we all know and to whom many of us are related, who was dying through no fault of her own. The visual is powerful, and it must be tapped for academic purposes as well as for social policy decisions.

Government's role stands out as one of the important changes over time as surveyed in this book. It was unwilling through the nineteenth century and the first half of the twentieth to involve itself in contesting Big Tobacco's control of smokers. One explanation for the eventual decision to intervene is that the societal costs of smoking are proving to be astronomical. A recent calculation by the federal government places smoking-related health care costs since 1955 in Canada at $50 billion.[5] The current annual cost of tobacco-related illnesses for the province of Ontario alone is estimated at more than $1.6 billion.[6] Partly in response to these steep costs, Ontario has recently launched a $50-billion lawsuit against tobacco companies Imperial Tobacco, JTL-Macdonald Corp., and Rothmans, Benson & Hedges Inc., along with their parent companies, to recover health care costs linked to smoking. This follows an American agreement between tobacco manufacturers and most state governments requiring manufacturers to pay $246 billion over 25 years toward the costs of treatment for ills caused by smoking.[7]

Government has taken a more active role as well by alerting Canadians to the many dangers of smoking. In January 2011, the federal government finally introduced more stringent requirements of tobacco companies to place enhanced warnings and grotesque pictures on cigarette packages in order to further enlighten the public about the effects of smoking. This follows six years and almost $4 million devoted to studies of the effects of packaging.[8] More government-sponsored research continues to be funded into the wide variety of health issues that either arise from or are exacerbated by smoking. There is now clear evidence, for example, that smokers beginning before the age of 15 have double the risk of premature death.[9]

How much of this research is finding its way to young people considering taking up smoking? We do not have evidence of the successful penetration of much of this research into the social world of adolescents, male or female. We do see the fruits of research funding in more vigorous and effective public campaigns to target youths at the community level, but without the support of the educational sector and new social media like Facebook, YouTube, and Twitter, any advances in reducing adolescent and youth smoking rates will be slow and fragile.

As for current popular culture's response to the challenge of smoking, there is a great deal of ambivalence. Media still show young women participating in this smoking rite while at the same time broadcasting the enormous costs of smoking. Generally, popular culture continues to celebrate many of the features of smoking. From the easy bonding and relaxed geniality of movies like Jim Jarmusch's *Coffee and Cigarettes* and the mild rebellion of *Thank You for Smoking* to television shows like *Mad Men* or reruns of *Sex and the City*, we all remain fascinated by smoking's cultural power.

What, then, is the way forward? Do we accept that modernity's grasp will not loosen any day soon and continue sacrificing our young women (and men) on the altar of body control and coolness as conferred by smoking? Or are we prepared to learn from the historical and cultural record that documents why young people and especially young women are drawn to smoking? What will it take to reduce smoking's magnetic attraction? I have argued throughout this book that the answer is surely not found in creating a health curriculum that ignores girls and young women and their reasons for smoking or that disparages their choices as "stupid."

This book has argued that young and mature women adopt smoking for good reasons: to control stress that is often not of their making, to construct and sometimes reconstruct a self image that aligns with modernist forces, to control their bodies, to give themselves pleasure in the face of pain and frustration, and to facilitate social exchange and interactions while building community, to name but a few. If we are to have any hope of mounting a truly effective anti-smoking campaign among young and mature women, we must acknowledge the legitimacy of their reasons for taking up the practice and be prepared to offer real alternatives to smoking. Furthermore, this campaign must be mounted through both the formal and informal educational systems as well as through popular and social media. Beyond crediting the real reasons why women smoke, what would an effective campaign of this kind involve? I propose here a "Top Ten" set of considerations.

1   An effective anti-tobacco campaign that finds its mark with girls and women would require a complete overhaul of the appallingly deficient school curriculum. It would mandate a gendered approach to anti-smoking education and other important social issues whereby

girls adopt dangerous habits like smoking earlier and for different reasons than boys do. If socialization is acknowledged to be different for girls than for boys, why would we think that one curriculum fits all?

2   A reworked and effective curriculum would call for an honest discussion with young women about the widely peer-discussed rewards of smoking, along with the many health costs both to themselves and their future children. Silence about the advantages and short-term pleasures of smoking does not allow for a credible anti-smoking message.

3   The factors that recommend smoking to young women must be contested by offering other approaches and solutions to real problems rather than presenting bland nostrums about the evils of "peer pressure" and the like. Neither the formal curriculum nor social messaging sites ever work in isolation from the culture of which they are a product. If the message is to carry any credibility with the young women we should be addressing, the pleasures and supports gained through smoking must be replaced by other meaningful rewards in a broad program of public education.

4   Fashioning a more convincing argument and ensuring that young women are exposed to it will require resources, and they are chronically in short supply in education of any sort. Yet there are more effective anti-smoking programs in this country than the school curriculum has been able to mount, and they should be accessed through collaborative partnerships. Health Canada has funded important gender-sensitive research since the late 1980s and has developed – often in partnerships – some very impressive educational programs. These programs should be made available to the most vulnerable of Canadian smokers. One of these groups is a captive educational audience: pre-adolescent girls. Even with such partnerships, smoking rates for young women will not drop overnight as the limited success of current programs shows. However, there is more chance of success than there is with scattershot and limited-duration cessation programs.

5   It has been amply demonstrated that tobacco manufacturers have developed some very persuasive marketing targeted directly at youths. Such successful "teaching" has emerged from well-funded research. Why have educational programs not used some of the same teaching techniques in their effort to dissuade youths from smoking? There is clear evidence as well that tobacco manufacturers have knowingly developed programs that are ineffective. (See chapter 3 for

a full discussion of "pseudo educational" strategies.) They too would be instructive for those searching for more convincing messages and pedagogy. We should learn from these approaches, especially where children and early adolescents are concerned, for they are at an age when experimentation with smoking occurs.

6 One reason that many young women turn to smoking is to exert control over weight and mood. The societal and media prescription for young women to be wraith-thin and to wear revealing clothing as a signal of rebellion, independence, and fashion-consciousness is ultimately destructive to young women's confidence and health. Yo-yo dieting has become a feature of even pre-teen girls' lives. The unrealistic standards of slenderness promulgated by an entertainment and fashion industry stocked with emaciated models as the standard of modern beauty exist alongside a fast-food industry that continues to fatten the population with empty calories. Understandably, young women are confused and frightened by standards that most cannot hope to achieve and thwarted in doing so by common food choices, also heavily advertised. As a society, we must contest this dangerous and cruel template for girls. If we do so successfully, we will weaken at least part of smoking's allure.

7 Another reason for young women to take up smoking is to alleviate anxiety and depression. Depression is more common in women than in men.[10] In the absence of better strategies to control moods, many young women experiment with smoking early in their lives. Early uptake of smoking is one factor that makes breaking the habit more difficult. We have a societal responsibility to provide better education for women in this area, from pre-teen to young adult women. Smoking would not become such an imbedded habit if young women were offered more support and alternative strategies for making them feel in greater control of their emotional lives.

8 For those young, middle-aged, or elderly women who choose to quit smoking, we must do better in providing gender-specific smoking cessation programming and support groups. For school-aged girl smokers, these programs should be provided in a school setting rather than dependent on community health services or the market. We have considerable data available to us about the kinds of support groups that are effective for girls and women in their quest to take control of their lives without tobacco. We know, for example, that for smoking controls to work with women, they need to be accompanied by techniques for stress management, healthy eating, and self-esteem training in a holistic approach. We should be making use of this

information and providing it to women at the critical stages of their lives when they would be inclined to begin smoking.

9 Second-hand smoke continues to kill too many innocent Canadians. It does so stealthily and over the long term but just as surely as if the victim had herself smoked. Heather Crowe's profile and story ought not to be forgotten, and the fact that she was exposed to this danger while working at a low-skill job as a single mother is not a coincidence. We should continue to forbid smoking in all public enclosed spaces and in as many private ones as possible. We must remain particularly mindful of the extra challenges faced by working-class women in their workplaces and homes.

10 While many of the people, associations, and mindsets of the past who fought tobacco have passed from the scene, we are not without institutions and strategies to continue this battle. The history of smoking and women offers key lessons of process, strategies, and above all, the importance of personal investment in fighting seemingly intractable problems. Even if the rhetoric and societal context has changed in the twenty-first century, there is much that we can learn from the past. We need to look to historical precedents to establish what worked and then model new strategies on old principles; we need to acknowledge what did not work, and then avoid replaying the same ineffective approaches.

The necessary struggle to reduce smoking's hold on women should not obscure the fact that historically, smoking symbolized for many women strength, passion, sophistication, independence, and rebellion. That image was first constructed in the 1920s when smoking helped to expand women's performative possibilities on the public stage through allowable gestures, objects, and attitudes, many of them empowering and some threatening. Even today, smoking offers young women an acceptable means to express their desires for personal and public authority and to do so through visual means. Through ritualized displays with the cigarette as an essential stage prop, these young women lay claim visually to a broad range of expressive techniques, including sophistication and glamour, sexuality, and authority in much the same way that their foremothers experimented with this potent blend. Sanctioning the empowerment of women without the many and severe health threats presented by smoking must become a goal for the entire society.

Notes

INTRODUCTION

1 Samet and Yoon, *Women and the Tobacco Epidemic*.
2 National Women's Law Center, *Making the Grade on Women's Health*.
3 Health Canada, *Mixed Messages*.
4 Cunningham, *Smoke & Mirrors*, 175.
5 Amos and Haglund, "From Social Taboo to 'Torch of Freedom.'"
6 Ernster, "Mixed Messages for Women."
7 Lennon et al., "Young Women as Smokers and Nonsmokers"; Nichter et al., "Smoking Experimentation and Initiation among Adolescent Girls: Qualitative and Quantitative Findings"; Lloyd and Lucas, *Smoking in Adolescent Images and Identities*.
8 Warburton, *Nicotine and the Smoker*.
9 Haines, "Smoke, in My Eyes."
10 Daykin, "Young Women and Smoking."
11 Glendinning and Inglis, "Smoking Behaviour in Youth."
12 Carpenter et al., *Designing Cigarettes for Women*.
13 Freidman, "The Female Smoker Market."
14 Greaves et al., "Smoking and Disordered Eating among Adolescent Girls," 165.
15 Ibid., 166.
16 Ibid., 165–7.
17 Burnham, *Bad Habits*, 993, esp. ch. 4.
18 MacDonald and Wright, "Cigarette Smoking and the Disenfranchisement of Adolescent Girls"; Wearing et al., "Adolescent Women, Identity and Smoking."
19 See, for example, Bridges, "Addictions: Booze and Butts."

20 LAC, *The Globe and Mail*, Makin, "Top Court Upholds Tobacco Advertising Laws," 29 June 2007.

21 Carpenter et al.

22 Currie et al., *Young People's Health in Context*.

23 Health Canada, *Canadian Tobacco Use Monitoring Survey*, 1996, 2000, 2005, 2006.

24 Statistics Canada, "Smokers by Sex, Provinces and Territories."

25 Poland et al., "The Social Context of Smoking."

26 Barbeau et al., "Smoking, Social Class, and Gender."

27 Shields, "Youth Smoking," 1.

28 Statistics Canada, *Au courant*.

29 Samet and Yoon.

30 US Department of Health and Human Services, "Women and Smoking."

31 This had been reported widely in *The Globe and Mail* in the early 1970s. See, for example, LAC, *The Globe and Mail*, "Cigaret Use Harms Fetus, Steinfeld Warns," 12 January 1971.

32 LAC, *The Globe and Mail*, "More Babies of Women Smokers Die, MD says," 8 June 1975.

33 See, for example, Health Canada, *Directions*, 12–13.

34 LAC, *The Globe and Mail*, "Teen Smokers Risk Breast Cancer," 2002.

35 Cook, "'Smokin' in the Boys' Room.'"

36 CBC Television Report, "A New Danger: Second-Hand Smoke," 1985.

37 Krueger et al., *The Health Impact of Smoking and Obesity*, 7.

38 LAC, *The Globe and Mail*, "Find More Lung Cancer in Women Who Smoke," 1966.

39 LAC, *The Globe and Mail*, "Women Smoking More Today," 1970.

40 LAC, *The Globe and Mail*, "Mouth Cancer Reported Increasing in Women," 1972.

41 LAC, *The Globe and Mail*, "Women Catching up to Men in Lung Diseases," 12 January 1980.

42 LAC, *The Globe and Mail*, "Toronto Study Connects Variety of Ailments to Women's Smoking," 30 April 1973.

43 LAC, *The Globe and Mail*, "Study Finds Nicotine Gathers in Breasts of Women Smokers," 1978.

44 Malmo, "Addressing Tobacco Dependency in Women's Substance Use Treatment," 324.

45 Vattimo, *The End of Modernity*, 7–8.

46 Crary, *Techniques of the Observer*, 10.

47 Ibid.

48 Ibid., 5.

49 Foucault, *Power/Knowledge*. This discussion is part of Foucault's notion of "geneology."

50 See, for example, Berger, *Ways of Seeing*, and Mulvey, "Visual Pleasure and Narrative Cinema."

51 Carson and Pajaczkowska, eds, *Feminist Visual Culture*, 18.

52 Klitzing, "Women Living in a Homeless Shelter."

53 Rutherford, *A World Made Sexy*, 42.

54 Crary, 13.

55 Chambers, "Family as Place."

56 Close, *Framing Identity*, xv.

57 Keith Walden documents young male freshman who dared to smoke in the presence of upperclassmen as punished by hazing. Walden, "Hazes, Hustles, Scraps and Stunts."

58 Routh, *In Style*, esp. 47–66.

59 Smith and Watson, "Reading Autobiography."

60 For a complex and revealing argument around the functions and means of "performance" for women, particularly "transgressive" women bridging established norms of propriety, see Butler, *Gender Trouble*, and Butler, "Performativity's Social Magic."

61 Butler, "Performativity's Social Magic."

62 Martin et al., *Technologies of the Self.*

63 Ibid., 18.

64 Rose, *Visual Methodologies*, 136.

65 Phillips and Harvey, *Discourse Analysis.*

66 Tinkler, *Smoke Signals*, 4.

67 See Close.

68 Reeves, "Through the Eye of the Camera."

69 Brandt, *The Cigarette Century*, 86.

70 Ibid., 87.

71 Mitchell and Reid-Walsh, "*Girl Culture.*"

72 Messaris, *Visual "Literacy,"* 165.

73 Barthes, *The Photographic Message*, 15–31.

74 Seppanen, *The Power of the Gaze*, 122–7.

75 See Forceville, "Pictorial Metaphor in Advertisements."

76 Tate, *Cigarette Wars*, 138.

77 These categories constituted the fields considered by Rebecca Haines in her research, for example. See Haines, "Smoke, in My Eyes," 81.

78 Cox, "Growth and Ownership in the International Tobacco Industry"; Cunningham, 175; Miles, *Coffin Nails and Corporate Strategies*; White, *Merchants of Death.*

79 Kruger, *Ashes to Ashes.*

80 Burnham, *Bad Habits*, esp. chap 4; Cook, "Educating for Temperance"; Cook, "Earnest Christian Women"; Gusfield, "The Social Symbolism of Smoking"; Gusfield, *Contested Meanings*; Tyrrell, *Dangerous Enemies.*

81 Burnham, "American Physicians and Tobacco Use."

82 See, for example, Gately, *La Diva Nicotina*; Hughes, *Learning to Smoke*; Miles, *Coffin Nails and Corporate Strategies*; Segrave, *Women and Smoking in America*; Tinkler, "Refinement and Respectable Consumption"; Warsh, "Smoke and Mirrors"; White, *Merchants of Death.*

83 Hilton, *Smoking in British Popular Culture.*

84 Tate.

85 Brandt.

86 Ibid., 12–13.

87 Rudy, *The Freedom to Smoke*.

88 Ibid., 108.

89 See, for example, Cook, "Evangelical Moral Reform"; Cook, "Educating for Temperance."

90 See especially Warsh, "Smoke and Mirrors;" see also Greaves, *Smoke Screen*.

91 Warsh, 183.

92 For the United States, see Brandt.

93 Tinkler, "Refinement and Respectable Consumption," and *Smoke Signals*.

94 Cunningham; Hilton; Strong-Boag, *The New Day Recalled*.

95 In her doctoral dissertation, Rebecca Haines finds only five qualitative studies explicitly addressing young women smokers in Canada. Haines, 2.

96 Nichter et al., "Gendered Dimensions of Smoking Among College Students."

97 Nichter et al., "Qualitative Research"; Tilleczek and Hine, "The Meaning of Smoking."

98 Carpenter et al.

99 Greaves, *Smoke Screen*, 1996.

100 Frohlich et al., "A Theoretical and Empirical Analysis of Context"; Frohlich et al., "Youth Smoking Initiation."

101 Mitchell and Amos, "Girls, Pecking Order and Smoking."

102 McCracken, "Got a Smoke?"

103 Kobus, "Peers and Adolescent Smoking."

104 Haines.

105 Ahijevych et al., "Factors Influencing Nicotine Half-Life."

106 Canadian Survey of Smoking Patterns, as quoted in Millar, "Place of Birth and Ethnic Status."

107 See, for example, Jategaonkar and Devries, "What We Don't Know about Gender."

CHAPTER ONE

1 Rudy, "Manufacturing French Canadian Tradition," 208.

2 Brandt, *The Cigarette Century*, 19.

3 Ibid.

4 Ibid., 21.

5 Rudy, "A Ritual Transformed," 263.

6 Hughes, *Learning to Smoke*, 66.

7 Ibid., 68.

8 Tate, *Cigarette Wars*, 11.

9 CBC Television, "How to Spit on Umpires' Feet without Getting Caught."

10 Burnham, *Bad Habits*, 88.

11 Rudy, "Manufacturing French Canadian Tradition," 9.

12 The eminent historian of alcohol, Joseph Gusfield, has argued that the American anti-tobacco movement was strongly moralistic during its genesis and that expressed in a different form, it remains so. He explores the construction of "devi-

ance" in tobacco use in relation to moralism. See Gusfield, "The Social Symbolism of Smoking," and *Contested Meanings*.

13 LAC, *Saturday Night*, "The Insidious Cigarette," 4 May 1912.
14 Bowman, "The Dangers and Delights of the Cigarette," 56.
15 This view was shared by Wilfrid Laurier, prime minister during this period. See LAC, Laurier, 846.
16 Brandt, 109ff.
17 See Cook, *"Through Sunshine and Shadow."*
18 LAC, *Saturday Night*, 8 February 1913.
19 LAC, *Maclean's* magazine, September 1911.
20 LAC, *Maclean's* magazine, June 1912.
21 LAC, *Saturday Night*, "The Insidious Cigarette," 4 May 1912.
22 To reinforce the notion of the discriminating consumer, one advertisement reads, "So rigid, so unremitting is the system of scrutiny enforced in the making of Tuckett's 'Club' Virginias that thousands of Cigarettes are discarded every day for slight, immaterial imperfections which would be overlooked by even the most critical smoker." LAC, *Saturday Night*, 6 September 1913.
23 Carpenter et al., *Designing Cigarettes for Women*, 839.
24 *Canadian Cigar and Tobacco Journal*, November 1932, 24, as quoted in Rudy, "A Ritual Transformed," 270.
25 LAC, *The Globe and Mail*, "Muscles, Blushes and Smoke," 5 February 1975.
26 Rudy, *The Freedom to Smoke*, 3.
27 Tate, 23.
28 Carpenter et al., 839.
29 Brandt, 23–5.
30 Ibid., 26.
31 Rudy, "Manufacturing French Canadian Tradition."
32 CBC Television, "Trouble in Tobacco Country," 29 June 1971.
33 LAC, "Is Tobacco Injurious?" *Canadian Cigar and Tobacco Journal*, March 1948.
34 See, for example, LAC, *The Globe and Mail*, "M.D. Says Dollars Push Smoking but It's Never Too Late to Stop," 7 November 1963.
35 Author's interview with respondent "IAA"; oral history study with older women having smoked for 40 years or more.
36 Rudy, "Manufacturing French Canadian Tradition," 221.
37 Tate, 93–4.
38 A.B. Hodgetts, *Decisive Decades*, 289.
39 Bowman, 76.
40 Warsh, "Smoke and Mirrors," 199; Jacobson, *Beating the Ladykillers*, 43. About 40 per cent of British women were smokers by 1950.
41 Rudy, *The Freedom to Smoke*, 148.
42 Rudy, "A Ritual Transformed," 259.
43 LAC, *The Monetary Times*, July 1955.
44 Ibid., 58–9.
45 Ibid., 168.

46 CBC Television, "Smoking Kills, Says U.S. Surgeon General," 12 January 1964.

47 Ibid.

48 Rates of doctors' smoking also slowly declined. A survey by the American Center of Disease Control showed that while 60 per cent of doctors admitted to smoking in the 1950s, the rate had been halved by the next decade. The article noted that the rate of doctors' smoking had dropped to 21 per cent in 1971. Survey of the American Center of Disease Control, 1977, as quoted in *Marketing* magazine, 4 July 1977, 16.

49 LAC, *The Financial Post*, 8 June 1963.

50 LAC, *The Financial Post*, 18 April 1984; LAC, *The Financial Post*, 24 October 1964.

51 CBC Television, "Do Cigarette Ads Cause Smoking?" 21 March 1965.

52 See, for example, LAC, *The Globe and Mail*, "Tobacco Question Warmly Debated by United Pastors," 22 May 1929.

53 Statistics Canada and Health and Welfare Canada, 1965–91, in Health Canada, *Directions: The Directional Paper of the National Strategy to Reduce Tobacco Use*, 1993, 10. A contemporary survey put the figure lower than this; *The Financial Post* reported that 34 per cent of women smoked in 1965 according to a survey by the Department of Health and Welfare (LAC, *The Financial Post*, 27 February 1965); an article in *The Business Quarterly* put the figure at 22.6 per cent (Delarue, "The Reasons for An Anti-Smoking Campaign," 93).

54 The trend was obvious enough that the press reported this from the late 1960s. See, for example, LAC, *The Financial Post*, 3 May 1969.

55 For American rates in that period, see US Department of Health, Education and Welfare, *The Smoking Digest*, Bethesda, MD: Office of Cancer Communications, National Cancer Institute, October 1977, 13.

56 LAC, *The Financial Post*, 28 March 1964.

57 LAC, *The Financial Post*, 17 October 1970; LAC, *The Financial Post*, 31 October 1970.

58 In 2001, 32 per cent of this age group is estimated to have smoked. Health Canada, *The National Strategy to Reduce Tobacco Use*, 2001.

59 See, for example, Health Canada, *Mixed Messages*, 1995; Health Canada, *Smoking Interventions in the Prenatal and Postpartum Periods*, 1995; Health Canada, *Tobacco Resource Material: A Selected Inventory*, 1995; Health Canada, *Francophone Women's Tobacco Use in Canada*, 1996; Health Canada, *Women and Tobacco: A Framework for Action*, 1995; Health Canada, *Smoking and Pregnancy: A Woman's Dilemma*, 1995.

60 Carpenter et al., 846–7.

61 Cook, "'Where There's Smoke, There's Fire.'"

62 LAC, Robertson, *Legislative Summary, Bill C-III: The Tobacco Sales to Young Persons Act, 1993*.

63 Cunningham, *Smoke & Mirrors*, 35.

64 Strange and Loo, *Making Good*, 77. See also Carstairs, *Jailed for Possession*.

65 Rudy, *The Freedom to Smoke*, 107.

66 Brandt, 51.

67 LAC, *Acts of the General Assembly of Her Majesty's Province of New Brunswick*, 1890, 1893.

68 LAC, *Statutes of the British Columbia Legislature*, 1891.

69 LAC, *Statutes of the Province of Ontario*, 1892.

70 LAC, *Ordinances of the North West Territories*, 1896. In that year, the "Public School Leaving" Hygiene and Temperance Examination included the following questions on tobacco: "2 (a) Why is the use of Tobacco particularly harmful to the young? (b) In adults what organs of the body are most likely to be affected by its use? How are they affected?" Report of the Council of Public Instruction of the North-West Territories of Canada, 1896, 73–4.

71 LAC, *Statutes of Nova Scotia*, 1900 and 1901.

72 LAC, *The Acts of the General Assembly of P.E.I.*, 1901.

73 Brandt, 60.

74 Cunningham, 44.

75 Ibid.

76 Ibid.

77 Ibid., 45.

78 Ibid., 46.

79 Ibid., 48.

80 Ibid.

81 Sinacore, *Health*, 341–2.

82 Cunningham, 50.

83 CBC Television, "Do Cigarette Ads Cause Smoking?" 21 March 1965.

84 Ibid.

85 Ibid.

86 CBC Television, "Trouble in Tobacco Country," 19 June 1971.

87 *The Globe and Mail* reported in 1973 that between 1965 and 1970, rates dropped for men under 55 while smoking by women of all ages increased. The rate for women between fifteen and nineteen had increased in that period from 19 to 25 per cent. LAC, *The Globe and Mail*, "Toronto Study Connects Variety of Ailments to Women's Smoking," 30 April 1973.

88 CBC Television, "Kicking the Habit," 25 June 1977.

89 LAC, *The Globe and Mail*, "Tip of the Hat to TTC for Cigaret Ad Ban," 16 July 1979; *Marketing* magazine, 27 August 1979, 14.

90 *Marketing* magazine, 31 March 1980, 2, and 9 June 1980, 2.

91 Ibid.

92 CBC Television, "Kicking the Habit," 25 June 1977.

93 CBC Television, "The Myth of the 'Light' Cigarette," 17 February 1983.

94 Ibid.

95 LAC, *The Financial Post*, 24 March 1962.

96 LAC, *The Financial Post*, 23 August 1975.

97 LAC, *Marketing* magazine, 19 February 1979, 16.

98 *Marketing* magazine, 7 May 1979, 8.

99 Ibid.

100 *Marketing* magazine, 20 September 1982, 2.
101 CBC Television, "A New Danger: Second-Hand Smoke," 4 March 1985.
102 Cunningham, 70–1.
103 Ibid., 71–8.
104 CBC Television, "On the Way to a Smoke-Free Canada," 22 April 1987.
105 Cunningham.
106 LAC, *Maclean's* magazine, 9 August 1993.
107 CBC Television, "Smuggled Smokes Flood the Market," 12 July 1991.
108 Ibid.
109 Menashe and Siegel, "The Power of a Frame."
110 LAC, *The Globe and Mail*, 31 December, 2010.
111 Vermond, "Smoke Busters."

CHAPTER TWO

1 AO, WCTU Collection. *Manual, Canadian Y.W.C.T.U. and Y.P.B.*, 12.
2 AO, WCTU Collection. *Minutes of the Convention of the Dominion W.C.T.U.*, 1891, 1909, 1914, 1927, 1980.
3 Cook, *"Through Sunshine and Shadow."*
4 Ibid.
5 See Hardesty, *Women Called to Witness.*
6 Cook, *"Through Sunshine and Shadow."*
7 Ibid., chapter 3.
8 Rudy, *The Freedom to Smoke*, 106–7.
9 Kerr, *Organized for Prohibition*, 48–50.
10 Clark, *Deliver Us from Evil*, 84–8.
11 Westfall, *Two Worlds.*
12 This was true of most provincial WCTUs until well after the Great War and of the Dominion WCTU until about 1905.
13 Willard, *Glimpses of Fifty Years*, 603.
14 AO, WCTU Collection. *Manual, Canadian Y.W.C.T.U. and Y.P.B.*, 4.
15 Cook, "The Ontario Young Woman's Christian Temperance Union."
16 Mimicking the holy trinity, WCTU and YWCTU materials often invoked a kind of shadow trinity of evils to be eliminated. Alcohol remained at the centre, with tobacco and bad language or sometimes poor character profiled as inevitable accompaniments.
17 GMA, "Pledge Book, Young Woman's Christian Temperance Union."
18 AO, WCTU Collection. *Manual, Canadian Y.W.C.T.U. and Y.P.B.*, 3.
19 AO, WCTU Collection. Clothier, "Is a YWCTU a Necessity?"
20 Tate, *Cigarette Wars*, 28.
21 LAC, *The Globe and Mail*, "Tobacco Question Warmly Debated by United Pastors," 22 May 1929.
22 See, for example, Richardson, *The Temperance Lesson Book*; Knight, *The Ontario Public School Hygiene*; and Fraser and Porter, *Ontario Public School Health Book.*

23 OYWCAA, *Minute Book of the Ottawa Branch.*

24 The LTL was the Loyal Temperance Legion, a youth group that overlapped the YWCTU in later years.

25 AO, WCTU Collection. Wilcox, "Two Boys and a Cigarette."

26 AO, WCTU Collection. Rittenhouse, "A New Regime."

27 AO, *The Canadian Mute,* 1 April 1892. I am grateful to Alessandra Iozzo-Duval for providing this reference.

28 C-HPC, untitled newspaper clipping, 14 June 1895.

29 Carr-Harris (née Wright), *Lights and Shades of Mission Work,* 36.

30 AO, WCTU Collection. *Annual Report of the Ontario W.C.T.U.,* 1889.

31 For more information on the Hull riots initiated by Bertha Wright, see Cook, "Through Sunshine and Shadow," 3–6.

32 OYWCAA, *Register of Inmates for the Home for Friendless Women,* 1888–94.

33 Walkowitz, *Prostitution and Victorian Society,* 221.

34 AO, WCTU Collection. *Annual Report of the Ontario W.C.T.U.,* 1889.

35 Cook, "Wet Canteens and Worrying Mothers."

36 Cook, "The Ontario Young Woman's Christian Temperance Union."

37 Bullen, "Hidden Workers."

38 AO, WCTU Collection. *Woman's Journal,* March 1890. For more information on Wright's approach to childhood education, see Cook, "Through Sunshine and Shadow," 171–4.

39 AO, WCTU Collection. *Minute Book for Newmarket W.C.T.U.,* 11 October 1910.

40 AO, MU 8427, 15 June 1922.

41 PAM, *Prohibition Watchword,* June 1924, 6.

42 Cook, "Through Sunshine and Shadow," 214.

43 AO, WCTU Collection. *Canadian White Ribbon Tidings,* 1 April 1905.

44 The *World's Y Hand-book* for 1906 suggested that members dress in the costumes of countries having YWCTUs. Each member was to be introduced with a report of what the Y did in her country, while the hostess wound strands of broad white ribbon around each representative. AO, WCTU Collection. MU 8471. "A World's Demonstration," *World's Y Hand-book.*

45 PAM, "The WCTU and Prohibition in Manitoba, 1883–1927."

46 Cook, *Shock Troops,* 607.

47 BR, Gray, *Queer Questions Quaintly Answered,* 112.

48 Ibid., 117.

49 LAC, *The Toronto Daily Star,* 2 June 1950. I am grateful to Lorna McLean for this reference.

CHAPTER THREE

1 *U.S. v. Philip Morris USA, In., et al.*

2 LAC, *The Globe and Mail,* Weeks, "Health: 'New Cigarettes,'" 20 February 2008. I am grateful to Joel Westheimer for bringing this article to my attention.

3 LAC, *The Globe and Mail,* 1 June 2010.

4 LAC, *The Globe and Mail*, Weeks, "Health: 'New Cigarettes,'" 20 February 2008.

5 The amendment is also termed the Cracking Down on Tobacco Marketing Aimed at Youth Act, 2009. Voon and Mitchell, "Regulating Tobacco Flavours." The federal legislation covers cigarettes, little cigars, and blunt wraps. It denies the use of caffeine, colouring agents, spices and herbs, sugars and sweeteners, vitamins, and taurine. It allows menthol, citric acid, ethanol, guar gum, and paraffin wax. The federal legislation is mirrored by three provincial amendments to their respective tobacco acts. In Ontario, the Smoke-Free Ontario Act was amended in 2010, covering cigarillos and tobacco products and prohibiting flavouring agents of all kinds, except menthol. Both New Brunswick in its 2009 amendment to the Tobacco Sales Act and the 2010 Saskatchewan amendment to its Tobacco Control Act cover cigarillos and tobacco products but include menthol in its prohibition. I am grateful to Graham Cook for this reference.

6 Research shows that American youths favour menthol-flavoured cigarettes at the rate of 44 per cent, while the general population in the United States consume 28 per cent of menthol-flavoured cigarettes. Voon and Mitchell, "Regulating Tobacco Flavours," 4.

7 The failure to include menthol on the list of prohibited additives in American legislation has resulted in the United States being sued at the World Trade Organization for discrimination because it has outlawed clove-flavoured tobacco products produced by such countries as Indonesia, the claimant in this case.

8 Mitchell, "Images of Exotic Women," 327.

9 Rutherford, *A World Made Sexy*, 39.

10 Ibid., 40.

11 Brandt, *The Cigarette Century*, 31–2.

12 Mitchell, 328.

13 Bowman, "The Dangers and Delights of the Cigarette," 71–3.

14 Mitchell, 328–9.

15 AO, WCTU Collection. *Minute Books of the Grey and Dufferin Counties*, 23 June 1926.

16 CBC Television, "Do Cigarette Ads Cause Smoking?" 21 March 1965.

17 LAC, *The Financial Post*, 6 December 1969.

18 LAC, *Commentator*, vol. 13, no. 3, March 1969, 30.

19 CBC Television, "No More Cigarette Ads for CBC," 11 May 1969.

20 LAC, *The Financial Post*, 6 June 1970, 1.

21 Ibid., 3.

22 Cunningham, *Smoke & Mirrors*, 58.

23 LAC, *Commentator*, vol. 13, no. 3, March 1969.

24 CBC Television, "Are Temp Cigarettes for Teens?" 26 September 1985.

25 McLaren, "How Tobacco Company 'Anti-Smoking' Ads Appeal to Teens."

26 Ibid.

27 LAC, *The Toronto Star*, 13 November 1999.

28 McLaren.

29 Boonn, "Big Surprise."

30 Wakefield et al., "Effect of Televised Tobacco Company-Funded Smoking Prevention Advertising."

31 *U.S. v. Philip Morris USA, Inc. et al.*, 1164, paragraph 3157.

32 Ibid., 1167, paragraph 3167.

33 Ibid., 1165, paragraph 3159.

34 Ibid., 1168, paragraph 3168.

35 Ibid., 1171–2, paragraphs 3180–3.

36 Ibid., 1165, paragraph 3160.

37 Ibid., 1171–2, paragraphs 3178–80.

38 Ibid., 1172–3, paragraph 3184.

39 Cook, *"Through Sunshine and Shadow."*

40 See Cook, *"Through Sunshine and Shadow,"* 54. See also Giles, "I Like Water Better."

41 AO, WCTU Collection. Bullock, *The Tobacco Toboggan*.

42 Chavasse, *Advice to a Mother*, 300.

43 BR, Gray, *Queer Questions Quaintly Answered*, 120.

44 OISE/UT, Cooke, "The Well-known and Popular Author," 187.

45 AO, WCTU Collection. Department of Medal Contests of the Dominion Woman's Christian Temperance Union, 4–6.

46 AO, WCTU Collection, MU 8285.

47 AO, WCTU Collection. Thompson, "The Things to Keep."

48 Cook, *At the Sharp End: Canadians Fighting the Great War, 1914–16*, 242–3.

49 PAM, Medal Contest Book, 48.

50 Tate, *Cigarette Wars*, 39.

51 The British Anti-Cigarette League was founded by Frank Johnson, editor of the *Sunday School Chronicle* and *Christian Outlook*, both of which were small British evangelical journals.

52 This approach was especially favoured by the Scouts. An article in *The Scout* intones, "No Smoking is a rule for every Scout. Scouts have something better to do than smoke and they want to keep fit." LAC, *The Scout*, "No Smoking," 463.

53 Welshman, "Images of Youth: The Issue of Juvenile Smoking, 1880–1914," 1,382.

54 Tate, 39.

55 FWM, The *A.C.A. Herald*.

56 Marks, *Revivals and Roller Rinks*, 144–5.

57 Airhart, "Ordering a New Nation," 119.

58 Bebbington, *Evangelicalism in Modern Britain*, 174.

59 SAA, "The Tobacco Devil," 6.

60 Tate, 51.

61 LAC, *Saturday Night*, "The Cigarette and Athletes," 22 September 1900, 7.

62 See Cook, "'Where There's Smoke, There's Fire.'"

63 Cook, *No Place to Run*, especially chapter 1, "Trial by Gas: 2nd Battle of Ypres," 11–35.

64 LAC, *Saturday Night*, "Trying to Make Smoking a Crime," 20 October 1918, 2.

65 LAC, *Lancet*, 1915, 11, 584.

66 LAC, *The Globe and Mail*, 5 April 1919.

67 See, for example, CWM, *Canadian Pay & Record Office Prisoners of War & Field Forces Tobacco & Cigarettes Fund*, "Send the Boys What They *Really Want*," no. 3.

68 *The Maple Leaf*, 6.

69 Tate, 66.

70 LAC, *The Scout*, "Chinstrap" and "Easily Led: Know Your Own Mind – Don't Be Swayed in All Directions by Others," 4 October 1913, 114.

71 LAC, *The Scout*, Baden-Powell, "Scout Yarns, A Weekly Pow-wow," 1921, 198.

72 Brandt, 57.

73 *The Ottawa Citizen*, 27 February 2010, A12.

CHAPTER FOUR

1 Interview, Allan Rock, University of Ottawa, 28 July 2011.

2 Hughes and Foster, *The Dominion Educator*, 821.

3 Sethna, "Men, Sex and Education."

4 Eyre, "Gender Relations in the Classroom."

5 Cook, "'Smokin' in the Boys' Room.'"

6 Henry Giroux defines the "hidden curriculum" as the "unstated norms, values, and beliefs that are transmitted … through the underlying structure of meaning" of a given learning site. Giroux, *Teachers as Intellectuals*, 23.

7 Apple and Christian-Smith, "The Politics of the Textbook," 23; Montgomery, "Banal Race-Thinking," and "Imagining the Antiracist State"; Temple, "People Who Are Different from You."

8 For more explanation of temperance ideas, and especially those of the Woman's Christian Temperance Union, the largest non-denominational women's organization devoted to health and hygiene, see Cook, "Earnest Christian Women," and "Sowing Seed for the Master."

9 Burnham, *Bad Habits*.

10 Cook, "From 'Evil Influence' to Social Facilitator."

11 Only public school textbooks were authorized for health instruction until the mid-1940s, when textbooks recommended for Grades 9 and 10 were also listed in Circular 14.

12 See, for example, Buckton, *Health in the House*.

13 Sutherland, *Children in English-Canadian Society*.

14 Ibid.

15 Cook, *"Through Sunshine and Shadow,"* 116–17.

16 Richardson, *The Temperance Lesson Book*, 98–100.

17 OISE/UT, *The Golden Rule Books*, 1916.

18 Cook, "'Smokin' in the Boys' Room.'"

19 FWM, Schrumpf-Pierron, *Tobacco & Physical Efficiency*.

20 See, for example, LAC, *Reports of Public Schools of British Columbia*, 1917, A30. BC called its course "Nature Lessons and Hygiene."

21 LAC, *The Canadian Lancet*, "The Time to Smoke," May 1919, and "Men Need Tobacco," February 1921.

22 Brandt, *The Cigarette Century.*

23 See, for example, Goldsmith, *Human Poisons.* See especially "Medical Men Speak," 47–53.

24 Solandt, *Highways to Health,* 52.

25 Wall, *The Nurture of Nature.*

26 O'Shea, *Tobacco and Mental Efficiency,* 213.

27 Ibid., 219.

28 Gregg, *Schoolroom Experiments with Tobacco.*

29 Fraser and Porter, *Ontario Public School Health Book,* esp. 107.

30 Fraser and Porter.

31 LAC, *Twenty-Fifth Annual Report of the Department of Education of the Province of Alberta.*

32 Solandt, 84–5, offers almost precisely the same arguments as in the previous decade.

33 AO, Ontario Minister of Education. *Programme of Studies for Grades 7 and 8 of the Public and Separate Schools.*

34 Schacter et al., *You're Growing Up Guidebook,* 4. There is no implication in this quotation that the WHO ever supported smoking, however.

35 Schacter et al.

36 Ibid., 314.

37 Phair and Speirs, *Good Health Today,* 318–22.

38 See, for example, LAC, York "Memo" Yearbook, York Memorial Collegiate Institute, 1951. I am grateful to Lorna McLean for providing this reference.

39 Phair and Speirs, 334–9.

40 Cunningham, *Smoke & Mirrors,* 44.

41 Ibid.

42 Ibid., 48.

43 Ibid.

44 Silverman et al., *Tomorrow Is Now.*

45 Hodgetts, *Decisive Decades,* 276.

46 Ricker et al., *The Modern Era,* 85.

47 Peart and Schaffter, *The Winds of Change,* 207.

48 It is interesting to note that when the topic of smoking and pregnancy are addressed in classroom resources, teaching strategies emphasize women's guilt. One pedagogical source encourages high school students to discuss this case study: "You are married and you have just learned your wife is pregnant. She is a pack-a-day smoker and she has no intention of quitting. As the father, you are concerned about the implications for your child. Describe three strategies you would employ to have your wife quit smoking. Come up with a master list from your class of strategies that can be used to encourage a pregnant woman to stop smoking. Which do you feel would be most effective and why?" Meeks et al., *Teaching Health Science,* 283. For a much superior treatment of smoking and pregnancy, see Berry and Lynn, *Biology of Ourselves,* 205, and Merki et al., *Glencoe Health,* 541.

49 Robertson et al., *Health Canada Series: Decisions for Health*, 50.

50 Ontario Physical and Health Education Association, *Health and Physical Education Curriculum Support Document*, 178. See also the otherwise useful support documents for Grades 5, 6, 7, and 8, all of which group tobacco with other drugs.

51 Hoodless, *Public School Domestic Science*, VI.

52 Recent research conducted by Wyn Millar and Robert Gidney indicates that relatively few schools in Ontario could provide domestic science classes at the elementary school level.

53 Gleason, "Disciplining the Student Body."

54 OISE/UT, *Duties of Teachers and Pupils*, 1909. Household science could be offered in the special lower school course in high school in place of agriculture.

55 OISE/UT, *Ontario Teachers' Manuals, Household Management*, 1916; *Household Science in Rural Schools*, 1918.

56 OISE/UT, Ontario Ministry of Education, "Programme of Studies for Grades VII and VIII," 96.

57 Ibid., 92.

58 Included in the late twentieth- and early twenty-first-century textbooks are: O'Leary-Reesor and Witte, *Food for Today*; Witte, *Food for Life*; Holloway and Meriog, *Individual and Family Living*; Fitzgerald and Witte, *Individual and Family Living*; Fitzgerald and Witte, *Parenting, Rewards and Responsibilities*; McCaffrey et al., *Parenting in Canada: Human Growth and Development*; Holloway et al., *Individuals and Families in a Diverse Society*; Thomson, *Food for Life* and teachers' guide; Foster et al., *Creative Living, Canadian Edition* and teachers' guide. I am grateful to Jane Witte for information on textbooks beyond 2000.

59 Humphries et al., *Foods and Textiles*, 169.

60 Brand, *Home Economics 1*, 123–4.

61 Ibid., "foreword."

62 Tameanko, *House and Home*, 7.

63 Eyre.

64 Harvey et al., *Try This on for Size!*, 101.

65 Cowan, *A Family Is ...*, 176.

66 Brinkley et al., *Teen Guide to Homemaking*; Foster et al.

67 Thomson, *Food for Life*, 358.

68 The transcripts of women teachers have been kindly provided to me by Dr Kristina Llewellyn, to whom I am most grateful. She gathered these interviews as part of her doctoral dissertation research.

69 This is a pseudonym.

70 McTaggart, "California Attacks the Problems of Smoking," 136–8; Speirs, "A Talk on 'Smoking' for Secondary School Principals," 23–5.

71 Cunningham, 50.

72 The Canadian legislation was paralleled by similar laws in the United States where many states had prohibited the sale of tobacco to children under sixteen by the early 1890s, in Australia, which invoked juvenile smoking legislation in all states between 1903 and 1917, and in Britain where the Children's Act of 1908

similarly prohibited the sale of tobacco to children under sixteen and policemen and park-keepers were to seize tobacco from children caught smoking in public. See Welshman, "Images of Youth."

73 "Cancer" is taken from the Latin word for "crab." Nevertheless, as a strategy to encourage readers of the pamphlet, it fails miserably.
74 Haines, "Smoke, in My Eyes," 130.
75 Haines.
76 Carpenter et al., *Designing Cigarettes for Women*, 839.
77 Ibid.
78 Haines, 145ff.
79 Ibid., 145.
80 Hughes, *Learning to Smoke*; Gately, *La Diva Nicotina*.
81 Haines.
82 Brandt.

CHAPTER FIVE

1 Rutherford, *A World Made Sexy*, introduction and chapters 1–4.
2 Strange and Loo, *Making Good*, 52.
3 Mitchell, "Images of Exotic Women," 333.
4 Ibid.
5 Jefferis and Nichols, *Search Lights on Health*, 440–1.
6 Cook, "Do Not ... Do Anything."
7 Barrie, *My Lady Nicotine*.
8 Tate, *Cigarette Wars*, 83.
9 Mitchell, 327–50.
10 Tinkler, *Smoke Signals*, 25–6.
11 Mitchell, 328.
12 I am grateful to Dr Sheldon Posen, curator for this exhibition, and to the Canadian Museum of Civilization for making these images available for inclusion in this study.
13 See chapter 9 for a full discussion of this theme.
14 Mitchell.
15 Willard, *Glimpses of Fifty Years*, 426–7.
16 Bowman, "The Dangers and Delights of the Cigarette," 69.
17 Ibid., 70.
18 Backhouse, *Colour-Coded*.
19 Bowman.
20 Tinkler, *Smoke Signals*.
21 Mawani, "Regulating the 'Respectable' Classes."
22 Pierson, "Archival Research as Refuge, Penance, and Revenge," 498.
23 Gehman, *Smoke over America*, 217.
24 Ibid., 219.
25 Keshen, "Wartime Jitters over Juveniles."

26 LAC, Jefferson, "These Are My Sisters."

27 LAC, "She Was My Girl," 22–3.

28 Strange and Loo, *True Crime, True North*, 65.

29 Oral history accounts IAA–7AA.

30 Gately, *La Diva Nicotina*, 248.

31 Haines, "Smoke, in My Eyes," 93ff.

32 Ibid., 97.

33 Carpenter et al., *Designing Cigarettes for Women*, 843–4.

CHAPTER SIX

1 Weinbaum et al., *The Modern Girl around the World*.

2 Matthews, *The Rise of the New Woman*, 13.

3 Tinkler, *Smoke Signals*, 31.

4 Rudy, "A Ritual Transformed," 267.

5 Carpenter et al., *Designing Cigarettes for Women*, 843–6.

6 Jarrett Rudy has shown that the same applies to Canadian francophone media and culture. See Rudy, "A Ritual Transformed," 272.

7 MacFadden, *The Truth About Tobacco*, 160.

8 For a modern version of this argument, see LAC, *The Globe and Mail*, "Muscles, Blushes and Smoke," 5 February 1975.

9 LAC, *The Globe and Mail*, "Women Smoking, Modern Dancing, Scored by Pastor," 12 April 1929, 18

10 LAC, *Woman's Journal*, 15 March 1901, in Cook, *"Through Sunshine and Shadow,"* 94.

11 See, for example, Gehman, *Smoke over America*, 161.

12 Van Noppen, *Death in Cellophane*, 15; LAC, *The Globe and Mail*, "More Babies of Women Smokers Die," 8 June 1975.

13 MacFadden, 158; Hewitt, *The Cigarette and You*, 43.

14 FWM, *The Cigarette News*, November 1930, 1–4.

15 FWM, *Smoking and Cosmetics – by a Medical Doctor and a Health Teacher*, 18.

16 Major, *The Crime against the Feet; Also on The Tobacco Habit*.

17 Van Noppen, 15.

18 Gehman, 161.

19 Lieb, *Safer Smoking*, 70–1.

20 LAC, *The Globe and Mail*, "Nonagenarian Is Disgusted by Women with Smoking Habit," 23 February 1935.

21 Gehman, 167.

22 Hopkins, *Gone up in Smoke*, 145–6.

23 LAC, *The Financial Post*, 6 December 1958.

24 For but one of many references, see Kellogg, *Tobaccoism*.

25 McClung, "Should Women Think?" 40–1.

26 One noted case was Maude Royden, head of Guild House for the Church of England, who had her lecture to the Women's Home Missionary Society of the Meth-

odist Episcopal Church of Oak Park, Illinois, cancelled because she was a smoker. Despite Royden's claim that "Cigaret smoking is of no religious importance," an American detractor noted that "smoking is not a general practise in this country [the United States] and is done not at all by the women of our churches." BR, *Literary Digest*, vol. 96, 28 January 1928, 28.

27 One example of this process is discussed by Jarrett Rudy with *tabac canadien* by British and American tobacco companies in the 1930s. See Rudy, "Manufacturing French Canadian Tradition."

28 Burnham, *Bad Habits*, esp. 1–112; Cunningham, *Smoke & Mirrors*; Gately, *La Diva Nicotina*, esp. ch. 13.

29 Brandt, *The Cigarette Century*, 90.

30 See, for example, similar images in the American press discussed by Warsh in "Smoke and Mirrors," 195.

31 LAC, AMICUS 3477896, "Famous Flower-Stylist Judith Garden, Florist with a Flair Agrees: Whether you're arranging flowers or choosing a cigarette … EXPERIENCE IS THE BEST TEACHER!" *Ladies' Home Journal*, November 1948, n.p. Before the 1950s, Canadian magazines advertised a mixture of Canadian, British, and, as in this case, American products.

32 Carpenter et al., *Designing Cigarettes for Women*, 839–43.

33 See for example, LAC, *Saturday Night*, 14 August 1920, 13, where the images are in the art deco style.

34 Tate, *Cigarette Wars*, 110.

35 DUA, diary and biography of Edith MacMechan Dobson, 1948.

36 Weight control figures so prominently in Polly's diary that one could call it an obsession.

37 DUA, diary of Edith MacMechan Dobson, 16 March 1948.

38 Tate, 104.

39 BR, Burke, "Women Cigarette Fiends," 19, 132.

40 Tate, 104.

41 BR, Burke, "Women Cigarette Fiends," 132.

42 RBRUBC, Emily Carr to Ruth Hymphrye, 20 March 1938, 2.

43 Tate, 104.

44 McCarthy, *A Fool in Paradise*.

45 Ibid., 195.

46 Ibid., 167.

47 Ibid., 218.

48 Ibid., 226.

49 The transcripts of women teachers have been kindly provided to me by Dr Kristina Llewellyn, to whom I am most grateful. She gathered these interviews as part of her doctoral dissertation research. The dissertation of which it is a part won a national award in 2007.

50 PAM, Charlotte Black diary, 1923–27; 1930–33.

51 All teachers' names are pseudonyms.

52 LC, Catherine Darby, pseudonym, taught from 1947 to 1978.

53 LC, Muriel Fraser, pseudonym, taught from 1947 to 1968.
54 Respondent 009: Kerry Callan-Jones, teacher and principal.
55 Respondent 008: wishes to remain anonymous.
56 Respondent 009: wishes to remain anonymous.
57 Respondent 010: Deborah Gorham, historian and educator.
58 DUA, Bernice Robb diary and biography.
59 DUA, Bernice Robb diary, 20 March 1935.
60 Haines, "Smoke, in My Eyes," 98.

CHAPTER SEVEN

1 Bowman, "The Dangers and Delights of the Cigarette," 81.
2 Carpenter et al., *Designing Cigarettes for Women*, 839.
3 CTA, SC 488, 1931–33.
4 Mitchell and Reid-Walsh, *Girl Culture*, 576.
5 Brandt, *The Cigarette Century*, 74.
6 Ibid., 77.
7 Brumberg, *The Body Project*.
8 Comacchio, *The Dominion of Youth*.
9 Bowman.
10 Brandt, 72.
11 Ertz, *Madame Claire*.
12 Vipond, "Best Sellers in English Canada."
13 Ertz, 46–7.
14 Ibid., 151.
15 Ibid., 9.
16 Ibid., 17.
17 Koehn, "Estée Lauder," 225.
18 Peiss, *Hope in a Jar*, 61–2.
19 Howard, "At the Curve Exchange."
20 Koehn, 219.
21 Sheehy, *The Silent Passage*.
22 LAC, *Chatelaine*, "Sorry, Miss Armour – but we must make way for younger girls," October 1933, 50.
23 Rothman and Rothman, *The Pursuit of Perfection*.
24 See Greaves, *Smoke Screen*.
25 LAC, *Chatelaine*, MacKay, "Those Pampered Bulges," May 1936, 50–1.
26 *Chronicle of the Cinema*, 191.
27 LAC, "Good Luck Margarine Hour," 26 March 1957.
28 LAC, *Canadian Home Journal*, Armstrong, "Kate Aitken's Spa," September 1953, 14–15.
29 LAC, *Business Week*, 14 November 1953, 54. R.J. Reynolds has denied the author use of this or any other cigarette advertisement in this publication.
30 LAC, *The Monetary Times*, July 1955, 58–9.

31 Mitchell and Reid-Walsh, XXVI.

CHAPTER EIGHT

1   Heron and Storey, eds, *On the Job*, 9.
2   Rudy, "A Ritual Transformed," 266.
3   PAA, Profile of Dr Mary Percy Jackson, 2005.
4   PAA, Letter from Dr Mary Percy Jackson to the Alumni Association, University of Birmingham, n.d.
5   For nursing, see McPherson, *Bedside Manners*; for teaching, see Prentice, "From Household to Schoolhouse"; for domestic service, see Barber, "The Women Ontario Welcomed."
6   Strong-Boag, "Women and Team Sport," 192–3.
7   Strong-Boag, *The New Day Recalled*, 62.
8   White, "Looking Back," 27.
9   Stephen, *Pick One Intelligent Girl*, 106–12.
10 In 1950, married women comprised 14.9 per cent of the workforce; by 1961, the rate stood at 21.9 per cent, with 29.5 per cent of the labour force occupied by all women, married and single. White, 34–5.
11 White, 40.
12 In 1921, of the total female waged workforce, 69.4 per cent were between ages 14 and 24; by 1931, the percentage in this youthful age group in waged labour had reached 73.9 per cent, and by 1941, the rate of youthful female waged labour had declined only slightly to 73.7 per cent. Series D107–122, Leacy, ed. *Historical Statistics of Canada*.
13 Rudy, "A Ritual Transformed," 265.
14 Cook, "'Liberation Sticks' or 'Coffin Nails'?"
15 See, for example, Cunningham, *Smoke & Mirrors*, 65.
16 This analysis is influenced by an argument proposed by Health Canada for the late twentieth-century girl and young woman. It proposes that smoking's allure offers support for five psychic needs of young women: acceptable displays of sexuality, sophistication, status, social acceptability, and slimness, the so-called five "S's".
17 Tinkler, *Smoke Signals*, 33.
18 Ibid., 22.
19 Carpenter et al., *Designing Cigarettes for Women*, 843–6.
20 Women's labour history for much of the period considered in this study remains underdeveloped. The first generation of Canadian labour history, including Kealey's work, much of which is summarized in his mid-1990s collection, *Workers and Canadian History*, Morton's *Working People*, Bercuson's *Canadian Labour History*, Heron and Storey's *On the Job*, and Palmer's *The Character of Class Struggle* largely ignored women workers' experiences except as they intersected with male interests and activities. In more recent years, the scholarship of historians like Bettina Bradbury, Joan Sangster, Lynne Marks, and Ruth Frager, to name but a few, have

added enormously to the historical record. Nevertheless, in pursuing a study of social practices like smoking in the workplace, the gaps are deep and wide.

21 Cassandra Tate finds a similar slow pace of acceptance of cigarette smoking by either men or women in the United States. See, for example, Tate, *Cigarette Wars*, chapter 5.

22 After the introduction of *Chatelaine* in March 1928, the *Canadian Home Journal* (which had been founded as *Canadian Homes and Gardens* in 1925) competed fiercely with it. For instance, in 1929 the *Canadian Home Journal* reported a circulation of 114,987 as against *Chatelaine*'s 74,278. By 1933, they were running neck-and-neck, with the *Journal* figures holding at 203,429 and *Chatelaine*'s at 198,303. By the following year, *Chatelaine* exceeded the *Journal*'s circulation by about 9,000, but they continued in fierce competition through the period, at which point the *Journal* again had a narrow lead. The family magazine *Star Weekly* outsold both women's magazines. Established in 1910, it had a readership of 198,064 by 1928. *McKim's Directory of Canadian Publications*, 1928 to 1939.

23 Valerie J. Korinek's fascinating study of *Chatelaine* in the 1950s and 1960s (*Roughing It in the Suburbs*) shows the magazine as instrumental in shaping the postwar middle class, but in the earlier period *Chatelaine* pitched its stories to all women, judging from the fiction, advice columns, and advertisements.

24 A good set of such magazines can be found at Library and Archives Canada, Ottawa.

25 LAC, *The Business and Professional Woman*, Per. Reg. 9873; A-60-7. Available from December 1930 as an unpublished newsletter and from December 1931 as a formal publication, it moved from a newsletter to a journal in September 1934. This journal, published in Winnipeg, was the publication of the Canadian branch of the International Federation of Business and Professional Women, centred in London, England.

26 The first advertisement was for W.D. & H.O. Wills's Gold Flake Cigarettes – "a shilling in London – a quarter here." LAC, *The Business and Professional Woman Newsletter*, 7. Gold Flake Cigarettes remained the only advertiser in this journal until 1940.

27 Strange and Loo, *True Crime, True North*.

28 Thompson and Seager, *Canada 1922–1939*, table X1b, as cited in Strong-Boag, *The New Day Recalled*, 53. The percentage in 1931 was 17.6 per cent.

29 In 1921, 49.6 per cent of the female workforce was clustered in these sectors; by 1931, the proportion had fallen to 43.9 per cent (mainly as a result of more women moving into domestic service in the early years of the Depression); and by 1941, it had climbed back up to 47.3 per cent. Heron and Storey, eds, 13. See also Strong-Boag, *The New Day Recalled*, 53.

30 LAC, *Maclean's*, McClung, "I'll Never Tell My Age Again!" 15 March 1926, 15.

31 LAC, *Chatelaine*, Eustace, "You Can't Love the Boss," June 1930, 6–7, 64–5.

32 Ibid., 64. Text bolded by author for emphasis.

33 LAC, *The Business and Professional Woman*, March 1936, advertisement for the C.H. Smith Company, Windsor, Ontario, 5.

34 LAC, *The Business and Professional Woman*, March 1937, 3.

35 Steedman, "Skill and Gender in the Canadian Clothing Industry."

36 Lowe, "Mechanization, Feminization, and Managerial Control."

37 Gelman, "The 'Feminization' of High Schools," 170–3.

38 LAC, *Canadian Home Journal*, Dare, "You Were Asking," October 1930, 96.

39 Chollat-Traquet, *Women and Tobacco*, 62.

40 The term "stress" was introduced by Hans Selye in the 1940s but did not find its way into advertising copy until some time after that. Hence, other terms like "soothing ragged nerves" are used in interwar advertisements.

41 Jacobson, *Beating the Ladykillers*.

42 See DUA, Diary B – 1919 – MS 2-686, A-60, diary of Ella Muriel Liscombe, 10 May 1934.

43 LAC, *Canadian Home Journal*, Dare, "You Were Asking," October 1930, 96.

44 LAC, "Her Own Fault," 1921.

45 See for example, LAC, *The Globe and Mail*, "Women Smoking, Modern Dancing, Scored by Pastor," 12 April 1929.

46 See, for example, LAC, *The Globe and Mail*, "A Few Facts about Fags," 31 May 1938.

47 DUA, Diary B – 1919 – MS 2-686, A-60, diary of Ella Muriel Liscombe.

48 After leaving the Bank of Montreal, Liscombe worked for many years in the General Office, Dominion Steel and Coal Corporation.

49 DUA, Diary B – 1919 – MS 2-686, A-60, diary of Ella Muriel Liscombe, 10 May 1934.

50 Colbert was one of the highest paid actresses in the 1930s.

51 Gately, *La Diva Nicotina*, 249.

52 DUA, Diary B – 1919 – MS 2-686, A-60, diary of Ella Muriel Liscombe, 29 January 1919.

53 Ibid., 12 February 1934.

54 Brandt, *The Cigarette Century*, 86.

55 DUA, Diary B – 1919 – MS 2-686, A-60, diary of Ella Muriel Liscombe, 19 March 1934.

56 Ibid., 11 January 1938.

57 Ibid., 11 August 1919.

58 CPC, Letter from Harriet Ethel Fry to John Fry, 2 February 1939. The author is grateful to Adele Matsalla for the gift of these letters.

59 CPC, Fry to Fry letter, 3 February, 1938.

60 CPC, Fry to Fry letter, 18 January 1938.

61 CPC, Fry to Fry letter, 4 December 1937.

62 CPC, Fry to Fry letter, January 1939.

63 CPC, Fry to Fry letter, 15 February 1939.

64 CPC, Fry to Fry letter, 20 October, 1936.

65 LAC, *The Globe and Mail*, "Cigarets and Alcohol Bad for Health, Morals of Women Who Indulge," 24 April 1937.

66 I am grateful to Dr Tim Cook, First World War historian at the Canadian War Museum, for his reference to this image.

67 Porter, "Women and Income Security," 291.

68 See LAC, *The Business and Professional Woman*, June 1934, 1.

69 Rudy, *The Freedom to Smoke*, 148.

70 LAC, *The Globe and Mail*, "Consideration," 18 December 1946.

71 I am grateful to Dr Sarah Glassford for this information and insight into the origins of the Pepper lighter and to Dr Amber Lloydlangston for the original reference.

72 *Ottawa Citizen*, 24 May 2010. http://www.ottawacitizen.com/life/century+promoting+Canada/3064571/story.html#ixzz0orA0QCKi. I am grateful to Lorna McLean for this reference.

73 Interview by author with Hallie Sloan, 1 February 2009.

74 Interview by author with Dr Sarah Glassford, 30 March 2010.

75 Interview by author with Hallie Sloan, 1 February 2009.

76 CWM, "Evelyn Pepper: The Florence Nightingale of Disaster Planning," obituary, *Ottawa Citizen*, 11 April 1998.

77 CWM, Guly, "Lives Lived Column: Evelyn Agnes Pepper," *The Globe and Mail*, 4 June 1998.

78 Ibid.

79 CWM, MacLean, "Evelyn Pepper," *Carillon*, October 1996, 3.

80 CWM, Guly, "Lives Lived Column: Evelyn Agnes Pepper," *The Globe and Mail*, 4 June 1998.

81 DUA, "Watching the CWACs."

82 MacDowell and Radforth, eds, *Canadian Working-Class History*, 271.

83 Interview with Respondent 2AA.

84 Morton, 188.

85 Porter, 292.

86 Morton, 215.

87 Ibid., 240.

88 Ibid., ch. 23.

89 Reiter, "Life in a Fast-Food Factory."

90 Haines, "Smoke, in My Eyes," 102ff.

91 LAC, *The Globe and Mail*, "Find More Lung Cancer in Women Who Smoke," 23 February 1966.

92 Hilton, *Smoking in British Popular Culture*, 35.

93 Tate, 106.

94 Cutex Liquid Polish was advertised in most women's magazines of the era.

95 Strong-Boag, *The New Day Recalled*, 62. See also Frager, "Class, Ethnicity, and Gender," 206.

96 Burnham, *Bad Habits*, 98.

CHAPTER NINE

1 In her study of British women's smoking patterns and visual culture, Penny Tinkler asserts that smoking was a primary marker of modernism. Tinkler, *Smoke Signals*, 84–5.

2 Cook, "From Flapper to Sophisticate."

3 ACA, Minutes of the Alma College Council, 9 June 1896. I am grateful to Stephen Francom, archivist at the Alma College Archives, for this information.

4 Austin, *Woman*, 450.

5 WLUA, *Board of Governors Minutes*, 15 November 1911.

6 This view is taken by, among others, Brandt, *The Cigarette Century*, ch. 3; Rudy, "A Ritual Transformed" and *The Freedom to Smoke*; Tate, *Cigarette Wars*; Warsh, "Smoke and Mirrors"; Cunningham, *Smoke & Mirrors*; Gately, *La Diva Nicotina*; Hughes, *Learning to Smoke*; Segrave, *Women and Smoking in America*.

7 While the analysis that follows argues that this ad and others like it were directed at the woman smoker (potential or actual), I do not have corroborating evidence from the producers for these specific advertisements. However, Allan Brandt provides much evidence that tobacco manufacturers consciously and consistently targeted women smokers by 1928, the date of these advertisements. See Brandt, *The Cigarette Century*, 72–5.

8 Ibid., 72.

9 Ibid., 75.

10 See, for example, LAC, Werner, "Cigars and the Women," *Harper's Weekly*, 3 December 1910, 16–17.

11 Carpenter et al., *Designing Cigarettes for Women*, 843–6.

12 Tate, *Cigarette Wars*, 106.

13 See also Cook, "From 'Evil Influence' to Social Facilitator."

14 See, for example, the authorized textbook for Ontario from 1893, Nattress, *Public School Physiology and Temperance*.

15 Richardson, *The Temperance Lesson Book*, 100. See also Henderson and Fraser, *Physiology and Hygiene Notes*.

16 FMW, Levy, *Tobacco Habit Easily Conquered*, 98.

17 Kellogg, *Tobaccoism*, 104.

18 See also Cook, "'Liberation Sticks' or 'Coffin Nails'?"

19 Kinnear, *In Subordination*, 31.

20 UMA, Note card, Auntie Maude to Charlotte Scott Black, "My Graduation Journal."

21 Close, *Framing Identity*, XII. Close explores how one female photographer uses her photograph album as a frame to produce a "self-aware spectacle," 75–95.

22 The percentage of women undergraduates in Ontario universities was far higher, however. In 1929, for example, 36.4 per cent of the undergraduate population was female at the University of Western Ontario. King, "The Experience of Women Students at Four Universities," 163. By 1931, more than half of the undergraduates at Victoria College were women. O'Grady, "Margaret Addison," 167. For Queen's University, Nicole Neatby notes that in 1919–20, 16.3 per cent of undergraduates were women, while by 1929–30 the percentage of female undergraduates had risen to 23.5 percent. However, for Canada as a whole, in 1920 only 1 per cent of Canadian women between ages twenty and twenty-four attended university. Neatby, "Preparing for the Working World," 333–4, 335.

23 Kinnear, *A Female Economy*, 59–60.

24 Kinnear, *In Subordination*, 33 and table 7, 176. See also Gillett, "Carrie Derick."

25 Gillett, *We Walked Very Warily*, 264.

26 Rudy, "A Ritual Transformed," 277–8.

27 BR, "Women and the Weed," 31–2.

28 Brumberg, *The Body Project*, 106.

29 Tate, III.

30 Tinkler, *Smoke Signals*, 23–4.

31 Pitsula, "Student Life at the Regina Campus," 135.

32 Neatby, "Preparing for the Working World," 342–4.

33 Prentice, "Three Women in Physics."

34 Interview with Hallie Sloan, who trained at the Vancouver General Hospital from 1937 to 1940, October 2008.

35 Pitsula, 134.

36 BR, Burke, "Women Cigarette Fiends," 19, 132.

37 Ibid., 29.

38 MacFadden, *The Truth about Tobacco*.

39 Edward Bernays, *The Truth about Tobacco*, quoted in Warsh, "Smoke and Mirrors," 198.

40 Brumberg, 105.

41 Comacchio, *The Dominion of Youth*, 11–13.

42 See, for example, Pitsula, "Student Life at the Regina Campus," and Comacchio, *The Dominion of Youth*.

43 Other universities placing their brand on cigarettes for fundraising drives included (at least) Queen's University in Kingston, Ontario, and Dalhousie University in Halifax, Nova Scotia.

44 *Ottawa Morning Citizen*, 12 August 1944.

45 Kiefer and Pierson, "The War Effort and Women Students at the University of Toronto, 1939–45."

46 Alcohol advertisements first appear in these yearbooks in 1941, but cigarette advertisements never appear in their pages.

47 RBRUBC, "Social Calendar," 52.

48 McKenzie, *Pauline Jewett*, 35.

49 Gibson and Graham, *To Serve and Yet Be Free*, 68, 75.

50 Neatby, 336.

51 McKenzie, 19.

52 In her article analyzing undergraduates' lives at Queen's University in the 1920s, Nicole Neatby deplores the scanty historiography of the 1920s female undergraduate experience. However, women's undergraduate lives during the Second World War and into the 1950s have been even less tracked.

53 Respondent 007.

54 Erickson, "Smoking Practices," 20–1.

55 Culling et al., "Smoking Patterns of University Students in Canada," 530–2.

56 Respondents 004, 005, and 006.

57 UWA, Lois McGratton scrapbook and photographs, "Party: 1963."

58 UWA, *Compendium*, '63, "A Study in Faces," 106.

59 See, for example, RBRUBC, *The Totem*, 1962, 153.

60 UWA, *Student Handbook*, 1961–62. Similar statements appear in handbooks from 1957 through the 1970s.

61 UWA, *University of Waterloo Student Village Handbook*, 1966–67, 14.

62 By this decade, the University of Ottawa was a public institution.

63 See figure 1.4.

64 CBC Radio, "Music in My Life," 11 December 1964.

65 McKenzie, 24.

66 Hemlow, "A Marty Scholar's Adventures," in McKenzie, *Pauline Jewett*, 24–5 in Parr, ed., *Still Running*.

67 Jewett's biographer, Judith McKenzie, reports that she first took up smoking while an undergraduate at Queen's University in the 1940s. McKenzie, 158.

68 LAC, *Vancouver Sun*, McMartin, "Life Lived Full of Fun, Purpose."

69 Respondent 0010.

70 Interview by author with Judy Rebick, 22 December 2010.

71 The yearbooks for Dalhousie University, *Pharos*, consulted were between 1950 and 1990.

72 Dawn Black, interview, Vancouver, 26 August 1997, in McKenzie, 134.

73 Interview with Judith McKenzie, August 2010.

CHAPTER TEN

1 LAC, CBC Television, interview between Pamela Wallin and Joni Mitchell, 19 February 1996.

2 Weller, *Girls Like Us*, 69.

3 Ibid., 136.

4 Ibid., 137.

5 Ibid.

6 LAC, CBC Television, interview between Pamela Wallin and Joni Mitchell, 19 February 1996.

7 Weller, 233.

8 I wish to acknowledge the scholarship of my colleague, Professsor Eileen O'Connor, in this summary of second-wave feminism.

9 Government of Canada, *Report of the Royal Commission on the Status of Women*.

10 The women's movement and the report of the Royal Commission on the Status of Women had in turn been inspired by philosophical and political debates about the lack of civil rights and liberties for African Americans, gays, and lesbians in the United States. The exclusion of "outlier" groups of Canadian women quickly became a mainstay of the feminist movement in this country as well. The sense of injustice faced by women was supported by protest movements against the war

in Vietnam and a growing abortion rights movement. See also Speers, "The Royal Commission on the Status of Women in Canada."

11 In this period, academic studies and social discourse blamed women's oppression primarily on male supremacy or "patriarchy" and not on other systemic forms of oppression, such as race, class, or governance structures. See, for example, Acton et al., *Women at Work*; Acheson et al., *Women and Legal Action*; Bradbury, "The Family Economy and Work"; Gillett, *We Walked Very Warily*; Latham and Pazdro, eds, *Not Just Pin Money*; Lowe, "Women, Work and the Office"; Prentice, "Writing Women into History"; Mitchinson, "Canadian Women and Church Missionary Societies."

12 Wild, "Joni Mitchell."

13 Whiteley, *Sexing the Groove*.

14 *Wikipedia*, "Joni Mitchell."

15 Brandt, *The Cigarette Century*, 84.

16 Ibid., 85.

17 Interview by author with Judy Rebick, 22 December 2011.

18 LAC, *Chatelaine*, March 1928, 16.

19 An article entitled, "Liquor and the Home" ran in *Chatelaine* in November 1948. This acknowledged the strong social pressures for both young men and women to drink with friends. LAC, *Chatelaine*, November 1948.

20 LAC, *Chatelaine*, Bennett, "The Bridge at High Leap," May 1939, 50, 54.

21 Carpenter et al., *Designing Cigarettes for Women*," 839–43.

22 After some debate about the "reading" of this advertisement, I have come to agree with Dr Ken Montgomery, whose argument this is.

23 LAC, *Châtelaine*, Roy, "*Grand-mère et la poupée*," October 1960, 25.

24 LAC, *Châtelaine*, Hébert, "Shannon," 35.

25 LAC, *Châtelaine*, Laurendeau, "*On croit se connaitre …*," January 1962, 24–5.

26 LAC, *Châtelaine*, "*Nos lectrices prennent position*," June 1970, 17.

27 LAC, *Châtelaine*, Tessier, "*La feminisme n'est pas héreditaire!*" December 1985, 45–8.

28 No advertisements by the R.J. Reynolds Company may be shown on their stated wishes.

29 Thom, *Inside Ms*, 36–7.

30 Ibid., 136.

31 Ibid., 38.

32 Ibid., 132.

33 No advertisements by the R.J. Reynolds Company may be shown on their stated wishes. Indeed, no advertisements from *Ms Magazine* have offered permission for publication.

34 See, for example, UOL, *Ms Magazine*, vol. 1–2, December 1973, 32–3.

35 Thom, 136.

36 Ibid., 137.

37 LAC, *Chatelaine*, *Medical News* health column, June 1982, 26.

38 LAC, *Chatelaine*, July 1982, 16.

39 LAC, *Chatelaine*, December 1982, 18.

40 Cunningham, *Smoke & Mirrors*, 67.
41 Haines, "Smoke, in My Eyes," 99.
42 Brandt, 86.
43 Mitchell and Reid-Walsh, eds, *Girl Culture*, 107.

CHAPTER ELEVEN

1 See, for example, Spelman, *Inessential Woman*; Silvera, *Silenced*; Klein, "We Are Who You Are."
2 See further Bannerji, "A Question of Silence"; *Enough: Aboriginal Women Speak Out*, as told to Janet Silman; Pierson, "Experience, Difference, Dominance and Voice."
3 Van Den Berg, ed., *Feminist Perspectives on Addictions*, 12.
4 Rudy, "A Ritual Transformed," 265.
5 DUA, MS 2-686, A-97, Lauretta Sluenwhite diary.
6 Ibid., 5 March 1936.
7 Ibid., 13 February 1936.
8 Cook et al., *Framing Our Past*, esp. part 6.
9 DUA, MS 2-686, A-97, Lauretta Sluenwhite diary.
10 Ibid., 26 February 1936.
11 Sangster, *Girl Trouble*, 29.
12 Ibid., 16.
13 Ibid., 34.
14 Ibid., 33–4.
15 See Backhouse, *Colour-Coded*.
16 Sangster, *Girl Trouble*, 23.
17 Strange and Loo, *Making Good*, 94; see also Backhouse, *Colour-Coded*, and Walker, *Racial Discrimination in Canada*.
18 AO, Drawings of the Mercer Reformatory.
19 For further discussion of Velma Demerson as a victim of sexual assault and the importance of her case, see Backhouse, *Carnal Crimes*, ch. 5, 105–30.
20 Demerson, *Incorrigible*.
21 Sangster, "Creating Social and Moral Citizens."
22 Erickson et al., "On the Street," 53.
23 Other studies have found a similar pattern, that between 80 and 90 per cent of alcohol and drug users also smoke. Malmo, "Addressing Tobacco Dependency," 324.
24 Erickson et al., "On the Street," 56.
25 Vermeiren et al., "Violence Exposure and Substance Use in Adolescents," 52–3.
26 Haines, "Smoke, in My Eyes," 125.
27 Ibid., 133–4.
28 There have been some significant advances in our knowledge within the past decade, however. Figuring importantly in adding to our understanding of how women see themselves are such collections as Poole and Greaves, *Highs & Lows*.

29 Canning, "Photographer as Witness," in Clarkes, *Heroines*.

30 See Razack, *Race, Space and the Law.*

31 Peace Arch Entertainment, *Heroines: A Photographic Obsession.*

32 Russell also starred as a journalist in *His Girl Friday* (1940).

33 Ellis, *Studies in the Psychology of Sex*, 222–30.

34 Tinkler, *Smoke Signals*, 21.

35 Castle, *The Apparitional Lesbian*, 91.

36 *USA Today*, "k.d. lang's World: Nothin' but a Drag."

37 Ibid.

38 Ibid.

39 Haines, "Smoke, in My Eyes," ch. 5.

40 Permission to reproduce any of these photographs has been denied.

41 Graham, "Women's Smoking and Family Health." See also her *When Life's a Drag.*

42 Mitchell and Amos, "Girls, Pecking Order and Smoking."

43 Haines, 127.

44 Ibid., 135.

45 Carpenter et al., *Designing Cigarettes for Women.*

CONCLUSION

1 In the latest survey, 13 per cent of students in Grades 10 to 12 claimed to be current smokers as compared with 11 per cent in the previous survey. Over the past two surveys, the rate of smoking among students in Grades 6 to 9 has also climbed. Health Canada, *Youth Smoking Survey*, 2010.

2 LAC, *The Globe and Mail*, 1 June 2010.

3 LAC, Macpherson, "The Great Equalizer," *Weekend Post*, 5 December 1998.

4 Kelland, "Smoking Could Kill 8 Million a Year in 20 Years."

5 LAC, *The Globe and Mail*, 30 September 2009.

6 Ibid.

7 Ibid.

8 LAC, *The Globe and Mail*, 31 December 2010.

9 Krueger et al., *The Health Impact of Smoking & Obesity*, 15.

10 LAC, Macpherson, "The Great Equalizer," *Weekend Post*, 5 December 1998.

Bibliography

PUBLISHED SOURCES

Acheson, Elizabeth, Mary Eberts, and Beth Symes, with Jennifer Stoddart. *Women and Legal Action: Precedents, Resources and Strategies for the Future*. Ottawa: Canadian Advisory Council on the Status of Women, 1984

Acton, Janice, Penny Goldsmith, and Bonnie Shepard. *Women at Work, 1850–1930*. Toronto: Canadian Women's Educational Press, 1974

Ahijevych, K.L., R.F. Tyndale, H.V. Weed, and K.K. Browning. "Factors Influencing Nicotine Half-Life during Smoking Abstinence in African American and Caucasian Women." *Nicotine and Tobacco Research* vol. 4, 2002, 423–31

Airhart, Phyllis D. "Ordering a New Nation and Reordering Protestantism, 1867–1914," in George A. Rawlyk, ed., *The Canadian Protestant Experience, 1760–1990*. Burlington, ON: Welch Publishing Company Inc., 1990

Amos, A., and M. Haglund. "From Social Taboo to 'Torch of Freedom': The Marketing of Cigarettes to Women." *Tobacco Control* vol. 9, 2009, 3–8

Apple, Michael W., and Linda K. Christian-Smith. "The Politics of the Textbook," in Michael W. Apple and Linda K. Christian-Smith, eds, *The Politics of the Textbook*. London and New York: Routledge, 1991

Austin, Principal, ed. *Woman: Her Character, Culture and Calling*. Brantford, ON: The Book & Bible House, 1890

Backhouse, Constance. *Carnal Crimes: Sexual Assault Law in Canada, 1900–1975*. Toronto: The Osgoode Society, 2008, ch. 5

– *Colour-Coded: A Legal History of Racism in Canada, 1900–1950*. Toronto: University of Toronto Press, 1999

Bannerji, Himani. "A Question of Silence: Reflections on Violence against Women in Communities of Color," in Enakshi Dua and Angela Robertson, eds, *Scratching the Surface: Canadian Anti-racist Feminist Thought*. London: The Women's Press, 1999

Barbeau, E.M., A. Leavy-Sperounis, and E.D. Bulback. "Smoking, Social Class, and Gender: What Can Public Health Learn from the Tobacco Industry about Disparities in Smoking?" *Tobacco Control* vol. 13, 2004, 115–20

Barber, Marilyn. "The Women Ontario Welcomed: Immigrant Domestics for Ontario Homes, 1870–1930," in Alison Prentice and Susan Mann Trofimenkoff, eds, *The Neglected Majority: Essays in Canadian Women's History*, vol. 2, 102–21. Toronto: McClelland and Stewart, 1985

Barrie, J.M. *My Lady Nicotine*. London, New York, and Toronto: Hodder and Stoughton, 1913

Barthes, Ronald. *The Photographic Message: In Image, Music, Text – Essays Selected and Translated by Stephen Heath*. London: Fontana, 1987, 15–31

Bebbington, David. *Evangelicalism in Modern Britain: A History from the 1730s to the 1980s*. Grand Rapids, MI: Baker Book House, 1989

Bercuson, David J. *Canadian Labour History: Selected Readings*. Toronto: Copp Clark Pitman, 1987

Berger, John. *Ways of Seeing*. London: Penguin Books, 1972

Berry, Gordon, and David Lynn. *Biology of Ourselves*, 2nd edition. Toronto: John Wiley & Sons, 1990

Boonn, Ann. "Big Surprise: Tobacco Company Prevention Campaigns Don't Work." Campaign for Tobacco-Free Kids, 26 January 2007; accessed at http://www.tobwis.org/uploads/media/Links-TobaccoIndustry Campaigns.pdf

Bowman, Nancy. "The Dangers and Delights of the Cigarette in American Society, 1880–1930," in Philip Scranton, ed., *Beauty and Business*, 54–86. New York: Routledge, 2001

Bradbury, Betinna. "The Family Economy and Work in an Industrializing City, Montreal, 1871." Canadian Historical Association, *Historical Papers*, 1979

Brand, Yvonne M. *Home Economics 1*. Toronto: J.M. Dent & Sons (Canada) Limited, 1968

Brandt, Allan M. *The Cigarette Century: The Rise, Fall, and Deadly Persistence of the Product That Defined America*. New York: Basic Books, 2007

Bridges, Andrew. "Addictions: Booze and Butts: Anti-smoking Drug May Also Curb Drinking, New Research Shows." *The Globe and Mail*, 11 July 2007, L4

Brinkley, Jeanne Hayden, Champion Chamberlain, and Valerie M. Frances. *Teen Guide to Homemaking*. Toronto: McGraw-Hill Ryerson, 1961, 1967, 1968, 1972, 1977, 1978

Brumberg, Joan Jacobs. *The Body Project: An Intimate History of American Girls*. New York: Vintage Books, 1997

Buckton, Catherine M. *Health in the House*, 6th edition. Toronto: W.G. Gage & Co., 1877

Bullen, John. "Hidden Workers: Child Labour and the Family Economy in Late Nineteenth-Century Urban Ontario," in Bettina Bradbury, ed., *Canadian Family History: Selected Readings*, 199–219. Toronto: Copp-Clark Pitman Ltd., 1992

Burnham, John C. "American Physicians and Tobacco Use: Two Surgeons General, 1929 and 1964." *Bulletin of Medical History* vol. 63, no. 1, 1989

– *Bad Habits: Drinking, Smoking, Taking Drugs, Gambling, Sexual Misbehaviour, and Swearing in American History*. New York and London: New York University Press, 1993

Butler, Judith. *Gender Trouble: Feminism and the Subversion of Identity*. London: Routledge, 1990

– "Performativity's Social Magic," in Theodore R. Schatzki and Wolfgang Natter, eds, *The Social and Political Body*, 29–48. New York and London: The Guilford Press, 1996

Canning, Patricia. "Photographer as Witness," in Lincoln Clarkes, *Heroines: Photographs*. Vancouver: Anvil Press, 2002

Carpenter, Carrie Murray, Geoffrey Ferris Wayne, and Gregory N. Connolly. *Designing Cigarettes for Women: New Findings from Tobacco Industry Documents*. Society for the Study of Addiction, 2005

Carr-Harris, Bertha. *Lights and Shades of Mission Work, or Leaves from a Worker's Note Book, Being Reminiscences of Seven Years Service at the Capital, 1885–1892*. Ottawa, 1892

Carson, Fiona, and Claire Pajaczkowska, eds. *Feminist Visual Culture*. London and New York: Routledge, 2001, cited in Claudia A. Mitchell and Jacqueline Reid-Walsh, eds, *Girl Culture: An Encyclopedia*, vol. 1. Westport, CT: Greenwood Press, 2008

Carstairs, Catherine. *Jailed for Possession: Illegal Drug Use, Regulation, and Power in Canada, 1920–61*. Toronto: University of Toronto Press, 2006

Castle, Terry. *The Apparitional Lesbian: Female Sexuality and Modern Culture*. New York: Columbia University Press, 1993

Chambers, Deborah. "Family as Place: Family Photograph Albums and the Domestication of Public and Private Space," in Joan M. Schwartz and James R. Ryan, eds, *Picturing Place: Photography and the Geographical Imagination*, 96–114. London: I.B. Tauris, 2003

Chavasse, Pye Henry. *Advice to a Mother on the Management of Her Children and on the Treatment on the Moment of Some of Their More Pressing Illnesses and Accidents*. Toronto: Willing & Williamson, 1880

Chollat-Traquet, C. *Women and Tobacco*. Geneva: World Health Organization, 1992

Chronicle of the Cinema. New York: DK Publishing, 1997

Clark, Norman. *Deliver Us from Evil: An Interpretation of American Prohibition*. New York: Norton, 1976

Clarkes, Lincoln. *Heroines: Photographs*. Vancouver: Anvil Press, 2002

Close, Susan. *Framing Identity: Social Practices of Photography in Canada (1880–1920)*. Winnipeg: Arbeiter Ring Publishing, 2007

Comacchio, Cynthia. *The Dominion of Youth: Adolescence and the Making of Modern Canada, 1920 to 1950*. Waterloo, ON: Wilfrid Laurier University Press, 2006

Cook, Sharon Anne. "Do Not … Do Anything That You Cannot Unblushingly Tell Your Mother: Gender and Social Purity in Canada." *Histoire sociale/Social History*, vol. 30, no. 60, 1997, 215–38

– "'Earnest Christian Women, Bent on Saving our Canadian Youth': The Ontario Woman's Christian Temperance Union and Scientific Temperance Instruction, 1881–1930." *Ontario History* vol. 86, 1994, 249–67

– "Educating for Temperance: The Woman's Christian Temperance Union and Ontario Children, 1880–1916." *Historical Studies in Education/Revue d'histoire de l'éducation* vol. 5, no. 2, Fall 1993, 251–77

– "Evangelical Moral Reform: Women and the War against Tobacco, 1874–1900," in Marguerite Van Die, ed., *Religion and Public Life: Historical and Comparative Themes*, 177–95. Toronto: University of Toronto Press, 2001

– "From 'Evil Influence' to Social Facilitator: Representations of Youth Smoking, Drinking, and Citizenship in Canadian Health Textbooks, 1890–1960." *Journal of Curriculum Studies* vol. 40, no. 6, 2008, 1–32

– "'From Flapper to Sophisticate': Canadian Women University Students as Smokers, 1920–60," in Edgar-André Montigny, ed., *The Real Dope: Social, Legal and Historical Perspectives on the Regulation of Drugs in Canada*, 83–122. Toronto: University of Toronto Press, 2011

– "'Liberation Sticks' or 'Coffin Nails'? Representations of the Working Woman and Cigarette Smoking in Canada, 1919–1939." *Canadian Bulletin of Medical History* vol. 24, no.2, 2007, 367–401

– "The Ontario Young Woman's Christian Temperance Union: A Study in Female Evangelicalism, 1874–1930," in M. Fardig Whiteley and E. Muir, eds, *Changing Roles of Women within the Christian Church in Canada*, 299–320. Toronto: University of Toronto Press, 1995

– "'Smokin' in the Boys' Room': Girls' Absence in Anti-Smoking Educational Literature," in Andrea Martinez and Meryn Stuart, eds, *Out of the Ivory Tower: Feminist Research for Social Change*, 25–48. Toronto: Sumach Press, 2003

– "'Sowing Seed for the Master': The Ontario W.C.T.U. and Evangelical Feminism, 1874–1930." *Journal of Canadian Studies* vol. 30, no. 3, 1995, 175–94

– *"Through Sunshine and Shadow": The Woman's Christian Temperance Union, Evangelicalism and Reform in Ontario, 1874–1930*. Montreal and Kingston: McGill-Queen's University Press, 1995

– "'Where There's Smoke, There's Fire': Tobacco Use and the Construction of the Canadian Citizen, 1890–1930." *The Social History of Alcohol and Drugs: An Interdisciplinary Journal* vol. 21, no. 1, Fall 2006, 69–95

Cook, Sharon Anne, Lorna R. McLean, and Kate O'Rourke, eds. *Framing Our Past: Canadian Women's History in the Twentieth Century*. Kingston and Montreal: McGill-Queen's University Press, 2001

Cook, Tim. *At the Sharp End: Canadians Fighting the Great War, 1914–16.* Toronto: Penguin Canada, 2007

– *No Place to Run: The Canadian Corps and Gas Warfare in the First World War.* Vancouver: University of British Columbia Press, 1999

– *Shock Troops: Canadians Fighting The Great War, 1917–18.* Toronto: Penguin Press, 2008

– "Wet Canteens and Worrying Mothers: Alcohol, Soldiers and Temperance Groups in the Great War." *Histoire sociale/Social History* vol. 35, no. 70, June 2003, 311–30

Cooke, Maud C. *Social Etiquette or Manners and Customs of Polite Society ... a Complete Guide to Self-Culture.* London, ON: McDermid & Logan, 1896

Cowan, Beverly. *A Family Is ...* Toronto: Copp Clark Pitman, 1979

Cox, Howard. "Growth and Ownership in the International Tobacco Industry: BAT 1902–27." *Business History* vol. 31, no. 11, 1989, 44–67

Crary, Jonathan. *Techniques of the Observer: On Vision and Modernity in the Nineteenth Century.* Cambridge, MA: MIT Press, 2001

Culling, Charles, Phillip Vassar, and A.M. Saunders. "Smoking Patterns of University Students in Canada." *The CMA Journal* vol. 83, 1960

Cunningham, Rob. *Smoke & Mirrors: The Canadian Tobacco War.* Ottawa: IDRC, 1996

Currie, C., C. Roberts, A. Morgan, R. Smith, W. Settertobulte, and O. Samdal, eds. *Young People's Health in Context. Health Policy for Children and Adolescents.* Copenhagen: WHO Europe, 2004

Daykin, N. "Young Women and Smoking: Towards a Sociological Account." *Health Promotion International* vol. 8, no. 2, 1993, 95–102

Delarue, Norman C. "The Reasons for an Anti-Smoking Campaign: A Challenge for Adult Commitment." *The Business Quarterly* vol. 35, no. 1, Spring 1970

Demerson, Velma. *Incorrigible.* Waterloo: Wilfrid Laurier University Press, 2002

Ellis, Havelock. *Studies in the Psychology of Sex*, vol. 1. New York: Random House, 1942

Enough: Aboriginal Women Speak Out, as told to Janet Silman. Toronto: Women's Press, 1987

Erickson, Arthur W.E. "Smoking Practices of First Year Education Students at the University of Alberta." *CAHPER* vol. 30, no. 1, October–November 1963

Erickson, Patricia G., Katharine King, and Ywit. "On the Street: Influences on Homelessness in Young Women," in Nancy Poole and Lorraine Greaves, eds, *Highs & Lows: Canadian Perspectives on Women and Substance Use.* Toronto: British Columbia Centre of Excellence for Women's Health, 2007

Ernster, V.L. "Mixed Messages for Women: A Social History of Cigarette Smoking and Advertising." *New York State Journal of Medicine* vol. 85, 1985, 335–40

Ertz, Susan. *Madame Claire.* Toronto: Longmans, Green & Co., 1923

Eyre, Linda. "Gender Relations in the Classroom: A Fresh Look at Coeducation," in Jane S. Gaskell and Arlene Tiger McLaren, eds, *Women and Education*, 2nd edition. Calgary: Detselig Enterprises Ltd, 1991

Fitzgerald, Hugh, and Janet Witte. *Individual and Family Living.* Toronto: Nelson, 2008

– *Parenting, Rewards and Responsibilities: First Canadian Edition.* Toronto: McGraw-Hill Ryerson, 2007

Forceville, Charles. "Pictorial Metaphor in Advertisements." *Metaphor and Symbolic Activity* vol. 9, no. 1, 1–29, cited in Janne Seppanen, *The Power of the Gaze,* 123–6. New York: Peter Lang, 2006

Foster, Josephine, M. Janice Hogan, Betty M. Herring, and Audrey G. Gieseking-Williams. *Creative Living: Canadian Edition.* Toronto: Collier Macmillan Canada, 1985; teachers' guide, 1986

Foucault, Michel. *Power/Knowledge.* New York: Vintage, 1980

Frager, Ruth A. "Class, Ethnicity, and Gender in the Eaton Strikes of 1912 and 1934," in Franca Iacovetta and Mariana Valverde, eds, *Gender Conflicts: New Essays in Women's History,* 189–228. Toronto: University of Toronto Press, 1992

Fraser, Donald T., and George T. Porter. *Ontario Public School Health Book.* Toronto: Copp Clark Co. Ltd, 1925

Freidman, V. "The Female Smoker Market," cited in Carrie Murray Carpenter, Geoffrey Ferris Wayne, and Gregory N. Connolly, *Designing Cigarettes for Women: New Findings from Tobacco Industry Documents,* 837–51. Society for the Study of Addiction, 2005

Frohlich, K.L., L. Potvin, L. Gauvin, and P. Chabot. "Youth Smoking Initiation: Disentangling Context from Composition." *Health and Place* vol. 8, no. 3, 2002, 153–66

Frohlich, K.L., L. Potvin, P. Chabot, and E. Coring. "A Theoretical and Empirical Analysis of Context: Neighborhoods, Smoking and Youth." *Social Science and Medicine* vol. 54, no. 9, 2002, 401–17

Gately, Iain. *La Diva Nicotina: The Story of How Tobacco Seduced the World.* London: Simon & Schuster, 2001

Gehman, Dr Jesse Mercer. *Smoke over America.* East Aurora, NY: The Roycrofters, 1943

Gelman, Susan. "The 'Feminization' of High Schools: The Problem of Women Secondary School Teachers in Ontario," in Sharon Anne Cook, Lorna R. McLean, and Kate O'Rourke, eds, *Framing Our Past: Canadian Women's History in the Twentieth Century.* Kingston and Montreal: McGill-Queen's University Press, 2001

Gibson, Frederick W., and Roger Graham. *To Serve and Yet Be Free.* Kingston and Montreal: McGill-Queen's University Press, 1983

Giles, Geoffrey J. "'I Like Water Better': A Comparative Study of Temperance Materials for Children in Britain, France and Germany." Paper presented to the International Congress on the Social History of Alcohol, London, Ontario, 1993.

Gillett, Margaret. "Carrie Derick (1862–1941) and the Chair of Botany at McGill," in Marianne Goszronyi Ainley, ed., *Despite the Odds: Essays on Canadian Women and Science,* 74–87. Montreal: Véhicule Press, 1990

– *We Walked Very Warily: A History of Women at McGill.* Montreal: Eden Press Women's Publications, 1981

Giroux, H.A. *Teachers as Intellectuals: Toward a Critical Pedagogy of Learning.* New York: Bergin and Garvey, 1998

Gleason, Mona. "Disciplining the Student Body and the Construction of Canadian Children's Bodies, 1930–1960." *History of Education Quarterly* vol. 41, no. 2, 2001, 189–215

– and Adele Perry, eds. *Rethinking Canada: The Promise of Women's History,* 5th edition. Toronto: Oxford University Press, 2006

Glendinning, A., and D. Inglis. "Smoking Behaviour in Youth: The problem of Low Self-Esteem?" *Journal of Adolescence* no. 22, 1999, 673–82

Goldsmith, William M. *Human Poisons: Individual and Racial Effects.* Winfield, KS: William M. Goldsmith, 1929

Government of Canada. *Report of the Royal Commission on the Status of Women in Canada.* Ottawa: Queen's Printer, 1970

Graham, Hilary. "Women's Smoking and Family Health." *Social Science and Medicine* vol. 25, no.1, 1987, 47–56

– *When Life's a Drag: Women Smoking and Disadvantage.* London: HMSO, 1993

Greaves, Lorraine. *Smoke Screen: Women, Smoking and Identity.* Halifax: Fernwood Press, 1996

– Natasha Jategaonkar, and Lucy McCullough. "Smoking and Disordered Eating among Adolescent Girls: Investigating the Links," in Nancy Poole and Lorraine Greaves, eds, *Highs & Lows: Canadian Perspectives on Women and Substance Use.* Toronto: British Columbia Centre of Excellence for Women's Health, 2007

Gregg, F.M. *Schoolroom Experiments with Tobacco.* Indianapolis: The No-Tobacco League of America, 1928

Gusfield, Joseph. *Contested Meanings: The Construction of Alcohol Problems.* Madison: University of Wisconsin Press, 1996

– "The Social Symbolism of Smoking," in S. Sugarman and R. Rabin, eds, *Smoking Policy: Law, Politics and Culture.* New York: Oxford University Press, 1993

Haines, Rebecca. "Smoke, in My Eyes: A Bourdieusian Account of Young Women's Tobacco Use." (PhD thesis, University of Toronto, 2008)

Hardesty, Nancy. *Women Called to Witness: Evangelical Feminism in the 19th Century.* Nashville: Abington Press, 1984

Harvey, Ann, Margaret Michaud, and Verna Lefebvre. *Try This on for Size!* Toronto: Copp Clark Publishing, 1976

Health Canada. *Canadian Tobacco Use Monitoring Survey.* 1996, 2000, 2005, 2006

– *Directions: The Directional Paper of the National Strategy to Reduce Tobacco Use.* Ottawa: Queen's Printer, 1993

– *Francophone Women's Tobacco Use in Canada.* Ottawa: Minister of Supply and Services Canada, 1996

– Health Canada National Campaigns, "Lung Cancer. Another Second-Hand Smoke Disease." 21 November 2007; accessed at http://www.hc-sc-gc.ca/hc-ps/tobac-tabac/res/media/camp_shelposter-eng.php

- "Matters of Good Taste." *Canadian High News* vol. 27, no. 3, 1966, 5
- *Mixed Messages*. Ottawa: Minister of Supply and Services Canada, 1995
- *The National Strategy to Reduce Tobacco Use*. Ottawa: Minister of Supply and Services Canada, 2001
- "Relax, Girls!" *Canadian High News* vol. 25, no. 6, March 1965, 4
- *Smoking and Pregnancy: A Woman's Dilemma*. Ottawa: Minister of Supply and Services Canada, 1995
- *Smoking Interventions in the Prenatal and Postpartum Periods*. Ottawa: Minister of Supply and Services Canada, 1995
- *Tobacco Resource Material: A Selected Inventory*. Ottawa: Minister of Supply and Services Canada, 1995
- *Women and Tobacco: A Framework for Action*. Ottawa: Minister of Supply and Services Canada, 1995
- *Youth Smoking Survey*. 2010

Henderson, G.E., and Chas. G. Fraser. *Physiology and Hygiene Notes*. Toronto: The Educational Publishing Company, 1897

Heron, Craig, and Robert Storey, eds. *On the Job: Confronting the Labour Process in Canada*. Kingston and Montreal: McGill-Queen's University Press, 1986

Hewitt, Donald W. *The Cigarette and You*. Mountain View, CA: Pacific Press Publishing Association, 1953

Hilton, Matthew. *Smoking in British Popular Culture, 1800–2000: Perfect Pleasures*. Manchester: Manchester University Press, 2000

Hodgetts, A.B. *Decisive Decades*. Toronto: Thomas Nelson & Co., 1960

Hoodless, Mrs J. *Public School Domestic Science*. Toronto: Copp Clark Co. Ltd, 1898

Holloway, Maureen, and E. Meriog. *Individual and Family Living*. Toronto: Nelson, 2001

Holloway, Maureen, Jane Witte, Marvin Zuker, and Garth Holloway. *Individuals and Families in a Diverse Society*. Toronto: McGraw-Hill Ryerson, 2003

Hopkins, Pryns. *Gone up in Smoke: An Analysis of Tobaccoism*. Culver City, CA: The Highland Press, 1948

Howard, Vicki. "At the Curve Exchange: Postwar Beauty Culture and Working Women at Maidenform," in Philip Scranton, ed, *Beauty and Business*, 195–216. New York: Routledge, 2001

Hughes, James Laughlin, and Ellsworth D. Foster, editors-in-chief, *The Dominion Educator*. Toronto: P.D. Palmer & Company, 1920

Hughes, Jason. *Learning to Smoke: Tobacco Use in the West*. Chicago and London: University of Chicago Press, 2003

Humphries, Mary E., Margaret Hilchie, M. Margaret E. Price, Elizabeth Chant Robertson, and Vivian M. Wilcox. *Foods and Textiles*. Toronto: W.J. Gage Ltd, 1965

Jacobson, Bobbie. *Beating the Ladykillers: Women and Smoking*. London: Pluto Press, 1986

Jategaonkar, Natasha, and Karen Devries. "What We Don't Know about Gender, Ethnocultural Communities and Smoking: The Case of South Asian Girls," in

Nancy Poole and Lorraine Greaves, eds, *Highs & Lows: Canadian Perspectives on Women and Substance Use*, 91–9. Toronto: British Columbia Centre of Excellence for Women's Health, 2007

Jefferis, Prof. B.G., and J.L. Nichols. *Search Lights on Health: Light on Dark Corners. A Complete Sexual Science and A Guide to Purity and Physical Manhood. Advice to Maiden, Wife and Mother. Love, Courtship and Marriage.* Toronto: J.L. Nichols Co. Ltd, n.d.

Kealey, Greg. *Workers and Canadian History.* Montreal and Kingston: McGill-Queen's University Press, 1995

Kelland, Kate. "Smoking Could Kill 8 Million a Year in 20 Years – WHO." *The Daily Gleaner*, 1 June 2011, A7

Kellogg, John Harvey. *Tobaccoism, or How Tobacco Kills.* Battle Creek, MI: The Modern Medicine Publishing Co., 1922

Kerr, K. Austen. *Organized for Prohibition: A New History of the Anti-Saloon League.* New Haven: Yale University Press, 1985

Keshen, Jeffrey. "Wartime Jitters over Juveniles: Canada's Delinquency Scare and Its Consequences, 1939–1945," in Jeffrey Keshen, ed., *The Age of Contention: Readings in Canadian Social History, 1900–1945*, 364–86. Toronto: Harcourt Brace, 1997

Kiefer, Nancy, and Ruth Roach Pierson. "The War Effort and Women Students at the University of Toronto, 1939–45," in Paul Axelrod and John Reid, eds, *Youth, University and Canadian Society: Essays on the Social History of Higher Education*, 161–83. Kingston and Montreal: McGill-Queen's University Press, 1989

King, Alyson E. "The Experience of Women Students at Four Universities, 1895–1930," in Sharon Anne Cook, Lorna R. McLean, and Kate O'Rourke, eds, *"Framing Our Past": Canadian Women's History in the Twentieth Century.* Montreal and Kingston: McGill-Queen's University Press, 2001

Kinnear, Mary. *A Female Economy: Women's Work in a Prairie Province, 1870–1970.* Montreal and Kingston: McGill-Queen's University Press, 1998

– *In Subordination: Professional Women, 1870–1970.* Montreal and Kingston: McGill-Queen's University Press, 1995

Klein, Bonnie Sherr. "'We Are Who You Are': Feminism and Disability." *Ms* vol. 3, no. 3, November/December 1992

Klitzing, S.W. "Women Living in a Homeless Shelter: Stress, Coping and Leisure." *Journal of Leisure Research* vol. 36, no. 4, 2004, 483–512

Knight, A.P. *The Ontario Public School Hygiene*, revised edition. Toronto: Copp Clark Co. Ltd, 1919

Kobus, K. "Peers and Adolescent Smoking." *Addiction* vol. 98, Suppl. 1, 2003, s37–s55

Koehn, Nancy. "Estee Lauder: Self-Definition and the Modern Cosmetics Market," in Robert Scranton, ed., *Beauty and Business.* New York: Routledge, 2001

Korinek, Valerie J. *Roughing It in the Suburbs.* Toronto: University of Toronto Press, 2000

Krueger, Hans, Dan Williams, Barbara Kaminsky, and David McLean. *The Health Impact of Smoking & Obesity and What to Do about It*. Toronto: University of Toronto Press, 2007

Kruger, Richard. *Ashes to Ashes: America's Hundred-Year Cigarette War, the Public Health, and the Unabashed Triumph of Philip Morris*. New York: Alfred A. Knopf, 1996

Latham, Barbara K., and Roberta J. Pazdro, eds. *Not Just Pin Money: Selected Essays on the History of Women's Work in British Columbia*. Victoria: Camosun College, 1984

Leacy, F.H., ed. *Historical Statistics of Canada*, 2nd edition. Ottawa: Statistics Canada, 1983

Lennon, A., C. Gallois, N. Owen, and L. McDermott. "Young Women as Smokers and Nonsmokers: A Qualitative Social Identity Approach." *Qualitative Health Research* vol. 15, no. 10, 2005, 1345–59

Lieb, Clarence William. *Safer Smoking: What Every Smoker Should Know and Do*. New York: Exposition Press, 1953

Lloyd, B., and K. Lucas. *Smoking in Adolescent Images and Identities*. London and New York: Routledge, 1998

Lowe, Graham S. "Mechanization, Feminization, and Managerial Control in the Early Twentieth-Century Canadian Office," in Craig Heron and Robert Storey, eds, *On the Job: Confronting the Labour Process in Canada*, 177–209. Kingston and Montreal: McGill-Queen's University Press, 1986

– "Women, Work and the Office: The Feminization of Clerical Occupations in Canada, 1901–1931." *Canadian Journal of Sociology* vol. 5, no. 4, 1980, 361–81

McCaffrey, Andrea, Laura Tryssenaar, Diane O'Shea, and Mary Cunningham. *Parenting in Canada: Human Growth and Development*. Toronto: Thomson Nelson, 2007

McCarthy, Doris. *A Fool in Paradise: An Artist's Early Life*. Toronto: MacFarlane, Walter & Ross, 1990

McClung, Nellie. "Should Women Think?" in Nellie McClung, *In Times Like These*. Toronto: McLeod and Allan, 1915

McCracken, G. "Got a Smoke? A Cultural Account of Tobacco Use in the Lives of Contemporary Teens." Toronto: Ontario Ministry of Health Tobacco Strategy, 1992

MacDonald, N., and N.E. Wright. "Cigarette Smoking and the Disenfranchisement of Adolescent Girls: A Discourse of Resistance?" *Health Care for Women International* vol. 23, no. 3, 2002, 281–305

MacDowell, Laurel Sefton, and Ian Radforth, eds. *Canadian Working-Class History: Selected Readings*, 3rd edition. Toronto: Canadian Scholars Press, 2006

MacFadden, Bernarr. *The Truth about Tobacco: How to Break the Habit*. New York: Physical Culture Corporation, 1924

McKenzie, Judith. *Pauline Jewett: A Passion for Canada*. Montreal and Kingston: McGill-Queen's University Press, 1999

McKim's Directory of Canadian Publications, 1928 to 1939

McLaren, Carrie. "How Tobacco Company 'Anti-Smoking' Ads Appeal to Teens." *Stay Free!* issue 17; accessed at http://www.ibiblio.org/pub/ electronic-publications/stay-free/archives/17/tobacco-anti-smoking.html

McPherson, Kathryn M. *Bedside Manners: The Transformation of Canadian Nursing, 1900–1990.* Toronto: University of Toronto Press, 1996

McTaggart, Aubrey C. "California Attacks the Problems of Smoking." *The B.C. Teacher* vol. 45, January 1966

Major, Alphonse. *The Crime against the Feet; Also on the Tobacco Habit.* New York: Alphonse Major, 1930s

Malmo, Gail. "Addressing Tobacco Dependency in Women's Substance Use Treatment," in Nancy Poole and Lorraine Greaves, eds, *Highs & Lows: Canadian Perspectives on Women and Substance Use.* Toronto: British Columbia Centre of Excellence for Women's Health, 2007

The Maple Leaf: The Magazine of the Canadian Expeditionary Force. (Published and sold for the benefit of Canadian Pay and Record Office Prisoners of War and Field Forces Cigarette and Tobacco Fund) vol. 2, no. 4, 1916

Marketing magazine. 23 August 1975; 4 July 1977; 7 May 1979; 27 August 1979; 31 March 1980; 9 June 1980; 20 September 1982

Marks, Lynne. *Revivals and Roller Rinks: Religion, Leisure and Identity in late Nineteenth-Century Ontario.* Toronto: University of Toronto Press, 1996

Martel, Caroline. "The Telephone Operator: From 'Information Central' to Endangered Species," in Sharon Anne Cook, Lorna R. McLean, and Kate O'Rourke, eds, *Framing Our Past: Canadian Women's History in the Twentieth Century*, 376–7. Kingston and Montreal: McGill-Queen's University Press, 2001

Martin, Luther H., Huck Gutman, and Patrick H. Hutton, eds. *Technologies of the Self: A Seminar with Michel Foucault.* Boston: University of Massachusetts Press, 1988

Matthews, Jean V. *The Rise of the New Woman: The Women's Movement in America, 1875–1930.* The American Ways Series. Chicago: Ivan R. Dee, 2003

Mawani, Renisa. "Regulating the 'Respectable' Classes: Venereal Disease, Gender, and Public Health Initiatives in Canada, 1914–35," in John McLaren, Robert Menzies, and Dorothy E. Chunn, eds, *Regulating Lives: Historical Essays on the State, Society, the Individual and the Law*, 170–95. Vancouver: University of British Columbia Press, 2002

Meeks, Linda Brower, Philip Sharon Heit, and Mitchell Pottebaum. *Teaching Health Science.* Dubuque, IA: Wm. C. Brown Company Publishers, 1981

Menashe, Claudia L., and Michael Siegel. "The Power of a Frame: An Analysis of Newspaper Coverage of Tobacco Issues – United States, 1985–1996." *Journal of Health Communication* vol. 3, no. 3, 1998, 307–25

Merki, Mary Bronson, Don Merki, and Gale Cornelia Flynn. *Glencoe Health: A Guide to Wellness.* Toronto: McGraw Hill, 1998

Messaris, Paul. *Visual "Literacy": Image, Mind and Reality.* Oxford: Westview Press, 1994

Miles, Robert H. *Coffin Nails and Corporate Strategies*. Englewood Cliffs, NJ: Prentice Hall, 1982

Millar, W.J. "Place of Birth and Ethnic Status: Factors Associated with Smoking Prevalence among Canadians." *Statistics Canada Health Reports*, vol. 4, no. 1, 1992, 7–25

Mitchell, Claudia A., and Jacqueline Reid-Walsh, eds. *Girl Culture: An Encyclopedia*, vol. 1. Westport, CT: Greenwood Press, 2008

Mitchell, Dolores. "Images of Exotic Women in Turn-of-the-Century Tobacco Art." *Feminist Studies* vol. 18, no. 2, Summer 1992, 327

Mitchell, L., and A. Amos. "Girls, Pecking Order and Smoking." *Social Science and Medicine* vol. 44, no. 12, 1997, 1,861–9

Mitchinson, Wendy. "Canadian Women and Church Missionary Societies in the Nineteenth Century: A Step towards Independence." *Atlantis* vol. 2, no. 2, part 2, Spring 1977

Montgomery, Kenneth. "Banal Race-Thinking: Ties of Blood, Canadian History Textbooks and Ethnic Nationalism." *Paedogigica Historica* vol. 41, no. 3, June 2005

– "Imagining the Antiracist State: Representations of Racism in Canadian History Textbooks." *Discourse: Studies in the Cultural Politics of Education* vol. 26, no. 4, December 2005, 427–42

Morton, Desmond. *Working People: An Illustrated History of the Canadian Labour Movement*, 5th edition. Montreal and Kingston: McGill-Queen's University Press, 2007

Mulvey, Laura. "Visual Pleasure and Narrative Cinema," in Brian Wallis, ed., *Art after Modernism, Rethinking Representation*, 361–73. New York: The New Museum of Contemporary Art, 1984

National Women's Law Center. *Making the Grade on Women's Health: Women and Smoking. A National and State-by-State Report Card*. National Women's Law Center website, 2005; accessed at http://www.nwlc.org/pdf/Women&SmokingReportCard2003.pdf

Nattress, William, MD. *Public School Physiology and Temperance*. Authorized by the Education Department, Ontario. Toronto: William Briggs, Wesley Buildings, 1893

Neatby, Nicole. "Preparing for the Working World: Women at Queen's during the 1920s," in Ruby Heap and Alison Prentice, eds, *Gender and Education in Ontario*. Toronto: Canadian Scholars Press, 1991

Nichter, M., M. Nichter, E.E. Lloyd-Richardson, B. Flaherty, A. Carkoglu, and N. Taylor. "Gendered Dimensions of Smoking among College Students." *Journal of Adolescent Research* vol. 21, no. 3, 2006, 215–43

Nichter, M., G. Quintero, M. Nichter, J. Mock, and S. Shakib. "Qualitative Research: Contributions to the Study of Drug Use, Drug Abuse, and Drug User–Related Interventions." *Substance Use & Misuse* vol. 39, 2004, 1,907–69

Nichter, M., N. Vuckovic, G. Quintero, and C. Ritenbaugh. "Smoking Experimentation and Initiation among Adolescent Girls: Qualitative and Quantitative Findings." *Tobacco Control* vol. 6, no. 4, 1997, 285–95

O'Grady, Jean. "Margaret Addison: Dean of Residence and Dean of Women at Victoria University, 1903–1931," in Sharon Anne Cook, Lorna R. McLean, and Kate O'Rourke, eds, *Framing Our Past: Canadian Women's History in the Twentieth Century*. Kingston and Montreal: McGill-Queen's University Press, 2001

O'Leary-Reesor, Lisa, and Jane Witte. *Food for Today*. Toronto: McGraw Hill Ryerson, 2008

Ontario Physical and Health Education Association. *Health and Physical Education Curriculum Support Document*. Grade 4. 2000

O'Shea, M.V. *Tobacco and Mental Efficiency*. New York: The Macmillan Company, 1923

Ottawa Citizen. 11 April 1998; 24 May 2010 (accessed at http://www.ottawacitizen.com/life/century+promoting+Canada/3064571/story.html#ixzz0orAoQCKi); 27 February 2010

Ottawa Morning Citizen. 12 August 1944, in Donald F. Davis and Barbara Lorenzkowski, "A Platform for Gender Tensions: Women Working and Riding on Canadian Urban Transit in the 1940s," in Mona Gleason and Adele Perry, eds, *Rethinking Canada: The Promise of Women's History*, 5th edition. Oxford: Oxford University Press, 2006

Palmer, Bryan. *The Character of Class Struggle: Essays in Canadian Working-Class History, 1850–1985*. Toronto: McClelland and Stewart, 1986

Parr, Joy, ed. *Still Running*. Kingston: Queen's University Alumni Association, 1987

Peace Arch Entertainment. *Heroines: A Photographic Obsession*. 2001

Peart, H.W., and J. Schaffter. *The Winds of Change*. Toronto: Ryerson Press, 1961

Peiss, Kathy. *Hope in a Jar: The Making of American Beauty Culture*. New York: Metropolitan Books, 1998

Phair, J.T., and N.R. Speirs. *Good Health Today*. Toronto: Ginn and Co., 1951 and 1958

Phillips, Nelson, and Cynthia Harvey. *Discourse Analysis: Investigating Processes of Social Construction*. Sage Qualitative Research Methods Series 50, 2002, 1–17

Pierson, Ruth Roach. "Archival Research as Refuge, Penance, and Revenge." *Queen's Quarterly: "Whispers of the Past: Life from the Archives"* vol. 14, no. 4, Winter 2007

– "Experience, Difference, Dominance and Voice in the Writing of Canadian Women's History," in Karen Ofen, Ruth Roach Pierson, and Jane Rendall, eds, *Writing Women's History: International Perspectives*. London: Macmillan, 1991

Pitsula, James M. "Student Life at the Regina Campus in the 1920s," in Paul Axelrod and John G. Reid, eds, *Youth, University and Canadian Society: Essays in the Social History of Higher Education*, 122–39. Montreal and Kingston: McGill-Queen's University Press, 1989

Poland, B., K. Frohlich, R.J. Haines, E. Mykhalovskiy, M. Rock, and R. Sparks. "The Social Context of Smoking: The Next Frontier in Tobacco Control?" *Tobacco Control* vol. 15, no. 1, 2006, 59–63

Poole, Nancy, and Lorraine Greaves, eds. *Highs & Lows: Canadian Perspectives on Women and Substance Use*. Toronto: British Columbia Centre of Excellence for Women's Health, 2007

Porter, Ann. "Women and Income Security in the Post-war Period: The Case of Unemployment Insurance, 1945–62," in Laura Selton MacDowell and Ian Radforth, eds, *Canadian Working-Class History*, 3rd edition. Toronto: Canadian Scholars Press, 2006

Prentice, Alison. "From Household to Schoolhouse: The Emergence of the Teacher as Servant of the State," in Ruby Heap and Alison Prentice, eds, *Gender and Education in Ontario*, 25–48. Toronto: Canadian Scholars Press, 1991

– "Three Women in Physics," in Elizabeth Smyth, Sandra Acker, Paula Bourne, and Alison Prentice, eds, *Challenging Professions: Historical and Contemporary Perspectives on Women's Professional Work*, 119–40. Toronto: University of Toronto Press, 1999

– "Writing Women into History: The History of Women's Work in Canada." *Atlantis 3* Spring 1978, 72–84

Razack, Sherene H., ed. *Race, Space and the Law: Unmapping a White Settler Society*. Toronto: Between the Lines, 2002

Reeves, Nicholas. "Through the Eye of the Camera – Contemporary Cinema Audiences and Their 'Experience' of War in the Film, *Battle of the Somme*," in Pater Laddle and Hugh Cecil, eds, *Facing Armageddon: The First World War Experience*, Leo Cooper, 1996, cited in Tim Cook, "Canada's Great War on Film: Lest We Forget (1935)," *Canadian Military History* vol. 1, no. 3, Summer 2005

Reiter, Ester. "Life in a Fast-Food Factory," in Laurel Sefton MacDowell and Ian Radforth, eds, *Canadian Working-Class History: Selected Readings*, 3rd edition, 426–38. Toronto: Canadian Scholars Press, 2006

Richardson, Benjamin Ward. *The Temperance Lesson Book: A Series of Short Lessons on Alcohol and Its Action on the Body: Designed for Reading in Schools and Families*. New York: National Temperance Society and Publication House, 1883

Ricker, J.C., J.T. Saywell, and E.E. Rose. *The Modern Era*. Toronto: Clarke, Irwin & Co., 1960

Robertson, Alan, Gordon Mutter, Jean Saunders, and Ronald Wakelin. *Health Canada Series: Decisions for Health*. Scarborough, ON: Nelson Canada, 1981

Robertson, E.C., S.S. Pritchard, R.E. Boden, U.N. Hawke, F.I. Heintz, and R.A.H. Kinsh. *Health, Science and You: Book 1*. Toronto and Montreal: Holt, Rinehart and Winston of Canada Ltd, 1967

Rose, G. *Visual Methodologies: An Introduction to the Interpretation of Visual Materials*. London: Sage, 2001.

Rothman, Sheila M., and David J. Rothman. *The Pursuit of Perfection: The Promise and Perils of Medical Enhancement*. New York: Pantheon Books, 2003

Routh, Caroline. *In Style: 100 Years of Canadian Women's Fashion*. Toronto: Stoddard, 1993

Rudy, Jarrett. *The Freedom to Smoke: Tobacco Consumption and Identity*. Montreal and Kingston: McGill-Queen's University Press, 2005

– "Manufacturing French Canadian Tradition: *Tabac canadien* and the Construction of French-Canadian Identity, 1880–1950." *Histoire sociale/Social History* vol. 39, no. 77, May 2006, 205–34

– "A Ritual Transformed: Women Smokers in Montreal, 1888–1950," in Bettina Bradbury and Tamara Myers, eds, *Negotiating Identities in 19th and 20th Century Montreal.* Vancouver: University of British Columbia Press, 2005

Rutherford, Paul. *A World Made Sexy: Freud to Madonna.* Toronto: University of Toronto Press, 2007

Samet, J., and S.Y. Yoon. *Women and the Tobacco Epidemic: Challenges for the 21st Century.* WHO Monograph. WHO/NMH/TFI/01.1; accessed at http://www.who.int/tobacco/media/en/WomenMonograph.pdf

Sangster, Joan. "Creating Social and Moral Citizens: Defining and Treating Delinquent Boys and Girls in English Canada, 1920–65," in Robert Adamoski, Dorothy E. Chun, and Robert Menzies, eds, *Contesting Canadian Citizenship: Historical Readings*, 337–59. Toronto: Broadview Press, 2002

– *Girl Trouble: Female Delinquency in English Canada.* Toronto: Between the Lines, 2002

Schacter, Helen, Harold Johns, and Archibald McKie. *You're Growing Up.* Toronto: W.G. Gage & Co., 1955

– *You're Growing Up Guidebook.* Toronto: W.G. Gage & Co., 1951

Segrave, Kerry. *Women and Smoking in America, 1880–1950.* Jefferson, NC, and London: McFarland and Co., 2005

Seppanen, Janne. *The Power of the Gaze: An Introduction to Visual Literacy.* New York: Peter Lang, 2006.

Sethna, Christabelle. "Men, Sex and Education: The Ontario Women's Temperance Union [sic] and Children's Sex Education, 1900–20." *Ontario History* vol. 88, no. 3, Sept. 1996, 185–206

Sheehy, Gail. *The Silent Passage: Menopause.* New York: Random House, 1992

Shields, Margot. "Youth Smoking." *Statistics Canada Health Reports* vol. 16, no. 3, May 2005

Silvera, Makeda. *Silenced.* Toronto: Sister Vision/Black Women and Women of Colour Press, 1989

Silverman, H., E. Chant Robertson, W.A. Hawke, and G.I. Heintz. *Tomorrow Is Now: Today's Psychology and Your Health.* Toronto and Montreal: Holt, Rinehart and Winston of Canada Ltd, 1971

Sinacore, John. *Health: A Quality of Life*, 2nd edition. New York: Macmillan Publishing Co., 1974

Smith, Sidonie, and Julia Watson. *Reading Autobiography: A Guide for Interpreting Life Narratives*, 165–79. Minneapolis: University of Minnesota Press, 2001

Solandt, Donald Y. *Highways to Health.* Toronto: The Ryerson Press, 1933

Speers, Kimberley. "The Royal Commission on the Status of Women in Canada, 1967–70: Liberal Feminism and Its Radical Implications," in Sharon Anne Cook, Lorna R. McLean, and Kate O'Rourke, eds, *Framing Our Past: Canadian Women's History in the Twentieth Century*, 252–7. Kingston and Montreal: McGill-Queen's University Press, 2001

Speirs, Rae. "A Talk on 'Smoking' for Secondary School Principals." *CAHPER* vol. 31, no. 4, April/May 1965

Spelman, Elizabeth V. *Inessential Woman: Problems of Exclusion in Feminist Thought*. Boston: Beacon Press, 1988

Statistics Canada. *Au courant*: *Newsletter of the Health Analysis and Measurement Group* (HAMG). www.statcan.gc.ca/pub/82-005-x/2002003/4060798-eng.htm.

– *Smokers by Sex, Provinces and Territories*. CANSIM table 105-0501 and Catalogue no. 82-221-X

Steedman, Mercedes. "Skill and Gender in the Canadian Clothing Industry, 1890–1940," in Craig Heron and Robert Storey, eds, *On the Job: Confronting the Labour Process in Canada*, 152–76. Kingston and Montreal: McGill-Queen's University Press, 1986

Stephen, Jennifer A. *Pick One Intelligent Girl: Employability, Domesticity, and the Gendering of Canada's Welfare State, 1939–1947*. Toronto: University of Toronto Press, 2007

Strange, Carolyn, and Tina Loo. *Making Good: Law and Moral Regulation in Canada, 1867–1939*. Toronto: University of Toronto Press, 1997

– *True Crime, True North: The Golden Age of Canadian Pulp Magazines*. Vancouver: Raincoast Books, 2004

Strong-Boag, Veronica. *The New Day Recalled: Lives of Girls and Women in English Canada, 1919–1939*, 342–60. Toronto: Copp Clark Pitman, 1988

– "Women and Team Sport," in Sharon Anne Cook, Lorna R. McLean, and Kate O'Rourke, eds, *Framing Our Past: Canadian Women's History in the Twentieth Century*, 192–3. Montreal and Kingston: McGill-Queen's University Press, 2001

Sutherland, Neil. *Children in English-Canadian Society: Framing the Twentieth-Century Consensus*. Waterloo, ON: Wilfrid Laurier University Press, 2000

Tameanko, Marvin. *House and Home*. Toronto: General Publishing Co. Ltd, 1968

Tate, Cassandra. *Cigarette Wars: The Triumph of "The Little White Slaver."* Oxford: Oxford University Press, 1990

Temple, Julia R. "People Who Are Different from You: Heterosexism in Quebec High School Textbooks." *Canadian Journal of Education* vol. 28, no. 3, 2005, 271–94

Thom, Mary. *Inside Ms: 25 Years of the Magazine and the Feminist Movement*. New York: Henry Holt and Company, 1997

Thompson, John H., and Alan Seager. *Canada 1922–1939: Decades of Discord*. Toronto: McClelland and Stewart, 1985

Thomson, P. *Food for Life*. Toronto: McGraw-Hill Ryerson, 1994; teachers' guide, 1995

Tilleczek, K.C., and D.W. Hine. "The Meaning of Smoking as Health and Social Risk in Adolescence." *Journal of Adolescence* vol. 29, 2006, 273–87

Tinkler, Penny. "Refinement and Respectable Consumption: The Acceptable Face of Women's Smoking in Britain, 1918–1970." *Gender & History*, vol. 15, no. 2, August 2003, 342–60

– *Smoke Signals: Women, Smoking and Visual Culture*. Oxford and New York: Berg, 2006

Tyrrell, Ian. *Dangerous Enemies: Tobacco and Its Opponents in Australia.* Sydney: University of New South Wales, 1999

U.S. v. Philip Morris USA, Inc., et al. No. 99-CV-02496GK (U.S. Dist. Ct. D.C.), Final Opinion, 17 August 2006

US Department of Health, Education and Welfare. *The Smoking Digest.* Bethesda, MD: Office of Cancer Communications, National Cancer Institute, October 1977

US Department of Health and Human Services, "Women and Smoking: A Report of the Surgeon General." Washington: US Department of Health and Human Services, 2004

USA Today. "k.d. lang's World: Nothin' but a Drag." 7 September 1997; accessed at http://dale.ckm.ucsf.edu:8080/j/k/d/jkd38d00/Sjkd38d00.pdf

Van Den Berg, Nan, ed. *Feminist Perspectives on Addictions.* New York: Springer, 1991

Van Noppen, Charles L. *Death in Cellophane, Part Two.* Greensboro, NC: Charles L. Van Noppen, 1938

Vattimo, Gianni. *The End of Modernity,* trans. Jon R. Snyder. Baltimore: Lavoisier, 1988

Vermeiren, R., M. Schwab-Stone, D. Deboutte, P. Leckman, and V. Ruchkin. "Violence Exposure and Substance Use in Adolescents: Findings from Three Countries." *Pediatrics,* vol. III, no. 3, 2003, 535–40, cited in Patricia G. Erickson, Katharine King, and Ywit, "On the Street: Influences on Homelessness in Young Women," in Nancy Poole and Lorraine Greaves, eds, *Highs & Lows: Canadian Perspectives on Woman and Substance Use.* Toronto: British Columbia Centre of Excellence for Women's Health, 2007

Vermond, Kira. "Smoke Busters." *University of Waterloo Magazine* Spring 2010, 28–31

Vipond, Mary. "Best Sellers in English Canada: 1919–1928." *Journal of Canadian Fiction* vol. 35, no. 36, 1986

Voon, Tania, and Andrew Mitchell. "Regulating Tobacco Flavours: Implications of WTO Law." *Boston University International Law Journal* vol. 29, no. 2, 2011; accessed at http://ssrn.com/abstract=1688690

Wakefield, M., Y. Terry-McElrath, S. Emery, H. Saffer, F. Chaloupka, G. Szczypka, B. Flay, Patrick M. O'Malley, and Lloyd Johnston. "Effect of Televised Tobacco Company–Funded Smoking Prevention Advertising on Youth Smoking-Related Beliefs, Intentions and Behaviours." *American Journal of Public Health* vol. 96, no. 12, December 2006, 2,154–60

Walden, Keith. "Hazes, Hustles, Scraps and Stunts," in Paul Axelrod and John G. Reid, eds, *Youth, University and Canadian Society: Essays in the Social History of Higher Education,* 94–121. Montreal and Kingston: McGill-Queen's University Press, 1989

Walker, James W. St George. *Racial Discrimination in Canada: The Black Experience.* Ottawa: Canadian Historical Association, 1985

Walkowitz, Judith. *Prostitution and Victorian Society*. Cambridge: Cambridge University Press, 1980

Wall, Sharon. *The Nurture of Nature: Childhood, Antimodernism, and Ontario's Summer Camps, 1920–55*. Vancouver: University of British Columbia Press, 2009

Warburton, D.M. *Nicotine and the Smoker*, cited in Carrie Murray Carpenter, Geoffrey Ferris Wayne, and Gregory N. Connolly, *Designing Cigarettes for Women: New Findings from Tobacco Industry Documents*, 837–51. Society for the Study of Addiction, 2005

Warsh, Cheryl Krasnick. "Smoke and Mirrors: Gender Representation in North American Tobacco and Alcohol Advertisements before 1950." *Histoire sociale/ Social History* vol. 31, no. 62, November 1998, 183–222

Wearing, B., S. Wearing, and K. Kelly. "Adolescent Women, Identity and Smoking: Leisure Experience as Resistance." *Sociology of Health and Illness* vol. 16, no. 5, 1994, 626–43

Weinbaum, Alys Eve, Lynn M. Thomas, Priti Ramamurthy, Uta G. Poiger, Doug Barlow, Madeleine Yue, and E. Tani, eds. *The Modern Girl around the World: Consumption, Modernity, and Globalization*. Next Wave: New World in Women's Studies. Durham, NC: Duke University Press, 2008

Weller, Sheila. *Girls Like Us: Carole King, Joni Mitchell, Carly Simon and the Journey of a Generation*. New York: Atria Books, 2008

Welshman, John. "Images of Youth: The Issue of Juvenile Smoking, 1880–1914." *Addiction* vol. 91, no. 990, 1996, 1379–86

Westfall, William. *Two Worlds: The Protestant Culture of Nineteenth-Century Ontario*. Montreal and Kingston: McGill-Queen's University Press, 1989

White, Julie. "Looking Back: A Brief History of Everything," in Gerald Hunt and David Rayside, eds, *Equity, Diversity, and Canadian Labour*. Toronto: University of Toronto Press, 2007

White, Larry C. *Merchants of Death: The American Tobacco Industry*. New York: William Morrow, Beech Tree Books, 1988

Whiteley, Sheila. *Sexing the Groove: Popular Music and Gender*. London and New York: Routledge, 1997

Wild, David. "Joni Mitchell." (reprint) *Rolling Stone*, 31 October 2002; accessed at http://jmdl.com/library/view.cfm?id=935

Willard, Frances E. *Glimpses of Fifty Years: The Autobiography of an American Woman, by Frances E. Willard*. Toronto: Rose Publishing Company, 1889

Witte, Jane. *Food for Life*. Toronto: McGraw-Hill Ryerson, 2008

ARCHIVAL AND UNPUBLISHED SOURCES

Alma College Archives [ACA]
Minutes of the Alma College Council, 9 June 1896

Archives of Ontario [AO]

WCTU Collection. *Annual Report of the Ontario W.C.T.U.* 1889

– Bullock, Helen I., *The Tobacco Toboggan*, National WCTU Leaflet no. 32

– *Canadian White Ribbon Tidings* 1 April 1905

– Department of Medal Contests of the Dominion Woman's Christian Temperance Union

– MG 10. Clothier, Ida C., "Is a Y.W.C.T.U. a Necessity?" Department Leaflets, YWCTU, no. 58, Evanston, IL: National WCTU, distributed in Canada by the Dominion WCTU Depository, London, Ontario, n.d., c. 1880

– *Minute Book for Newmarket W.C.T.U.*, 1910

– *Minutes of the Convention of the Dominion W.C.T.U.* 1891, 1909, 1914, 1927, 1980

– *Minute Books of the Grey and Dufferin Counties*, 23 June 1926

– MU 8285

– MU 8425. *Minute Book of the Ottawa Branch*, report by recording secretary on annual convention in London, Ontario, 19, 20 October 1881

– MU 8427. 15 June 1922.

– MU 8471. *Manual, Canadian Y.W.C.T.U. and Y.P.B*, n.d., likely c. 1931

– MU 8471. "A World's Demonstration," *World's Y Hand-book*

– Rittenhouse, Maud, "A New Regime," Chicago, IL, National WCTU, National Leaflet 104, distributed by the Dominion WCTU Literature Depository in London, Ontario, n.d., c. 1900

– Thompson, Thomas Roberts, "The Things to Keep," in Jane W. Colbeck, compiler, *The Dominion W.C.T.U. Reciter*

– Wilcox, Ella Wheeler, "Two Boys and a Cigarette," in Mrs G.R. Dolan and Advisory Committee, compiler, *The Cigarette Menace: A Manual for L.T.L. Leaders*, Regina: Saskatchewan WCTU

– *Woman's Journal* March 1890

The Canadian Mute vol. 1, no. 4, 1 April 1892, 4

L236. Drawings of the Mercer Reformatory for 1922 – drawing of entire structure and grounds; 1940 – plan of second floor; 1941 – alteration of classroom to recreational centre

Ontario Minister of Education, *Programme of Studies for Grades 7 and 8 of the Public and Separate Schools*, Toronto, 1942

The Baldwin Room, Metropolitan Toronto Reference Library [BR]

Burke, Harry, "Women Cigarette Fiends," *The Ladies' Home Journal* vol. 39, June 1922

Gray, Reta, *Queer Questions Quaintly Answered; or, Creative Mysteries Made Plain to Children*, Toronto: J.J. Nichols & Co., 1899

Literary Digest vol. 96, 28 January 1928

"Women and the Weed," *Literary Digest* vol. 87, 19 December 1925

Canadian Museum of Civilization [CMC]

"Canada in a Box: Cigar Containers That Store Our Past, 1883–1935," accessed at http://www.civilization.ca/cmc/exhibitions/tresors/cigares/cigar-boxes-e.shtml

Canadian War Museum [CWM]

Canadian Pay & Record Office Prisoners of War & Field Forces Tobacco & Cigarettes Fund, "Send the Boys What They *Really Want*," no. 3

"Evelyn Pepper: The Florence Nightingale of Disaster Planning," obituary, *Ottawa Citizen*, 11 April 1998

Guly, Christopher, "Lives Lived Column: Evelyn Agnes Pepper," *The Globe and Mail*, 4 June 1998

MacLean, Teresa, "Evelyn Pepper," *Carillon*, October 1996

Carr-Harris Private Collection [C-HPC]

Untitled newspaper clipping, 14 June 1895

CBC Radio

"Music in My Life," 11 December 1987, quoted in Judith McKenzie, *Pauline Jewett: A Passion for Canada*, 30, Kingston and Montreal: McGill-Queen's University Press, 1999, 30

CBC Television

"Are Temp Cigarettes for Teens?" *The Journal*, 26 September 1985. CBC Digital Archives, 3 minutes, 55 seconds, http://archives.cbc.ca/version_print.asp?page-1&lDLan=1&idcLlP=14246&lDDossier

"Do Cigarette Ads Cause Smoking?" 21 March 1965. CBC Digital Archives, 8 minutes, 9 seconds, http://archives.cbc.ca/version_print.asp?page-1&lDLan=1&idcLlP=14246&lDDossier

"How to Spit on Umpires' Feet without Getting Caught," *90 Minutes Live*, 18 May 1977 and commentary on production, 2004. CBC Digital Archives, 3 minutes, 7 seconds, http://archives.cbc.ca/version_print.asp?page-1&lDLan=1&idcLlP=14246&lDDossier

Interview between Pamela Wallin and Joni Mitchell, 19 February 1996. CBC Digital Archives, 8 minutes, 6 seconds, http://archives.cbc.ca/version_print.asp?page-1&lDLan=1&idcLlP=14246&lDDossier

"Kicking the Habit," *Newsmagazine*, 25 July 1977. CBC Digital Archives, 10 minutes, 5 seconds, http://archives.cbc.ca/version_print.asp?page-1&lDLan=1&idcLlP=14246&lDDossier

"The Myth of the 'Light' Cigarette," *The Journal*, 17 February 1983 and additional commentary. CBC Digital Archives, 6 minutes, 18 seconds, http://archives.cbc.ca/version_print.asp?page-1&lDLan=1&idcLlP=14246&lDDossier

"No More Cigarette Ads for CBC," 11 May 1969. CBC Digital Archives, 16 minutes, 44 seconds, http://archives.cbc.ca/version_print.asp?page-1&IDLan=1&idc LIP=14246&IDDossier

"On the Way to a Smoke-Free Canada," *The National*, 22 April 1987 and additional commentary. CBC Digital Archives, 5 minutes, 4 seconds, http://archives.cbc.ca/version_print.asp?page-1&IDLan=1&idc LIP=14246&IDDossier

"Smoking Kills, Says US Surgeon General," 12 January 1964. CBC Digital Archives, 13 minutes, 15 seconds, http://archives.cbc.ca/version_print.asp?page-1&ID Lan=1&idcLIP=14246&IDDossier

"Smuggled Smokes Flood the Market," *The Journal*, 12 July 1991 and additional commentary. CBC Digital Archives, 5 minutes, 4 seconds, http://archives.cbc.ca/version_print.asp?page-1&IDLan=1& idcLIP=14246&IDDossier

"Trouble in Tobacco Country," CBC Television News, 29 June 1971. CBC Digital Archives, 2 minutes, 49 seconds, http://archives.cbc.ca/version_print.asp? page-1&IDLan=1&idcLIP=14246&IDDossier

City of Toronto Archives [CTA]

Cook Private Collection [CPC]
Letters from Harriet Ethel Fry to John Fry, 20 October 1936; 4 December 1937; 18 January 1938; 3 February 1938; January 1939; 2 February 1939; 15 February 1939

Dalhousie University Archives [DUA]
Diary B – 1919 – MS 2-686, A-60, diary of Ella Muriel Liscombe
MS 2-686, A-97, Lauretta Sluenwhite diary, Pine Grove, Lunenberg County, 1920s–1938
MS 2-686, A-123, "Watching the CWACS: The Diary of a Service Woman in W.W.II"
MS 2-707, Diary and biography of Edith MacMechan Dobson, 1948
MS 2-711, Photograph album of Bernice Robb, 1920s
MS 2-712, Bernice Robb diary and biography, 1930–70
Pharos Yearbook, 1961, 1962, 1973, 1976–77

Frances Willard Museum and Library Research Center [FWM]
The A.C.A. Herald, the "Official Organ of the Anti-Cigaret Alliance of America"
The Cigarette News, November 1930
Levy, Mac, *Tobacco Habit Easily Conquered*, New York: Albro Society, Inc., 1916
Schrumpf-Pierron, Pierre, *Tobacco & Physical Efficiency: A Digest of Clinical Data*, New York: Paul B. Hoeber, 1927
Smoking and Cosmetics – by a Medical Doctor and a Health Teacher, New York: Rational Living, 1936

Glenbow Museum Archives [GMA]
WCTU Collection. M 1705, BD.3, W872B, file 32, "Pledge Book, Young Woman's Christian Temperance Union"

Hudson's Bay Company Archives [HBCA]

Library and Archives Canada [LAC]
Acts of the General Assembly of Her Majesty's Province of New Brunswick, 1890, 1893
The Acts of the General Assembly of P.E.I., 1901
AMICUS 3477896. "Famous Flower-Stylist Judith Garden, Florist with a Flair Agrees: Whether you're arranging flowers or choosing a cigarette ... EXPERIENCE IS THE BEST TEACHER!" *Ladies' Home Journal*, November 1948, n.p.
The Business and Professional Woman, Per. Reg. 9873; A-60-7: June 1934; March 1936; March 1937
The Business and Professional Woman Newsletter
Business Week 14 November 1953, 54
Canadian Cigar and Tobacco Journal:
    "Is Tobacco Injurious?" graphic, Tobacco Usage, vol. 55, no. 3, March 1948, 20
Canadian Home Journal:
    Armstrong, Alice, "Kate Aitken's Spa," September 1953, 14–15
    Dare, Eleanor, "You Were Asking: A Page of Problems – Personal, Household and Otherwise," October 1930
    Woods, Rex, "Macdonald Lassie," cover, 1936
The Canadian Lancet:
    "Men Need Tobacco," vol. 56, no. 6, February 1921, 336–7
    "The Time to Smoke," vol. 52, no. 9, May 1919, 436
(The) Chatelaine:
    vol. 1, no. 1, March 1928; November 1948; July 1982, 16; December 1982, 18.
    Bennett, Melanie, "The Bridge at High Leap," May 1939, 50, 54
    Eustace, C.J, "You Can't Love the Boss," June 1930, 6–7, 64–5
    "Liquor and the Home," November 1948
    MacKay, Alice, "Those Pampered Bulges," May 1936, 50–1
    "Sorry, Miss Armour – but we must make way for younger girls," October 1933, 50
Châtelaine:
    Hamelin, Jean, "En tête d'affiche: 4 femmes," vol. 1, no. 1, October 1960
    Hébert, Anne, "Shannon," vol. 1, no. 1, October 1960
    Laurendeau, André, "On croit se connaitre ...," January 1962
    "Nos lectrices prennent position: le rôle des femmes dans l'animation sociale – Au sien des comités de citoyens, les militantes se multiplient. Quels moyens nouveaux utilisent-elles pour transformer la société?" June 1970
    Roy, Gabrielle, "Grand-mère et la poupée," vol. 1, no. 1, October 1960
    Tessier, Catherine, "La feminisme n'est pas héreditaire!" December 1985, 45–8
Commentator vol. 13, no. 3, March 1969, 30

The Financial Post:

6 December 1958, front page; 24 March 1962, 49; 8 June 1963, 49; 28 March 1964, 2; 24 October 1964, 17; 27 February 1965, 23; 3 May 1969, editorial; 6 December 1969, front page; 6 June 1970, 1, 6; 17 October 1970, 13; 31 October 1970, 1; 23 August 1975, 12; 18 April 1984, 1

The Globe and Mail:

5 April 1919; 30 September 2009, A10; 1 June 2010, L4; 31 December 2010, L6

"Cigaret Use Harms Fetus, Steinfeld Warns," 12 January 1971

"Cigarets and Alcohol Bad for Health, Morals of Women Who Indulge," 24 April 1937, 15

"Consideration," 18 December 1946, 9

"A Few Facts about Fags," 31 May 1938, 13

"Find More Lung Cancer in Women Who Smoke," 23 February 1966, 11

Makin, Kirk, "Top Court Upholds Tobacco Advertising Laws: Anti-smoking Lobbyists Claim Ruling Opens Doors for a Full Ad Ban," 29 June 2007

"M.D. Says Dollars Push Smoking but It's Never Too Late to Stop," 7 November 1963, 16

"More Babies of Women Smokers Die, MD Says," 8 June 1975

"Mouth Cancer Reported Increasing in Women," 8 September 1972

"Muscles, Blushes and Smoke," 5 February 1975, editorial page

"Nonagenarian Is Disgusted by Women with Smoking Habit," 23 February 1935, 12

"Study Finds Nicotine Gathers in Breasts of Women Smokers," 3 January 1978, 12

"Teen Smokers Risk Breast Cancer," 4 October 2002

"Tip of the Hat to TTC for Cigaret Ad Ban," 16 July 1979, 12

"Tobacco Question Warmly Debated by United Pastors," 22 May 1929, 26

"Toronto Study Connects Variety of Ailments to Women's Smoking," 30 April 1973, 29

"U.S. Plans to Warn Moms Who Smoke," 12 January 1979

Weeks, Carly, "Health: 'New Cigarettes': Under Federal Scrutiny – Critics Call for Curbs on Starter Smokes – Fruit-Flavoured Cigarillos Popular with Teens Are Not Required to Carry Warnings about Nicotine," 20 February 2008

"Women Catching up to Men in Lung Diseases," 15 January 1980, 13

"Women Smoking, Modern Dancing, Scored by Pastor," 12 April 1929, 18

"Women Smoking More Today," 26 January 1970

"Good Luck Margarine Hour," 26 March 1957. MG 30D206, vol. 31

"Her Own Fault," Ontario Government Motion Picture Bureau, 1921. ISN 99688

Jefferson, Lara, "These Are My Sisters," *Sisters of the Damned*, Toronto: Crowe Editions, #21, Alval Publishers of Canada Limited, 1949, n.p. Box 3, 10054

Lancet 1915, 11, 584

Laurier, W., *Hansard: House of Commons Debates*, 1 April 1903, 846

Maclean's:

September 1911; June 1912; 9 August 1993

McClung, Nellie L., "I'll Never Tell My Age Again!" 15 March 1926, 15
    "When a Girl's Thirty," 1 January 1926, 16–17
McMartin, Pete, "Life Lived Full of Fun, Purpose," *Vancouver Sun*, 7 July 1992
Macpherson, Sandra, "The Great Equalizer," *Weekend Post*, 5 December 1998
Marketing magazine, 19 February 1979
The Monetary Times, July 1955, 58–9
Report of the Council of Public Instruction of the North-West Territories of Canada, 1896, *Ordinances of the North West Territories*, 1896
Reports of Public Schools of British Columbia, 1917, A30
Robertson, James R. Law, and Government Division, Library of Parliament, *Legislative Summary, Bill C-111: The Tobacco Sales to Young Persons Act, 1993*
Saturday Night:
    8 February 1913, 1; 14 August 1920
    "The Cigarette and Athletes," 22 September 1900
    "The Insidious Cigarette," 4 May 1912, 31
    "Trying to Make Smoking a Crime," 20 October 1918
    "Tuckett's Cigarettes," 6 September 1913
The Scout:
    Baden-Powell, Sir Robert, Bt, "Scout Yarns, A Weekly Pow-wow," 1921
    "Chinstrap," 4 October 1913
    "Easily Led: Know Your Own Mind – Don't Be Swayed in All Directions by Others," 4 October 1913
    "No Smoking," 16 January 1914
"She Was My Girl," *Sensational Love Experiences* vol. 8, no. 7, April 1949, 22–3. Box 11
Statutes of Nova Scotia, 1900 and 1901
Statutes of the British Columbia Legislature, 1891
Statutes of the Province of Ontario, 1892
The Toronto Daily Star:
    2 June 1950, 3; 13 November 1999
Twenty-Fifth Annual Report of the Department of Education of the Province of Alberta, 1930
Werner, Carl. "Cigars and the Women," *Harper's Weekly* vol. 54, 3 December 1910, 16–17
Woman's Journal, 15 March 1901
York "Memo" Yearbook, York Memorial Collegiate Institute, 1951, n.p.

Llewellyn Collection [LC]
Catherine Darby, pseudonym, taught from 1947 to 1978
Muriel Fraser, pseudonym, taught from 1947 to 1968

McCord Museum Archives [MMA]

McGill University Archives [MUA]

McKenzie Collection [MC]

Oakville Museum [OM]

Ontario Institute for Studies in Education/University of Toronto, Thomas Fisher Rare Book Room [OISE/UT]
Cooke, Maud, "The Well-known and Popular Author," 187
The Golden Rule Books, 1916, Teachers' Manual
Household Science in Rural Schools, vol. 10, Toronto: William Briggs, 1918
Ontario Department of Education, *Duties of Teachers and Pupils: For the Use of the Teachers-in-Training in the Faculties of Education and the Normal and Model Schools of Ontario*, Toronto: L.K. Cameron, Printer to the King's Most Excellent Majesty, 1909
Ontario Teachers' Manuals, Household Management, vol. 9 and 10, Toronto: Copp Clark Co. Ltd, 1916
"Programme of Studies for Grades VII and VIII," Toronto: Minister of Education, 1939

Ottawa Young Woman's Christian Association Archives [OYWCAA]
Minute Book of the Ottawa Branch, report by recording secretary on annual convention in London, Ontario, 19, 20 October 1881
Register of Inmates for the Home for Friendless Women, 1888–94

Personal Interviews
Dr Sarah Glassford, Hallie Sloan, Judy Rebick, Dr Judith McKenzie, Allan Rock

Provincial Archives of Alberta [PAA]
Profile of Dr Mary Percy Jackson, OC, ChB, LLD, "Celebrating 100 Years of Organized Medicine in Alberta in 2005" Exhibition, 2005
Letter from Dr Mary Percy Jackson to the Alumni Association, University of Birmingham, n.d.

Provincial Archives of Manitoba [PAM]
Charlotte Black diary, 1923–27, 1930–33
P4636. "The WCTU and Prohibition in Manitoba, 1883–1927"
P4639. Canadian Woman's Christian Temperance Union, Medal Contest Book, 1979
P4639. Manitoba Woman's Christian Temperance Union, *Prohibition Watchword*, June 1924

Queen's University Archives [QUA]

Rare Book Room, University of British Columbia [RBRUBC]
Emily Carr letter to Ruth Hymphrye, 20 March 1938

"Social Calendar," *The Tillicum*, 52
The Totem, 1962

The Salvation Army Archives [SAA]
"The Tobacco Devil," *The War Cry*, 17 September 1910

Thesis
Cook, Sharon Anne Cook, "A Helping Hand and Shelter: Anglo-Protestant Social Service Agencies in Ottawa, 1880–1910" (MA thesis, Carleton University, Ottawa, 1987)

University of Alberta Archives [UAA]

University of Manitoba Archives and Special Collections [UMA]
MSS SC 89. Note card, Auntie Maude to Charlotte Black, "My Graduation Journal," scrapbook, May 1925

University of Ottawa Archives [UOA]

University of Ottawa Library [UOL]
Ms Magazine, vol. 1–2, December 1973, 32–3

University of Waterloo Archives [UWA]
B97 – 0038, file 11. Lois McGratton scrapbook and photographs, "Party: 1963"
Compendium '63, "A Study in Faces," 106
Student Handbook 1961–62
University of Waterloo Student Village Handbook, 1966–67

Wilfrid Laurier University Archives [WLUA]
Evangelical Lutheran Seminary of Canada, Board of Governors Minutes, 15 November 1911

Index